AF409763

RATA SABHĀWA OF NUWARAKALAVIYA

Judicature in a Princely Province
An Ethnographical and Historical Reading

LOKUBANDA TILLAKARATNE

WORKS BY AUTHOR

- *Gammedde Ninnadaya* (in Sinhala, 2022).
- *Rata Sabhāwa Hewath Variga Sabhāwa* (in Sinhala. Approved by National Library Board (2019)
- *Echoes of the Millstone* (2015)
- *Monterey Withthi* (tr. in Sinhala, John Steinbeck's *Cannery Row*) (2009)
- *Pulse of the Jungle* (2000)
- *Amerikawata Ena Obata* (With Dr. Niranjala Tillakaratne, in Sinhala, 1990)

A concise version of this book, *Rata Sabhāwa* (2020), was published by the author in Sinhala by Sarasaviya Publishers, Nugegoda.
Printed and bound in the United States of America.
ISBN 9798218157654 – Book
ISBN 9798218157661 – eBook
Library of Congress Control Number: 2023905150
Author: Tillakaratne, Lokubanda
Subjects: Sri Lanka History; Culture and Traditions; Caste Practices; Ancient Rural Judicial Systems; Indian Subcontinent.

Cover art by Bhadraji Mahinda Jayatilaka
Book design by Niranjala Tillakaratne

To Niranjala and Mihiri
My Inspiration

Until lions have their own historians, the history of the hunt will
always glorify the hunter.
— *African Proverb.*

ABBREVIATIONS AND NOTES ON SINHALA WORD USAGE AND STYLES.

AGA – Assistant Government Agent
BTA – Buddhist Temporalities Act or Ordinance
CGA – Ceylon Government Archive
CO – Colonial Office Papers in the Public Record Office, Kew, London
DRO – Divisional Revenue Officer
IWMI – International Water Management Institute
JRAS – Journal of the Royal Asiatic Society
JRSA – Journal of the Royal Society of Arts
LTTE – Liberation Tigers of Tamil Elam
MP – Member of the Parliament
n.d. – undated.
NLR – New Law Reports
Qtd. – quoted
pl – Plural
RAS – Royal Asiatic Society
RS – Rata Sabhāwa
S. – Singular
SLNA – Sri Lanka National Archives
Sans. – Sanskrit.
SSS – *Sinhala Sirit Sangrahaya*
Vv – Verses.

Notes on Diacritics:
- ā as in path.
- á as in cat.
- ä as in valve.
- ō as in toe.
- é as in wave.

For the transliteration of Sinhala words in singular (s) or plural (pl.) are noted as such at first occurrence. Often plural of some titles and ranks are shown with the suffix *-varu* (Ratemahat*varu*). The plural of a word with the suffix *ya* (e.g., toppi*ya*) is given with an *i* (e.g., toppi). In footnotes, only first reference to the author appears as: Last and First name, year(s) of publication, *title*, and page number. Subsequent occurrences will have only the last name, year of publication, shortened title (if necessary), and page number(s). Literary works, words and expressions in Sri Lankan vernacular, title names, except when they form a part of the name of a person or place with prefix or suffix are given in italics.

CONTENTS

Source: John D'Oyly, 1835

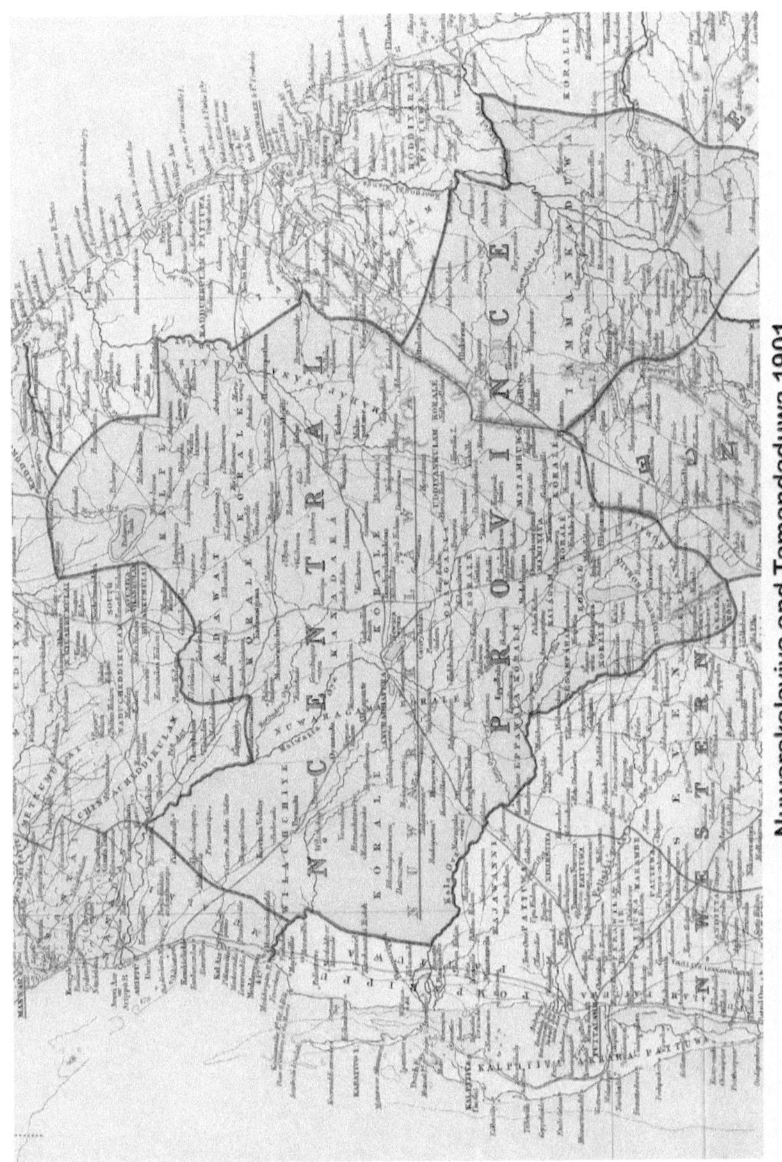

Nuwarakalaviya and Tamandaduwa 1901.

David Rumsey Historical Map Collection, Edward Stanford Ltd., London

ACKNOWLEDGEMENTS

While I was writing *Echoes of the Millstone* (2015), I found a corpus of writers who had written briefly about Rata Sabhāwa. As their interest in this institution did not stretch beyond a few pages within the scope of the main narrative, and after I stumbled upon a living link to the Rata Sabhāwa from my mother's chance gesture once which I will note later, I wanted to know more about it. I wanted to bring to surface the pre-eminent, or rather foundational text compiled thus far about this subject by Kapuruhami Madukanda Ratemahattayā and the role of the fraternity of his peers. Hence, I feel I have honored them by delving into study a tradition that was their way of life, their law at the time, their story which had dropped from the collective memory of our generation.

Elapsed decades did not give me the luxury of meeting and listening to a participant in a Rata Sabhāwa. Even if I were lucky to stumble upon a hearsay about Rata Sabhāwa, it was different from hearing a personal story, because as anthropologists often found, a villager hearing something may recall it differently three or four years later.

Without the benefit of hindsight, we can only follow leads wherever they take us to look folklore and literature compiled by earlier writers. The literature may not be just on the Rata Sabhā traditions and functions, but other areas that focus on the merits of this subject which helps sift through to get a closer understanding of life of previous generations. I hope numerous anecdotal notes I found of the times, particularly between 18th and 20th centuries, give a three-dimensional view of the era the Sabhā functioned.

My work was akin to making a pointillist painting of the past on a large, blank canvass. I only had a concoction of dots from which a perceptible portrait had to be produced. The first dot was the humbling moment when my mother placed the *mohotti bámma* of my great-grandfather on my head years ago.

History unwritten is susceptible to distortion or forgotten altogether. Most oral histories or material information about Rata Sabhāwa having been lost to the tides of time, it is an understatement that writing about it was an intimidating undertaking. But along the way, I was encouraged and humbled by the support I received from everyone I contacted. They dug into family archives and made available to me precious photos and personal writings of their ancestors going back to the 16th century. Whenever I came across anecdotal information, in written or oral form, I did not hesitate to include it, for they provided me, and I have no doubt the readers, with an opportunity to visit the past in real time.

My father-in-law L.B.S. Wickramasinghe who passed away due to the dreadful COVID was one of my living resources of early 20th century Kandyan history. I miss him. I cannot thank enough for Nanda Kumarihamy Wijeratne Mahadivulwewa for assisting me in the very early stages of my research providing me pivotal information about her grandfather, historian, and ethnologist son of Nuwarakalaviya - Kapuruhami Kapurubandara Madukanda Dissava, who, early in the 19th century, brought out the story of Rata Sabhāwa from obscurity. Principal R.B. Dissanayake introduced me to Dissava's relatives at Madukanda. Vinodh and Dushmantha Madukanda, and Post mistress Kamuarihamy flocked around me to provide every bit of information and personal items they could find on their great-grandfather. Nanda Kumari Jayampathi Herath and Gamini Anurajith Herath of Tirappane also helped me in finding much needed information about their great grandfather Alittane Kōrāla. D.B. Diwakara Mahadivulwewa was helpful in details of land distribution to middles class during last years of the British colonial administration. I was able to find unwritten folklore and family photos with the assistance of Themiya Loku Bandara Hurulle, Janaka Bulankulame, Sharana Bulankulame, Ravana (Ravi) Wijeyeratne, Ananda Markalanda, family of Alittane Kōrāla, K.B. Seneviratne, Sanath Panabokke and Turtle Bunbury, great-great-grandson of R.W. Ievers. Professor Emeritus U.B. Karunananda of University of Kelaniya, Professor Emeritus C.M. Madduma Bandara of University of Peradeniya, Assistant Librarians Pradeep Epa and Ajantha Dharmaratne of the University of Peradeniya, personnel at the library at the University of California, Los Angeles (UCLA) had helped me in finding sources and facts and provided encouragement. P.B. "Chutta" Senevirathna dug into the bowers of his memory and wrote for me the *Madukande Gedara Kavi* by Kapuruhami Ratemahattayā. Madduma Banda Tillakaratne, my brother was my savior to find photographs and other resourceful contacts. Dr. M.U.A. Tennakoon's insightful comments and suggestions were mightily helpful for the preparation of the final manuscript. I am also ever so thankful to him for agreeing to write the Foreword for this book, which is an up-to-date compendium of Nuwarakalaviya, past and present. I am indebted to the fantastic work of my wife Dr. Niranjala Tillakaratne and my daughter Dr. Mihiri Tillakaratne for formatting, photos, illustrations, and tables of this book.

Finally, all mistakes, if any, found here are mine. This book would have been only a dream if not for the support from the loves of my life, Niranjala, and Mihiri. The mother and daughter are the toughest critics of what I put in writing in the pages to follow.

Lokubanda Tillakaratne
Maradankalla & Los Angeles

Fig. 1. Rata Sabhāwa in Session. Art by Bhadraji Mahinda Jayatilaka

FOREWORD
M. U. A. Tennakoon, PhD, DSc.

Those in Rajarata inclusive of Nuwarakalaviya have a long history not just to memorize important dates and events associated with it and while away time, but to critically examine them repeatedly to draw useful lessons to complete their present task functions well and more importantly to plan and execute their future task functions still better.

NUWARAKALAVIYA OF YESTERYEARS. No one exactly knew when the old Nuwarakalaviya came into existence as an administrative region of the Kandyan kingdom and what were its precise boundaries. According to the folkloristic tradition of belief, Nuwarakalaviya as its pivotal point of administration in the north central part of the island was that chunk of land roughly falling within the imaginary triangle formed by Nuwaraweva, Kalaweva and Padaviya reservoirs. Of these three great reservoirs, Kalaweva was the last to build during the reign of King Dhatusena in the latter half of the fifth century A.D. If so, the term Nuwarakalaviya would have been in use since the construction of Kalaweva and not before.

During the early British period of administration of the island of Ceylon, Oswald Brodie once the Assistant Government Agent of the Anuradhapura District attempted, somewhat convincingly but still imperfectly, to describe Nuwarakalaviya as that administrative unit of Ceylon with set boundaries as on the following lines:

I. One running from a point one mile north of Dambulla to another at about five and twenty miles west of Trincomalee.

II. A second from the last-mentioned spot on the ninety fifth mile post south of Jaffna.

III. A third running thence to within six miles to Arippu.

IV. A fourth proceeding from thence south-south-west to a place about twelve miles west of Pomparippu.

V. A fifth joining this last-mentioned point with that near Dambulla.

Within these boundaries, Brodie's estimated land area of Nuwarakalaviya was 29,900 sq. miles, where a great *Ellanga* (cascade) based tank civilization thrived even before the third century B.C. A testimony to this is the Basavakkulama tank constructed in the city of Anuradhapura, in 247 B.C. These *Ellanga*-based tanks in micro- or meso-valleys starting from highlands or summits (*mudunna*) and ending at minor streams or rivers far down, enabled the early settlers to construct tanks one after the other, where rain water was collected, stored, allowed excess water to pass over the tank spills and frugally controlled the release of stored water through the tank sluices for crop irrigation in downstream lands. These tanks were and still are the life givers to all living beings, including humans and plants.

In the so-called Nuwarakalaviya, the tank density increased over time, cultivation areas expanded, and population grew from about the third century B.C. up to about the seventh century A.D. Due to soil depletion and repeated cultivation, soil exhaustion due to serious droughts and more importantly due to political invasions and plundering of wealth by the South Indian conquerors, there appeared a progressive out movement of settlements from the immediate environ of the city of Anuradhapura in Nuwarakalaviya, towards the better-watered areas of virgin soils more towards the eastern and north-eastern parts of Anuradhapura, then to the present area of the Polonnaruwa District and finally to the central Hill Country.

Nevertheless, a small segment of the population remained steadfast to their original village settlements stubbornly refusing to move out of the Anuradhapura environs while a vast majority of people were moving out of it abandoning their traditional settlements. Those who remained behind over centuries had a struggling life amidst deterioration of irrigated agriculture. Eventually they struggled to survive on *chena* cultivation, hunting and gathering. If not for these indigenous people's long survival struggles, those who trickled later in to the Nuwarakalaviya from the Hill Country after losing their lands to the British coffee planters from about 1825 to the middle of the nineteenth century and those rebellious persons who left the Hill Country to the Nuwarakalaviya to escape the tyrannical drafts of able bodied men by the Sinhala kings to fight the British as well as the British themselves who were actively seeking to crush the rebels fighting against the British, notably soon after the rebellion of the 1818 and other minor uprisings afterwards against them, would not have had any other safe haven to land in to re-establish new settled lives.

These newcomers, rather the intruders to the Nuwarakalaviya from the Hill Country and its immediate environs, first settled down alongside the indigenous people in existing villages or soon developed village settlements on their own, to settle down peacefully. When they came to Nuwarakalaviya with some experience in irrigated farming in their ancestral lands in the Hill Country, it was possible for them to blend that knowledge with the prevailing irrigation devices in Nuwarakalaviya with the support of the indigenes settlers there, which further strengthened the unique *Ellanga*–based system of irrigated agriculture (Tennakoon, 1974).

It is sad to note that the difficult contributions made by these indigenous people and their descendants over the centuries to sustain the *Ellanga*-based irrigated civilization have not been adequately appreciated either by the descendant of those new settlers or by the twentieth century administrators of Nuwarakalaviya. Some of them even ridiculed these indigenous people as village aborigines (*gam veddo*). These truly indigenous people in Nuwarakalaviya were not related to those indigenous people (*Ādivāsin*) in Bintenna and its surrounding areas to the east of Mahaweli Ganga. They were of a different stock of people with a long history of their own to be proud of.

The author of this book is the first person to hint in relation to his reference to Kukulawa community that these indigenous people of Nuwarakalaviya belong to a long line of respectable descendants coming from the days of the establishment of the Anuradhapura city or even before. Like all others, they too had their own social organizations such as *Variga Sabhā* or *Variga Sammuthy* of many villages of same stock within a perimeter from which they could reach a *Variga Sabhā* venue within half days walk that is about 20 to 25 miles maximum. An amalgamation of several *Variga Sabhā* sometimes called a *Rata Sabhāwa* usually presided over by *Ratemahattayā* (Lord of the Rata) next to the District Government Agent in rank under the British rule. Although Nuwarakalaviya then was important for a settled life for those indigenous and lately arrived settlers from the Hill Country, it was somewhat of marginal significance to the kings who ruled the country from Kandy. During the time of king Sri Wickrama Rajasinghe, Polonnaruwa *Disawani* was sixth in the rank of importance to the king while Nuwarakalaviya was seventeenth in the rank. Therefore, Nuwarakalaviya was placed under a lowly ranked *Dissava*, invariably a less favored by the ruling monarch in Kandy, without allocating even an official residence in Nuwarakalaviya for him and he was required to live in a hamlet closer to the king's palace in Kandy. When the designated *Dissava* was to visit Nuwarakalaviya on official duties, his family members were required to be virtually under house arrest where they lived in or near Kandy. In fact, the assigned *Dissava* hardly visited or did not visit Nuwarakalaviya at all during his tenure.

The kings' governing of Nuwarakalaviya from Kandy through their less favored *Dissavaru*, remained very nominal. The Kandyan kings' negligence of Nuwarakalaviya, the heart of Buddhist civilization in this country, was blatantly made evident in the annual procession of the Tooth Relics of Lord Buddha held in Kandy by not giving a representation for the *Dissava* in charge of Nuwarakalaviya. Within the rim of the Kandyan Kingdom, Nuwarakalaviya was considered by the kings in Kandy merely a peripheral zone of low economic value but useful as a buffer for lessening the pressure of Tamil rulers of Jaffna in the extreme north of the island. This enabled the Vanniyar Chiefs to run the affairs of Nuwarakalaviya at their free will with a retinue of lesser duty-bearers appointed as they liked.

If the Nuwarakalaviya Vanniyar Chiefs acknowledge the Kandyan king's nominal suzerainty with occasional appearances before the kings in Kandy with offers of some routine gifts, this vast region was just allowed to be with least royal interest or interventions from Kandy. Thus, the virtually neglected land, remained something like a yam struggling to survive in a very thin soil band pressed by three mighty rock slabs from three sides – the costal control of the European powers, the Tamil rulers' pressure exerted from the Jaffna peninsula in the north and the step-motherly treatment of the Kandyan kings. Thus, the people of Nuwarakalaviya had to survive and manage their legal, economic, and social lives largely under the command, control and wishes of hereditary Vanniyar Chiefs through the Rata Sabhāwa, which the author so elegantly described.

The author has indeed made a profound study of this people-based organization in terms of its functions and responsibilities of its pantheon of office- and duty-bearers such as *Ratemahattayā, Kōrāla. Mohottāla, Badderāla, Gamarāla* and *Henayā* (washerman). *Henayā* was important because he had to ceremonially ensure that clean white clothes for elegant decoration of a shed erected to hold all *Rata Sabha* ceremonial events, including the ancient etiquette-bound partaking of the departing meal offered to all participants. *Henayā* was also the last to be consulted by the judgers and jurors of a *Rata Sabhāwa* complaint adjudicated, to ensure whether the judgment arrived at, is fair and to get the usually expected "yes" endorsement from him.

Perhaps the best firsthand account of the intent and purpose of the Rata Sabhāwa, that was in vogue in 1909/1910, seems to have been enumerated by Kapuruhami Madukanda Dissava, which was very much later, published in the *Journal of Royal Asiatic Society (Ceylon)* Volume xxxviii. In enumerating twenty-five offences and disrespectful acts that came within the jurisdiction of a Rata Sabhāwa, the first nine have been dealt exclusively with women's violation of group (caste) purity through their immoral and socially disagreeable sexual relationships intended or had with males within or outside due *varige (clan)* and their disastrous consequences.

The males in any group or a *varige* (clan) were very much concerned with women's possible misbehaviors, because in the author's own words, everyone hoped to have a conflict-free marriage and protect the *varige* purity which was a beacon for social stability and kinship fundamentals that alleviated threats and inconveniences born out of any aberrant deed or unacceptable practice. *Rata Sabhāwa* indeed functioned to uphold social morality that was essential for the wellbeing of those isolated and jungle-clad small village communities in this 'no man's land' type, Nuwarakalaviya in the distant past. *Rata Sabhāwa* with its pantheon of office- and duty-bearers disappeared in the 1930s.

ANURADHAPURA DISTRICT INCLUSIVE OF NUWARAKALAVIYA TODAY. In place of socially cohesive village republics with ancient social organizations and group dynamics in active operation in the past, a new form of national and regional governance, sometimes with an overabundance of law makers, law enforcers and administrative executives above the actual duty-bearers of all sorts at village, district and national levels came into force under the British rule throughout the early twentieth century. Since independence in 1948 this administrative heaviness has worsened. Today in respect of a village, there are as many as twenty-five officials descending to guide over all developments in it! With all of them in operation, village and district development activities have gone haywire unlike in better managed private sector. With lethargy, incompetence, indiscipline, bribery and corruption, the over-staffed government service is either moving at snail's speed or does not move at all. Undue political intervention in administration even by usurping the administrating executives' freedom in decision making together with increased bribery, corruption and nepotism of the law-making politicians have made the country's economic and social standard to fall into a deep abyss.

Although in the name of democracy, the citizens have sent their representatives to the parliament and provincial councils. Have these representatives done enough for the rural masses that they represent at these national and provincial bodies? Political family banditry, launching glorified gigantic projects with foreign borrowings at high interest rates ghostly standing hither and thither as white elephants without much contribution to the national economic growth or to the wellbeing of the masses, giving massive direct tax concessions to a favored few at times making them fabulously rich illegally, incompetent financial management causing severely increased balance of payment difficulties, decreased foreign reserves, failure to repay foreign debts, inability to control inflation all round and because of many other reasons Sri Lanka is slipping fast down to the rock bottom of poverty amidst an unending political chaos. All of the above are affecting the Anuradhapura District like any other district in the country, but the most serious one that immediately affects this predominantly agricultural district with more than 90 per cent of the population engaged in grain farming is that dreamy and arrogant agricultural policy favoring organic farming based on some wrong advice and banning the import of chemical fertilizer and other agro-chemicals which reduced grain and vegetable production by more than 40 per cent during the last three seasons of farming. This has created not only food insecurity but a chain of other consequences such as immediate food scarcity, family health deterioration, constraining children's education, rising family indebtedness and increase of property mortgages and sales. As a sequel of all this, there emerged a long-lasting cry for an economic and social system change, defying the political party in power loaded with too old or lowly educated or both old and lowly educated political representatives.

Some of these people's representatives in the country are lowly educated in the sense that they have not gone beyond GCE ordinary or GCE advanced level. Their capacity for law making and guiding district administrators and even village level duty-bearers is disappointingly low. They do not accept this reality and foolhardily try to show others that they know everything. The worst thing is that they are not willing to take professional advice from the available subject specialists. These lowly educated politicians simply turn a deaf year to subject specialists' suggestions even when offered.

Some of those subject specialist professionals live and work hovering over the capital city or the universities and research institutes elsewhere. May be that they know their preferred subject areas well, but the question is whether they widely apply that knowledge to foster grass-root level development all round. This calls for a broad-based selection of professionals from the districts as well, to entrust them with planning and implementation of those plans because they know the ground realities thoroughly. This applies to Anuradhapura District as well as to the other outlying districts.

Admittedly, higher education achievers were rather limited in the Anuradhapura District during the first half of the twentieth century, but the conditions have vastly improved during the latter part of the twentieth century and thereafter. The local parliamentary and provincial council representatives of the Anuradhapura District know this very well though they follow a policy of not seeing them, not hearing about them, and not even speaking about them. Increase of educated persons in the district is seen as a threat to the standing of lowly educated politicians which is an unwarranted fear.

Late Mr. Ratna B. Ekanayake in 2011 published a 266-page book called *Wev Bendi Danawwe Nihanda Pera Gammankaruwo* in which the higher educational achievements of 36 selected persons, their subject specializations achieved in their earned first-degree examinations and postgraduate degrees in local and foreign universities have been well documented. Some have even achieved double doctorates in their chosen fields of studies. Their professional achievements as research writers, planners, administrators, Ministry secretaries, agriculture specialists, soil scientist, irrigation and construction engineers, irrigation management specialists, university professors and lecturers including a vice chancellor, vocational training directors, ambassadors, lawyers including a Chief Justice, doctors, bank heads including a Central Bank Governor and one director general of Regional Development Banks, several senior employees in State and private banks, heads of many corporations, financial managers, including a Director General of National

Budget, Chief Secretaries of Provincial Councils and excelled senior heads of Government Departments, leading Businessmen and many others. However, the politicians never bothered to access such available information and seek professional support for the overall development of the district.

As the genuine professionals are grossly involved in their chosen activities, one cannot expect them to come meekly before the lowly educated politicians paying homage to them. It is up to the politicians to get professionals' support on invitations extended to them, seeking their support. Professionals are also unwilling to be rudely dictated to by politicians and their immediate shady supporters. Unless the professionals are cordially invited to help the politicians, they will continue to avoid curry-favoring the politicians and more particularly to reach them through those lowly educated undesirable supporters of the politicians, as the helpless ordinary villagers are destined to do today. In fact, that is the reason why there exists a yawning gap between the politicians and the professionals.

There is one thing that the professionals can and should do in this regard. That is raising constructive voices in private and public about the development needs. It seems that this is beginning to take shape at present. The politicians on their part need to give an increasingly cordial hearing mostly to the local professional experts and try to make use of their advice more often. Unless such 'give-and-take' stances are adopted by both professional experts and politicians takes place in the Anuradhapura District, the progress of the present task functions for development of the district either remain dwarfed or go more chaotic.

FOR A BETTER TOMORROW. As a prelude to this Foreword, it has been noted that we need to draw useful lessons from history more importantly to plan and execute our future task functions still better than our present functions. This requires many parliamentary and regional policy changes that are mutually inclusive, to pull up the severely ailing economy and its consequential worsening of social behavior going towards a worst situation like sinking in a mass of quicksand. The on-going youth uprising *(aragalaya)*[1] is a loud and clear warning of this disaster, raised first in cities but with government's calculated suppression, it is rapidly going into the rural masses in all nooks and corners with the support of many other discontent groups. An attempt to suppress it is not the answer. Show the people that the government is taking wise policy decisions to make the economy and society both healthy. The following are some of the essential needs in this regard.

(i)   Conduct parliamentary and provincial council elections soon. Delaying them for the benefit of those in power in the present parliament and provincial councils is likely to increase the animosity and anger of the economically suffering voters highly influenced by youth, in a background of international voicing about the economic and political stability needed in the country for a new economic revival.

(ii)   For the future elections, nomination should not be granted to the undesirable persons such as government's fund-abusers, those accused of bribery and corruption, illegally national resource exploiters, drug

---

[1] Peaceful public protests took place in Colombo in 2022.

dealers or supporters of others dealing with drugs, proven immoral characters, very lowly educated and too old persons.

(iii)   Nominate not more than one blood-related person of sound character from an immediate or extended family to contest for a parliamentary or a provincial council seat and do not nominate one person to contest for more than one constituency.

(iv)   More than 50 per cent of the population in this country being women, assign at least a 25 per cent of all nominations of any political party for an election. For a provincial council election in particular women from the same province subject to the conditions in (ii) and (iii) above be nominated from each contesting political party. If this assigned number of women nomination-seekers are unattainable to meet, devise a system to meet the shortfalls as appointed female members later, also subject to (ii) and (iii) above. This device is generally expected to have female election-victors relatively free of bribery and corruption as women are by and large free from those evils.

(v)   Set up a National Youth Commission with nine sub-components for the nine provinces' representation under the command of a competent professional body (not under a politically shaded body) to understand the real youth grievances which can vary from province to province, and then seek fitting solutions for youth in each province, without any prejudice, political or otherwise, as youth forms a very large segment of the country's population that should not and cannot be just ignored or hated.

(vi)   Development projects need to be well-identified, prioritized to serve mostly the masses, subject to critical financial auditing and letting the public know all about projects from the start to completion of them through effective and regular monitoring and evaluation of them.

(vii)   It should be the responsibility of the new government that comes into power in the next general election to be responsible to maintain a healthy balance of payment, an increase of foreign reserves, a contained inflation, a national asset protection and a credible financial management all round fostering economic and social responsibilities of the government which positively affect the people both at national and regional levels.

(viii)   In the face of the non-availability of heavy metals, fuel, and the ever-changing technology and stiff competition for manufactured goods of developing countries in the world market, more emphasis must be laid on the development of agriculture and agro-based small and medium scale industries with properly harnessed knowledge and advice of the subject specialist. That effort should not be made on political whims and fancies anymore. In boosting agriculture, act in advance to withstand likely climate changes due to floods in the wet zone and likely droughts in the dry zone where drainage and irrigation must be improved respectively. Early preparedness for such likely natural disasters is necessary.

(ix) Strong social organizations of agricultural communities in the past, well sustained their economic and social activities. As R. W. Ievers in 1899 demonstrated in his *Manual of the North Central Province*, these communities in the Anuradhapura District were engaged in proper and timely cultivation systems with frugal use of tank water during the dry spells, proper sowing and harvesting of crops and adhering to all rituals associated with farming. Lokubanda Tillakaratne, in his ethnological and historical reading of *Rata Sabhāwa of Nuwarakalaviya* in 2023 shows how important it was for the upkeep of a strong social organization in an agricultural community. Due to economic, social, and political changes these organizations have gone out of screen and in place of them new economic and social organization need to be formed both with the fusion of worthwhile concepts still traceable in the old organizations and newly emerging cohesive development concepts for the economic, social, and political betterment of rural agricultural communities. In fact, this is happening in small scales in Sri Lanka today. Cases in point are *Manudam Mehewara* headed by the *Sarwodaya* movement, *Vanithabhimana* movement sponsored by the National Development Bank and *Gammedda* movement sponsored by the Maharaja Organization together with Sirasa Television Channel.

(x) In addition to them like the old *Rata Sabhāwa*, establish *Ellanga Sabhā* constituting all villages in a micro- or meso-valley compact physical development units based on tank irrigation to foster agricultural economic rejuvenation with social cohesion sans (already ebbing) racial and caste differences in the great North Central Dry Zone plain including the Anuradhapura District. As the average number of village tank in an *Ellangava* has been found to be eight by Panabokke in 1999, an *Ellanga Sabha* would be an ideal unit of management with active participation of its residents with good leadership emerged from it and active provincial council support. It would also be an ideal management stage for the now discontented youth to come in and get constructively engaged on their own in their homeland peacefully shedding their right or wrong belief that *Colambata kiri gamata kekiri* (best to the urbanites, scraps to us the villagers).

15, January 2023
muatennakoon@gmail.com

1. INTRODUCTION

*D*ecades ago, one day, as I was playing with other kids on the front yard of our *gemandiya* (housing compound) in the village, my mother brought out a circular bundle, faded and wrinkled, a family relic made of linen. It looked like an upside-down cooking pan. When asked, she told us it belonged to her late grandfather. She then casually placed it on my head as other kids stood around hoping to a get a chance to try it on. It was, as I came to know later, *mohotti bámma*, the unassuming headgear and the insignia of authority, and belonged to my great-grandfather who was the Mohottāla, head of his clan (Varige) of 18 villages of close kins.

I had no idea who Mohottāla was nor what he looked like. As years piled up behind me, I could not miss this inconsequential moment when I saw someone wearing a headscarf or a hat, until some years ago I came across a seminal piece of writing by Kapuruhami Madukanda Ratemahattayā (?-1943) about a village assembly called Rata Sabhāwa or Variga Sabhāwa practiced in Nuwarakalaviya. This *Ratemahattayā* (Master of Rata – Country; pl. Ratemahatvaru, Ralahaminvahansela) had written how Mohottālas, and other village officials resolved conflicts and dispensed justice to their fellow villagers. As I began to explore it more, I realized my great grandfather was associated with something special to him, his community, and his ancestors. This newfound information gave me energy to continue to find more about this assembly.

Often the following pages may read like a collection of anecdotes and notes. Because when I decided to write about this tradition, I had very little resources to work with. All the officials, in whatever capacity they functioned, and people who were present watching how this system worked were two generations removed. Although the history of religious involvement in this province for centuries was well documented, literature and scholarship on day-to-day life of its people and their social institutions like Rata Sabhāwa had been in the fringe. At best they appeared as subtexts in other ethnographic narratives. Thus, recovery of its history in the context of greater Sri Lanka has been a difficult and challenging task to interested scholars and to those whose ancestors had a stake in it. Thus, I had only a very few trails to follow. I found, "without leaving documentary debris to sift through, task of recording and examining the lived experience of these people required listening attentively to the resonances of their spoken thoughts which endured"[1] through the years.

Rata Sabhāwa or Variga Sabhāwa was an ancient judicial system in Sri Lankan villages, mainly in Nuwarakalaviya province. This book tries to explore how this tradition came about, how it worked, who its actors were and how it ceased to exist. By doing so, I peeked deep into the history of the region. When the Rata Sabhāwa was in full gear, it was not a perpetual Eden of Judiciary, but was beneficial to the

---

NOTES

[1] Anand A. Yang, 1987, Conversation of Rumors: The Language of Popular Mentalites in Late Nineteenth-Century Colonial India. *Journal of Social History*, Vol. 20, No. 3, pp.485-505.

people in the region in their good times and bad times.

This institution may not look like a *prima facie* case of judicial exploration, but evolved with nascent elements of a modern court, with its own home-grown 'laws', best called as traditions and customs mostly indigenous to the region. Bryce Ryan (1953) called it a "formal quasi-legal judicial machinery," while E. R. Leach (1961, 1968) found it as a "corporate type of social group."

In addition to what is written already about the Rata Sabhāwa tradition or exists as oral history, my first plan was to contact any descendants of Chiefs or *mulādenivaru* (minor officials) who were involved in conducting these Sabha, and to find any archival records and any physical evidence to see or learn about to share with others. I did not discount the general interest public would have to know about them. I also dwelt to see the relationship between Nuwarakalaviya and the Kandy King who had appointed a *Dissava* (Senior Chief; Governor of a large tract of country; pl. *Dissavaru*) for Nuwarakalaviya region where he did not reside nor have property inherited by himself or granted by the King. I discuss contradistinctively the extent of involvement of Nuwarakalaviya *Maha Vanniya* (Senior-most Chief with plenipotentiary powers in Nuwarakalaviya) or his deputy *Ratemahattayā* (Chief) with Kandyan Court and other powers in Maritime provinces. I found interesting revelations and the state of relationship existed among traditional leaders of Nuwarakalaviya, Kandy King and colonial administrations.

The advantage and central function of the Rata Sabhāwa tradition was to maintain law and order in communities, resolve conflicts between individuals, families, *variga* clans (s. *Varige*, adj. *variga*) and villages and sustain differentiated caste schemes to make social order manageable. Given its entrenched stature, Rata Sabhāwa was the *lex terrae*, the law of the land (in Nuwarakalaviya). It was a law privy to the villagers in the region. In many ways, what represented the inner space of cultural universe which expressed the character of the people in the province was the Rata Sabhāwa 'law.' But as this institution remained a cloistered fact of life in the village, its configuration in the national awareness remained diffusive.

Rata Sabhāwa or Variga Sabhāwa tradition evolved to fill the vacuum of rural governance created when the Sinhala Kings vacated Nuwarakalaviya and moved south following the invasions by South Indian elements. Some elders suggest that the customs of Rata Sabhā that functioned at the time of its demise in early 20th century started by King Buwanekabahu II in the Hasthisilapura (Kurunegala) kingdom in 14th century.[2]

Rata Sabhāwa had all the ingredients and characteristics of a court sans the written laws and procedures. Even without any exposure to Western or Eastern law principles, Nuwarakalaviya Chiefs and *mulādānivaru/kāriyakarawannō*, also called *sulu mulādānivaru* (lesser officials) (s. *mulādāniya*)[3] made use of precedents of centuries old customs and traditions rooted in communities largely in the province and to some

---

[2] D.B. Rajakaruna, Indigenous Doctor of Kekatiyagollewa cited in Hettiarachchi, D. E. 2019, 1979, ed. *Sinhala Sirith Sangrahaya*, p. 33.

[3] In Kandyan districts these numbered about 28 (Vimalananda, T, 1963, *Udarata Maha Keralla*, p. 424). In the pages to follow, *Chief* denotes one who holds an elite title (Ratemahattayā, Dissava, Maha Vanniyā, Vanniya and Adikārama) with executive powers over a district granted by the King or Maha Vanniyā.

extent in Kandyan highlands to make sound and equitable decisions. There was no training for *mulādenivaru*. Their training was the apprenticeship of life's experience which everyone in the community shared. So, there were no surprises at the Sabhāwa. The laws – customs – they discussed were all in the open, known and practiced by everyone.

Common belief is that our traditions and customs were partially influenced and shaped by what were found in some parts of India. Thus, William Robertson's writings in 1812 about traditions existed in the Indian subcontinent aptly describe the beginnings of the community-based institutions like Rata Sabhāwa:

> [...] long before the positive statues, there is gradually formed, a body of customary or common law, by which judicial proceedings are directed, and every decision conformable to it is submitted to with reverence as the result of the accumulated wisdom and experience of ages. (p. 271)

Even if there were no "written laws" the Chiefs and their minor officials could refer to, norms practiced for a long time were nearly always accepted as law. Traditionalism also granted authority to those who worked to sustain it. Authority also is derived from heroism and exemplary character or charisma of a person as we found in Keppetipola during the war against the British in 1818 when he commanded the respect of the people, and grudgingly, the British colonial administration.[4] Legitimacy to conduct Rata Sabhāwa business stemmed from the "persistence of cultural forms that may be attributed as much to the exercise of power as to the spontaneous consensus about values, and acknowledgement of the openness of the historical process."[5] Elena Kagan, Supreme Court Justice of the Unites States noted, "Overall, the way the Court retains legitimacy and fosters public confidence is by acting like a court."[6] Moreover, the legitimacy[7] of the Rata Sabhāwa system seems to fall under a concept called 'consensual consent folk theory' whereby government received its legitimacy under the consent of the governed.[8]

Villagers agreed to abide by the practice (of the Sabhāwa system) following long standing customs and folk traditions, its zeitgeist.[9] With consistent and faithful adherence to tradition, cultural foundations like Rata Sabhāwa provided moral authority for their relevance and existence. Richard H. Fallon, Jr. (2018) wrote:

> A morally legitimate regime is one with the power to alter normative obligations… In order to have that moral power, a legal regime must satisfy certain moral conditions. Conversely, if the overall body of law within a legal regime falls beneath some standard, or if morality would forbid conformity to enough of its dictates, it will lack legitimate authority in the moral sense, even if it enjoys broad support among its population. (p.24)

---

[4] In Kandyan folklore, his heroics had elevated him to a deific state known as Monarawila Aluth Deyyo.

[5] Brow, James, 1996, *Demons and Development: The Struggle for Community in a Sri Lankan Village* p. 24.

[6] Caplan, Lincoln (2022), Justice Elena Kagan in Dissent, qtd. in *Harvard Magazine*. November-December 2022.

[7] *Leg*, the root of the Latin word *legitimus* (lawful) comes from *lex* – law.

[8] Arthur I. Applbaum, 2019, *Harvard Magazine*, November-December 2022. p. 34.

[9] General state of cultural, political, and moral mood of a particular time.

Even without written laws, nor an alternative, the Rata Sabhāwa stood square in the middle of the village as the institution to look up to, and its customs gave it legitimacy, and a sense of indigeneity whereby it created a *us* or *ourselves* feeling. This happened while the Dutch and British colonial laws functioned concurrently, two one-lane roads heading side by side in one direction through the same forest.

With their fidelity to the cultural norms, Rata Sabha was presided over by *Maha Vanniya, Ratemahattayā,* under them the *kāriyakarawannō* (lesser officials), while people who looked up to them provided the inviolability of the authority traditions demanded. Such consent was boosted by a certain state of mindset as seen from statements made by these officials who attributed their authority to a royal referendum given to *Vannivaru,* the Chiefs, in the 14th century.

To place the Sabhāwa in its traditional confines, I decided to begin with its geographical demarcations and folklore narrations in Chapter 2. They show the breadth of this institution's influence within and beyond the boundaries of the province. Because in reality the geographical area this judicial system practiced included not just the Nuwarakalaviya, but Tamankaduwa areas in the North Central Province, some northern areas of Matale in the Central Province, Hath Kōrale Districts in North Western Province, and Sinhala Pattu (s. *Pattuwa,* a Province) of Vavuniya District in the Northern Province.[10]

In general, two kinds of people's gatherings convened on an ad hoc basis to resolve an issue brought before them. Usually, these gatherings were called Rata Sabha, variga courts or caste courts. Albeit the sociologists' belief that the knowledge of the existence of a common ancestor creates stronger bonds in a community, sharing similar experiences also leads to diverse groups (families) coming together to form a new identity, a variga clan in this case, which can also augment the strength of a people in a locality. The common origin of the experience enhances the situation they are now in and when they find others around them willing to conform to it, the bond gets stronger. Examples to these community principles can be found incorporated into the ability of Rata Sabhāwa or Variga Sabhāwa to settle contentious issues amicably with the members of the same caste, and assuredly take a stand against discordant inter-group activities, e.g., cases of inter-caste unions and punish the offenders involved in such situations. I will discuss this in Chapter 3.

Chapter 4 investigates slightly different collectives of people in other areas of the country set up to resolve their community issues as well. For example, the *Gan Sabe* (Village Court) practiced in Kandyan Highlands as described by British Governor's Resident Representative, (*Rāsident Tena*) in Kandy, John D'Oyly (1774-1824) (1929), aptly matches the ingredients of the Rata Sabhāwa concept existed in Nuwarakalaviya in early decades of the 19th century:

> This Court is frequently held both in the Dissavonies and the Upper Districts, and consists of an assembly of the Principal and

---

[10] According to T.B. Ekanayake, a *mulādāniya* (a minor title holder) from Kekirawa who submitted an essay in 1932 for the SSS, also known as Wickramasinghe Manuscripts, the following areas practiced the Rata Sabhāwa tradition: North Central Province, Vanni Hath Pattuwa, Demala Hath Pattuwa, Hiriyala Hath Pattuwa (Nikawagampaha Kōrale; Divigandahaya Kōrale and Otota Kōrale), and North Matale (Kandapalla & Inamaluwa Kōrale Districts) (Hettiarachchi, ed. 1979, 2019, p. 50).

experienced Men of a Village, who met at an Ambalama or a shady
tree or other Central Place upon the occurrence of any Civil or
Criminal matter, as Disputes regarding Limits, Debts, Petty Thefts,
Quarrels etc., and after Enquiring into the Case, if possible settle it
amicably, declaring a Party which is in default, adjudge Restitution
or Compensation and dismissing with Reproof and Admonition,
their Endeavors being directed to Compromise and not to
Punishment. [...] a fine is sometimes levied for some offences, and
in some dissvonies is shared with the other assessors [*sic*].[11] (p. 28)

In addition, I put forward in this chapter my explication of the uniqueness of
Nuwarakalaviya, and its rulers and independence enjoyed by its institutions. Rata
Sabhāwa of Nuwarakalaviya operated as an independent entity. Only sometimes
officials from other Rata Sabhā participated as invited guests. It was answerable to
no other authority, not even the King, but *Vannihuru* (*Vanniyars* or *Vannivaru* in
regional vernacular) and *Ratemahatvaru* alone.[12] This was partly due to implicit belief
of *Vannihuru* (and the villagers) that they had independence to deliver justice in their
districts.[13]

While the three main sub kingdoms (*rata*) in the country: Pihiti, Maya and
Ruhunu (*Three Sinhale*) remained as one kingdom in the reckoning of the people,
practicalities spelled otherwise. Even though the country is an island, Shirani
Bandaranayake noted the lack of any commonality between its three ancient
kingdoms. "[…] in relation to the administrative matters there seems to have been
no inter-relationship between these kingdoms."[14] By perusing further, I found even
within one kingdom, i.e., the Kandyan in particular, geographical isolation played
some areas to be quasi-independent as seen from the role of Rata Sabhāwa in
Nuwarakalaviya and its immediate neighboring areas in King's dominions like Matale
and Hath Kōrale (Kurunegala) which submitted to practices generally not shared by
other areas of the Kandyan highlands.

Rata Sabhāwa crafted and often embraced some practices, traditions, customs,
and even precedents overseeing the justice which made it possible for *Mohottāla* or
in a special case, Maha Vanniyā (Head of the Vanni region) or *Ratemahattayā* (Head

---

[11] D'Oyly was in Sri Lanka since 1802 as Resident and later as the first Commissioner of Kandyan
provinces. He died in Kandy on May 25, 1824. Well versed in Sinhala, he had a major role in
drafting the Kandyan Constitution in 1815. His role in the fall of Kandy as the Resident is subject
to multiple interpretations. Gananath Obeyesekere called him "master spy; king-breaker" (*The
Doomed King*…2017, pp. 23, 212) while Brendon and Yasmine Gooneratne (1999) wrote that he
"had become deeply attached to the island and its people" and was "devoted to Ceylon… (*This
Inscrutable Englishman: Sir John D'Oyly (1774-1824*, p. 226)." But his *Sketch of Kandyan laws* (1833, 1835)
is the foundational document on the subject.

[12] Folklore suggests Vanni name for the region was first coined by King Buwanekabahu v. British
Civil Servant R. W. Ievers (1899) in *Manual of the North Central Province* said *Vannihuru* claim descent
from seven Bandaras who came from the Indian subcontinent during the reign of King Maha Sen
(274-301 AD), p. 92.

13 D'Oyly, John, 1835, p. 230.

[14] Shirani Bandaranayake, 1986, *The Devolution of Government in Sri Lanka: Legal Aspects of the
Relationship Between Central and Local Government; An Historical and Comparative Study*. (Unpublished
Doctoral Dissertation, University of London), p. 22.

of a Region) to give final decision at a Sabhā session. All participants in this Sabhāwa willingly acquiesced that these officials as having power to act as final arbiters.

In Nuwarakalaviya, the passel of *mulādānivaru/kāriyakarawannō* which consisted of *Lékam Rāla, Mohottāla, Badderāla, Arachirāla, Undiya Rāla, Vel Vidāne, Veda Rāla, Nákath Rāla, Gamarāla* and *Héna Māma* (*Henayā* – washerman) did the bulk of groundwork in the two Sabhā – Rata and Variga. Their dedication to duty was of high order as they believed the title bestowed upon them as an honor. I have seen the level of importance my maternal grandfather (Fig. 37) placed on his humble and unpaid work as a *Vel Vidāne* of the village.

Considering there were 17 divisions called *Kōrales*[15] in the province, each headed by a *Kōrala*,[16] it is safe to assume there must have been at least two dozen functioning Rata Sabhā in the late 19th and early 20th centuries. They had authority granted by the traditional system of Chieftains and officials who met *en banc* in the presence of the people. In 1899, R. W. Ievers, Government Agent in Anuradhapura, wrote that the vernacular term *Ratemahattayā* title was previously called *Mudiyanse* who headed a *pattuwa* (pl. *pattu*) or a district in Nuwarakalaviya. However, after 1834, a Head of a *pattuwa* began to be called *Kōrala*.[17] The explicit power of Chieftains and officials allowed them to find an accused in the wrong or innocent. Often such a verdict is appealed to the *Ratemahattayā* or Dissava, or in ancient times, to the King of the region.

I will discuss the crimes and punishments existed in Sri Lanka in the past in Chapter 5. Acts defined or traditionally accepted as 'crimes' perhaps could have been called infractions of minor scale in modern standards. In the case of Nuwarakalaviya, nevertheless, they received full attention of the community and in turn its enforcer of social order – the Rata Sabhāwa. Sabhāwa believed in the main that all villagers were equal under its laws, customs, and traditions. When applying the rules and dispensing justice, Rata Sabhāwa did not act on the principle of *parium judicium* – trial by jury per se.[18] Nonetheless, in a way, and interestingly, I found the Rata Sabhāwa or Variga Sabhāwa had which I call a 'jury of one' – the *henayā*. At least for one phase of the hearing went directly through him. Some punishments in general existed in the country then were not much different from the medieval methods practiced in other countries as well. Although Rata Sabhāwa was involved in solving mild forms of intransigeances like breaches and infractions punishable by

---

[15] Several *Kōrale* divisions formed a *Rata* or *Pattuwa* which was headed by a Ratemahattayā.

[16] Ievers, R. W. 1899, p. 42.

[17] Ievers, 1899, p. 61.

[18] Even before deposing the Kandy King, English in Maritime Provinces had jury trial with 13 peers. It was introduced to Sri Lanka with the efforts of Sir Alexander Johnston by the Charter of August 6th, 1810 (William Skeen, Govt. Printer, *Collection of Legislative Acts of the Ceylon Government*, 1853, Sec. X, p. 125). It soon gained popularity among the native population. The 1818-19 painting, *The Supreme Court on the Judicature of Ceylon* (James Stephanoff, 1787 -1874) at Yale Center for British Art shows the diverse populace that was participating in a jury trial in Colombo (Fig. 26). In 1834, in the notable case of treason against Molligoda Adikārama, Dunuwila Dissava and few others, the jury was composed of six Europeans and seven natives of high rank from the Maritime Provinces. The accused Chiefs refused to have a jury of Kandyans! When the native jurors unanimously voted to acquit the accused, the Chief Justice "was surprised by the verdict" (Marshall, Henry, 1846, 1954, *Ceylon: A general Description...* p. 169).

detention, imprisonment, or social ostracism, Maha Vanniyā or Ratemahatvaru also had to deal with instances of crimes of vicious nature like robbery or murder. What punishment they could have imposed upon the accused had not been put in writing. Exceptions for such situations are ancient inscriptions on stone slabs or walls or Sannas or Sittu (Pali: *citta* - will, intention) – notes written on strips of processed palm leaves for a specific transaction or an edict where punishments like imprecations or curses were written down often. In my review, a general description of crimes, and punishment for unsociable behavior will throw light to the larger picture of law and order in the country along with the role of Rata Sabhāwa in it.

Villagers, existing for centuries or newly formed, were caste-conscious in many ways. In Chapter 6, I discuss these dynamics and how villages remained differentiated in the context of distance between, and caste composition of people in them. Rata Sabhāwa functioned in a *gama* (s.) or a group of *gam* (pl.) community with its physical formats, as needed. Gananath Obeyesekere (1967) stated Gama as a "Collection of land holdings (p. 13)." In Nuwarakalaviya, it is an agricultural republic, each with its tank and the fields below, self-governing, relatively independent of State control, but scarcely having the "hierarchy of power" as seen in a Kandyan village – minor official > Chief > and finally, the King. In Nuwarakalaviya, it was called a *paraveni gama* (freehold village) and fits this description in the context of the Rata Sabhāwa tradition independent of the region it practiced. A collection of contiguous plots of land called 'an estate,' with a common name, owned and held by one feudal Chief was a *nindagama* (pl. *nindagam*), a village granted to him by the King. It is important to note, therefore, that a *gama* owned solely by a Chief may not fall under the authority of a Rata Sabhāwa. Villages endowed by the King to temples and priests are also exempt from Rata Sabhāwa overview. There is no record that Europeans or Burghers in Nuwarakalaviya ever appeared before a Rata Sabhāwa.

New villages were built from ground up or renovated by a group of individuals, usually with the process called *gam bándeema*.[19] One reason for *gam bándeema* occasion in Nuwarakalaviya was when an inhabited village was deserted or abandoned and left to fallow because of diseases or haunted by devils or subjected to the anger of deity Pulleyar.[20, 21] Generations later, a new group of villagers who may be strangers to the area come and revive the village by repairing its abandoned infrastructure and establishing communication with the neighboring villages to link up with the jurisdiction of its Rata Sabhāwa.. Afterwards instead of the *Mohottāla*,[22] the Chief

---

[19] See Codrington, H. W., 1938, *Ancient Land Tenure and Revenue in Ceylon*, p. 63 for a detail description of Gam Bendeema exercise.

[20] Leonard Woolf (1913) (p. 176) in *Village in the Jungle*, the fictitious story based near Hambantota in Southern Sri Lanka with similar living and climatic conditions as Nuwarakalaviya, gives a vivid picture how a lone village in a jungle gets abandoned forever. "[…] The years had brought evil, death, and decay upon the village. …Disease and hunger visited each year. … No man, traveler or headman or trader, ever came to the village now. Disease and death took the old first […]. At last, they yielded to the jungle. They packed up their few possessions and left the village forever."

[21] Lewis, J.P. 1895b, Folklore from North Ceylon, *Folklore*, Vol. 6, No. 2 (June 1895), pp. 176-185. pp. 176-185.

[22] About 14 diverse Mohottāla types have been identified. Ven. Medauyangoda Wimalakeerthi (1955). *Sinhala Ānduwa*, p. 62.

himself may conduct hearings in the Rata Sabhāwa until matters of its jurisdiction (if comes up) are resolved.

The bedrock of social structure and sustenance of Nuwarakalaviya was its oral traditions as there were hardly any written volumes about them in 19th century or earlier for people to follow. To sustain traditions, customs, and etiquette of the community as an existential stabilizer of orderly survival, Rata Sabhāwa played an immensely valuable role. It insulated these traditions, maintained trusting social conventions, but rarely written, to prevent them from getting run over by forces detrimental to the welfare of the community. Anthropologist Megan Biesele (1993) said, "Though speech doesn't fossilize, it is clear that oral traditions consistently preserve enough material to be recognizable over time as the 'same tradition' while processing and incorporating new material."[23] It is transferable archaeology of a people's way of life. It participated in the community in a major way in maintaining kinship creed, caste purity and status quo of a *Varige*. In its rudimentary way, shying away from social disorder and even violence, Rata Sabhāwa achieved a functional society. Elizabeth Marshall Thomas said of the violence in *Ju/wasi* bushmen clans in Kalahari: "what they had that we seem to lack was a successful method of containing it."[24] In respect to maintaining harmony amongst its people, Rata Sabhāwa fits this description in amplest ways. Chapter 7 reviews written information in all forms existed in ancient Sri Lanka and up to the time feudal system disappeared in early 20th century.

Particularly interesting are the two written sources in the early 20th century that dwelt into social traditions of the region. The earliest was the seminal essay *Rata Sabhāwa* by Kapuruhami Madukanda Ratemahattayā in 1911 (in Sinhala, unpublished, and published posthumously in the Journal Royal Asiatic Society in 1948).[25] Then in 1932, for a writing competition launched by C. L. Wickramasinghe, Govt. Agent at Anuradhapura, 32 essayists from the province submitted compositions discussing the folklore and their personal experiences of the customs and social codes in the province. These essayists were office holders of traditional institutions like Rata Sabhāwa, *gamwasama* (*gamarāla*, head of the village), the *wewa* (*Vel Vidāne*, caretaker of the village tank), or professionals like indigenous doctors, *patabándō* (s. *patabándā*) or *mulādānivaru/kāriyakarawannō* (Appendix C) or simply autodidacts of the time. Exposure to formal writing, much less structured education was a rarity in villages then.[26]

These essays came to be known as Wickramasinghe Manuscripts. Later they were handed to the Royal Asiatic Society in Colombo. Manuscripts were a testament to the authority of the elders who were involved in Rata Sabhāwa or other administrative traditions that provided and maintained a culture of civility

---

[23] Qtd. in Elizabeth Marshall Thomas, 2006, *The Old Way*, p. 207.

[24] Thomas, 2006, p. 228.

[25] Kapuruhami, K.A. (1948). Rata Sabhāwa, *Journal of the Royal Asiatic Society* (*Ceylon*), Vol. 28, No. 106, 42-68. Sinhala translation of this is found in Lokubanda Tillakaratne, *Rata Sabhāwa* (Sinhala) Sarasavi Books, 2019.

[26] Schooling was a sorry affair and not a widely available option or privilege to majority of people in Nuwarakalaviya and other remote parts of the country. Living proof was my mother who was illiterate, and father who attended school only up to 6th grade.

demanding good conduct in people. Although the essayists lived in villages far away and isolated from urban centers, they wrote authoritatively about the customs in Nuwarakalaviya with sophistication showing their extraordinary erudition and experience.

Authors of the Wickramasinghe Manuscripts bemoaned and noted that after the British took full control of the administration of the country, attention to Rata Sabhāwa began to decline in favor of colonial legal machinations devised to maintain agricultural and irrigation infrastructure, laws on tort, some criminal offences, and to act on civil conflicts between people. E.R. Leach (1968) wrote that after the introduction of the Divisional Revenue Officers (DRO) system in 1938, the Chiefs "lost interest in the maintenance of the Nuwarakalaviya *variga* institutions" (p. 78). At the same time, without the authority of the new *lex terrae* vested in them, and the Roman Dutch law traditions adapted to encompass the whole island, the disbanded Chiefs were not going to take a chance in conducting an anachronistic and unsanctioned system of private tribunals and taxing people (by way of fines) which could have been interpreted as an extra judicial activity.

How it continued to prosper even without a *lex scripta*, written code of laws, to sustain consistency on a larger and continuously changing stage is a question for another time. Whereas the pre-modern writers have written mostly glorious accounts of the District and Chiefs of the past, my observations often seem to take on a critical dimension. Often it was unavoidable. Chapter 8 describes the Chiefs and how titles were granted. Throughout the history, even as the Anuradhapura kingdom was slowly migrating south, its Chiefs did not abandon their precious charges, e.g., the Sacred Bodhi Tree (*Ficus religiosa*) and other religious and cultural monuments and institutions painstakingly protected by previous Kings. Rata Sabhāwa, supplemented Chiefs' work though not directly involved with some of their tasks but maintaining some aspects of social institutions.

There were conductors leading the traditions and customs of Rata Sabhāwa. The functionary leader, supervisor or the one who held the stewardship of a Rata Sabhāwa was the traditional hereditary feudal Chief in the province, addressed in any of the following titular appellations: *Maha Dissāva*,[27] *Ratemahattayā* , *Vanni Bandara*, *Vanniyā* or *Vanni Unnehe*.[28] As *Vanniyars* of Malabar origin (Southwestern Coastal region of India) gradually moved further north beyond Nuwarakalaviya, the last three titles and *Maha Vanni Unnehe* (ruler of the Vanni) seem to have been in effect

---

[27] Offices of Dissāva of Nuwarakalaviya and Tamankaduwa, appointed by the King, were abolished by British in 1818 (Pieris, R 1956, p. 250 n57).

[28] According to written accounts and Tamil fables, *Vanniyars* were brought to Sri Lanka by Kulak-Koddan (Kallakkolam), the Indian Maha Raja who was in Sri Lanka on a pilgrimage during the time of King Pandu (c 500 BC). The *Vanniyars* were summoned to the island to cultivate lands for the benefit of the (Hindu) temples. After a series of internecine conflicts among their own factions, the *Vanniyars* decided to select seven among themselves as Chieftains with sovereign power (C. Brito, 1879, 2007, *Yalpana-Vaipava-Malai or The History of the Kingdom of Jaffna*, p. 6 & 7). In 1848, an old lady claimed to be the last descendent of this line of *Vanniyars* lived in the fort of Jaffna with a small hereditary estate and ancestral possessions (James Emerson Tennent 1860, *Ceylon: An Account of the Island, Physical, Historical and Topographical...* Vol. 2, p. 510). Ievers (1899) suggests that as of 1270 AD, Anuradhapura, already irrelevant as the kingdom had moved to Polonnaruwa three centuries earlier, was in Maha Vanni region ruled by *Vanniyars* (p. 37).

since 1270. Unnehe is an honorific in the level of Minister or someone of similar or superior ranking. Ievers (1899) says Chiefs in Nuwarakalaviya continued to be called as such until 1833 when the British began conferring titles to Sri Lankan elites (p. 37). While *Ratemahattayā* or *Vannihuru* held the controlling power of the tradition of Rata Sabhāwa, a passel of minor ranks of officials appointed by them – *Kōrāla, Mohottāla, Badderāla, Lēkama* (scribe)[29] and different caste representatives providing caste-related functions did bulk of the work.

Unlike the English or Indian titular classes, it is important to note that the Chiefs in Sri Lanka did not have hereditary or inherited rights to a title. But the reality was a different story. Centuries ago, Sri Lankan titles were granted at the pleasure of the King. That usually happened when a Chief maintained the good grace of the King. Then almost always his replacement was his eldest son. King had no compunction in granting him a title whether the grantee had the ability to discharge his responsibilities. Ievers reported some Chiefs with no ability to read or write. The King also had no protocol regarding dismissal of an official regardless of his rank. But he did it anyway. During colonial times too, for their own reason to appease the sitting Chief, his immediate relatives were more likely to become a beneficiary of the rulers' benevolence in the process. Such putative entitlement was rooted deeply in the acquiesced visceral mindset of Sri Lanka. As recently as in the first decade of the 21st century, some newspaper writers were calling the grandson of a former Chief a 'crown prince,' though he had below average education and no proven competency in any profession. Ironically, the Chieftain tradition had disappeared a decade before the 'prince' was born.

Chiefs executed the King's verbal commands, the supreme laws of the land that were etched in the collective reckoning of his subjects. Since the title remained in the family, often over centuries, it was usual the honor to gain enough exposure to have written them as hereditary. In England or most European countries, for instance, once granted by the King the title becomes inherited right of the family until it runs out of male issues to continue. A good example is Sir John D'Oyly (1774-1824) who was granted a baronet title, "*D'Oyly of Kandy*" in 1821. He never married and had no heirs. With his death in Kandy after a bout of fever, his baronetcy became extinct.

Only exception to the above tradition I believe, at least in the perspective of Sri Lanka, is the head of the Nuwarawawe Bulankulame family of Anuradhapura, who is the traditional and long standing lay guardian of the Sacred Bodhi Tree, albeit his title as *Maha Vanniya* too was invalidated when the feudal system was abolished in mid 1930s. This tradition was implicitly incorporated in to an Act of Parliament allowing his descendants to continue a major role in the selection of *Anunāyake* (Chief Monk) of the *Atamasthāna* (Eight Holy Places of Worship).[30] Such a tradition is not known or associated with defunct Chieftaincies elsewhere in the country.

---

[29] During the Dutch times, this appears to have ranked 3rd in the line of titles in *Kanda Uda Kattuwa*.
[30] *Atamasthāna* is a uniquely independent Buddhist religious establishment operated under the tenets of age-old traditions and customs. It consisted of the Sri Maha Bodhi Tree, Lowamahaprasada – the ancient monastery on 1600 granite pillars, Ruwanweliseya (stupa), Thuparamaya (stupa), Mirisawetiya (stupa), Jethawanarama (stupa), Lankarama (stupa) and Abhayagri (stupa) - a collective

Leach (1968) found that the folklore of the region also suggests that the said families are "descendants from the 18th century *Vanniyā* – the Lord of the Vanni – whose baronial state was almost that of an independent prince" (p. 19)." According to pre-modern writings, and in their own claims, the two Nuwarakalaviya families, Nuwarawawe, eponymous after the Nuwaraweva reservoir, and Bulankulame, after the Bulankulama tank, come from the same primogeniture called Suriyawansa Bodhiguptha.[31] This place them in a different taxonomic of standing among former Chieftaincies. Nuwarawawe Bulankulame's deep affiliation with the Bodhi Tree allows them to claim it a unique situation than their former peers.

Rata Sabhāwa was a community event. It functioned with characteristics that regulated its members who expected to retain the fellowship and a sense of belonging for larger communal wellbeing. According to James Brow (1996), it came with the understanding that:

> Such communalization was [...] a simultaneous and sometimes contentious process of inclusion and of exclusion, in the course of which differences among those who are incorporated are often erased or obscured, while differences between insiders and outsiders may be loudly proclaimed. (P. 19)

The functional reach of the Rata Sabhāwa or Variga Sabhāwa extended across all caste denominations in Nuwarakalaviya. Only their mechanics consisted of differences based on varying caste principles. Alchemy for Rata Sabhāwa and Variga Sabhāwa came within the concepts of love and respect for each other, and desire and perseverance for equality the village community expected for and from each other. They relied on themselves and the Chiefs and *mulādānivaru* of all levels, i.e., from *henayā* to Maha Vanniyā, to make it work. Although there had been some exceptional situations, *mulādānivaru* in general considered their participation in these assemblies as an unfettered but ethical responsibility and commitment to justice and community. The higher social status as *patabándō* – those were appointed as officials by wrapping a silver or copper frontlet called *pata tahaduwa* around the forehead by the King or a Chief under the feudatory customs – placed them at a higher podium of exposure to deliver justice. They based their duty on the Three Pure Types of Authority which derived on the grounds of, as Weber (1978) wrote: 1. Legal; 2. Traditional; and 3. Charismatic (p. 215).

Understanding the reasons for the Rata Sabhāwa can only be achieved with diligently searching for caste traditions, customs, and particularly the woman's place in the community and bureaucracies that were in existence in the last two centuries

---

of much revered historic and religious monuments located in Anuradhapura. Its collective administrative functions were done by a committee consisting *Maha Vanni Unnehe*, Head of the Nuwarawawe Bulankulame family, three Ratemahatvaru in Nuwarakalaviya, *Kōrālas* and the Chief Prelate who was called *Anunāyake* of the *Atamasthāna* without any influence or participation of the government since the times of King Kirti Sri Raja Singhe (1747-1782). In 1889, with the enactment of the Buddhist Temporalities Ordinance No. 3, the government stepped in. The Atamasthāna committee lost much of its independence to manage and operate its affairs on its own terms.

[31] Ievers, 1899, p. 43. In early decades of 21st century, the two families coalesced as one and now call Nuwarawawe Bulankulame with one Head. It appears these families had used names *Suriyakula Suriyawansa Bodhigupta,* and *Suriyakumara* intermittently in the past.

and retracing them back to the Medieval Times. In Chapter 9, I look at this and how Rata Sabhāwa customs have influenced women's standing in society, among other factors. There were more laws women were expected or required to abide by than men and these conditions notoriously placed a woman into a restrictive and burdened life in the community back then. Especially remarkable is the restrictions placed on women to marry. I discuss these laws which were quite common centuries ago.

Rata Sabhā customs involved monetary issues. Unlike the Gam Sabhā held in a Kandyan village closer to the palace, generally, fines collected at the Rata Sabhā sessions were not presented to the King. In the case of the former, either the Chief or the villager himself required to take King's share to the royal treasury. In Nuwarakalaviya, officials in the Sabhā sessions divided the collected fines among themselves and villagers. In Chapter 10, I will discuss the monetary aspects and how the Chiefs and officials benefitted in other ways.

A Rata Sabhāwa in session is described in Chapter 11. I have used graphical ways to present the seating arrangement and other protocols. Sequence of stages of the session and duties of each of the official are also given for clarity.

It is not my intention to seek whether there existed localized councils or collectives like the Rata Sabhāwa in other parts of the country with some influence over people. However, it is only reasonable to suggest that Rata Sabhāwa or Variga Sabhāwa functioned as a widespread and firmly anchored concept only in Nuwarakalaviya and its bordering districts in the Dry Zone.[32] These courts enjoyed their own form of autonomy and responsibility to keep social order, which are characteristic of Nuwarakalaviya being an independent and princely region different from other provinces not too far back in the past. But paucity of extensive written material expounding sustained practices of such customs gives us little to conclude otherwise, but to think that they could well have been done under procedures only practiced within the purview of their local ways. Occasionally, if we find the use of the phrase Rata Sabhāwa in other regions, it may be nothing more than a figurative reference to a "council" or "meeting" of that "country" (*rata*).

Villages isolated as they were, and impediments like distance between communities providing no means and desire to write about them, sadly we have rare glimpses of oral accounts that existed until about 1970s to show how these institutions operated. By the turn of the 21st century, we only had a handful of very old villagers with their dream-like memory of the youth then, seeing a group of elders with avuncular self and an aura of authority, each sitting on different layers of reed mats in a '*Maduwa*' (a makeshift shed with flat roof, and walls covered in coconut fronts) and talking about things they had no idea of.

Complexities and inevitability of the march of time swallowed most memories of Rata Sabhāwa, and here we are, trying to build its once colorful mosaic with bits of anecdotal and sparsely written accounts as described under the literature history. Many years later, in a changed society now, we cannot criticize whether this institution was proper or necessary for the needs of the times it existed. We can only compare traditions surrounding it that have evolved into what they are today in the

---

[32] Pieris, R. 1956, p. 150.

diverse legal and cultural winds. To understand the perspectives of Old Village was to understand firsthand the Rata Sabhāwa we were accustomed to hearing about.

Generations of Sri Lankans who lived through Rata Sabhawa were not immune from changes introduced by sources from Europe and the Subcontinent or changes evolved within the fertile grounds in communities. Even the Kandyan Kingship, which was hailed as *Surya Vansa* (of the Sun Race) could not dodge this trend. With the death of King Narendra Singha in 1739 without heir apparent, suddenly his bloodline of succession stood ominously without an agnatic primogeniture. The King's wife was a Nayakkar queen, probably of Vaduga caste. Soon, her Nayakkar brother became the King as Sri Vijaya Rajasinghe. This major event in Sri Lankan monarchy succession imbued a direct Indian identity without any blood-shed or war, historian K. M. De Silva wrote that the accession of the Nayakkar dynasty was 'a change accommodated with the minimum of adjustment.'

These changes, nonetheless, had not affected Nuwarakalaviya much as it maintained a neutral and independent region throughout which I shall discuss in coming chapters. But a South Indian form of potentates taking reigns in the country in the 18th century after being absent for centuries was the completion of a full circle foreign influence. However, the Nayakkar line of monarchy too ended in 1815 when the British deposed King Sri Wickrama Rajasinghe. Changes in culture, religion, superstitions, and folklore continued during these times. Some of these changes are still evident in the country two centuries later. Meanwhile Nuwarakalaviya remained in a supposedly deserted but a de facto sovereign state.

With calculated stratagems, the new rulers set the stage for full-scale changes in the way of life, law, customs, and economy in the colony. Without any countering force, Sri Lankans adjusted and realigned with many Western ways, gradually, and often enthusiastically. Yet in close to 150 years of British rule, only a few Sri Lankan institutions remained unaffected. One among them was Rata Sabhawa.

However, in early 20th century, Kapuruhami Madukanda Ratemahattayā observed the changes around him slowly encroaching into the customs and traditions that remained unchanged during British rule. Caste traditions began to fall asunder, in part with the egalitarian British laws and their influence on inter-community relationships. The Ratemahattayā lamented how such changes might affect Rata Sabhawa. But more people began to like the codified British judicial processes over traditional judicial processes Rata Sabhawa and Gam Sabhawa represented.

By 1938, when the Civil Service system in Sri Lanka instituted major modifications, traditional patrons of the Rata Sabhawa, the native elites – Chiefs and *mulādenivaru* – found their niche in the community becoming less influential and not in need. In Chapter 12, I discuss these changes, and how the Chiefs and *mulādenivaru* disengaged from the old self and realigned with the evolving society we see today.

I conclude the post-Rata Sabhāwa Nuwarakalaviya in Chapter 13. Rata Sabhāwa saw its end at the hands of the government itself. The new changes introduced to Sri Lankan Civil Service stated above turned out be the fatal inflection moment in the Rata Sabhāwa and nearly all other feudal customs in the country. Leaving the titular class powerless and meaningless seems like a routine and one of many changes British had been introducing during their rule, particularly in Nuwarakalaviya. A byproduct of this was the ending of powers and privileges enjoyed by the native Chiefs, and spurring inveterate traditions associated with these titles to fall into disuse. But a closer look in the province points to its momentousness and keenly felt impact on the life and culture of the people. It did not give the institution of Rata Sabhāwa a Darwinian dimension to evolve into something else. In turn, the Civil Service system effectively wrote the requiem for a long-standing cultural institution in Nuwarakalaviya. With the disbandment of the native titular class, Rata Sabhāwa or Variga Sabhāwa lost its steering. It lost standing in the village and ceased to be relevant in the lives of its residents. People lost the opportunity to resolve conflicts in simple ways.

Chapter 14 is a portion of the Kapuruhami Madukanda Ratemahattayā's exclusive description of the Rata Sabhawa tradition as it existed in the early decades of the 20th century. This text sets the underpinning of a centuries old tradition that is now lost in the community memory and customs of the few generations that came after 1930s. It will identify in authoritative fashion crimes, violations, and breaches of behavior norms, and etiquette of the people of Nuwarakalaviya, Tamankaduwa and their adjacent areas.

Finally, the appendices will show results of my direct and indirect contacts with some of the descendants of the Chiefs and minor officials, names of an inconspicuous and ordinary group of village elders, rather autodidacts, who I call 'pundits made under the Damba tree' referring to the shady tree in the school yard where spill-over classes assembled often in the village school in early 20th century. Their contribution is as superior and valuable as any other written account about the province. While analyzing the stories and histories of functional Rata Sabhāwa, I could not disregard the fact that Nuwarakalaviya remained as the keeper of Raja Rata, the Country of Kings, long regarded in last few centuries as irrelevant in the Sri Lankan identity. What I found astonishingly unique is that Nuwarakalaviya and its institutions like the Rata Sabhāwa and its fabled irrigation reservoir system helped keep their forgotten history relevant in the country. The Raja Rata and its lords, although not having the warrant of the Kings revered elsewhere in the country, retained their identities as they did through the reigns of nearly 90 Kings in the greater country intact albeit abandoned and often forgotten in the collective memory of later permutations of political ideologies.

2. NUWARAKALAVIYA: A MONTAGE

*N*uwarakalaviya was one of the 12 *Dissavanis* (Divisions) in the times of the Kandyan Kingdom. This discussion is about its boundaries, folklore about the origin of the name and other miscellaneous issues like how it existed in the heydays of Rata Sabhāwa and Variga Sabhāwa.

The region occupies a large portion of North Central Province (NCP) which was created by the British colonial administration on September 6, 1873, with Anuradhapura as its seat of government. But the region remained in the vernacular under the name Nuwarakalaviya centuries before the arrival of colonists. Computing the information found in the 1852 census, Brodie, (1894) found there were 3.7 houses or 11 individuals per square mile in Nuwarakalaviya (pp. 136-161). Although having a low population, it stretched nearly 200 kilometers from sea to sea and encompassed about 2900 square miles of symphonically verdant landscape.

Although standing as a porous but still effective buffer keeping intruders from the India in check for millennia, its integral role as the major contributor to Sri Lankan history had not been written fully. Nuwarakalaviya has the distinction of being home to at least seven Kingdoms[1] and 90 Kings. *Nuwara* is a suffix used to denote a place a King had a palace or during his regular travels stayed and held Court in a temporary palace called *gaman maligawa* (travelling palace). Today, the larger country it is in is Raja Rata. No other region in the country can claim this distinction.

Anuradhapura has been the capital city of Nuwarakalaviya since ancient times. Thus, a brief introductory description of this city will aptly usher us to the wholesome nature of the region. J. Ferguson, Editor of *Ceylon Observer* for nearly 50 years wrote in 1893 that Anuradhapura, center of Nuwarakalaviya as a:

> [...] scene restful to the eyes, beautiful in its ways, yet chiefly attractive for its historical interest. [...] a world of stone pillars, the forest-covered parks, glistening tanks, and the wide-extending jungle to the far distance background of hills, might well speak of Anuradhapura as the monumental, forest-shaded city of the plains in North-Central Ceylon. [...] a vision of mystery and romance in the presence of two-thousand years of history. [...] In the monsoon season, with Malwatu Oya running banks high and all nature refreshed and at its best, Anuradhapura may be placed above most other low-country towns in Ceylon, as enjoying 'The melodies of woods and winds and water' [*sic*] (p. 360).

This was Nuwarakalaviya in a nutshell. History of the region goes back to country's first kingdom, Anuradhapura,[2] King Pandukābhaya started in 474 BC.

NOTES

[1] Anuradhapura Nuwara, Upatissa Nuwara, Topawewa Nuwara, Ritigala Nuwara, Tammanna Nuwara, Vijithapura Nuwara and Ulagalla Nuwara (H. A. P. Abeywardena, 1978, *Kada-Im Poth Vimarsanaya*, p. 109.

[2] Ptolemy called it *Anur Ogrammum Regnum.*

Around 307-267 BC, Arahant sage Bhikkhu Mahinda, son of Emperor Asoka of India, arrived in Mihintale and introduced Buddhism to the country. Mihintale is about 10 kilometers east of Anuradhapura in the heart of the province. Millenia later when the seat of the government moved south or to other regions of the country, *Maha Vannivaru,* and their deputy *Vanniyās* as local Chiefs moved in to fill the void and helped keep it together for the next 7-8 centuries. In the Vanni region, Nuwarakalaviya was known as the '*Maha Vanni*' which probably explains why the Chief there was called Maha Vanniyā.

Fig. 2. Gaja Singhe Flag (*Maha Kodiya*) of Nuwarakalaviya.

Just as in physical appearance or demarcated by political ideologies, cultural norms, or religious beliefs, a place or an area in Sri Lanka can be bounded by many other nuances about it that are embedded in the perception of community. Nuwarakalaviya people believe their region lies within the boundaries of the country protected by its guardian deity *Ayyanār* who is said to have come from India. Tamankaduwa, the adjoining sister province of Nuwarakalaviya, is protected by *Minneri Deyyo,* believed to be the incarnation of King Mahasen who built the Minneriya reservoir, and many other major irrigations works.

Communities identify with their boundaries based on the idioms of spiritual and religious pantheon they believe protect the area. For those who call themselves belong to Kandyan highlands or Nuwarakalaviya, the presumed and well-known physical divide between them lies on a marker, a bridge to be exact, on Dambulu Oya (river) north of the city of Dambulla on A9 highway connecting Kandy and Jaffna. This is also the present political boundary between North Central and the Central Provinces. In cultural and religious lore, the area north of the bridge is under the protection of Sri Maha Bodhi (Sacred Bo Tree) in Anuradhapura and south of the bridge encompassing all the hill country is under the protection of *Sri Daladāwa,* the Sacred Tooth Relic, housed in the city of Kandy. If one sees a vehicle on the A9 highway displaying a large and colorful sticker "*Daladā Samidu Phitai,*" (May the

Sacred Tooth Relic protect you!) or *"Jaya Sri Maha Bodhi Pihitai,"* (May the Sacred Bodhi Tree protect you!), the operator of vehicle is announcing the larger community he belongs to – Kandyan highlands or Nuwarakalaviya, respectively.

Even a small village community can be confined within specific boundaries as small as a few kilometers around it by the decree of its protective deity which may not be known a few villages away. For instance, residents of Samādhigama, a village of 60 houses near Kahatagasdigiliya in Anuradhapura district created in 1980 under the *Udāgama* (Village Awakening) program believed their village was under the guardianship of an unnamed deity.[3] In 1980s, a woman named Seelawathie in the village was possessed by this deity. The community was bound together by the calls of the deity who spoke to them through Seelawathie after she went into trance on *kemmura* days, the days rituals for deities and demons are performed.

Although the communities were demarcated by their physical boundaries, a village can lose some aspects of its 'identity' by administrative actions of the government while retaining the boundaries as in the case of Kanadara and Kallanchiya Kōrales to be discussed later.

Thus, a distant rural community can erase its identity from official records, literally. It happened in 1956 when a Post Office was opened in my birth village. Until then, its name was Maradankadawala in all government records and even in our horoscopes – strips of processed palm leaves. We were excited that the iridescence of the government's kindness is descending right into the middle of our village - information processing warehouse - post office.

But before long, by a quirky mix-up, another Maradankadawala, a bazaar 30 miles south of our village on route A9 came calling asking us to meet its postman on his postal route to collect our letters. Its post office had been operating many years before ours. The postal department had no idea it had duplicated the big brother Maradankadawala on A9 route obfuscating from the map its rural brother with the same name. The old Maradankadawala stuffed all letters addressed to my village into bags of their own and gave us a choice: either change the name of our village or lose our pride, the Post Office. Elders all feared that this loss would be apocalyptic, not just for our pride, but our symbol of worldly recognition. Reminiscing his tedious weekly trip 10 miles back and forth to Mihintale to pick up our letters, an elder stood up and proposed the name 'Maradankalla' and restored the free flow of information to us. Consequently, the postal authorities in one short pen stroke changed our birthplace and infused new biodata to our horoscopes.

BOUNDARIES OF NUWARAKALAVIYA. Folklore and colonial Civil Servants have drawn boundaries of Nuwarakalaviya in multiple ways. Most are not dedicated boundary marks but descriptions that one can put together and translate as a boundary line. Samuel Baker (1855) walked through the forested areas of the country often by following "notches" cut on trees along the path by villagers.[4] D'Oyly determined Nuwarakalaviya as the region in North Central Province less the

---

[3] Brow, 1996. P. 190.
[4] Samuel Baker, 1855. *Eight Years in Ceylon.* p.21.

Tamankaduwa district (p. x).[5] In the middle of the 19th century, A. O. Brodie, the British Engineer cum Archaeologist had pointedly recorded the boundaries reproduced earlier in the Foreword by M. U. A. Tennakoon who also adds chronological dimension to the etymology of *Nuwarakalaviya*.

To make these boundary lines, it is quite plausible Brodie was sticking to what Sujith Sivasundaram called 'recycling of indigeneity,' the colonial practice of revisiting the know-how already existing among villagers to foster their long-term strategies. R. W. Ievers (1899) quotes the diary of the first Government Agent of Anuradhapura J. F. Dickson (1873 - 1876, 1881).   It refers to a Kapuruhami Nekathrāla of Nekattegama providing the latter with boundary points between Nuwarakalaviya and Hath Kōrale existed during the time of Buwanekabahu:

I.   Weudapokutu Siyambalagaha.

II.   Deduru-Oya Neligankadulla.

III.   Deduru-Oya Tunmodarakadulla.

IV.   Deduru-Oya Ambagassewa Mankandiya.

V.   Deduru-Oya Witikullekadulla.[6]

Closer to home, in 1886, boundaries of Anuradhapura city were set as: From West: Bund of Tissaweva tank; South: Wessagiri Vihare; East: Malwatu Oya (river); and North: a line drawn from Malwatu Oya due west on circular road north of Jetawanarama.[7]

BOUNDARIES OF TAMANKADUWA. While my theme of this review is centered upon the Nuwarakalaviya, I append here for general reference boundaries of its sister district Tamankaduwa that forms the eastern part of the North Central Province. John F. Dickson, the first Government Agent (GA) marked the Tamankaduwa boundaries as follows:

I.   On the South, Nugagaha-ela *alias* Aliadi-ara, 1 mile from Yakkure. On the East, sun and moon cut on a palu tree, about 3 miles beyond Makuppe.

II.   On the Northeast, the Yodayabemma *alias* Yodayenkattu, 8 miles beyond Mawila.

III.   On the Trincomalee road, a sun and moon on an ebony tree.

IV.   Between Tamankaduwa and Mahapotana Kōrale, Kahatagashinna, part of the ridge which extends from the head of Gantalawa away to the Sigiri boundary near Habarana, the stone heaps half a mile south of Habarana Rest House on Minneriya road. Towards Sigiriya between Tamankaduwa and Matale, the ridge of Konduruwakanda continued from Habarana boundary on to Diyakapilladamana on Laggala side. Then along the ridge to the *Hen-ganga* [sic].[8]

---

[5] D'Oyly, 1917, *The Diary of Mr. John D'Oyly, 1810-1815: With Introduction & Notes by H. W. Codrington* p. x.

[6] Ievers, 1899, p. 19.

[7] Ievers, 1899, p. 74.

[8] Dickson Diary qtd. in Ievers, 1899, p. 20. Such boundary recording was still in practice in the mid-20th century Sri Lanka. I saw on a surveyor's plan executed in early 1962 a jack tree and an anthill marked as boundaries in a deed of land transfer in Talatu Oya town near Kandy!

Nuwarakalaviya occupied most of the Vanni region which extended south from the border of the southern-most principality of Jaffnapatam. Scholars think Nuwarakalaviya district was surrounded by five Vanni districts: Jaffnapatam in the North; Trincomalee in the East; Mukkuwa Chieftaincies in Batticaloa in the East and Puttalama on the Northwest and Vedda Chieftancies.[9] Both Sinhala and Vedda Chieftaincies occupy these districts, and except Puttalama, they extended south covering eastern half of the country down to Yala National Park and Panama. The western half of the Vanni districts extended from Mantota (about Mannar) to the northern borders of Kotte kingdom.[10] Historians suggest, anyone either appointed by the Kotte King for Vanni regions in the south of the district or inherited the Chieftainship from nobility already in the Vanni principalities, was called *Vanniyars* or *Vannihuru*.

Save for few principalities near Jaffna, other *Vanniyās* paid some forms of tribute to Kotte and Kings in Kandy. In early times, there were stations called *kadawat* (s. *kadawata*, also called *Murathul*[11] or *Murapola*) positioned intermittently on strategic locations on the boundary lines between two territories. They were controlled by different potentates.[12] In early colonial times they were called 'Land-Pass Customs.' Presents were exchanged and travel documents (usually clay tokens) were examined at these *kadawat* in areas under control of *Vannihuru*.[13] D'Oyly in 1815 noted Maha Vanniyā controlled four *Kadawat*.[14] Robert Knox, the English sailor held prisoner for 20 years by Kandy King in mid-17th century, marked in his map of Sri Lanka four places where *kadawat* in Nuwarakalaviya were located: at a spot which I believe close to present-day Vilachchiya — about 15 kilometers northwest from Anuradhapura on Malwatu Oya along which he made his escape; two places called *saut pan* (Dutch: Zout — Salt) and *Salt Pannen* sitting juxtaposed to each other west of Nikaweratiya border in the easterly direction from Kalpitiya lagoon and Hurulle in the East.

Interestingly, though in 1681 when boundary lines between districts were not as clear, Knox's map mirrors his knowledge of Nuwarakalaviya covered in a sea of forest. He had made at least 8-10 reconnaissance trips to Nuwarakalaviya region to map out his escape route. Once he came up to Hurulle (*Hourley* or *Houerlgh*). Knox (1681, 1995) wrote that King's dominion extended up to Hurulle (p. 154). About

---

[9] De Silva, K. M. D., 1981, *A History of Sri Lanka.* p. 85 n6.

[10] De Silva, K. M.D., 1981, p. 99.

[11] In *Mukkara Hatana*, written in the 17th century, now in the Hugh Neville Collection in the British Museum.

[12] During King's reign in the City of Kandy, in the highlands or in Colombo in the Maritime Provinces, *kadawat* were located on city streets or strategic locations like mountain passes in the countryside or river and stream crossings. After crossing the Mahaweli river on the way to Kandy in 1800 for an audience with the King, British General Macdowall passed seven guard points between Gannoruwa Bo tree near present day botanical garden and Katukale close to present-day clock tower. Along this 4-mile stretch on what came to be known as Peradeniya Road, there were five guard gates suggesting they must have functioned more as a security check points than anything else (Jonville, Mons. 1948, Macdowall's Embassy, 1800, *JRAS*, Vol. 38, No. 105, pp. 1-21).

[13] In premodern times, a passport was usually a piece of clay token with a symbol engraved on it to identify the owner holding it (Knox, 1681, 1995, p. 55).

[14] Qtd. in Ievers, 1899, p. 112.

150 years later, at the time of fall of Kandy, there were number of such *kadawat* spread across the Vanni country reflecting its boundaries. These were located at Virasole, Vilachchiya Alut Kadawata, Ilukwewa (along the old road to Trincomalee past Sigiriya in Matale District) Serenewera, Ebagalma, Kalugallegama and Wagollewa.[15]

CLAIMS OF POPULATION SPREAD. Throughout its history, Nuwarakalaviya was a region that had experienced multiple encroachments from people of different ethnicities from the Subcontinent, understandably similar in some ways but diverse in many aspects. There are also various interpretations and theories about their centuries-old occupation. Some writers have claimed Tamils and Malabars occupied a better portion of the region while some suggest it was mostly Sinhalese. Such a mix obviously led to marriages across ethnic lines over the centuries. There are no population statistics, or other forms of evidence even to begin to review the extent of this practice. It is well-known from folklore and written accounts that occasionally in the past, South Indians of non-Tamil origin – Mukkuwas, Vanniyas, Vagai, Raja Vanniyas, Malabars, Indigenous Veddas, Villi Durai, Maravars, Pallavas and Arabs – too could just hop on a boat and paddle East the two dozen kilometers to the northwest coast of Sri Lanka. They then occupied large swaths of the coast first, later spreading out to the interior to blend in with the indigenous population.

With the knowledge accumulated so far about human migration patterns and characteristics, all the above scenarios can be deemed realistic. Scattered clusters of diverse peoples occupying a large area across the forested land from sea to sea is something we can expect when no firm and well entrenched central authority maintained a presence to regulate it for extended time periods. Robert Knox trekking through Nuwarakalaviya to Arippu in northwest coast in late 17th century found Malabar (Karnataka and Kerala) as the lingua franca northward of Anuradhapura. As princes, Chiefs, and even locally potent lords ruled the region intermittently, any writing about the population characteristics of a particular region without tangible evidence needs to be taken with a caveat. Governor Robert Wilmot-Horton wrote to the Colonial Secretary in 1833 that the region "contains a much larger population than was suspected to exist, and which in general found to be better circumstances than those of the neighboring Maritime Provinces." The Governor also found the inhabitants maintain a "very considerable commercial intercourse." Some exports found markets in India.[16]

But closer examination of the permanent structures standing, even in dilapidated state, in the Nuwarakalaviya proper (Anuradhapura and Tamankaduwa districts, and some parts of the Hath Kōrale) reveals that the alleged reach of influence of the Chiefs with indisputably South Indian origin is a suggestion far removed from tangible evidence. It is true that Nuwarakalaviya has a preponderance of structures and remnants of buildings influenced both Buddhistic and Hindu pantheon showing North and South Indian architectural influence. This can be argued as an indication of a dual orientation to which the people of this region had

---

[15] Ievers, 1899, p. 112.

[16] Governor's letter on Jan 14, 1833, to Colonial Secretary, qtd. in Sujit Sivasundaram, 2013, *Islanded*, p. 156.

been exposed through the centuries. In Jaffna peninsula too, architecture with similar characteristics, and ancient Buddhist and Hindu-influenced styles show the nature of intermingled population dynamics and religious approaches prevailed in the area in the past.

Being isolated as it was, the linguistic history of Nuwarakalaviya shows evidence of presence of many languages throughout the history. In September 1679, Knox encountered people including the 'Governor' of Nuwarakalaviya, quite likely Maha Vanniyā in Anuradhapura. They did not speak Sinhala – the language of Kandyan highlands.[17] It is also possible Elu language, a precursor of Sinhala, could also have been used in certain corners of Nuwarakalaviya. Centuries ago, contact with the Indian subcontinent was intense, the coastal and northern half in Sri Lanka found in addition to Elu an admixture of diverse languages like Sinhala, Tamil, Malabar, Malayalam, Arabic and a pidgin language – a mix of Malayalam, Karnataka, Konkani, and Tamil spoken by *Rodiya* or *Ahikuntika* people, a peripatetic and untouchable untouchable tribe. This is evidence that a corpus of languages that trickled into this region even up to modern times, mirrored its demographic diversity.

Due to South Indian influence, it was natural Nuwarakalaviya to be seen as a melting pot of traces of disparate cultural, linguistic, and demographic trends. Having had a flow of exchange of cultural and social norms between peoples in this large tract of land helps this supposition. Just as the Kandyan Kings' extraordinary love to send for potential brides from royal families in East and Western Ghats region of India, the Chiefs in Nuwarakalaviya had shown inclination to look for brides from the royal or elite families in other parts of the Vanni. When Vanni was carved out as small princely regions, the *Vanniyars* and Chiefs there regarded the wholesomeness of the country as one land. Regardless of the unsettling issues arising often between groups of people, intercultural and interethnic endogamy had happened then, happens now and we can assure ourselves it to happen in the future as well.

The lack of marked boundaries like permanent waterways, distinct land barriers, and impenetrable forest made it easy for this process to take place, giving new meaning to the people in the region as centuries passed. In 1785, Kumarasinghe Vanniya, the eldest son of Nuwara Vanniya of the Nuwarakalaviya District married the sister of Pandara Vannya (Bandara Vanniya) of Mullativu.[18] Chiefs' association with Mullativu area was not unusual. Lewis (1895) noted that in 1839, Tamarawewa Vanniya, later *Ratemahattayā* of eastern Nuwarakalaviya, visited Vattappalai Kovil near Mullativu (120 kilometers) with 100 villages (p. 265). I shall note later, a Maha Vanniyā once married a South Indian princess and roused Kandy King's ire.

WHAT IS IN A NAME? Folklore is rich with how Nuwarakalaviya got its name. This name seems to appear in writings and usage only after the Polonnaruwa period which ended in 1293 AD. It was called the province of *Noure Calava* in the turn of 19th century.[19] In the map of Robert Knox, Nuwarakalaviya is written as *Newe*

---

[17] Knox, 1681, p. 159.

[18] Moothoothamby Pillai, A. *Yalpana Kammuthy*, p. 187, cited in *Vanni and the Vanniyas with Map of the Vanni Districts*, C. S. Navaratnam, 1960, p. 29.

[19] Robert Percival, 1803, *An Account of the Island of Ceylon*, p. 237.

Calava. In old Portuguese maps this area was written as *Norcalabra.* During certain times of its history, this province had also been called as Nuwaravanniya or Maha Vanni.[20] One name that had gained deeper traction is anagrammatically derived from parts of the names of three iconic irrigation reservoirs in the province: *NUWARA*weva (1st century BC) in the city of Anuradhapura, *KALA*weva (5th century A.D.) about 30 kilometers East of the city, and pada *VIYA* weva (6th century A.D.) about 75 kilometers Northeast of the city.

According to another story recounted by Robert Knox (1681, 1995) in the 17th century, due to its large reservoirs, citizens of *Neurecalava* [*sic*] were able to grow abundance of corn (rice?). When a famine swept across the neighboring kingdom of *Cournegal* (Kurunegala) in *Hotcourley* (Hath Kōrale) King asked for assistance from his northern neighbor – Anuradhapura. In response, its neighborly citizens drove a team of pack animals (*tawalam*) to *Cournegal* (Kurunegala) with a large stock of corn. The King of Kurunegala was so pleased with the citizens' gesture and asked them what he could do to appreciate their help. When they said they had everything except *kaha miris* – turmeric and pepper, the King gladly gave them it as a gift. When the citizens brought the rewards home to Anuradhapura, they found the quantity was insufficient to be shared by all. The only solution for this conundrum was to grind them and dissolve the mixture in the river and ask everyone to get buckets full of yellow (*kaha*) water. They dissolved the paste in the water, and the river flowing through the city, *Nuwara,* too became yellow, *kaha lava.* The story does not stop there. After taking what the citizens did as an insult, the King became angry. But he kept it to himself. Later when he visited the province, he asked how their country became so prosperous. They replied they have a large reservoir made with a half-moon shaped stone dam across the river and use its water for irrigation. The King took note of this and went home. There, he asked his magicians to destroy the dam. After the dam was destroyed, the province became a wasteland and had to depend only on rainwater ever since (p. 111).

In the middle of the 19th century, Simon Cassie Chitty (1834, 1989), born in Kalpitiya and worked as a court interpreter in Puttalama in Northwestern province added another shade to this tale. The people of Nuwarakalava [*sic*] thought King sending turmeric and pepper to them as a contemptuous gesture. They thus coated the two spices on their bodies and bathed in Kalawa Oya (Kala Oya which feeds Kalaweva). It made the water turn yellow, thus the name.[21]

A 20-page palm-leaf book, an extension to the *Rajavaliya* covering the period from Buwanekabahu VI (Vijayabahu VI?) to Buwanekabahu VII (1534 – 1542) and found in 1889 with Munnankulame (probably Monnekulama) Mudiyanse of Wanni District in the Northwestern Province alludes to certain Princes in it in the past making reparations to large tanks Kalaweva and Balaluweva (now joined as one reservoir).[22] Resemblance of some versions of these three accounts between Knox and Munnankulame Mudiyanse extending over a period of two and half centuries is telling.

---

[20] Hettiarachchi, D.E, ed. 1979, *Sinhala Sirith Sangrahaya,* p. iv.
[21] Simon Casie Chitty, 1834, 1989, *Ceylon Gazetteer,* p. 191.
[22] Wickremasinghe, 1900, p. 79, para 73, in British Museum Collection.

Nuwaragam Palatha abounds with tales that ascribes the Nuwarakalaviya name to the heartbreak that descended upon the capital city of Anuradhapura Nuwara a thousand years ago when the Kings abandoned it and relocated to Polonnaruwa, 100 kilometers to the east. Beginning around the 13th century, the seat of the kingdom moved further south to the central parts of the country. Residents of Anuradhapura never got their kingdom back and watched as other cities with Kingdoms elsewhere prosper while their once elysian home, Nuwara and its religious monuments and irrigation reservoirs become entombed in thick forest, *káláva*, thus the name *Nuwara Kaláva*!

No wonder the multitude of writers jotted down how this fabled forest looked like. In 1877, J. F. Dickson, Government Agent of Anuradhapura found the city where "monuments buried in jungle and forest, many of them difficult to access even on foot."[23] Even as late as last decades of the 19th century, H. C. P. Bell, the Archaeological Commissioner wrote of the progress he was making on excavations in a stupa in the old city of Anuradhapura: "I have said above, 4 to 5 feet crust needs removing. What think you when [...] we have gone down 10 to 12 feet below the surface as it was before we commenced operation there, and hardly reached the foundations yet!"[24]

DIVISIONS. Nuwarakalaviya had two divisions in the past: Kayila Pattuwa and Kilakkumulai. Kayila Pattuwa is a corruption of the word Kaluwila Pattuwa named after the village of Kaluwila which Robert Knox in the 17th century visited as he was heading to the Northwest coast during his escape from Kandy. Kaluwila was a *nindagama* of the of Nuwarawawe *Vanni Unnehe* (*Ratemahattayà*) clan, also called the *Hatpattu Maha Vanni Unnehe*. Kaluwila Pattuwa consisted of two *Kōrales* – Nuwaragam and Vilachchiya. Kilakkumulai (in Tamil) is in the eastern division. It included Kändä, Kanadarā and Kadawat Kōrales.

It is important to keep in mind that since the early years of the 19th century, boundaries of Nuwarakalaviya had been drawn, re-drawn, and occasionally taken out by the colonial administrators. They had little help. It is conceivable that without a source document, but only scattered fields of archaeological ruins, the administrators only had the benefit of clues about the region's spread and history. They came to know about them from mostly folklore or even fancies of loquacious individuals in villages. At the time of ratifying the Kandyan treaty with the British in 1815, Galagoda who was a signatory to it as Dissava of Nuwarakalaviya too had very little to do with the province except an ambassadorial role on behalf of the King.

Within weeks of signing the treaty, on April 15, 1815, the Board of Commissioners for Kandy was formed, and reorganization of Kandyan provinces began.[25] The Board grouped the provinces into five divisions. At that time, the

---

[23] Ievers, 1899, p.74.

[24] Bell, H. C. P., qtd. in J. Ferguson, 1898, *Ceylon in 1893*, p. 371.

[25] In the Ceylon Government Almanacs of 1817 and 1818 the Kandyan Provinces were listed as follows: Four Kōrale, Hat Kōrale, Uva, Matale, Sabaragamuwa, Tun Kōrale, Walapone, Udapalata, Nuwarakalaviya, Wellassa, Tamankaduwa, Bintenna, Udunuwara, Yatinuwara, Tumpane, Harispattuwa, Dumbara, Hewaheta, Kotmale and Upper Bulatgama, Minneri, and Lower

eastern division of Nuwarakalaviya consisted of Hurulu, Tamarawewa, Maminiya and Ulagalla pattu. It was under the purview of the Government Agent, Matale or Nalanda. *Maha Vanni Unnehe* administered the Nuwarakalaviya as of 1815 while domiciled in Anuradhapura. The Dissava appointed for this province by the King usually resided in Kandy. It is not clear what role he played other than as an implied overlord.   It is known that the *Vanni Unnehe* tradition existed in Nuwarakalaviya long before Kandy had Kings. But after 1833, during Governor Horton's tenure when the British further consolidated the role of appointing such Chiefs, *Maha Vanni Unnehe* was given the title of *Dissava* as well in line with similar titles granted elsewhere in the country.

Titles of Maha Vanniyā, *Vanni Unnehe* or *Vanni Mudiyanse* continued to be used in the vernacular even after the area north of Dambulla up to Vavuniya which in general included Nuwarakalaviya was annexed to the Northern Province. The same order established a District Court in Anuradhapura. The annexation also caused a lot of displeasure among the officials and *Ratemahatvaru* in the province.

In mid-19th century, each four *palat* (s. *palata*) of Nuwarakalaviya – Nuwaragam, Hurulu, Kalagam, Tamankaduwa – was under a *Mudiyanse*, a title equal to *Ratemahattayā*. Each *palata* had divisions or districts called *pattu* (s. *pattuwa*) and each *pattuwa* had multiple *Kōrales* (s. *Kōrale*). These four *palata*s initially comprised of seven *pattu* (thus the *Hath Pattu Maha Vanni*) consisting of 20 *Kōrale* districts and 75 *tulān* (s. *tulāna*, a collection of few villages) called *Arachi Vasam*, later called *gam muladeni vasam*, few of which formed a *Kōrale*.[26] Ievers reported Tamankaduwa Palata had 12 *pattu*s. A *Kōrāla* was the head of each *Kōrale* district. It was a title a level higher than a *mulādäniya* but one lower than a *Ratemahattayā* or a *Mudiyanse*. A graphic representation of the Chiefs in Nuwarakalaviya and Tamankaduwa is shown in Fig. 4.[27]

In 1873, Nuwarakalaviya became a region to reckon with: Together with Tamanakaduwa, it was declared as the North Central Province. It had three districts: Nuwarakalaviya, Tamankaduwa (detached from Eastern Province) and Demala Hatpattu of Hath Kōrale. The region was covered in thick forest with ancient monuments hidden throughout, half of them buried in mounds of broken bricks and sand. It covered an area of 4047 square miles. At the time of its establishment, this province was the largest in area but smallest in population.[28] On January 1, 1875, the Demala Hatpattu was annexed to Northwestern Province.

Nuwarakalaviya, although described as having a landscape with no discernible character, has random hillocks popping up breaking the monotony of its green expanse, enriching the delightful sight. The tallest mountain in Nuwarakalaviya is Ritigala (766m) in Ulagalla Kōrale. In the early days of the British rule, Ritigala area

---

Bulatgama (P. Arunachalam, 1910, Kandyan provinces. *JRAS (Ceylon Branch)*, Vol. 22, No. 63, pp. 103 -123.

[26] Ievers, 1899, pp. 2 & 80. Seven *pattu* are Kirulu, Omdow, Kelagam, Maminiya, Motombuwa, Undiyankulama and Hurulu.

[27] As government policies changed over time, often some districts merged to make one unit. Therefore, numbers of *pattu* or palath could vary from time to time in diverse written or oral accounts.

[28] Ievers, 1899, p. 1.

was in consideration for the seat of the Government Agent. But the idea was abandoned in favor of Anuradhapura for its proximity to Jaffna and the Pearl Fishery near Mannar and centrally located for business. By now, however, the British could not disregard the historical importance of the city. On the other hand, the Ritigala idea may have been in contention since the main Colombo-Trincomalee Road and communication to Kandy passed by close to this area. Not just ancient monuments, the characteristic of the province is that it is sprinkled with tanks and natural ponds. Thus, the region is also called in popular vernacular as the *Wev Bendi Rajya* (Kingdom of Tanks). Ancient hydro-engineers built them with such remarkable design, in early 1980s, C. M. Madduma Bandara identified one such feature in their distinctive pattern he called 'Tank Cascade System.'[29]

During the colonial times, the impenetrable forest cover and distance insulated Nuwarakalaviya from the Maritime Provinces. Since the arrival of colonists, citizens of Nuwarakalaviya began to call the littoral with the moniker *pātha rata* (lower country), a euphemistic expression tagging it as 'the lesser country' and its inhabitants with the caste label *pāthayō*, the lower or lesser people. Most notable of these castes were *Karawa, Halagama* (*Salagama*), and *Durawa*. As shown later, anyone subjugated by the colonial powers was regarded as lower in caste and rank hierarchy under the Rata Sabhā and variga customs in the 19th century. During that time, villages in other parts of the country continued to lose their identity due to colonial influence. J.F. Dickson, Government Agent of Anuradhapura who highlighted Nuwarakalaviya village with this annotation in 1877: "[…] here the Oriental Village remained still pure and simple type while in the rest of Ceylon it has disappeared under the influence of foreign government and the jurisdiction of English courts. …Villages have been left buried in their virgin forest and neglected and failed to share the general progress which has been going forward around them."[30]

In 1823 Lieut. Colonel Stackpoole spent a month in Nuwarakalaviya and found "the people seem well disposed and peaceably inclined." He found no criminal cases or disputes. "The inhabitants live harmoniously and in good fellowship.[31]" Brodie (1894) claimed the people of Nuwarakalaviya the gentlest he had found. Grave crimes were unheard of. Reginald Jones Bateman of the Ceylon Service described in 1919 in *Refuge from Civilization* that the villagers of this district (Mullativu adjacent to Nuwarakalaviya) as " the most honest, friendly, and generous people in the world."

He also added, "The Vanni villager, except when he is beginning to get into contact with civilization, always tells the truth [*sic*].[32]" As these attributes shined the larger picture, Samuel Baker (1855) was so enchanted with the island, he ended his *Eight Years in Ceylon* with the epiphonema: "For me Ceylon has always had a charm, and I shall ever retain a vivid interest in the colony."[33]

---

[29] Madduma Bandara, C. M., 1985, Catchment Ecosystems and Village Tank Cascades… *Strategies for River Basin Development*, pp. 99-113.

[30] Qtd. in Ievers, 1899, p. 74.

[31] Lt. Col. Stackpoole qtd. in Ievers, 1899, p. 53.

[32] Reginald Jones-Bateman (1919) qtd. in Toussaint, J. R., 1934, Literature and the Ceylon Civil Service. *Journal of the Dutch Burgher Union of Ceylon.* Vol. 23, No. 3, pp. 113-143.

[33] Baker, 1855, 1983, p. 221.

Dissava: Directly Reporting to the King. Administrative role or involvement with Nuwarakalaviya is not clear. No home or *nindagam* owned in the province.

***Hatpattu Maha Vanni Unnehe* of Nuwarakalaviya (1)**
Also called Vanni Bandara, Bandara Vanniya/*Maha Vanniyā*. A hereditary title specific to the Vanni Rata. Claims descent from a prince who came with the Bodhi Tree. Some say *Vanniyars* came from the Coast of India. Had free hand with the rule of the province, like one heading a princely State (a *yuva raja?*).

***Vannivaru* of Palath (3)**
Nuwaragam, Hurulu & Kalagam Palath. Often called Ratemahattayā. Later in the British times, he headed multiple Kōrale Districts. Appointed Kōrālas.

***Vanni Mudiyanse* of *Pattu* (7)**
Appointed by Maha Vanni Unnehe. Like Ratemahattayā, enjoyed seniority and more power by virtue of his historic relationship with the Bodhi Tree. Appointed *kāriyakarawannō* or patabándo.

***Kōrāla* (17)**
Headed a Kōrale District which included multiple *tulan.*

Arachirāla, Headman a.k.a *Lékama* of a *tulāna* consisting of few villages.	*Mohottāla Baddarāla Lékama.(Walawwe Mohottala*	*Vel Vidāne* (Irrigation &Agriculture) *Gamarāla* (administrative & social order)

Fig. 3. Chain of command of Nuwarakalaviya Chieftains during Kandyan King's & early British times (Ievers, 1899, p. 79, Karunananda, 1990, p. 138). Illustration: Niranjala Tillakaratne.

According to A.M. Ferguson (1868) in *Ceylon Directory*, during the period 1861-1863, only 4 crimes were sent for trial from the Anuradhapura magistracy in Nuwarakalaviya. For the same period the rest of the 12 magistracies in Kandyan Districts stretching from Dambulla, Badulla, Nuwara Eliya, Nawalapitiya, Kegalle, Pussellawa, Kegalle, have sent 268 cases for trial, mostly of 'theftuous' [*sic*] nature (p. 137).

But this is not to say that the villagers were all saintly. If anything, sadly though, the villagers would not allow us to give them a pass. Brodie (1894) also found gentleness typical of the villagers gets asunder sometimes. They still retained a good degree of aggressiveness to survive among themselves and in the harsh environs that cloaked them. "It is true they (Nuwarakalaviya villagers) quarrel a lot, but such squabbles are of trifling kind. They use all manner of abusive words, terms, pull each other's hair, and shriek, and in the end run away from each other when the matter ends" p. (136-161). This still did not come to the level of needing a sophisticated enforcement of social order.

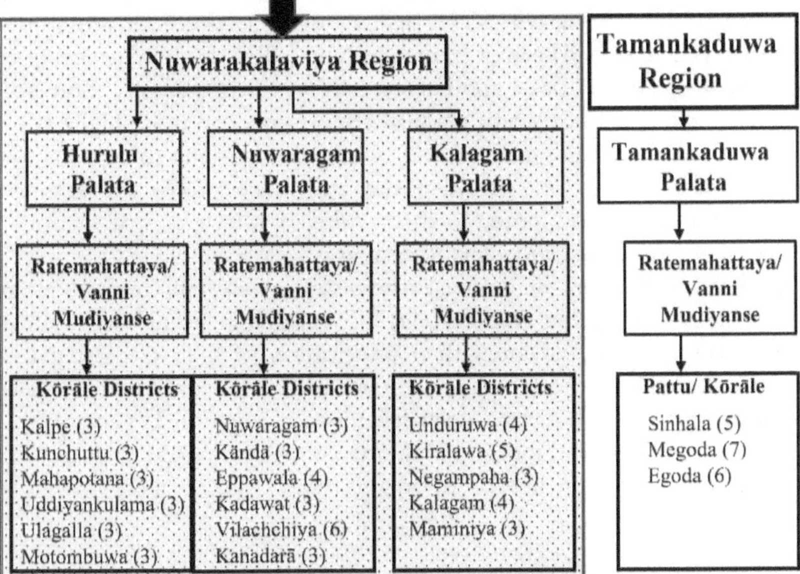

Fig. 4. Chiefs, *Mulādānivaru*, Districts in North Central Province   late in the 19th century. The number of *Tulan* in each *Kōrale* is in parenthesis. (Ievers 1899, Karunananda 2009). Illustration: Niranjala Tillakaratne.

When the North Central Province was created, indigenous institutions like Rata Sabhāwa had been maintaining social order already with remarkable success. Rata Sabhāwa system remained central to the villagers to manage their affairs internally and communally. Reginald Jones-Bateman observed in 1919, "In the town of Anuradhapura order is maintained by one town constable; in the rest of the province no police are required."[34] It was a time of innocence, and with the horizontal love among people, they could have easily sustained a peaceful living even without a constable. But this was not always the case elsewhere in the country.[35] Here the people even gave their labor gratuitously for common objects and were rewarded by not being taxed, unlike in other provinces. The community appreciated the dedication of its members.

Few decades after capturing Kandy, the British finally began concentrating on development of Nuwarakalaviya. The bulk of the irrigation infrastructure of the province was ruined or had been overtaken by jungle. British found restoring cultural and religious monuments was a good investment towards this goal. Some officials bent on reinforcing justification of colonial claim to occupy and rule the country as a colony made diversions to ascribe its deleterious state to the corrupt Kings of the country, down to the last one they deposed, and suggested that villagers for their lethargic or indolent habits, turned to chena cultivation (swidden cultivation) which led to destruction of forest and valuable timber resources.

Another fraternity of the colonial administrators showing moral high ground thought that attributing the responsibility of upgrading the infrastructure to the Colonial government would strengthen justification of their obligation to effect repairs and improvement to thousands of tanks.[36] Either way, with the devastating lessons learned in the 1803 war – insufficient knowledge of its geography – the Government was interested more in mapping and surveying the country[37] but not much in knowing its culture and social organization.

---

[34] Government Agent Dickson qtd. in Ievers, 1899, p. 75.

[35] J.P. Lewis notes of an incident during the religious festival at the Vattappalai temple dedicated to Hindu deity Kannakai Amman, a few miles from Mullaitivu, 130 kilometers Northeast of Anuradhapura. The mass of devotees "struggling to find a good place" for the *puja* had to be calmed down by using a small stick (1895b, pp. 176-185).

[36] Brow, 2011. *The Anthropologist and the Native...* ed. H. L. Seneviratne, pp. 128-130.

[37] Sivasundaram, 2007, Tales of the Land: British Geography and Kandyan Resistance [...], *Modern Asian Studies* Vol. 41, No. 5, pp. 925-965.

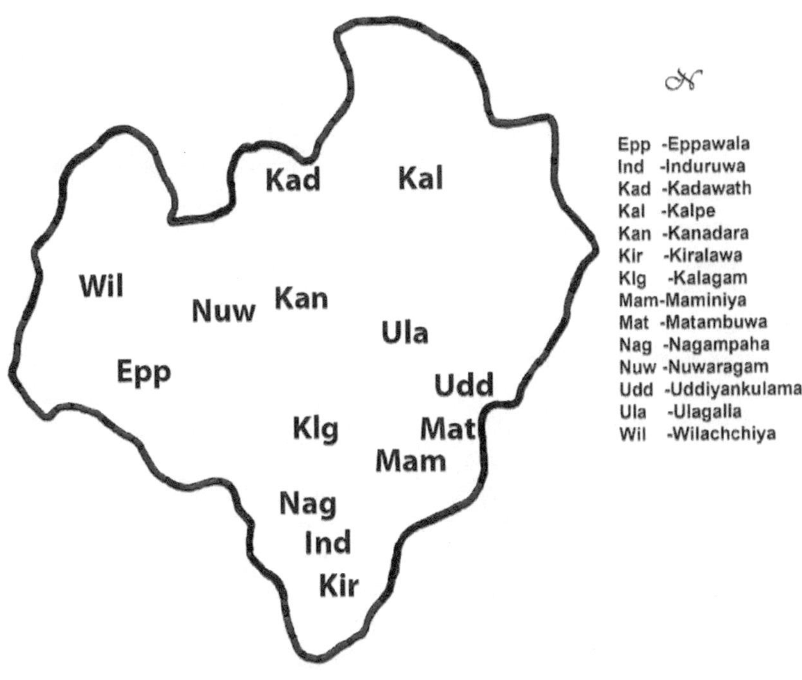

Fig. 5
. Partial list of Kōrale Divisions of Nuwarakalaviya c 1894. Edmond
Standford, Long Acre, London.
Illustration: Niranjala Tillakaratne.

3. VARIGA SABHĀWA OR RATA SABHĀWA?

a Varige was naturally a group of people belonging to a similar caste structure but may not have close kinships. But kinship possibilities remained open. In preference to kins (*näyō*), they may be called just *varigakkārayō* or *gankārayō*. I call it an extension of *pavula* (family or clan) which Nur Yalman called a 'micro-caste'[1] in diverse degrees of connections. Anthropologists have called these collectivist arrangements. Researching in Sri Lanka in 1963 and 1967 in Morapitiya village (a fictitious name), Marguerite Robinson called *Varige* coming from the mother.[2] On the other hand, a variga is a neighborhood of communities or villages coalesced, what Max Weber called one with "a feeling of belonging together."[3] It could also be extrapolated as community with "affective and cognitive components, both a feeling of solidarity and understanding of shared identity."[4]

A *Varige* usually was identified with a name. One consisting of 18 villages in several Tulān supervised by three *Kōrales* was called just that: *Gam Daha Ata Varige* (Clan of Eighteen Villages) (Fig. 34). Some Variga were each named after an anchor village. Thus, Gonewe Varige in Kändä Kōrale was in Gonewa. Divullābe *Varige* was made up of villages around the village of Divullābe. In Hurulu Palatha in Nuwarakalaviya, a *Varige* can have subgroups e.g., *Maha Varige* – a *Varige* with multiple villages (great *Varige*), *Meda Varige* – a *Varige* in the middle and, a *Sulu Varige* (lesser *Varige*) – a *varige* with one village.[5]

Tradition required all villages to be subjected to the jurisdiction of a Rata Sabhāwa of a *rata* (district or province or convention attended by a Chief) and a Variga Sabhāwa in order to retain sharing the right of belonging and to be able to preserve the solidarity with *ape átto, apé kattiya, apé minissu* or *apé Varige*, which is how villagers called being '*of us.*' In Nuwarakalaviya, a Rata Sabhāwa jurisdiction covered a group of villages of similar *Variga*. This was made possible with a sense of belonging to the village (community) consisted of equality, democracy, cultural homogeneity, social harmony, cohesion, and hope of material prosperity for all.[6] A village which completed the *gam bándeema* phase, may join a nearby *Varige* to strengthen their standing in the community if favored by its members. For someone not familiar with the social norms, this situation can easily be seen as an instance where the sphere of all things traditional in his own community trespassing the deep contours of his personal life. As a practical matter, a strain of logical community existence guided the *mulādänivaru* to bring fair and successful conclusion to cases where community traditions conflicted with real-life situations.

NOTES

[1] Yalman, Nur, 1967, *Under the Bo Tree,* Berkeley: UC Press, p. 202.

[2] Robinson, Marguerite, 1968, Some Observations on the Kandyan Sinhalese Kinship System. In *Man.* Sep. Vol. 3 No. 3, pp. 402-423.

[3] Max Weber, 1978, *Economy and Society*, p. 42.

[4] James Brow, 1996. *Demons and Development: The Struggle for Community in a Sri Lankan Village,* p. 50.

[5] A. P. A. Gunasekara, 2004, *Horowpothane Palaveni DRO* (Sinhala), p. 138.

[6] James Brow, 1996, p. 81.

In general, the Rata Sabhāwa functioned as the wheelhouse of a community maintaining its wellbeing and the consistency of caste customs. This concept was practiced until mid-20th century in Nuwarakalaviya and adjacent areas in Sri Lanka. This was not a concept prevalent in Kanda Uda Rata where the caste, not *Varige*, ruled the division of groups. I will discuss in a later chapter the manner of caste location in Kanda Uda Rata and Nuwarakalaviya. The term 'custom' needs careful examination. Charles Winick (1970) called it as:

> A group behavior pattern [...] established by tradition, by contemporary social habits, or religious precepts as differentiated from a legally enforced institution. Customs are enforced by social disapproval of their violation [...]. They lack the coercive backing of the State and the sanctions of the mores.... Mores are accepted behavior patterns but usually subject to change slowly. It is conducive to society's welfare. The breach is punished more severely and formally unlike the folkway which is observed traditions that are punished informally [*sic*]. (pp. 148, 218, 369)

They shared and abided by homogenous customs and strictures of the *Varige* they belonged to, and to a larger extent, related to each other or could establish kinship relationships by endogamous unions without any restrictions. These restrictions can be commonly accepted taboos, i.e., incest,[7] caste, and on some occasions, religion, geographic location, and exogamous unions. Variga members believed such a coalition strengthened the existence and standing of the group in the larger society.

According to a 95-year-old villager I was fortunate to talk to,[8] Rata Sabhā or *Variga Sabhā* – the fiber of the social organization, assiduously kept the concept of variga (clan) system relevant and important by discharging their executive functions through a body of local officials.

Some ask if Rata Sabhāwa and *Variga Sabhāwa* is one and the same or two different institutions. My view is that they are two sides of a coin. Based on the rules, procedures, practices, and theory that guided their functions, considering them as one and the same does not shift their identities off-track much. Nearly 75 years ago, in the subtitle and the glossary appended at the end of his landmark paper, Kapuruhami Madukanda Ratemahattayā whom I call one of the last pillars of authority representing the traditions of both these *Sabhā*, had referred to the Rata Sabhāwa as *Rata Sammutiya* or *Variga Sammutiya* (clan convention).[9] In principal, but with some exceptions as shown later, the name used to call it on a given instance depended upon the location it was held, and the title and rank of the person presiding over it at the time. Officials for these two Sabhā must be from the same caste.

In some areas of Nuwarakalaviya, the Sabhāwa was referred to in different terms. When it was assembled for, and in a higher caste village (village of *rate áttŏ*), it

---

[7] In 17th century, Kings in Sri Lanka practiced incest regularly (Knox, 1681, 1995, p. 38).

[8] S.B. Kapuruhami, (personal communication), June 6, 2002.

[9] K.A. Kapuruhami, 1948, Rata Sabhāwa, *JARS* (*Ceylon*), Vol.38, No. 106, pp. 42-68. He wrote the manuscript in Sinhala around 1909-1910 or he discussed its traditions existed during that time.

is also known as Rata Sabhāwa. Although these Sabhā had different names, their functions and purposes were the same. Unless specifically required otherwise, herein after both will be referred to in the text as Rata Sabhāwa.

A *Sabhāwa* is called a Rata Sabhāwa:
- I.   When it was held in the courthouse in the residence of *Ratemahattayā*.
- II.   When it was held in a village, *Ratemahattayā* comes and presides over, usually to resolve a conflict between two villages or two variga, or

A *Sabhāwa* is called a Variga Sabhāwa:
- III.   When a *Mohottāla* presides over it in the village to resolve an issue between two individuals.
- IV.   *Navandannā Ayage Sabhāwa*: The Sabhāwa of lower caste (*Vanan Inan*) people. D. B. Rajakaruna of Kekatiyagollewa tells that the leading officer of the Henayinge (of *Henayā*) Sabhāwa like *Navandannā Ayage Sabhāwa* is known as *Mulāchāriyā*.[10] But S.B. Ratwatte Kōrāla of Kalaweva had noted an exception. If a Sabhā session consists of the full cast of *mulādāniwaru*, and the five *vanam* (castes), i.e., *vidāne, kadayā* (pingo carrier), *henayā, pandithayā* (who works on gold and precious metal) and *gurunnehe* (*guruvo* – drummers), it can also be called a Rata Sabhāwa.[11] It seems that in this instance the diverse caste participation had earned it the need to be addressed with a higher status. Rata Sabhāwa is a 'Council of Chiefs.'[12] Vicissitudes of naming preferences thus depend upon the characteristics of the officials participating and place it was held.

When *Ratemahattayā* visited a village for a Rata Sabhāwa session, it was a festive occasion for the villagers. A *Ratemahattayā* may ask a *Mohottāla* to hold a Rata Sabhāwa in a village or *Mohottāla* himself may call a Sabhāwa. In this case, after concluding the session he sent a report (a *sittu*) to *Ratemahattayā*. I will go into details on the festivities of a Sabhāwa in a later chapter.

In both these situations, festivities, procession, decorations of the assembly hall and the makeup of the participants may be similar in many ways. But when the *Ratemahattayā* is present, the gravitas of all aspects of the assembly are distinctly sharper. Save for occasional use of the courthouse situated in the walawwa (Fig. 6), most Rata Sabhā or Variga Sabhā were held in the village as needed.

In another instance, when *Mohottāla* is unable to resolve a conflict in village level and refers it to the attention of his superior authority, such an assembly is also called a Rata Sabhāwa. "Places where justice is heard and served by the Chief of the

---

[10] Rajakaruna, D.B. cited in Hettiarachchi, ed. 1979, p. 15.

[11] Rajakaruna, D.B. cited in Hettiarachchi, ed. 1979, p. 10.

[12] Hettiarachchi, ed. 1978-79, Wickramasinghe Collection of Manuscripts, *JRAS* (Sri Lanka), 24 (*new series*), pp. 1-24.

rata (district, province) are known as Rata Sabhāwa."[13] And a Sabhā assembled for projects that are vital for the rata are also called Rata Sabhā.

Although Sabhāwa is a fundamental and seemingly a compartmentalized organization as related to the caste and variga affairs, often a *Mohottāla* may participate in a Sabhāwa out of his village or jurisdiction, *Varige* area, or a different caste community. While a *Mohottāla* of a *Goigama* caste has the authority to conduct hearings of a lower caste village, a lower caste person does not get the same reciprocal privilege. Rata Sabhāwa for a lower caste does not get the "*Rata*" prefix which usually denotes *rate átto* – higher caste persons.

Fig. 6. Court House at Madukanda Kuda Walawwa.
Photo: Niranjala Tillakaratne.

It was the tradition then to designate and call anything involving *Ratemahattayā* with the prefix *Rate-* to emphasize its importance and the underlying prestige. Furthermore, where a Chief or a similar personage is conducting an event or grace it with his presence, the custom was not to bestow it with a commoner designation, but with one that reflected its worth and high regard for its pedigree.[14]

A temporary shed in the village, roofed and walled with woven coconut fronds, or permanent structure in *Ratemahattayā*'s residence where the Sabhāwa was held was called a *Maduwa*. Building the *Maduwa* was the responsibility of the resident official in the village – *Mohottāla, gamarāla* or *Vel Vidāne*. Persons who were under orders of a ban were not allowed to participate in these activities. When the *Mohottāla* is presiding over a Sabhāwa in this *Maduwa*, it becomes a distinguished assembly, a *Sabhā Ranjané* [15] (Fig. 1) a word of art for an elevated or a dazzling assembly. The same Sabhāwa is called *Maha Maduwa*[16] to indicate the presence of a Chief like

---

[13] Hettiarachchi, D. E. ed. 1979, pp. 1, 10.

[14] In the folktale, *gamarāla and the Washerman* found in Northwestern Province, such a Sabhā was called *Rate Wissa* (assessors), Parker, H. 1910, 1982, *Village Folktales of Ceylon* Vol. I, p. 315; D'Oyly, 1929, p. 28.

[15] Kapuruhami, 1948, pp. 42-68.

[16] S. B. Ratwatte Kōrāla of Kalaweva cited in Hettiarachchi, 2019, 1979, p. 32.

Ratemahattayā or *Maha Vanni Unnehe*. Prefix *Maha-* is more than a collocation of a word. It denotes something being "special or imperious." Common examples found in Sinhala vernacular are: *Maha Wāsala* (palace), *Maha Naduwa* (judicial proceeding before or by the King), *Maha Gabadāwa* (storehouse of the palace), *Maha Aramudala* (royal treasury), *Maha Walawwa* (manor house of the elder or senior Chief),[17] *Maha Adikārama* (Chief Minister)[18] and *Maha Nilame* (senior Chief), and even affable *Maha Denamutta* (wise person) in Sri Lankan folktales.

Being of a lesser officer rank (*Sulu Mulādäni*), even the *Mohottāla* gets accorded the prefix *walawwe-* (of the manor house) when he assists on secretarial and logistical matters at *Ratemahattayā*'s house. In such instances, he is also known as *rate-lēkama*. He becomes *Dissāve Mohottāla* or *Walawwe Mohottāla* if he does similar work in the Dissāva's walawwa (See page 195).

A Sabhāwa is convened by the *Mohottāla* to sort out conflicts like *kula pali*,[19] *kula nadu* or discord between two individuals in the village. When it is conducted by any of the lesser officials like *Mohottāla* and *Baddarāla* for a similar issue, it was the custom of the villagers to call it just a *Sammutiya* or *Variga Sammutiya*. Since *Mohottāla* is commonly regarded as the head of a *Varige*, it is plausible a Sabhāwa convened by him to discuss *variga* concerns was also referred to as *Variga Sabhāwa*.

DISPARATE VARIGA CONCEPTS. Use of the term "*Varige*" (*W(V)aruge*) by a different ethnic subgroup – Vedda folks (*Ādivasin*) – in a different region in Sri Lanka also needs examination. Since earliest times and up to early decades of the 20th century, *Ādivasin* were forest-dwellers. They lived in ephemeral shelters and as such were always on the move following the game. The montane districts of Kandyan kingdom do not practice the so-called Nuwarakalaviya *Vedda* traditions. The Vedda folks who are also known as *Vanniyala ätto* or *Ādivāsin* in the Uva and Eastern provinces and their bordering areas also use the word '*Varige*.' Their variga concept has a different connotation.[20] Their Variga also have names. Since these people were hunter-gatherers and did not have a village to identify with, they identified by referring to their clan's name (an animal or location) which is attached as a prefix to the word '*Varige*.' Examples are Uru Varige, Ambala Varige, Morane Varige and Tala Varige. C.G.& Brenda Seligmann listed nine such Variga names Vedda folks belong to. The main purpose of their *Varige* is to identify and recognize each band (clan) of people. It is not a concept founded with guiding measures intended to support the stability of the band. When one member in a community committed to an exogamic marriage, there was no danger of being punished or banished from the band.

After conducting research in Kukulawa and few other villages in Nuwarakalaviya, James Brow labelled these villages as belonging to Vedda (Ādivasin)

---

[17] The manor house of Kapuruhami Madukanda Ratemahattayā is an example for this. After he was elevated to the title of Dissava in 1933, he continued to live in the same house. It was then called Maha Walawwa.(Fig. 51) His son was later appointed as the Ratemahattayā and built a new manor house in the adjoining lot. It is called the Kuda Walawwa (*kuda* – lesser) (Fig. 6, 52). The two houses are still occupied by their descendants. Those who are knowledgeable about the history of such houses in Sri Lanka continue to call it as walawwa regardless of the status of the current occupants.

[18] Sans. *adhikāra* – high official.

[19] *Giya kula, ā kula, wetunu kula, kiv kula, kä kula, ath veradi, kata veradi,* and *bath veradi*.

[20] Seligmann C. G. and Brenda, Z., 1911, 1993, *The Veddas*, p.74.

Variga (*gam veddo*).[21] This is a misnomer, probably reached by using narrow and hazy criteria. Kukulawa is 150 kilometers north of Uva province where traditional Vedda folks live. I live only 10 kilometers from Kukulawa. They hardly live or look like a caricature of Veddas.

Besides the identification tag bestowed upon the Anuradhapura 'Vedda' villages as a singular (ethnic) group merely because "they call(ed) themselves" so and "so called by their neighbors" or "they looked like so," they also practiced customs and traditions like Rata Sabhā and Variga Sabhā in the same way as other villages in Nuwarakalaviya. These villagers did not have linguistic or social similarities with Vedda folks in Uva. 'Vedda' in Nuwarakalaviya in academic or day-to-day vernacular do not reveal kinship relations with the Ādivasin of Uva. The so-called 'Veddas' of Anuradhapura led an agriculture-based livelihood. They owned paddies and cleared plots yearly in the forest around the village for *héna* cultivation. Whenever opportunity was granted, they hunted and fished using both The Old Way (with apologies to Elizabeth Marshall Thomas) and modern methods. They built permanent settlements – villages – by building permanent dwelling structures. They made gardens around the house and cleared strips of forest as chenas. Boundaries of these settlements are clearly marked. They shared forest resources with other villages around theirs.

Ādivasin, on the other hand, did not practice conventional agricultural livelihood until middle of the 20th century as described above. They "disliked settling down."[22] If they had to remain in a place for few days or weeks, they took shelter in caves or temporary enclosures – 'rough' shelters of sticks covered with twigs and situated in strategic locations, because they led primarily a peripatetic lifestyle like ancient humans. When food became scarce in an area, or water sources became dry, they just picked up and moved on. Male members of the Ādivasin fearing that the visitors might see their women did not allow anyone, mostly Moormen, who came to their campsite to trade. The visitor had to stay at a special location outside the camp. One other major difference between the two groups is that the so-called 'Vedda' villagers in Anuradhapura practiced patrilineal naming customs exclusively like rest of the district, while the Ādivasin practiced matrilineal traditions. However, by the end of 19th century, *Ādivasin's* lifestyle began to change. By then Danigala Ādivasin of Nilgala area showed sign of modernization like conventional agricultural practices, e.g., planting banana gardens.[23]

Although villages in Nuwarakalaviya district were shielded to a larger extent by forest, and residents in them occasionally showed similar styles of living as Veddas, that do not qualify as the medium to identify them with other forest dwelling groups. Vedda folks did not grow their own food in contrast to the Nuwarakalaviya people. Furthermore, the ethnic identity of the Vedda folks has been accepted as a singular category. A study of different ethnic groups in Sri Lanka in 2014 found Vedda populations in Rathugala, Dambana, Dalukana, Henanigala, and Pallebedda (all in

---

[21] Brow, James, 1978, *Vedda Villages of Anuradhapura: A Historical Anthropology of a Community in Sri Lanka.* p. xi. University of Washington Press, Seattle.

[22] Seligmann, C. G. and Brenda, Z., 1911, 1993, p. 36.

[23] Seligmann, C. G. and Brenda, Z., 1911, 1993, p. 37.

Uva Province) were clearly separated genetically from other Sri Lankan ethnic groups.[24]

Many decades before observers attached the inference of 'Vedda' to the few isolated villages in Anuradhapura, R. W. Ievers who is regarded as the first observer to provide the best informative insight to the history and culture of Nuwarakalaviya stated in no uncertain terms that "There are no wild Veddas now in this Province. The Veddas of Hurulu Palatha live in villages in no respect different from their neighbors."[25] Therefore, if a Vedda Varige tag is ascribed upon villages like Kukulewa, it contradicts with any descriptions of Variga identities of villages like it elsewhere in Nuwarakalaviya.

In contrast to Ādivasin, a *Varige* in Nuwarakalaviya constructed its procedures and laws specific to their needs for orderly existence within the community and with other Variga communities. Endogamy was one rule the Rata Sabhāwa in Nuwarakalaviya applied to its *variga* customs. Someone accused and subsequently found guilty of exogamy is expelled from the *Varige* or gets fined 500 *ridi* by the Rata Sabhāwa or Variga Sabhāwa. It is the largest fine the Sabhāwa could impose on a person found guilty of any breach under its purview. This situation is remarkable as the guilt extends not only to the accused, but to his or her blood relatives. Then they are also imposed a fine of 100-25 *ridi* for the breach. If there are no mitigating facts to clarify the situation, and if the accused couple is unable to pay the fine, it is incumbent upon the Sabhāwa to expel them from the *Varige*. In vernacular this is called *tolonchi karanawa*.

But there is no evidence that the Ādivasin of Bintenna in Uva province practiced Rata Sabhāwa or Variga Sabhā traditions as in or of Nuwarakalaviya. They also did not have the functional elements of Rata Sabhāwa — where titled Chiefs, *Vannihuru*, and officials like *Mohottāla* or *Badderāla* in the district actively participated to keep order about their affairs. Ādivasin only had band leaders and elders. Had there been any, no reference to it in multiple writings is surprising.

Thus, the stark contradistinction of the two peoples cannot be emphasized more. If designating a group of villages in Nuwarakalaviya as 'Vedda villages' as if one had a 'eureka' moment — stumbling up on a new group of people — and for no other reason than probably taking hints from unsubstantiated comments by travelers who in the past most likely had formulated their opinions by mere sight of a people in their most rudimentary hunter-gatherer state is of concern to most, particularly to these villagers themselves for distorting their identity. Labelling villages as Vedda villages in Anuradhapura have also generated confusion not just among anthropologists but among residents in these villages as well. When I talked to the villagers in Kukulawa, they were surprised to hear their village was identified with this surprising ethnic moniker. I found out that they are not happy with the moniker and the connotations attached to it. If Leach (1961, 1968) used a similarly imprecise and hazy viewfinder, he could have easily used a more captivating suffix for his classic, *Pul Eliya.*

---

[24] Ranaweera, L., et al., 2014. *Journal of Human Genetics* (59), 28–36.
[25] Ievers, 1899, p. 93.

Predicating such views based on the meagre lifestyle these villagers lead, while all their expressions of customs and traditions are diametrical opposites of traditional Vedda folks in parts of Uva province must only be confirmed by further studies and lengthy discourse so that we do not have uncertainties about their identity as an exclusive ethnic group, which I humbly believe at this moment, they are not.[26] The 2014 study cited earlier showing different genetic makeup of Ādivasin stands alone as the guide which helps us to sort out this confusion surrounding the moniker attached to an inconspicuous community of people in Nuwarakalaviya.

M.U.A Tennakoon, a pioneering authority in village life and rural irrigation systems in Sri Lanka remarkably enlightened me on this further. He wrote:

> People of Kukulewa, Valaave, Diviya Uda Bendaweva, Rambakepuweva, Kokpetiyawa and 30 such villages of the same stock of people are the original village settlers from the days of Anuradhapura kingdom who stubbornly refused to move to Polonnaruwa, Kandyan Hill Country kingdom proper or to the South. They remained steadfast to their village tanks, maintained them as much as they could amidst droughts, diseases, and poverty. Hunger and misery all around. If they too moved out of Nuwarakalaviya, there wouldn't have been a Nuwarakalaviya for people to talk about later. They saved Nuwarakalaviya village settlements as much as they could, even being gradually degraded to levels of hunting and gathering paupers in mere survival. They had no relationship to Dambana Adivaasi stock. We must acknowledge them with gratitude the services that they rendered in making the Nuwarakalaviya settlement live for nearly eight centuries till British took over its administration sometime after the signing of the Kandyan Convention in March 1815 [*sic*].[27]

---

[26] See James Brow (1978), *Vedda Villages of Anuradhapura.*

[27] Written communication, November 7, 2022.

4. VARIANTS, CHIEFS, A PRINCELY PROVINCE

a disquisition of Rata Sabhāwa of Nuwarakalaviya, a province seemingly isolated but princely in importance, stature and history would be seen as an inadequate effort without a preview of the customs and traditions in the communities existed in early times and the composition and role of feudal leaders involved in maintaining those customs. Many such customs, officialism and officialdom seem to have found roots in the Indian subcontinent. Indian epic *Mahabharata* mentions of a *grāmani*, leader or *gamarāla* of the village whose duty as the name suggests was to administer the affairs of the *grāma* (*gama* – village). In the Indian classic *Arthasasthra*, philosopher Kautilya mentions demarcating groups of villages as *pancha grāma* (five villages), *dasa grāma* (ten villages) and the like, forming a *mandala* (group, committee) of villages with one assigned as the main or anchoring village.[1]

Although unexampled and not much known about the procedures of administering justice in a community in ancient times in Sri Lanka, oral histories, certain words in use and phrases deciphered from rock inscriptions and palm leaf books show that long time ago people participated in a somewhat formless local system of authority to maintain order in their midst by clumping communities into early forms of 'districts' or 'precincts.' And the King, or a central authority, seems to have tolerated a degree of decentralization of the dressings of rural justice which we see in some fashion in institutions like Rata Sabhāwa.

As time passed, these councils evolved with culture and traditions of the respective countries. Towards the end of the Anuradhapura period, there were councils called *Sabhā* in villagers where a *lēkamge* or *liyanarāla* (scribe/secretary)[2] documented laws the council applied to maintain order. A *sabhāpathi* headed the council, but its make-up or responsibilities were vaguely known.[3] Similar to *Mohottāla* in a *Varige*, a *damilaadhikāri* was appointed to oversee villages where Tamils who were in King's service lived.[4] Committees were created in villages to oversee the forest; another for agricultural lands.

James Emerson Tennent tells of a collection of stone pillars that were remnants of a building that housed *Gam Sabhāwa*, a council of municipality, near Jetawanaramaya in Polonnaruwa. This council held meetings to administer justice and resolve disputes between citizens. He says such *Gam Sabhā* still exist in Sri Lanka in secluded districts arbitrating issues relating to property and morals. Distanced and

---

NOTES

[1] Abeyawardana, 1978, p. 12.

[2] Abeyawardana (1978) found the title of secretary mentioned in different terms in different *Kadaim poth* (Boundary Books) of Sri Lanka. Examples are, Lékamgei Samdaruwan (p.8), Jayamaha Lékhaka (p. 24), *Lékamgei* Aettan (p.24), Lékam Payyanda (p.145), Lékam Mahatkama (p.148), Aramadule Lékam (p. 155) and Hannasrāla or *Sannasrala* (p. 230). Sumitta who accompanied Bodhi Tree to Sri Lanka was appointed as *Jayamahalena* by King Devanampiyatissa.

[3] Nicholas and Paranavitana, 1961, p. 167.

[4] Abeywardena, 1978, p.152.

secluded from King's judicial oversight, the pre-British Nuwarakalaviya no doubt had workable rural bodies headed by Chiefs and *mulādenivaru* to resolve conflicts in the community. Tennent believed these officials were like officials of Panchayat in India or "elders of the gate" in ancient Jewish and Roman traditions.[5] The Panchayat[6] in India and Nepal, *Kgolta* in Botswana and *Baojia* system in China[7] are similar citizens' tribunals having functions like Rata Sabhāwa. Panchayat is led by a *Sarpanch* (Panchayat Pradhan) and his deputy called Upa-Pradhan. During Chola dynasty in South India, Chola-Mandalam bodies were like village bodies of Panchayat or early versions of village Sabhās. Judging from the Chola and other Indian inspirations that etched furrows in Sri Lankan history, there is no doubt some aspects of the Mandalam, Panchayat or other forms of tribunals helped culture early Sri Lankan village life as well.

K. N. Choksy appropriately starts the 1955 *Report of the Commission of Local Government* with this telling summary of the ancient system of local governments in Sri Lanka as quoted in Bandaranayake (1986):

> We would say that the systems of local government in ancient Ceylon would appear to have been of a patriarchal type, in which the affairs of every village were directed and controlled by its natural leaders whose decisions were accepted and obeyed by the community in general. The village elders met from time to time at a convenient spot, where surrounded by those who cared to hear and see and criticize their proceedings, they deliberated on affairs of common interest, adjusted civil disputes, and awarded punishments to ordinary offenders against person and property. Cases of serious crime were reserved for the consideration of the King himself. These Village Councils of ancient Ceylon known as "Gam Sabhā" were not controlled or directed by the King or any central authority. We are not certain whether there were formal rules of procedure laid down but matters of common interest were fully discussed by the Village Councils, and the decisions of the majority were accepted by the community without dissent. There were too, in time, larger councils known as "Rata Sabhā," which dealt with matters affecting a whole district or province. The fundamental ideas of democracy seem to have been in active operation in these institutions [*sic*]. (p. 21)

GAM SABHĀWA. **A VILLAGE BODY**. Often Rata Sabhāwa was classed as a district level body while *Gam Sabhāwa* remained a village-level body. Since the

---

[5] Tennent, 1860, p. 595.

[6] Panchayat (Council of Five) in rural India is a concept in each village where residents get together in the presence of elders and discuss and resolve conflicts influencing their lives. Unlike Rata Sabhāwa, Panchayat is a legally sanctioned institution with up to 3-5 years term limits for members.

[7] In the Ming Dynasty (1368-1644) China, families were belonged a collective of neighborhood organizations called *baojia*. Ten families grouped as a *jia* and ten *jia* were grouped as a *bao*. These were a form of precincts or districts formed for administration (Sourced from Yuval Noah Harari, 2015, *Sapiens: A Brief History of Humankind*, p. 357; https://www.britannica.com/topic/baojia)

former included several villages that formed a *Varige*, e.g., Gam Daha Ata Varige (Clan of Eighteen Villages) and functioned under the supervision of two *Ratemahatvaru*, it no doubt elicited elements of an institution covering an area stretching beyond a single village, seldom beyond the boundaries of an administrative district in the colonial context (Fig. 34). Brow (1978) writes *Vedda Varige* of Kukulawa near Maha Kanadarāwa off Anuradhapura-Trincomalee Road was said to contain four communities or villages (p. 48). Furthermore, its functions involved more of the maintenance of social order-cum-conflict resolution but not quotidian affairs of a village.

On the other hand, except during the colonial administration which provided legislative direction with written rules, the *Gam Sabhāwa* (seldom written in texts as *Gan Sabhāwa* or *Gam Sabe*) in a village in Nuwarakalaviya was the continuation of traditions and customs, without the benefit of written laws from the King, or the Maha Vanniyā. *Gam Sabhāwa* existed in different forms from ancient times or since the inception of the village, the *gam bándeema*. A group of elders led by *gamarāla* (head of the village), *Vel Vidāne* (coordinator of paddy fields related issues) and the *Lékama* aided by few senior villagers or heads of families in an advisory role formed an entity for the upkeep of order, irrigation matters, agricultural and other interests of the village. It was in general a court of arbitration.

In the case of colonial regions, although there were few reports of village bodies like the one in Panadura in 1848[8], from 16th to 18th centuries, grievances were resolved by writing petitions to the government officials. As far back as 1636, a petition was submitted to Captain-General Dieogo de Melo de Castro against the Sinhala and Portuguese officials for failing to protect and promote Sinhala customs as agreed upon at the Malvana Convention of 1598.[9]

As a kid in 1950s, I remember watching how my grandfather, the *Vel Vidāne*, summoning the villagers to his house for the *kanna meetima* (meeting of the paddy season) held just before the rainy season. The group sat on reed mats and discussed the timetable to start the work regimen in the paddy fields and issues that would follow during the growing season. Everyone had a voice, and decisions such as when to open the *kota horowwa* (sluice gate), when to clear ditches to irrigate fields and other related tasks were made after long deliberations. In the context of protocol and purpose, they were *Gam Sabhā* in pure form as well sans the involvement of a Chief.

In 17th century, Knox wrote about the existence of a '*gam sabi*.' He called them "town-consultations" [*sic*].[10] After a century and a half later, King Sri Wickrama Raja Singhe during his final years, encouraged and approved local councils called *Rata Sabē* and *Gam Sabē*. But his disgruntled Chiefs showed lukewarm interest and favor

---

[8] Goonesekere, R. K. W. 1958, The Eclipse of the Village Court. *Ceylon Journal of Historical and Social Studies,* Vol. 1, No. 2, pp. 138-154.

[9] Abeysinghe, T.B.H. 1964, Myth of the Malvana Convention, *Ceylon Journal of Historical and Social Studies,* Vol. 7 No. 1 (Jan-June), pp. 67-72.

[10] Knox, 1681, 1995, p. 52.

to the idea.[11]

While the Rata Sabhāwa was the mainstay legal institution in Nuwarakalaviya, in most Kandyan villages *Gam Sabe* (*Gam Sabhāwa*) performed somewhat similar judicial and social functions. In this case, every head of the family, regardless of his wealth or rank, was mandated to participate by default in its decision-making processes. No application – *bulathurulla* (pl. *bulathurulu*) or other form of entry protocol – was required. Unlike the Rata Sabhāwa, residents in general incurred no expenses to hold the *Gam Sabe*. It was a body supported by group participation of villagers for management of their community affairs.

In Kandyan highlands, a decision of the *Gam Sabe* could be appealed to the "Rata Sabhāwa" which is not the same Sabhāwa as in Nuwarakalaviya which did not have a secondary Sabhā to appeal. Rata Sabhāwa of Kandyan country comprised of "intelligent delegates from each village." That is not to say that the delegates and officials of the Rata Sabhāwa in Nuwarakalaviya were otherwise. As their long-standing traditions show, they were as good as any person of judicial capacity. If the decision of the Nuwarakalaviya Rata Sabhāwa were not to the liking of the affected villagers, they could appeal to the *Kōrāla*. If not satisfied with his decision, they appealed to *Walawwe Mohottāla* (a rank like *Ratemahattayā* in Nuwarakalaviya). An appeal can proceed all the way up the ladder to Maha Vanniyā, *Dissava*, *Adikārama*, and finally to the King. But as will be shown later, an appeal to the King was rarely made.

Abuses of judicial decision-making seemed to be acute in the distant *Dissavani*s than in and around Kandy where being closer to the King was a forewarning for the Chiefs and *mulādänivaru* to be objective in their activities. Yet, *Ratemahatvaru* in Kandyan highlands could conduct independent hearings (courts) and sometimes acted "without check or control" and with the two-fold attributes of judge of law and fact.[12] Villager always had the option of going to the palace (*Maha Wāsala*, used as a synecdoche for the King) if he thinks the decision of his hearing was not fair! This must have been rampant as folk poetry too had referred to abuses by *mulādänivaru*. In one such poem, a villager bemoans the injustice caused to him by a mid-range title holder named Atapattuwe Mudali, and questions why the sun rises in a country which does not have justice![13]

In isolated regions like Nuwarakalaviya or Uva, *Ratemahattayā* had the freedom to conduct judicial and administrative matters as he wishes. Therefore, those who appeared before a Rata Sabhāwa were mindful to hazard the ire or displeasure of the officials. This situation further exacerbated as there were no written rules and fixed protocols on *Maduwé Chārithra*, the customs of court session for the villagers (and *mulādänivaru*) to abide by.

There are reports that a few years after the commencement of administration of justice by the new colonial administration in Kandy, with the Proclamation of November 21, 1818, the Judicial Commissioner and Government Agents occasionally referred disputes to the *Gam Sabe*. The government's decision on the

---

[11] Pridham, Charles,1849, *A Historical, Political and Statistical Account of Ceylon…* Vol. I, p. 219.

[12] Pridham, 1849, p. 220.

[13] Siripala, Norman, 1990, Quoting *Vinoda Kavya Sangrahaya*, p. 127, in *Govi Gedara Jana Kavi*, p. 247.

matter was then based on the decision of the *Gam Sabe*.[14] Under the Ordinance 2, of 1835, the colonial government allowed a headman, often called *Lékama* to convene few villagers to a *Gam Sabe* and enquire cases of Cattle Trespass and assess damage sustained.[15] There are instances in post-Rata Sabhāwa Sri Lanka when retired *Kōrāla*s still received these complaints from villagers. A *sittu*-like note written on paper by Alittane Kōrāla in Ulagalla Kōrale in mid-20th century describes a complaint of cattle trespass and the punishment he levied on the owner of the herd (Fig. 49).

The headman held *Gam Sabe* Court often under a large shady tree in the village or an *ambalama* (pl. *ambalam*, also called *madam*) – the small road-side rest stops without hospitality service for travelers. The shady tree where villagers convened was usually located in the center of the village.[16] *Ambalama* has a permanent roof, and short walls to sit on. As shown in later pages, and as embodied in the architecture of some *ambalam* (Fig. 44), seating arrangement of travelers in these locations has followed a caste hierarchical tradition existed at the time.[17]

Issues discussed in *Gam Sabe* were disputes, debts, and petty offences.[18] The *Sabe* assisted in arbitration and "directed to compromise and not to punish."[19] Although both functioned as very low-level tribunals, there were differences between *Gam Sabe* and Rata Sabhāwa of Nuwarakalaviya. Rata Sabhāwa had its leader in the *Mohottāla* or *Ratemahattayā*. At the time of its dissolution in 1938, functions of the Rata Sabhāwa included comportment-related issues (etiquette), personal disputes, general conduct, and attention to decorum within the Sabhāwa. At the end of a Sabhāwa session, the feast given to participants and officials was prepared by the respondent with rice provided by *gamarāla*.[20]

A. C. Lawrie,[21] being a Justice himself, had also been looking out for native judicial customs and traditions in and around Kandy. He found the *Gam Sabe* was

---

[14] Goonesekere, 1958, p. 140.

[15] Ferguson, A.M., 1868, *Ceylon Directory: Calendar and Compendium of Useful Information for 1866 and 1868*, p. 58.

[16] Knox (1681, 1995) calls it *gam sabi* or 'town consultations' (p. 52); *Gansabe* - D'Oyly, 1833,1835, p. 231. Henry Marshall also gives the order of the appeal process. Firstly, neighbors take up a dispute. If the villager seeking redress is not satisfied, then he takes it to the *Kōrāla* of the area and then to *Mohottāla*. If not satisfied still, the next stop is the *Dissāva*. If necessary, final stop is before the King in Kandy (1846, 1954, p. 32).

[17] Such roadside rests were common in South India. They were called Chouree (Chatra – umbrella), Choultry or Chavadi.

[18] Codrington, 1938, P. 2.

[19] Goonesekere, 1958, p. 140; D'Oyly, 1833, 1835, p. 232.

[20] Pieris, R., 1956, p. 150.

[21] Scotsman Archibald Campbell Lawrie (1837-1914) was a legal scholar in Sri Lanka from 1873 to 1901 and had worked in Kandy as the District Judge from 1873 to 1892. In addition to being a judge, he had a passion for historical records. While working in Kandy he had access to cases that had been decided in the court. He extracted information from evidentiary material, including *Sannas, ola* books, and *sittu* that were filed by litigants on record as evidence of land ownership which was the subject of litigation in most civil cases at the time. He then compiled them into 974-page two-volume masterpiece, *A Gazetteer of the Central Province of Ceylon (Excluding Walapone)* in 1896 & 1898.

held on the spot sometimes.[22] It also had reed mats laid out in a circular pattern for participants to sit, but no food was provided to them. According to John D'Oyly, in village courts (he must have been referring to the turn of the 19th century *Gam Sabe* existed in Kandyan country) the principal inhabitants in the village constituted a jury.[23]

VILLAGE COMMITTEE AND VILLAGE TRIBUNAL. In the second half the 19th century, Governor Henry Ward thought that restoration of traditional customs by community involvement with *Gam Sabhāwa* was an important instrument in governing. He proposed a plan for this in 1861, and in 1871, Governor Hercules Robinson introduced Act 26 creating Village Committees and Village Tribunals.

The Village Tribunal consisted of five members from the village with certain basic qualifications – over 25yrs of age, having property in the village and other distinctive attributes. Its jurisdiction extended to one village or a cluster of villages. Members elected the Tribunal President. The difference between the Village Committee and the Tribunal was that members of the latter received a small renumeration. District Court sometimes referred issues like disputed land boundaries or land encroachment and host of quotidian conflicts to the Village Committee or the Tribunal to be resolved. Subsequently, the court received the resolutions from the Tribunal. A Fiscal officer, *Piscal Rālahāmi,* collected any fines imposed upon the convicted and submitted them to the Government Agent. This job continued to the 1950s collecting fees due to *Gam Sabhāwa* too from villagers.

Villagers elected 6 members for the Committee from among them for a 3-year term. The tribunal Councilors also had a similar term in office. The Committee and Village Tribunal reported to the Government Agent as two distinct officially sanctioned entities. Meanwhile Rata Sabhāwa remained a tradition under the purview of only the Chiefs. The whole idea of the Committee seems to be that it was a small court to which regular courts outsourced some of their work. All present at the meeting could vote. A majority vote required to convict a person. In case of ties, the President of the Tribunal had power to use his vote as he sees fit. Village Committee had power to fine Rs. 10, and Rs. 5 for each day the breach continued. Village Tribunal had the power to fine up to Rs. 20. Results of the case is then sent in writing to the Kachcheri with a copy of it to the Government Agent.[24] The councilors lost their position if they did not attend the meetings regularly or committed a crime.

Operational areas of Rata Sabhāwa, Variga Sabhāwa or the Village Tribunals corresponded with the existing boundaries of areas under the jurisdiction of the Nuwarakalaviya Chiefs – *Ratemahatvaru* in Kandy and *Vannivaru* who the government called Chief Headmen, though they had no role whatsoever in the functions of the Committee. All 'Natives' (any citizen other than Europeans and Burghers) fell under their jurisdiction. Upon receiving a request from at least 10 villagers, the Government Agent called for a public meeting of the Committee at a

---

[22] A. C. Lawrie cited in Jennings, Ivor, July 1952, Notes on Kandyan Laws… *University of Ceylon Review* Vol. 10, No. 3, pp. 185-220.

[23] D'Oyly, 1833, 1835, p. 235.

[24] Makeup and functions of the Village Committees and Village Tribunals are sourced from *Legislative Enactments of Ceylon 1870-75.* 1875, pp 83-94.

time and place chosen by him. Such hearing did not interfere with villagers convening the old Rata Sabhāwa or *Gam Sabe* outlined hereinbefore.

Committee had authority to make rules on both Civil and Criminal matters. In a sense, it was a rule-making body. Usually, it established protocol for the operation of the Tribunal. These rules were made within the framework of existing traditions and customs, covering irrigation and day-to-day affairs and customs of the people. The Committee also examined and decided upon acts defined as offences by the Governor and the Committee. These two bodies were meant to reduce protracted and expensive litigation, particularly involving irrigation affairs. These included, but not limited to, branding of cattle, refusal to participate in repair work of the tank bund, irrigation canals, culverts, old *edanda* (bridge of one log placed across a stream) petty theft, forgery, fraud, and any infamous crimes. Customs like marriage, a main staple in the Rata Sabhāwa, did not fall under the overview of the Committee.

RATA SABHĀ AND SACERDOTAL ISSUES. Rata Sabhāwa of Nuwarakalaviya had stayed out of the issues of Buddhist sacerdotal establishment because clerical disciplinary affairs were under the purview of the Sangha Sabhā (ecclesiastical courts).[25] But in *Kiria* vs *Poola* (c 1859), a monk giving evidence said that in ancient times a priest in the village got involved in laymen's affairs and presided over the *Gam Sabhāwa*.[26] It is not known whether this happened in Nuwarakalaviya or in Kandyan region.

Asgiriya temple in Kandy was familiar with such tribunals. There are records of its *Mahanayake Thero* (Head Priest) convening and presiding over a *Gam Sabhāwa* several times in 19th century. He asked the Vidāne to summon 10-15 villagers to assemble in the temple. The Thero then held hearings before issuing a *Sittu* (order).[27] He and a committee of resident monks met and reviewed allegations against monks who had received ordination at the Temple Chapter. In such an instance, after the review, if charges were found credible, the committee had the power to admonish or censure or if necessary, even depose the bhikkhu.[28] Usually, laity did not participate in these hearings because they were about priestly discipline. The Temple kept some form of record of such hearings. D'Oyly states that in tribunals held in Kandyan country, the decisions were written in a *Sittu* called *Witti Wattoru*. It is therefore possible that the Asgiriya temple tribunals too could have prepared such written accounts of their decisions.

King also got involved often when the issue is between a laymen and temple concerning its lands. He then appointed a special lay official called *Hantiye Nilame* to review and give a ruling.[29] Although some higher tribunals of laity commissioned by the King consisted of two *Adikaramvaru, Dissavaru, rate rālas* (*Ratemahatvaru*) and the *Maha Mohottāla*, in some instances, if a need arises, a prominent bhikkhu who had no official capacity was asked to participate.[30] In a description given in verbatim by a *henayā* village leader about a caste court, Variga Sabhāwa, convened to hear a

---

[25] Thambiah, H. W., 1962, Buddhist Ecclesiastical Law. *JRAS*, Vol. 8, No. 1, pp. 71-107.

[26] Lorensz Law Reports III, 1859 p. 143 qtd. in Bandaranayake, 1986, p. 36.

[27] Goonesekere, 1958, p. 142.

[28] Lawrie, A. C. 1896, p. 71.

[29] Lawrie, A. C. 1896, p. 71.

[30] de Silva, K. M. D., 1981, p. 145.

case of sexual relation between a Bhikkhu and two women, at the end of the hearing, the Bhikkhu was fined Rs. 200 and disrobed.[31]

After the British Colonial government abolished the *rājakāriya* (corvée labor or King's work, service tenure)[32] in 1832, it had tacitly let the *Gam Sabe* fall into disuse and sealed the destiny of similar practices including Rata Sabhāwa of Nuwarakalaviya. But as we found out later, it would refuse to drop out of existence just yet. Many decades later, it was still pulsing in some villages in Nuwarakalaviya.

Thus, towards the latter parts of the 19th century, the *Gam Sabhāwa* sanctioned by the Colonial government and Rata Sabhāwa as described by Kapuruhami Madukanda Ratemahattayā existed as a binary, two unrelated entities — the former an official institution, the latter simply as a native tradition unsanctioned and without official recognition or blessings.

Moreover, since the start of Courts of Request and Police Courts earlier in 1843,[33] villagers' perception of the *Gam Sabhāwa* changed and propensity for litigations, especially criminal cases brought by villagers in the Request and Police courts went up. As a result of this compelling alternative, the *Gam Sabhāwa* concept had begun less and less persuasive to villagers.[34] There is no doubt the caste-neutrality seen in the British legal system and corruption of native members of the *Gam Sabhāwa* must have given impetus for people to seek redress from the novelty of these courts. People also praised the fairness of the British legal system which enabled "the lowest (of the society) to make a complaint against the highest on any oppression."[35] Nira Wickramasinghe wrote: "Apart from the alleged lack of moral principle among the natives, the reason for this flurry of judicial activity could be attributed to the feeling among the people that the land tenure system as well as social laws and hierarchies were now uncertain and could be contested."[36]

SAKKIBALANDA. This is another Sabhāwa assembled in the village with individuals having distinguished résumé. This 'tribunal' too had some degree of judicial powers. Some called it a High Court, but the duties were like those of a coroner-by-committee. It was called *Sakkibalanda* (to search for evidence or facts). Its membership usually consisted of the officials like *Lékama*, *Kōrala* and *vidāne*.[37]

When a dead body was discovered anywhere within the boundaries of the village, uncovering the cause of death was the primary task of this committee. After 1822, in similar cases in the Kandyan provinces, British introduced the inquest by a

---

[31] Ryan, 1953, p. 249.

[32] In Kings' times and few decades into the British colonial administration, *rājakāriya* work was exacted from "all males who could throw a stone over their houses" (Arthur Perera, 1917, p. 26). But with the Act number 8 of 1848, the British instituted their own form of *rājakāriya* wherein all native males between 15 and 55 years were mandated to provide 6 consecutive days of labor a year. Those who can pay three shillings were allowed commutation of such labor (*Collection of Legislative Acts... 1854*, p. 358.

[33] Ordinance 10 and 11, respectively. *Collection of Legislative Acts ...*, 1854. p. 156.

[34] Mills, 1933, p. 136; R. K. W. Goonesekere, 1958, p. 142.

[35] A. O. Brodie qtd. in Ievers,1899, p. 55.

[36] Wickramasinghe, Nira, 2020, *Slave in a Palanquin*, p. 186 citing Colebrooke-Cameron Report of 1832.

[37] Codrington, H. W. 1938, p. 3; Charles Pridham, 1849, p. 220; John Davy, 1821, 2006, *An Account of the Interior of Ceylon.* P 180, 181).

jury of at least nine English and Burgher nationals.[38] Few years later, this jury was reorganized to consist mainly of principal inhabitants of the village.[39]

The native Chief was supposed to first make inquiries and report to the Government Agent.[40] If the death was a suicide by hanging, which was usually regarded as a 'high crime' like homicide and treason,[41] a fine of 50 ridi was imposed upon the residents of the village which was shared by the committee members and the *Dissava*. There will be no fine if the person committed suicide was known to be not of sound mind. The dead body cannot be disposed of until the fine was paid, which fact has parallel shades of a *tahanam* or *tahanchi* - ban, modern day equivalent being 'free on bail with conditions,' a feature in a Rata Sabhāwa which will be written about in coming pages.

EARLY OFFICE HOLDERS AND CHIEFS. Two millennia ago, King Pandukābhaya (377-307 BC) in Anuradhapura, the city which would be the seat of Kings for the next 15 centuries, appointed his uncle Abhaya as its night-time administrator. His title was *nagaraguttika* (Guardian of the City) or *nagara-laddā* (Recipient of the City). In the 12th year of his reign, Pandukābhaya also created four suburbs[42] in his city and established boundaries for villages.[43] There is no doubt these four suburbs or precincts, too had some form of leadership to run their day-to-day affairs.

After Pandukābhaya's grandson Devānampiyatissa (247-207 BC)[44] became the ruler, the south branch of Sacred Bodhi Tree in Jambudweepa (India) was brought to the city of Anuradhapura. It was escorted by eight princes[45] and a retinue of people belonging to 18 castes. *Mahavamsa* states these princes were of *Setthi*) caste and earned the name *bodhāharanakula* (caste of the Bodhi Tree holders).[46] Citing H.Ellawala, Shirley Pulle Tissera suggests that the word Chetty in Sri Lanka is identified with the word Sethi in pali, Hetti or Situ in Sinhala and that "Prince Sumitta and his seven brothers who came to Lanka to guard the sacred Bo Tree were sons of a Deva Sethi from Vedissa City in Avanthi. Therefore, their sister

---

[38] By the Charter of 1833, the colonial government increased the Jury composition to 13 men, *Legal Enactments*, 1875, p. 84.

[39] D'Oyly, 1833, 1835, p. 235.

[40] *Collection of Legislative Acts,* 1853, p. 275.

[41] Pieris, R., 1956, p. 143.

[42] *Mahawansa* n.d. 1912, 2003, X. 88. 74.

[43] Obeysekere, Donald, 1911, 1999, *Outlines of Ceylon History*, p. 13.

[44] Geiger, Wilhelm, 1912, *Mahawansa*, p. xxxvii; *C.W.* Nicholas and S. Paranavitana, 1961, *A Concise History of Ceylon*, (1961), p. 341, gives this date as 210-250 BC.

[45] Bodhiguttadeva (Protection of the Bodhi Tree), 2. Sumittadeva (Protection of the Bodhi Tree), 3. Chandraguttadeva (Play the golden drum for the Bodhi Tree), 4. Devaguttadeva (Carry golden pitcher at the Bodhi Procession distributing blessed water), 5. Suryaguttadeva (Pour water to the Bodhi Tree from golden pitcher), 6. Gotamadeva (Holds parasol, *sesath*, to Bodhi Tree, 7. Juteendradeva (Guarding the Bodhi Tree) and 8. Dharmaguttadeva (Blow the conch at the Bodhi Tree). They were known as Bodhiwansadeva princes. (Ven. Matale Sri Upananda, Undated booklet, Printed and published by S. Rajapakse, Semage Industries, Rajagiriya. P. 13.; Ven. Medauyangoda Wimalakeerthi, 1955. p. 222.

[46] Turnour, George.1836, p. 132. Pali: *Dhāra* – Bear; Hold. *Dhāraka* – One who hold or possesses.

(Queen of King Asoka and mother of Mahinda and Sangamitta) was also a Sethi."[47] *Dipawansa* notes them as Bodhi Guards of warrior clans.[48] Host of other Brahmana Rālas (nobles, also called *Mudalihuru*)[49] and commoners of 18 castes came with the Bodhi Tree. King appointed Bodhigutta and Sumitta[50] to supervise wards in the purlieu of Anuradhapura city.[51] He rightly thought that dividing a city into precincts was an effective administrative idea. Bodhigutta was titled *Lēkam mahalena* and Sumitta was called *Jayamahalena* (Chief Secretary for War).[52] They were also charged with administering the people of 18 castes mentioned before.[53] It is possible these two wards acquired different names later.

Some of the commoners who looked after the Sacred Bodhi Tree and provided its ancillary services were called *villidurai* (an off root of them called *kontadurai* moved to Sabaragamuwa region) and their descendants are still said to be living in Anuradhapura area.[54] As they live in villages owned by *vihara* (temples) in Nuwarakalaviya they are also called *viharagamkārayo*. While appreciating their dedication and troubles in bringing the Sacred Bodhi Tree, there is no doubt the King realized that there was a need for officials to oversee the caste dynamics between the newcomers and other diverse groups already living in the kingdom. This highlights the depth and characteristics of administration of precincts, i.e., villages and castes structure in ancient Sri Lanka. King's idea of dividing the city into precincts must have been necessitated based on these realities. There are varying accounts about where others who came with the Sacred Bodhi Tree settled.

Nearly two millennia later, however, *Matale Kada-Im Potha* (Matale Boundary Book), believed to have been written a millennia later during or after Gampola period, i.e., in 14th and 15th centuries, notes that they took residence in villages in Matale area.[55]

According to folklore in Nuwarakalaviya, beginning from the Medieval Times, administrative positions were given to persons belonging to families with honorific names or titles such as Raja Nayaka, Raja Paksa, Raja Karuna, Raja Tilaka, Tri Sinhala, Sri Vijaya Sundara, Atta Nayaka, Keerthi Tissa, and Bandara.[56]

Véválketiya inscription, a polished granite pillar believed to have been made during King Udaya IV (946-954 AD) located about 20 kilometers on Medawachchiya-Horowpothana road north of Mihintale mentions on several lines

---

[47] (https://thuppahis.com/2013/07/14/the-colombo-chetties-of-sri-lanka-three-essays/

[48] Oldenberg, Hermann, 1879, 2001, *Deepawamsa* p. 195.

[49] Abeywardena, 1978, p.224.

[50] Verse 27 of the *Perakumbasirita* by Totagamuwe Sri Rahula refers to a Sevulu Vijaya Bahu. Edward W. Perera (1910) suggests he is descended from Sumitta, maternal uncle of Mahinda Thera (citing Sri Rahula in *Kavyasekharaya* Part 14, vv 61, 62). King Devānampiyatissa appointed him as the Secretary of War. (The Age of Sri Parakrama Bahu VI 1412-7 A.D. *The Journal of the Ceylon Branch of the Royal Asiatic Society of Great Britain & Ireland*, Vol. 22, No. 63, pp. 6-45.

[51] *Mahawansa*, 1912, 2003, X. 88.74.

[52] M.B. Ariyapala, 1956, 1997. *Society in Mediaeval Ceylon*, p. 117.

[53] Hettiarachchi, D. E., ed. 1979, p. 2.

[54] Ryan, 1953, p. 126.

[55] Abeywardena, 1978, p. 128.

[56] Hettiarachchi, D. E., ed. 1979, p. 2.

a ten-village group called *dasa gam*.[57,58] Although it is not clear of the administrative structure and leaders of this *dasa gam* 'district,' inscribers of this pillar no doubt would have been proud to learn that nearly 10 centuries later, their compatriots – a *Varige* in the present-day group of Gam Daha Ata (Clan of Eighteen Villages) in the 3-Korale region (Kanadara, Kändä and Ulagalla) just 20 kilometers to the South would bear dear some semblances to the treasured traditions of their village collective.

My village Maradankalla is part of this collective. My great-grandfather Seneviratne Banda was the last *Mohottāla* (*mulādäniya*/ *kāriyakarawannā*) of the Rata Sabhāwa of this group of villages (Lokubanda Tillakaratne, 2015, *Echoes of the Millstone*, p. 3). Despite these 18 villages forming a unit based on their variga identity, they belonged to different administrative districts such as *tulāna* and *Kōrale* governed by the British colonial administration. H(S)orabora (Hopitigamu) inscription, also called Badulla Inscription where it is in display now, refers to an "eight village committee men and eight forest committee men with a *Lékamge* (secretary)." H. W. Codrington (1938) believes, however, these men functioned more as a form of administrative body drafting rules (p. 3). In this respect, Rata Sabhāwa or *Gam Sabe* look to be different in that they functioned only as a court system under the umbrella of existing oral traditions overseeing customs and social decorum.

The first duty of King Vijayabahu I (1055-1110 AD) after ascending to the throne was to "provide for proper administration of justice" for which no attention seemed to have been given in prior years. He created a *sabhāpathi* (Chief of the Council).[59] Each large city had such councils.[60] Officials in them functioned like "father or mother to people" without "fear, favor, hatred or ignorance." King Nissankamalla (1187-1196 AD) created *Dharmadhikarana* (Courts of Justice). Nicholas and Paranavitana also paralleled the feudal officials in these as a jury which after considering evidence of parties involved "expressed their opinion." Following this the presiding officer (probably like *Mohottāla* in Rata Sabhā?) announced the decision.

CHIEFS. Next reference to Sinhala nobility in Nuwarakalaviya or *Vannivaru* in the northern region comes in the 13th century.[61] *Mahavamsa* tells of rich princes of Vanni[62] during the reign of King Parakramabahu II (1240-1275 AD). A

---

[57] By comparing the remarkable similarities of grammatical characteristics in the text on the first few lines of both Mihintale and Véválketiya inscriptions, Muller (1883) thinks both inscriptions are likely have been made during the reign of Siri Sangabo Abhaya or Mahinda III (801-804 AD) (p. 58).

[58] Muller, Edward, 1883, *Ancient Inscriptions in Ceylon*, p. 85.

[59] C.W. Nicholas & S. Paranavitana, 1961, p. 260.

[60] It is interesting some large cities in other countries now have similar system of town administration. For instance, City of Los Angeles in California (Est. 1781, Pop. 4 million) now has 99 Neighborhood Councils, each with nine volunteer members elected by the residents of each neighborhood to serve as their representatives for a 4-year term. These council members are different from the regular elected and paid City Council members that number only 15. Neighborhood council meets monthly and listen to residents' concerns ranging from streets repairs to beautifying the neighborhood and other small-scale projects that they believe will enhance the profile of and bring benefits to their community.

[61] Nicholas and Paranavitana, 1961, p. 278.

[62] Sylvan region sandwiched between Jaffna Pattam and northern boundary of Nuwarakalaviya.

Nuwarakalaviya *mulādāni* named D. B. Rajakaruna who was an indigenous doctor at Kekatiyagollewa and an essayist in the Wickramasinghe Manuscripts competition in 1932, which later became *Sinhala Sirith Sangrahaya* (SSS), wrote that after the end of the Anuradhapura and Polonnaruwa periods, Buwanekabahu II (or V?) had used Rata Sabhā system in the year 1303 AD at Hasthisilapura (Kurunegala).[63]

Folklore of the region also appends stories to King Buwanekabahu in the year of Saka 1358 or AD 1558(?). According to R. K. Tillakarathna Mohotti of Kahatagasdigiliya,[64] the King had summoned Vanni Bandaravaru and directed them to hold Rata Sabhā to investigate those who intermix with different castes. This King also appointed *Mohottālas*, *Baddarālas* and other lesser officials.

There were 18 *Vanniyās* in the very thinly populated area between Jaffna and Kanda Uda Rata (Kandyan region) during Parakramabahu VI.[65] They were also called Raja Vanniyā (Senior Vanniya) and *Kumara Vanniya* (Junior Vanniya) [*sic*].[66] Mukkuwas in Puttalama who were believed to be partly Mohamadens, partly Christians and claim to have crossed Ganges at Ayodhya centuries earlier to settle in the area during Dutch occupation were also called *Vanniyās*.[67] Some suggest them as descending from Malabars and settled in this district. The region was ruled by 12 *Vanniyās*.[68] King of Sitawaka had created a Royal tribunal at Puttalama called *Muttrakudam* and appointed 18 Mukkuwas as its members under a *Dissava*.[69] This could be considered as their own Rata Sabhāwa, which was presided over by a *Kanakapulle* and *Vidane* appointed by the King's Dissāva. These *Vanniyās* apparently did not have jurisdictions of their own but investigated and settled small disputes of Mukkuwas.[70]

It has been known that *Vanniyas* of North Central Province were unpleasant for paralleling them with Kandyan Chiefs.[71] In a diary entry in 1851, Brohier quotes a *Vanniyā* Chief flouting the Kandyan Chiefs: "they (*Vanniyās*) were in Vanni (most of North Central Province) long before the "Bo-tree!"[72] But in the Rata Sabhā context, *Vanniyā*, *Ratemahattaya*, and *Dissavaru* were functionally similar; the distinction being just terminological, and attitudes privately held by the *Vanniyās* about their hill-country counterparts and vice versa.

---

[63] D.B. Rajakaruna, qtd. In Hettiarachchi, ed. 1979, p.10.

[64] The gold medalist in 1932 essay competition conducted by Government Agent of Anuradhapura.

[65] Lewis, J. P. 1895, 1993, p. 16.

[66] D'Oyly,1929, p. 51; Gunasekara, B., 1900, 1954, *Rajavaliya or Historical Narrative of Sinhalese Kings from Vijaya to Vimala Dharma Sooriya II* p. 77.

[67] Paul E. Pieris, 1918, p. 123.

[68] Paul E. Pieris, 1918, p. 123. Mukkuwas (Mukkaras) seem to have influenced Sri Lankan politics (and life) centuries before. A *Vitti Potha* (Book of Incidents) mentions an invasion by *Kāka Mukkaru* from India (Wickremasinghe, 1900, p. 74). Verse 75 of *Parakumbasirita* by Totagamuwe Sri Rahula refers to Parakramabahu VI (1412-1467) defeating Mukkaras (cited in Perera, Edward W, 1910, pp. 6-45). This is also chronicled in a palm leaf manuscript called *Mukkara Hatana* now in the Hugh Neville collection in British Museum (Or. 6606 - 139).

[69] Chitty, 1834, p. 277.

[70] Paul E. Pieris, 1918, p. 123.

[71] Ryan, 1953, p. 243.

[72] Ievers, 1899, p. 92.

The *Kōrāla*, a title sandwiched between *mulādānivaru/kāriyakarawannō* and *Ratemahattayā*, had been in existence during Kandyan King's times in Kanda Uda Rata. King did not seem to make any efforts to grant *Kōrāla* titles in Nuwarakalaviya. But with his muted attention to Nuwarakalaviya, he was happy to appoint only a *Dissava* for the province. Only the British began appointing the *Kōrāla*s across the province starting from around 1833.

In pre-modern Sri Lanka, it was a common survival necessity that every community or a group of them needed a leader or a Chief to act as its anchor. But the leader or a Chief of a people comes for other reasons as well. There are leaders or Chiefs who hold the responsibility on a temporary basis. Democratically elected persons with term limits in modern times are examples of this category. In theory, they are supposed to perform administrative functions and make rules within the framework of the power entrusted to them during their tenure. In time, these rules can become part of the tradition and culture of the multitude. There are other leaders who are Kings or Queens who can be just traditional and cultural Heads of State as we see in some countries in modern times. They help sustain the pride and identity of the subjects who cling to the idea of them as being special or even divine. In such case, someone else like democratically elected prime minister who is not of royal blood line does the actual governing of the people.

The Chief's family derives its name from customs and traditions that existed in the area in ancient times. After a major irrigation tank or a religious edifice was built in early Sri Lanka, it had been the practice of the King to appoint a leading citizen as its caretaker. Such a person was called a *nayaka, na, rat na* or *Ratemahattayā*. Naturally, the people in the area then began to associate the name of the tank or the community with the person who now has an elevated profile.[73] In addition to being the caretaker with the reservoir related affairs, these Chiefs also were responsible for maintaining order by being the caretaker of the customs and social traditions of the larger area and the resources of the tank or the other edifices. Often, the caretaker role of the large tank may not be spelled out, but for reason of traditions, the namesake Chief had a large acreage on his own under the tank. For this privilege, he was expected to guarantee the safety of the tank at a higher level.

An uncomplicated but equally effective form of leadership is found in lesser-known places like the bushmen communities in Namibian savanna. They do not have a 'leader,' but someone took the role to provide guidance for real life situations. For example, a person of experience is at the head of a band on an uncomplicated but equally effective form of leadership is found in lesser-known places like the bushmen communities in Namibian savanna. They do not have a 'leader,' but someone took the role to provide guidance for real life situations. For example, a person of experience is at the head of a band on a hunting trip, always walking in single file, and a similarly able elder in the rear for safety from lions and other predators lurking in the bush. Some leaders, not bushmen, may fall within the definition of the adage that 'all meat belongs to the hunter' where the hunter keeps the lion's share of everything. In the case of bushmen, after returning to the camp after a hunt, they shared daily food collection equally with the leader and everyone

---

[73] Corresponding caretaker of a small rural tank is *Gamarāla*, or *Vel Vidāne*.

including those who did not go on the trip. Kandyan Chiefs seemed to have had a 'large stock of meat!'

The Chiefs of the pre-modern Sri Lanka were attuned to cultural and traditional roles while providing forms of administrative functions to maintain the social order in shape by keeping these foundations firm. Thus, in fairness to the Chiefs in the distant province of Nuwarakalaviya, they achieved this task by celebrating its customs and traditions with institutions like Rata Sabhāwa, prevailing caste norms (*kula sirith*), *rājakāriya*, and being patrons of the religion.

Since the King appoints the Chiefs in the Kandyan kingdom, it is pertinent to comment on the selection of the King himself. Towards the later years of the line of royalty in Kandy, selection of the King had taken a tradition of its own. When the reigning King died, it appears two districts in the outskirts of Kandy, Udunuwara and Yatinuwara, had a major role in the selection process. People in these districts (particularly in the village of Daskara in Udunuwara area looked after the King's paddy fields on Daskara Veediya (Yatinuwara Veediya) and lived on this street for convenience. As the Nayakkars were in line for succession for the monarchy over a century, at the selection ceremony of the new King, *Maha Adikarama* (First Adikar – Prime Minister) pointed out to the villagers from the Daskara Veediya the Nayakkar who had the claim (usually top of the line of succession) to the throne. They then show their preference by paying homage to would be King. Undoubtedly, the villagers were influenced by the Adikar and other Chiefs in attendance.[74] This reminds us that asking for or seeking involvement of a third party for confirmation of an important moment had been a tradition then in Sri Lanka. A custom, not necessarily similar in context and scale is the referring of the judgement imposed by the Rata Sabhāwa on an accused for confirmation by the *henayā* in attendance before the penalty can take effect.

At the time of its fall in 1815, Kandy Kingdom had two *Adikāramvaru*, Chiefs of the Prime Minister level in the kingdom. These two were the most senior Chiefs, King's *Curia Regis*.[75] Some accounts note a third parallel title called *Siya Pattu Maha Nilame*.[76] The city of Kandy was divided into two precincts: on either side of the Swarnakalyana Veediya (present-day King's Street). The northern part of it was under the Pallegampahe Adikārama (the First *Adikarama*) and Eastern part was under the Udagampahe *Adikārama* (the Second *Adikarama*). *Hirage Kankanama*, and four *Veediye Arachchis* (Headmen of the Street) assisted them with administrative functions in these two precincts on behalf of the King. The title name *Veediye Arachchis* survived in the Sinhala lexicon at least through 1960s. I remember the *Arachirāla* of Mihintale was called *Veedi Arachila*, no doubt a reference to the bazaar bragging its quartet of lonely streets which intersect it in the center! This title disappeared when the *Grama Sevaka* system was introduced in the early 1960s. It evolved further into the present-day title of *grama niladhari* (village officer).

---

[74] Turner, L.J.B. 1918, p. 76.
[75] D'Oyly, 1833, 1835, p. 194.
[76] Ekanâyaka, A. de Silva, 1876, *JRAS*, New Series, Vol. 8, No.2, pp. 297-304.

Chiefs who were appointed by the King to head his Dissāvanis – twelve of them – and their subdivisions called *rata* or *pattu*[77] all came from Kandyan families who identified themselves as *Radala*, a sub-group of the Goigama caste. *Matale Kada-Im Potha* chronicling the Etipola Dissava's victory over the Dutch in Trincomalee (Thrimangalawa) in the 17 century gives an idea of the order of rank and of importance of titles that were granted by a King Godapola Wijayapala (Fig. 8). He is said to be a regional prince and brother of Kandy King Raja Singhe II.[78]

Fig. 7. Kandyan Chief and wife with attendants holding the decorative sun shields (*sesath*) c.1880. Gloria Katz and Willard Huyck. Los Angeles county Museum of Art.

There is one notable fact regarding the appointment procedure of Chiefs in Sri Lanka needs comment. In the case of aristocracy in Kandyan country, a woman having granted a Chieftain title is unheard of. However, in a rare and a singular instance about 150 years ago, according to a case decided in District Court, Anuradhapura, the closest a woman came to clearing this anomalous hurdle was following the death of her husband, Nuwarawawe Suriyakumara Wannisinghe Bulankulame Maha Vanniyā. In the vacuum created after the *Maha Vanniya's* passing, a dispute erupted in the family as male members refused to accept his widow Owille Kumarihamy as the head of the clan which would have given her the

---

77 D'Oyly, 1929, p. 6.
78 Abeywardena, 1978, p. 150.

right to represent the family in all matters. This conflict extended to other Chiefs as well.

By tradition, among the responsibilities of *Maha Vanniya* was the heading the committee which nominated the Anunāyake of Atamasthāna. Kumarihamy went to Government Agent of Northern Province and to court where she was legally declared heir to her late husband's estate, including right to represent him to lead the *Anunāyake* selection committee.[79] In early 1870s, after Nuwarawawe Banda, the Maha Vanniyā at the time, died without issue and his widow Owille Kumarihamy became the heir to the family interests and property.

APPOINTEE	TITLE	INSIGNIA & ITEMS
Etipola.	MATALE MAHA DISSAVA	Five guns and a flag
Uduphille Kulatunga Mudiyanse	MATALE DISSAVA ADIKARAMA	Whip and a Cane
Alahakone Mohottāla	LÉKAM MAHATKAMA	Golden Stylus and a flag.
Aluwihare Wanisekera Mudiyanse	MATALE RATEMAHATKAMA	Flag; Head of 8 Muhandiram Divisions
Ehelepola Banneheka Mudiyanse	UDUGODA RATEMAHATKAMA	Flag, Head of two Muhandiram Divisions
Alutgama Banneheka Mudiyanse	WAGAPANAHA KŌRALEMAHATKAMA & MUHANDIRAM WASAMA	Flag
Mawathapola Devundegedara Melpitiya	KODITUWAKKU NILAYA	Not listed.
Paranagama Kōrālayā	TUNKORALE LEKAM PAYINNDAYA	*Palingu Pahada* (crystal pebble) *Mewara Heramitya* (walking-stick)

Fig. 8. Rank/importance of titles in descending order in Matale Dissava awarded in 17th century by Godapola Wijayapala, an independent prince in Matale; After H.A.P. Abeyawardene, 1978, p. 150.[80]; Wickramasinghe, Don, 1900, p. 82, para 76. Illustration by Niranjala Tillakaratne.

---

[79] SLNA 41/187, 27 May 1872 & SLNA 41/251, 27 Aug. 1872, cited in Karunananda, 1993, p. 144. Also sourced from a family document shared with me by Ravana (Ravi) Wijeyeratne, 2021.
[80] See D'Oyly, 1833, 1835, pp. 191-252 for titles and duties existed at the time of the fall of Kandy.

Naturally, the Chiefs' seniority, or the place in the chain of command within their own fraternity was based on multiple factors such as significance of a heroic act, number of divisions or units of villages in each Chief's control and the relationship to the Atamasthāna. The Nuwarawawe Bulankulame family, usually Maha Vanniyā (found invoked in Rata Sabhā incantations) said to have come from in ancient times, was regarded as the senior to other Chiefs in Nuwarakalaviya. Chief Nuwarawawe *Ratemahattayā* lived in his house below the Nuwarawawe reservoir east of the old city of Anuradhapura. In old records, the area was called Nugara or Nuwara.[81]

CHIEFS: SEPARATE BUT EQUAL. Chiefs in Nuwarakalaviya had royal patronage in the past. When King Vijaya Bahu IV (1267/68-1270) of present-day Dambadeniya visited Anuradhapura, *Vanniyars* came to see him with *dākum* (audience before the King or a Chief with tributary payments). With less topographical encumbrances, communication means between Dambadeniya and Anuradhapura were better. So, a royal visit to the latter from the former was more convenient than from Kandy. The King then presented them with *Andoli* (palanquin or *dōlāwa, pallakkiya*), white umbrellas, chowrie (*chamara, pavan path*), and emblems of princes of Maha Vanni.[82] They paid a consolidated emolument of *dākum* tribute to the King on an annual basis.[83] But a few centuries later, unlike the *Dissavaru* based in Kandy, the Nuwarakalaviya Chiefs seem to have distanced and began not participating in the protocol of presenting the annual *Wāhal Kada* to the palace – a pingo taken to the palace with items such as rice, coconut, ash pumpkin and reed mats.[84] Being distanced as such, if the Chiefs made occasional pilgrimages to Kandy Court, the King was satisfied with the effort and it was seen as an adequate act of acquiescence. King was less intolerable how they ran the province.

In 1815, after signing of the Treaty, Kandyan country was divided into five divisions and civil authority in them was exercised as before by native *Dissavaru* and *Vannihuru*.[85] This is an implied reference and interpretation of ground realities by a senior British official, i.e., that *Vannihuru* of Nuwarakalaviya with its institutions including Rata Sabhāwa were worthy of recognition manifestly as a binary of the *Dissavaru* of Kandy, in separate but equal terms. Referencing and grouping Chiefs in Kandyan highlands and *Vannihuru* in Nuwarakalaviya together demonstrate that the British had abundant reasons to regard the Chiefs as having characteristics to be of two distinct entities but equal responsibilities and standing.

No *Vanniyā* – either Maha Vanniyā or any of his deputies – was present in Kandy at the signing of the Treaty of 1815. Galagoda Dissava who did not have a residence or lands in Nuwarakalaviya or any active participation in its affairs but was

---

[81] According to a family member, before the Nuwarawawe tank renovation in the 19th century, the ancient walawwa was located below the tank. Later when this was demolished to make room for renovation activities, the stone lintels of the main door of the house were said to have removed and mounted on a doorway at the Isurumuniya temple complex.

[82] Obeyesekere, Donald, 1911, 1999, p. 187.

[83] Ralph Pieris, 1956, p. 250 n57, p. 117.

[84] Vimalananda, 1963, p. 408.

[85] Ievers, 1899, p. 62.

titled only as its *Dissava* rather nominally signed his name on the Treaty 16 days later. But it did not take away Maha Vanniyā's historic standing as the true head and the administrator of the province. D'Oyly, who was responsible for logistics of writing the Treaty in English and translating it to Sinhala for Chiefs' signature must have thought that Nuwarakalaviya was a different entity and there was no need to have its Chief or a deputy Chief present while all manner of Chiefs and officials from similarly distant (Uva, Sabaragamuwa) *Dissavani*s were required to be present in Kandy on the signing day. Obviously, with the sensitivity and urgency of the moment and to avoid Chiefs changing their mind as deposed King was still being processed as a prisoner in Colombo, getting ratification of the treaty document was of utmost importance to Governor Brownrigg (1812-1820) and D'Oyly. Waiting for more clarification of the standing of King's Nuwarakalaviya Dissava with Nuwarakalaviya proper or worrying about it was secondary to the victors. Had Galagoda Dissava not signed it representing Nuwarakalaviya, British still would have walked into Anuradhapura within days as Kandy was still in shock and some Chiefs a la Ehelepola even ready to help if necessary, securing it (Nuwarakalaviya) for his new masters.

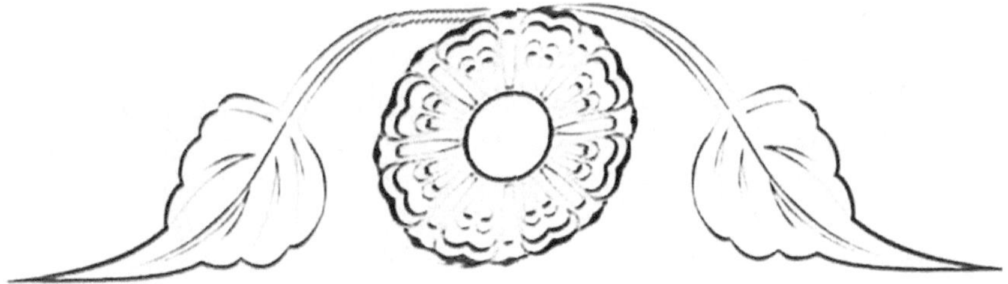

Fig. 9. Family Crest of Nuwarawawe Bulankulame, Source: Ravana (Ravi) Wijeyeratne; Reproduced by Niranjala Tillakaratne.

But Galagoda was not there at the signing. He and Ehelepola were in Kandy from day one but waited until March 18 to sign the treaty, D'Oyly (1917) wrote in his Diary (p. 237). Ehelepola probably had his own reasons – he was still dreaming of the Kingship and discussing his grievances with D'Oyly after losing 10 relatives recently (p. 231) while an asylee in Colombo and seeking compensation for property he lost. He was also eying King's black horse (p. 214)! The reason for delay in Galagoda signing the treaty has never been explained. Was he second guessing his own title? Was he under the impression that he was only performing an ambassadorial role in Nuwarakalaviya for the King as it was not part of Kandy proper? Or he was only an honorary *Dissava* title, and he did not think there was a need for him to be present on March 2nd signing ceremony?

Even with the reassurances etched out in the Treaty, the colonists' instincts of potential trouble in the future proved to be correct. On July 18, 1818, just three years after the Treaty, Ekneligoda Nilame from Sabaragamuwa tipped-off Lt. Col. Hardy on an *ola* page – a secret missive written on a palm leaf – saying that Kandyan

Chiefs were plotting to overthrow the Colonial government![86] In pre-colonial times, such missives were called *káda path*.[87] This missive was the result of friction between colonists and the natives that would manifest into a turning point with Kandyan Chiefs losing patience and trust in British. It led to the tempestuous revolt, the War of 1818. Thirty years of eternity later, Matale erupted revolting, and the murderous side of the colonial rule came to full view (See page 129-130).

It is important to note that day after signing the treaty, *Dissavaru* and other high-ranking Chiefs swore allegiance to Governor in the Audience Hall. From later writings, however, it was found that the Chiefs were unaware that their allegiance had no reciprocity. Lakshmi Kiran Daniels (1992) wrote that "The British had no intention of unequivocally accepting the pledges of allegiance of the former chieftains and headmen – their eager acquiescence to the new hegemony" (p. 27). Disruptions that erupted years later took the British by surprise, and their official communications later prove their ambiguity about Chiefs' allegiance. Daniels quotes a letter from a British civil servant John Baily to the Secretary of State, "The policy of our government has always been to curtail the power of the Chiefs and to destroy that paramount influence which under a despotic Government they naturally possessed."[88]

Thus began the gradual end of Kandyan Bandarawaliya (Kandyan Chiefs' Guild) or *Vanniperuwa* (Vanni Chiefs' Guild), also called *Mudaliperuwa* (Nobility Class by Descent) of Nuwarakalaviya and beginning of restructuring the Kandyan institutions and people's lives by the new orientalism through the colonial machinery. In the end, having gone through a variety of changes with all variants and their subordinate titles, the class of Sri Lankan nobility ended in 1938. With that, all indigenous institutions directed or headed by the Chiefs came to a stop.

A PRINCELY PROVINCE. Nuwarakalaviya held ingredients to be called a princely province. King's role in it was peripheral and relaxed. In his wisdom, he appointed a *Dissava* for Nuwarakalaviya, but expected him to reside in Kandy as other Chiefs did. "Not uncommonly that this *Dissava* never visited his province but remained at court... [*sic*]."[89] But the role of this *Dissava* in the province had never been made clear. King also deputized a supervisory role of Nuwarakalaviya to First *Adikārama*.[90] If anything, there is no evidence that the King invested much interest in his *Dissava* to live in the Nuwarakalaviya province. While all his *Dissavaru* were ordered to reside within walking distance to the palace, why did the King not ask Maha Vanniyā to have a residence in Kandy?

---

[86] Letter of Governor Robert Brownrigg to Secretary of State Earl Bathurst dated Nov. 5, 1816, qtd. in Vimalananda, T. *The Great Rebellion of 1818,* 1970, p. 1.

[87] *Mukkara Hatana* (Mukkara War), the 17th century palm leaf manuscript in Hugh Neville Collection, British Museum (Or. 6606 – 139), reproduced in M.D. Raghavan, *The Karava of Ceylon,* p. 178.

[88] CO 54/471, Bailey to Lord Blanchford, 19 December 1871, quoted in Daniels, Lakshmi Kiran, 1992, *Privilege and Policy: The Indigenous Elite and the Colonial Education System in Ceylon, 1912-1948.* (Unpublished Doctoral Dissertation). Oxford University. Retrieved from *https://ora.ox.ac.uk/*

[89] Ievers, 1899, p. 59.

[90] D'Oyly, 1833, 1835, pp. 191-235.

Given the muted level of participation and superintendence by the King's *Dissava* over the administration of the Nuwarakalaviya *Dissavani*, I hazard to interpret his role as non-executive, but an emissary-type on location. By appointing his own *Dissava*, a representative with no historical or deep family roots in the province and without any ceremonial or discernible role in its administrative, religious, or cultural affairs, the King's intention could not have been clearer. But having the First *Adikārama* in a supervisory role for the province proves that the King still regarded the region as special and important. Therefore, he wanted a show of presence in the province.

Whenever *Dissava* visited Nuwarakalaviya, D'Oyly noted a few interesting customs that existed in the province. During this visit Maha Vanniyā could not or would not" use his palanquin or show the customary pomp and pageantry such as drummers and *kasakarayo* (whip-crackers)." I believe this is no more than a gesture of common courtesy and goodwill extended by the *Vanniyā* to the King's representative for his trouble in making the grueling trip of 145 kilometers from Kandy to Anuradhapura. Tradition of such civilities had been in existence in the region as far back as King Dutugamunu's time (161-137 BC). He ordered all citizens to stop music and drumming when walking past the monument he built on the spot where the Tamil King Elara was cremated (*Mahawansa* XXV. 175.74). According to folklore in Nuwarakalaviya, when Pilimatalawa *Adikārama* was in hiding in Anuradhapura following the 1818 rebellion, as he passed the monument of King Elara, he alighted the palanquin and walked past it as a mark of respect to the slain King's memory (Ievers, 1899, p. 51). When a *Dissava* visits *Dissavani* of an *Adikārama*, he must stop beating drums within sight of *Adikārama's* house (D'Oyly,1835, pp. 191-235).

Maha Vanniyā, to say the least, was independent than any of his fellow *Dissavaru*. Often, he even showed his high-handedness or lack of awe for the Court. Once he stopped Madura-bound princess who was once a potential bride for the King but rejected later as not good (See page 192). King implicitly regarded him as a singularly separate entity. His Kandy-based *Dissava* had little power over revenue from the province, and his rank was symbolic. Nuwarakalaviya people regarded him only as a 'King's Man' with no role in appointing the *Anunāyake* of the Eight Holy Places in Anuradhapura, one of the few highest sacerdotal titles in Sri Lanka. "Effective authority of Vanni districts lay with *Vanniyars* rather than the *Dissavaru* appointed by the King."[91]

Therefore, I suggest that the Rata Sabhāwa must have been a "foreign" notion to *Dissava* from Kandy whose office in Nuwarakalaviya was considered by historians as largely insignificant and adumbral. I have no doubt the King's Nuwarakalaviya Dissava title was of the same kind as riding sidesaddle – partial and loosely engaged. He was not overly excited to be in this district away from the comforts of his home in Kandy. With this built-in disconnect, it is not surprising that the extent of the *Dissava's* acquaintance with the inner workings of the province was to remain low in comparison to the Chiefs residing in the district.

---

[91] de Silva, K. M. D., 1981, p. 145.

Besides the lack of interest, difficult travel conditions and even fear of insalubrious conditions like malaria were not very encouraging reasons for a Kandyan Chieftain to attempt trips to Anuradhapura or Polonnaruwa on regular basis. In modern vernacular, it could well be a 'punishment transfer,' a dreaded metaphor in the present-day. Besides, had *Dissava* wanted to visit 'his' province more often, the King's general fear and suspicion of the Chiefs' potential for plotting secret endeavors against him while in Nuwarakalaviya diminished any possibility of his giving his blessings for such recurring trips. Furthermore, roundtrip to Nuwarakalaviya usually took a week.[92] Instead, the Chief was happy to keep something little more than an ambassadorial glow but receive all the perks as a *Dissava* in another *Dissavani*.

The silence of Kandyan *Dissava* in Nuwarakalaviya folklore is not surprising.[93] No record exists of his participation, or whether he levied any punishments on an accused person at a Sabhāwa in Nuwarakalaviya. There is no record of *Dissava* advising or being involved in administrative functions of *Vannihuru*, *Ratemahatvaru* and *Kōrāla*s of Nuwarakalaviya. Had a *Dissava* owned *nindagam* in the Nuwarakalaviya region – a rare instance at that – with its paucity of reliable water resources, their crop output hardly came closer to what he would take from his lands in the hill country with year-round water supply. So, the *Dissava* prided himself in the title as an honor and a feather in his cap to represent Nuwarakalaviya in the Court.

Kandyan Dissava of Nuwarakalaviya was a "King's representative" and a "mere nominal Overlord."[94] King indirectly let the Nuwarakalaviya know that 'I am interested in your affairs but not involved in your affairs.' Thus, he appointed his representative "*Dissave Mohottāla* to represent his interests" in the province.[95] It was not lost in the King's mind that regardless of the apparent isolation and independence of the province and his own detachment from its direct affairs, the Kandyan people had not forgotten the role of Nuwarakalaviya as the root of their civilization and the city of Anuradhapura, the home of their venerated religious and

---

[92] Three examples will shed light on the measure of travel time between places in Kandyan times. (1) In the time of King Kirti Sri Raja Singhe (1747-1782 AD) it took four weeks for a letter from Batticaloa to reach Colombo (Pieris, P.E. 1918, 2018, *Ceylon and the Hollanders 1658-1796*, p. 98); In 1795, after British overpowered the Dutch in Trincomalee, Robert Andrews walked two weeks to Kandy to deliver a letter from Lord Hobart to the King (Pieris, P.E. 1918, 2018, p. 162). (2) On October 28, 1818, immediately after he was rounded-up at a place near Parawahagama, Manewa off Kalaweva in Anuradhapura district, Keppetipola Dissava told Lt. William O'Neal that he walked 20 days from Dumbara (sandwiched between Kandy and Matale districts) to join Pilimatalawa on that morning (Lt. O'Neal's letter with the same date to his commanding officer Capt. Fraser camped near Parawahagama, qtd. in Vimalananda, p. 308; Pieris, P.E. 1950, *Sinhale and the Patriots 1815-1818* p. 394; Ievers, p. 52). (3) On September 22, 1679, Robert Knox (1681, 1995) sneaked out of Eladetta (*Elledat*), 15 kilometers south of Kandy and his last place of residence, and walked through Bandarakoswatte (*Bonder Cooswat*), Nikaweratiya (*Nicavar*), Parawaha (*Parroah*), Kaluwila (*Colliwilla*), Anuradhapura (*Anarodgburro*) and reached Arippu (*Arrepa*) near Mannar on the South-west coast on Oct. 18, 1679.

[93] The storied visit of Keppetipola, Pilimatalawa and Madugalle – illustrious Chieftains in Kandy to Nuwarakalaviya – is an exception. They found Nuwarakalaviya as their last refuge while on the run from the British after being accused of orchestrating the Kandyan War of 1818.

[94] Ralph Pieris, 1956, p. 249.

[95] Ralph Pieris, 1956, p. 251.

cultural icon – the Sacred Bodhi Tree. So, by naming a *Dissava*, the King ensured that he was represented in Nuwarakalaviya at least as a symbolic gesture. As time passed, personal acquaintances of Kandyan *Dissavaru* and Nuwarakalaviya nobility grew, and mutually beneficial kinship relationships flourished.

MARCH OF HISTORY. During the Anuradhapura and Polonnaruwa periods, the King enjoyed absolute sovereignty over the three provinces (*ratas*, s. *rata*) – Pihiti Rata, Maya Rata and Ruhunu Rata. They encompassed the whole island. Pihiti Rata consisted of Nuwarakalaviya and Tamankaduwa areas and made the bulk of the Dry Zone. The Maya rata and Ruhunu rata were distant provinces in the Southwest and Southeast of the country respectively and faced little threats of invasion from Indian invaders. The King installed a Prince, called *Yuva Raja* (Sub King) for each of these *ratas*, and according to folklore and historical accounts, he lived in his assigned province. The King's capital was one of two vibrant cities in the kingdom, either Anuradhapura or Polonnaruwa, in that order. They were in the center of the kingdom with minimum geographical impediments for control. Even with occasional intrusions by South Indian invading elements, this area still mattered in the context of beginnings of Sri Lanka's inveterate culture and religion. Without treacherous mountainous passes and deep ravines to walk through, the region was communicable with roads, yet on bare terms.

There are two examples, physical and documented, to show proof of long-distance travel conveniences rather necessities during this illustrious Sri Lankan history. Passage of two Kings, Pandukābhaya (377-307 BC) and Dutugamunu (161-137 BC), 275 years apart, (former heading south and latter north) through the same village, Kahala-gama (Kahapathwilagama, also called Pajjota Nagara) near Kasa Pabbata (hill), 15 kilometers southwest of Anuradhapura, is evidence that a well-established permanent road system existed through Nuwarakalaviya, and beyond.[96]

Without any geographical barriers for expansion and with ease of water storage and distribution implanted with remarkable advances of hydrology far better than in the mountainous regions, Nuwarakalaviya achieved the status of a self-sufficient and self-ruling region. During this golden period, Kandyan country remained a dark and impassable land mass. Kandyan highlands allowed its abundant streams empty into the sea, untamed and unused. The magnificent spectacle of huge historic reservoirs and religious edifices in both main cities of Nuwarakalaviya and lack thereof in Kandyan highlands demonstrate not only the literal distance, but advancement claimed by the former.

But over time political fortunes of Nuwarakalaviya began to deteriorate. Onslaught of pressure from the Indian mainland was too much to counter and the province reached the breaking point. The result of this was the center of political gravity shifting out of the Dry Zone altogether, this time to Southwest. Economic degradation, long droughts, disease (especially malaria, cholera and *Parangi* - Yaws), and political turmoil have all been identified as factors contributing to this development. The cities of Anuradhapura and Polonnaruwa left in ruins, and much of the Dry Zone became isolated and in poverty. Population drastically thinned out,

---

[96] *Mahawansa*, n.d. 1912, ed. 2003, X.27 & Appendix C, p. 288; XXV.50. Kahala-gama (Kahapathwilagama) is my father's birth village.

tanks fell into disrepair, while many villages and temples fell victims to vandalism and desertion.[97] Most of the stone pillars standing or buried in Nuwarakalaviya and found later by generations up to the present century are remnants of this (hi)story. But for the Sri Lankans across the land, fate of Nuwarakalaviya was a bitter thought to share.

Threats to political stability in the province came mainly from audacious and expansionist South Indian Kings and regional overlords. After establishing power, they realized they had to face destructive potencies in the southwest and southeast of the island. Frequent incursions from these Sinhala rulers continued.[98] With their own internecine political turmoil back home and Sinhala Kings getting upper hand, the South Indian invading Kings lost the desire to hold on to power in Sri Lanka. Unable to continue, they dissolved into obscurity.

As the South Indian enterprise in the northern half of the country declined after late Middle Ages (13th, 14th, and 15th centuries), the area became a wasteland leaving only a smattering of populations centered around the ruined religious edifices and irrigation reservoirs, some were still in working order after escaping the dual winds of destruction brought by the invaders and nature. In the interregnum, the resulting power vacuum in the mostly acephalous and scattered communities was filled by lesser rulers, native and Malabar overlords who people later began to call nobles or Chiefs, carved out tracks of land as their suzerainties in these isolated areas.

Among these rulers were *Vanniyars*, Vanni Bandaras and immigrant groups like Mukkuwas. Vanniyās had power since "ancient times."[99] Brow (1996) writes, "… *Vanniyās* enjoyed virtually autonomous power in the region and made little more than formal acknowledgement of any superior authority. Nuwarakalaviya thus came to form part of a broad arc of country, remote from center of power and supporting only sparse population" (p. 37). Chiefs in Nuwarakalaviya and littoral in the northern half of the country acted as a buffer between diverse political forces while maintaining their isolation rather independence.

Nayakkar Kings now prospering in the central highlands lost influence over the region and made efforts to bring it under their control in the 18th century.[100] Until then Kandyan and Kotte Kings must have been relieved of this informal force, which was native to the core in the northern half of the land, but independent and powerful enough to remain as a buffer, though unintended, an epiphenomenal force with southern rulers to hold on to their kingdoms without fear of intrusion from the Subcontinent. And "(They) settled in this wild territory (but) carved out kingdoms for themselves and defied the authority of successive Sinhalese rulers.[101]"

The Chiefs in these distant provinces, though, reciprocated with the rulers in Kotte and Kandy, on occasions by indifference or being diplomatic as a strategy of survival. On Kings' part, they prided in a polity consisting of "partially autonomous

---

[97] Brow, 1996, p. 37.
[98] Bertolacci, 1817, p. 12.
[99] D'Oyly, 1929, p. 27.
[100] Sivasundaram, 2013, p. 148.
[101] Edward W. Perera, 1910, pp. 6-45.

entities, each of which retained significant control over its own internal affairs."[102] In any case, the Nuwarakalaviya Chiefs enjoyed the remoteness of the province to their advantage and rule with little or no interference, a distant form of laissez-faire theme adopted by the Kings in the south of the island. The *Vannihuru*, while maintaining autonomy from Kings in Kandy and Kotte, were open and ready to be conciliatory when they came across unavoidable circumstances. Provocations or wars by the *Vanniyars* against the King were unheard of, which also shows that the *Vanniyars* ruled without an active and sophisticated army.

The regional identity held by *Vannihuru* as being separate and independent seems to have extended to people of Nuwarakalaviya as well. After *kada-im* books, believed to have been written in 3-4 centuries earlier, A. O. Brodie, an engineer and one of the earliest colonists to write down the boundaries of Nuwarakalaviya, noted in mid-19th century that people of this region as "having a great dislike to strangers and to bustle." By not being in favor of the Road Ordinance of the British, they even did not welcome their road construction program.[103] They must have thought, rightly so, that opening the country with roads would bring in unsavory disturbances. Many residents preferred to live alone in their own cloistered enclaves without any interruption.

The residents of Nuwarakalaviya were entrusted with evidence of the ingenuity of their ancestors. Remarkable religious, engineering, and cultural structures spread out in the area stand as proof of this. The presence of these edifices, even in ruined state and swallowed by forest or buried in earth, influenced, and shaped precolonial Nuwarakalaviya institutions of which its citizens were proud of. Part of this enthusiasm was exemplified in regional ballads like *vandana kavi* (Poems of Pilgrimage), *Kadawara Puwata* (Story of Kadawara), *Ratnamali Vistaraya* (Story of the Ratnamali), *Ruwanvali Dagab Varnanava* (Tribute to Ruwanvali Stupa), *Solosmastana Vanadanava* (Praise of Sixteen Holy Places).[104] Thus historian Sujith Sivasundaram (2013) noted:

> Anuradhapura had a place in spiritual cartography of the island. …The historic artifacts of Nuwarakalaviya mediated in the formation of social communities and practices in the immediate locality, even as they symbolized the region far afield… These multivalent narrations urge a healthy skepticism of a reductionism which looks out from Kandy or Colombo alone. (p. 146)

Such reductionist views were true then where Kandyan Court shifted the role of history of Nuwarakalaviya to their mountainous protectorate and explained it with their eyes. It is true, in the present time as well when the region's efforts to climb the totem pole of relevance continue to miss the attention of the rulers. Sivasundaram wrote that "Kandyan Kingship was a territorialized discourse." The Nayakkar kings (in the 18th and 19th centuries) "hoped to bring the provinces (including Nuwarakalaviya) directly under the spiritual superintendence of the

---

[102] Brow, 1996, p. 39.

[103] Brodie, 1894, p. 154.

[104] Palm leaf manuscripts found in Colombo Museum Library, sourced from Sivasundaram (2013). Also see review of some Sinhala Ballads in L. D. Barnett (1916), *Alphabetical Guide to Sinhalese Folklore from Ballad Sources*, *The Indian Antiquary*, Vol. 45, pp. 1-105.

capital in Kandy to unify the island as a political entity."[105] Yet, the Sinhala kings in the central and western parts of the country did have a flimsy appetite for proactive involvement in Nuwarakalaviya which was insulated with an expansive stretch of forest with its reputation as an insalubrious region. They cocooned in their kingdoms in the southern and central areas of the country, were out of touch with Nuwarakalaviya, but plumbed in the thought that they were the rulers of the Raja Rata region, another cognomen for the province. Fittingly, though, the district continued the isolation in the northern areas. It could not have maintained anything other than a marginal interest with the King in Kandy, or later, the colonists in the Maritime Provinces.

Well entrenched in their kingdoms in the South, rulers of Kandyan highlands and colonial powers had no interest or inducement to abandon the stability they enjoyed. This attitude had an infectious influence on the public as well. As I will discuss in later pages, the 14th century *Sandésa* poets' failure to include the northern half of the country in the itineraries of their avian messengers cum letter-carriers is a good example of the elision of Nuwarakalaviya narrative expounded by the Southern intellectuals. But having the honor of nurturing over 90 Kings during its history, this province existing in obscurity could not distance it from the Kandyan Kings' wishes. They tuned to imitate the glorious aura of past Kingships of Raja Rata. Pressed with this persistent mindset of Kandyan Kings, some citizens in Nuwarakalaviya began to treat Kandy as representing them, both in heritage and space in the larger framework of the country, though the loose temporal divide between the two regions as evinced from their customs, and cultural nuances remained manifestly accented. When the British colonial administration finally extended its reach to Kandy in 1815, the demise of the monarchy there was immediate, but in areas like Nuwarakalaviya or some fringe parts of Sabaragamuwa, the Kingship idea did not die. It sustained for a long period.[106] And for the people who continued to live in Nuwarakalaviya, the Kingship based in Kandy, at a week's travel back and forth, was a token concept. Although imagery of Kandyan Kingship still flourished in the minds of Nuwarakalaviya people as much as in the bordering areas, the influence of the Kingship was a distant reality same way as an unseen mythical exalted being.[107] But in the mythmaking customs of Nuwarakalaviya, even if the people there had not seen the King, they joined Kandyans calling him a *'Deyyo'* (deity) as in *Rasin Deyyo* in reference to King Raja Singhe. Any semblance of divide and distance between two regions began to diffuse with the agency of colonial policies and approach.

Although there was no representation of Nuwarakalaviya at the annual Kandy Perahera,[108] Kings in Kandy have shown tepid interest to travel to Nuwarakalaviya. Only three have visited Nuwarakalaviya during all of 18th century.[109] Notwithstanding what some 18th and 19th century writers have alluded to, Kandyan

---

[105] Sivasundaram, 2013, p. 138.

[106] Sivasundaram, 2013, p. 138.

[107] Brow,1996, P. 39.

[108] In *Dalada Pelahera Alankaraya* [*sic*] n.d. pamphlet, and information provided by T.B. Paranatala to H. C. P. Bell, 1904, p. 126.

[109] Sivasundaram, 2013, p. 139.

Kings seemed to have found reasons, though, regarded as immediate, worthy, and outlandish to make an annual visit to Nawakkaduwa, an ordinary village on a sandy strip of beach in Kalpitiya/Puttalama lagoon close to Puttalama on the west coast. This village was known for the manufacture of salt, a popular import of Kandyan country. It is also the birthplace of *Raja Vanni Unnehe*.[110] King Buwanekabahu V of Kotte appointed one of the seven Vanni Bandaras who came from India, Rathran Kumarasinghe Vanni Bandara, to rule Nawakkaduwa and Puttalama.[111] This stretch of the coast was strategically and economically important to both the Maritime Provinces and Kandy. As far back as 1720, the harbor at Puttalama belonged to Kandy while the one at Kalpitiya, 40 kilometers north, was controlled by the Dutch.[112,113]

D'Oyly (1917) noted that "King went to Hath Kōrale (present-day Northwestern Province) for the purpose of enforcing his Commands of redressing Injuries & placing the Country in Order... to proceed (via Kurunegala) to Puttalama, & Celebrate his *kadu bandina mangalle* (Sword Tying Festival) there as former Kings were accustomed to do, there and at Kotta- [*sic*]" (p. 115). Possibly, it was a re-enactment of coronation that took place in Kandy, and perhaps an implicit show of power to residents (and rulers) in Maritime Provinces.

Chiefs built provincial palaces - the *gaman maligawa* for the King when he was on short visits out of the city. Notable travelling palaces were in Kundasale, Hanguranketa, Nillambe, Attapitiya in Sabaragamuwa province, Kurunegala, some places in Uva province and close to Maritime boundary of Hath Kōrale. They sent out word in their districts through lesser officials to assemble hundreds of people to build these temporary homes, but worthy and fit to be a royal adobe lest the Chief finds his head on his palms, literally, if the King was displeased of its workmanship. Folklore in Nuwarakalaviya does not refer to a *gaman maligawa* in the region. However, an attendant named Kawrala in the King's service stated in a *tal potha* (palm book) written in 1753 that he once accompanied the King to Nawakkaduwa, Anuradhapura, Kudiramale, and Kataragama.[114] It is likely that Kawrala, grandson of Hetti Appu of Uda Talawinna near Kandy, must have thought or got confused with the archaeological sites they passed along the way were part of Anuradhapura or it was not far from their route to Kudiramale. If Kawrala did not exaggerate, the coastline along Puttalama and Kalpitiya seems to be the closest the King ever got to Nuwarakalaviya which had slipped down in the scale of importance in the thinking of Kandyan Court.

---

[110] Wimalakeerthi. 1955, *Sinhala Ānduwa*, p. 52.

[111] Hettiarachchi, 1979, 2019, p. 34.

[112] Leupe, 1862, 1889, p. 117.

[113] *Nawa* – New, *Kaduwa* – Sword (or *Nawa* – nine). Chitty (1834, 1989) provides different versions of how this place got the name. Navakadu in Tamil is 'forest of Jambu tree,' but in Sinhala the word is derived from 'the place of shipwreck.' While some may suggest both these definitions are 'fanciful,' they trace it to mean 'nine swords,' recalling that no less than nine kings have come here to dip in the sea as part of a coronation and an ablution ritual. The place is known to abound excellent water springs as well (p. 282). In a region dry most of the time, it is possible having a well-fed source of freshwater in the neighborhood to wash off after swimming in and spending time by the sea must have been another reason the King thought of coming here.

[114] Lawrie, 1898, p. 809.

Often in cultures in which a person's name appears at the bottom of a list, or one standing at the end of a line or behind a crowd usually signified lower in importance or influence proportionately. Thus, being listed as 16th in the list of 17 *Dissavani*s in Kandyan times indicates the insignificant position Nuwarakalaviya held, at least in the minds of the Kandyan Court, while neighboring Tamankaduwa was placed at a respectable 6th.[115] In the case of Tamankaduwa, however, it was not lost to the ruler in Kandy that communications with Trincomalee, the most important eastern harbor, cut through Tamankaduwa,[116] thus the apparent lofty treatment of the province. Therefore, King's Dissava of Tamankaduwa actively took part in the administration of the *Dissavani*.[117]

When the Sinhala kingdoms moved gradually out of Anuradhapura and Polonnaruwa, the Kings introduced *kadawat*, land pass points, along the border of his kingdom to control movement of people and goods. A *kadawata* was important to a ruler as a sign of geographic demarcation of his territory. Particularly, two land-pass points at Vilachchiya, northwest of Anuradhapura, and Ilukwewa near Sigiriya reminds me that they were intended to announce that the area from that point onward was beyond King's command. In and around Kandy and along the route to Colombo, King was privy to secretly guarded stratagems. British forces trying to defeat the King found that he had "guarded knowledge about topography" of the mountainous region[118] which helped him keep the invading forces at bay. Thus, the mountainous core of the new Kandyan kingdom provided a haven for Kings to rule without external harassment while the northern areas remained isolated and distanced, exposed to threats, and left to mend for themselves.

Sujit Sivasundaram (2013) noted that the "early British travel in Sri Lanka was an attempt to bring unruly territories such as Anuradhapura to order" (p. 171). 'Unruly' here was an unsubstantiated definition. I believe the opposite to this definition holds true. In 1870, L. Liesching, Anuradhapura Magistrate who observed the 20000 Poson pilgrims who flock to the city every year wrote that they "come and go without a single policeman being here." As the pilgrims occupied the verandahs of government buildings, no one ever attempted to steal the Kachcheri safe which was a little metal box waited upon by three watchers.[119]

Naturally, if a need arose, only choice of the scattered communities in the isolated northern half of the country was to turn to the Kandyan kingdom for some level of protection and identity while at the same time yielding to local princes, *Vannivaru*, for guardianship of regional institutions and edifices that included not just cultural but religious collectives like Atamasthāna in the city. Which *Vannivaru* did. But it is doubtful whether the Nuwarakalaviya citizens got a good value for the bargain from the King. The isolated province remained alone and separate as ever.

One rather telling reality was that before the British began administering the province, only form of organized conflict resolution body in Nuwarakalaviya was Rata Sabhāwa. Such institutions enjoying legitimacy by long standing custom and

---

[115] Bertolacci, Anthony, 1817, p. 465.

[116] Ievers, 1899, p. 202.

[117] Ievers, 1899, p. 40.

[118] Sivasundaram, 2007, p. 925-965.

[119] Qtd. in Ievers, 1899, p. 43.

tradition in the area continued without King's magisterial involvement. Instead, Maha Vanniyā delegated district level administration to *Ratemahatvaru*. Meanwhile, the King in Kandy did not do an effective governing in this distant wooded province. Only having the *Dissava* in Kandy was his link to protect his 'self-proclaimed' sovereignty to the province.

But the province held a unique advantage which the King with his mountainous territories did not have, i.e., the ports and salterns in the Maritime Provinces, controlled by the Dutch East India Company, and later the British. They were accessed easily along footpaths only a *tawalam* can pass through the flat country of Nuwarakalaviya. On the other hand, to reach the sources of essential commodities, the King's trade routes lay through stretches of mountainous passes, but land along the coast was controlled by the colonial rulers. This situation always presented encumbrances to Kandyans. For example, as seen on the 17th century map of Sri Lanka, Knox (1681, 1995) shows two *kadawat* – posts on boundaries – near Kalpitiya salterns near each other. Kandyan *tawalam* en route to the coast for salt and salted dry fish had to pass these points. Did the two *kadawat* represent a de-militarized buffer zone?

But the Nuwarakalaviya boundaries along the coastline were porous and thus its residents faced less impediments to reach small scale ports and salterns on the northwest and northeast coastal belt. Dutch also were comfortable with the merchants from Nuwarakalaviya because they were few and less hostile to the colonists. It was an area enveloped in jungle and controlled by local overlords they considered non-confrontational.

Even though Vanni princes had some degree of fidelity invested in Dutch, so, too, were they yearning to have the good grace of the King to secure advantages and prestige. For the King too, appointing a *Dissava* for Nuwarakalaviya provided a medium through which he was able to overcome the inconveniences the territory presented and reinforce the claim to the title as the ruler of the whole country.

Distance from Kandy, and population scarcity in Nuwarakalaviya and Tamankaduwa were reasons for the two districts to remain less attractive for King's sustained interest. As the province remained less and less relevant, and disease and famine-like threats remained endemic, the Kandy King's control and suzerainty, and attention to and familiarity with the localities remained at a nominal level. Lack of familiarity was well seen in a *Sri Sannasa* (pl. *Sannas*) written by the order of the King Sri Wijaya Raja Singhe in 1745 and given to Ehelepola Mudiyannehe granting him the title of *Dissava* of Nuwarakalaviya and Tamankaduwa. Inexplicably, all villages endowed to the new *Dissava* were in a different *Dissavani* – Matale.[120] Moreover, unlike those villages closer to Kandy, the King himself did not have *gabadagam* (royal villages) in both Nuwarakalaviya and Tamankaduwa.[121] This leads us to believe that probably he had little information about villages in these two *Dissavanis*, or it exemplified the measure of his general disconnect with the region. Such disconnect is also reflected by the unusual difference of the amount of *dākum* paid by Chiefs in Kandyan country and the Maha Vanniyā, an indicator of the difference existed

---

[120] Lawrie, 1896, Vol. I, p. 200.
[121] Pieris, R, 1956, p. 44.

between the King and the Maha Vanniyā in particular, and Nuwarakalaviya Chiefs in general. While each *Dissava* of Hatara Korale, Uva, and Hath Korale – the most important *Dissavanis* of the kingdom – paid 12000 ridi to the King as annual New Year *dákum*, the Maha Vanniyā paid only 1000 ridi![122]

As some areas stretched further and further away from the Center so much so, they remained insulated to outside influence even decades after the British took total control of the country. Such temporal isolation must have led some communities in forested stretches to remain, "for all intents and purposes acephalous administrative units."[123] Huruluwewa area, in the past known as "[…] *Hourly* (Hurulle) the remotest of the king's dominions [...]"[124] remained far away from the King's boundary. From Huruluwewa,[125] ostensibly the northernmost point of the Kandyan kingdom, it is about 42 kilometers northwest to Anuradhapura, the center of Nuwarakalaviya. Even as late as 1817, in Captain Schneider's map reproduced in Bertolacci (1817), marked Nuwarakalaviya and adjacent provinces as "unknown countenance region."

Quoting Mr. Bournand, a civil servant in 18th century Dutch East India Company, Bertolacci stated that "Wanniships of Soerlie (Hurulle) and Nogerie (Nugara, Nuwarakalaviya), [...] and Weddas, from Maagamme (Magama) in the South, to Coklay (Kokilai) river at the northern side of the island, does not contain more than ten thousand people [*sic*]."[126] It was a measure of how thinly populated this nether province covering about 5000 square miles was. In *Eleven Years in Ceylon*, Forbes too quotes Nuwarakalaviya as a "remote province."[127] As shown earlier, the population spread the province was thin and far in between.[128]

As late as 1832, British officials rarely visited the area, and control of the region by the government was "little more than nominal."[129] In the 1843 map of Sri Lanka on the front matter of *Recollections of Ceylon* by James Selkirk (1844), the region around Anuradhapura is written as "*Country Almost Uninhabited.*" It was called a *pālu rata*, a deserted country, by late 19th century writers.[130] Bandaranayake (1986) wrote about the lose control exerted by the center on these frontier regions:

> [...] It should be mentioned that the aspirations of these controlling powers were thwarted by physical factors such as the island's peculiar physical features, and inadequacies in the means of communication at the disposal of the King at the centre of the country to impose his control effectively on a day-to-day basis at the village level [*sic*]. (p. 43)

Another example of the extent to which the Nuwarakalaviya and its major institutions maintained isolation but demonstrable independence from either the King, rest of the country, or later the colonial governments is the state of the

---

[122] Vimalananda. T. 1963, p. 318, quoting an old document in Colombo Museum.

[123] De Silva, K. M. D., 1981, p. 145.

[124] Knox, 1681, 1995, p. 62.

[125] In *Mahawansa* (XXXVII. 47): Challura Vapi, built by King Mahasen.

[126] Bertolacci, 1817, p. 64.

[127] Forbes, Major, 1840, *Eleven Years in Ceylon* Vol. I. p. 71.

[128] Brodie, 1894, pp. 136-161.

[129] Ievers, 1899, p. 63.

[130] Obeyesekere, 2017, p. 38.

Anunāyake (Chief monk) of the Atamasthāna (Eight Holy Places) in Anuradhapura. This priestly position was selected by a committee of monks and laymen from Nuwarakalaviya. The committee operated quite independently since ancient times until the British instituted the Buddhist Temporalities Ordinance (BTA) No. 3 of 1889. Anunāyake title, one of the powerful and pre-eminent in Sri Lanka's religious institutions had evolved on a system unique to itself.[131] A distinctive feature in the state of this title was that until the late decades when the religious affairs of the country received more attention with legislation like the BTA, Mahanayake of any other Buddhist clerical chapters in Kandy or King's *Dissava* for the province had no role, participation, or overseeing the selection process. It was a process managed exclusively by Maha Vanniyā and a few other Chiefs in the region. King having no discernible role in this prominent tradition shows the singular independence and autonomy enjoyed by the Chiefs in Nuwarakalaviya. With this too, Nuwarakalaviya earns the honor to be called a 'princely province'.

Colonial writers too took note of this when they cast Anuradhapura as in ruined and abandoned state while quite surprisingly, but understandably, Sri Pada (Adam's Peak) in Sabaragamuwa province was written as heavily frequented by pilgrims.[132] Adam's Peak was the first Sri Lankan landmass that was visible from sea when the tired travelers, the earliest 'orientalists' got a glimpse of the inviting coconut tree-lined shore in Southwest Sri Lanka. There is no doubt the first glimpse by visitors to this unique location was so remarkable that it heavily influenced their writings about Sri Lanka later. Early morning on December 18th 1803, aboard the sailing ship *Olive* few leagues or so from Galle harbor, George Viscount Valentia described the Adam's Peak as it came to view over the smoky hills in the distance: "... fog clearing away, from a distant of four miles we discovered Point de Galle, backed by a chain of round-topped hills covered to the summit with wood; and beyond them a still loftier range, with Adam's Peak rising to an acute point" (p. 266). He would only find out later that Anuradhapura, over 300 kilometers to the north, was an equally enchanting city, though abandoned and in the depth of a sea of forest.

But until as late as three years after capturing Kandy, and save for few marginal contacts through the Assistant Government Agent at Mannar, the British seem to have allowed Nuwarakalaviya to run its own business as an autonomous region. The payroll for the Chiefs of Kandyan districts proposed by the Kandyan Commission Board member D'Oyly in October 1818 is an example for this ostensibly disconnect between the colonists and this distant province. D'Oyly suggested to the Governor that "no salaries be allowed" to Vanniya of Nuwarakalaviya and Tamankaduwa,[133] an apparent insignificance, disregard or 'separateness' ascribed to the Vanni Chiefs at least during these early years of administration. D'Oyly must have extracted this feeling from the Kandyan Chiefs themselves as they were the only conduit through which the true standing of Nuwarakalaviya drew in, at least in their reckoning. D'Oyly's list of prospective recipients of salary contained only the Chiefs and

---

[131] Karunananda, 1993, p. 147.

[132] Sivasundaram, 2013, p. 136.

[133] Vimalananda, 1970, pp. 353.

mulādānivaru/kāriyakarawannō in the area consisting of Kandy, Uva, Hath Kōrale and other parts of the hill country.

After some time, the threat level from Nuwarakalaviya to the British occupation in Sri Lanka was relatively low compared to the hotbed hilly districts around Kandy. As folklore suggests, a few suspected Kandyan rebels were taking refuge in the Anuradhapura area. The story of Keppetipola, Pilimatalawa and Madugalle, while on the run from the British, showing up at a house near Parawaha in Kalaweva area is well known. As for Maha Vanniyā, there is no record of him being involved in preparations or planning of the rebellion. But as the struggle in 1817 got momentum, Nuwarawawe Vanni Unnehe "joined the disaffected Chiefs of the up-country."[134] What this could mean in my view is that as up-country Chiefs stood up against the British, and Maha Vanniyā did not side with the British for his own reasons of solidarity with Kandyans unlike some Kandyan Chiefs did during that time. But his resistance was noted by the British as at a lower degree. For the brotherhood of Chiefs in Kandy and Vanni, i.e., Nuwarakalaviya in 1818, British were the common intruders.

In 1819, *The Asiatic Journal* quoted the *Ceylon Gazette* of 5th December 1818 dispatch which said, "we are happy to learn that the Moodiance of Nuarecalava, the only district where the least remnant of hostility left, has sent Lieut. Sweeting a proposal of an unconditional surrender [*sic*]."[135] This was Chief Nuwarawawe Mudiyanse whose role did not involve attacking any British positions as there were none in the vicinity of Anuradhapura. This also shows that the British too had reasons to believe that Nuwarakalaviya existed as an independent self-governing entity, thus to make a special note in a dispatch about the surrender of Mudiyanse who probably did it after realizing the futility in showing any disfavor to the government, the iron grip of which on its subjects tightening. As Kandyan resistance was falling asunder, he accepted the fact that it was foolish to continue even token resistance, better yet alone.

Meanwhile, when the rebellion of 1818 ended, British considered all Chiefs representing districts and *Dissavanis* as surrendered by default, and except for senior members, no specific announcement for each Chief was made. Nuwarakalaviye Mudiyanse was arrested on September 20, 1818, and imprisoned in Galle accused of participating in the Kandyan War.[136] Upon release in 1834, he returned to Anuradhapura and restored to *Maha Vanniya* title. He died in 1839.[137]No other Chief from Nuwarakalaviya appears to have been in this predicament, i.e., alleged participation in the War with the British. In fairness to Maha Vanniyā, harassments, arrests, and judicial process of the British at the time were blemished in so many ways as seen from the trial of rebels in another rebellion in Matale 30 years later (See page 129).

Nuwarakalaviya traditional and cultural government was still in the hands of Maha Vanniyā and his deputies, the *Ratemahatvaru* and *Kōrāla*s, during British times.

---

[134] Ievers, 1899, p. 49.

[135] *Asiatic Journal and Monthly Register... 1819*, Vol. 8, pp. 92-95.

[136] Governor Robert Brownrigg's letter to Bathurst on April 24, 1819, qtd. in Vimalananda, 1970, p. 420.

[137] Ievers, 1899, p. 66.

Maha Vanniyā's social and political capital in the district was his ability and latitude to act as an independent prince. It helped him to maintain the institution of Rata Sabhāwa without any opposition from the colonial government, populace, and tradition.[138] The British too was aware of this as seen from the missives exchanged between the senior officials on location. Earlier in 1815, few months after the fall of Kandy, D'Oyly wrote to the government advising against relinquishing the four *kadawat* (gravets) "possessed" by *Vanniya* of Nuwarakalaviya for fear that "it will diminish his dignity" and loss of respectability he relished from the merchants arriving (in) his "territory to wait upon him."[139] Conversely, the King "possessed" all gravets in the Kandyan highlands.

Kandyan Chiefs often faced situations where their dignity was put to labor by the British. Once during a little-known action by the British, senior Kandyan Chiefs were subjected to an instance of belittling their dignity they have not experienced before. On the day after signing the Treaty, the Governor was waiting in Audience Hall with Ehelepola to meet the "Superior Chiefs." As the Chiefs came forward, Ehelepola asked them to kneel before the Governor. Governor looked on while elderly men fell on their knees before him. Next day they told D'Oyly that senior Chiefs had not kneeled even before their former King and complained about this humiliation. Ehelepola demanded they continue the practice as he was going to do it himself the next day. But after some discussions, the confusion was resolved and the need to kneel before the British officials was removed.[140] Even it was resolved, to go into that confusing phase of a formality was evidence that the British harbored traces of indifference to Kandyan Chiefs.

The *Vannivaru,* including Nuwarawawe Bulankulame, represented the region by virtue of 'inheritance' through ages of customs and traditions that granted them authority to rule the province. Kandy King was not part of this process. Nuwarakalaviya citizens regarded *Vannivaru* as their guardians and elders who were expected to assist and guide them in maintaining unity and upholding supremacy of their local institutions of culture, religion, economics, and maintaining their overlordship.

Nevertheless, as much as the King of Kandy was invoked as a villainous character, it is correct to say the dealings of Chiefs in remote provinces like Nuwarakalaviya with the King were of mixed nature. Oftentimes these Chiefs found themselves out of step with King's grace. On two occasions the missteps of some Chiefs drew anger in the King. Fearing reprisal, Chief in question, Nuwarakalaviye Mudiyanse took off to Mullativu once and another time to Mannar, both colonial protectorates at the time.[141] Mullativu area seems to have been a popular destination of Nuwarakalaviya Chiefs as J.P. Lewis reported an instance of Tamarawewa

---

138 Welimuwapothana Mohottāla authoring his essay for the Wickramasinghe Manuscripts in 1932 noted that *Vanniyars* of Vanni Hatpattu were independent Chiefs until about 13th century. It is possible he based his opinion on the prevailing folklore in the area. Welimuwapothana is in the Hurulu Pattuwa, about 60 kilometers east of Anuradhapura.

139 Ievers, 1899, p. 113.

140 D'Oyly, 1917, p. 224.

141 Ievers, 1899, p. 49.

Ratemahattayā of Eastern Nuwarakalaviya visiting Mullativu area in 1839 (See page 183 n4).

Distance to Kandy, and independence the *Maha Vanniya* enjoyed in the province often got the best of him. He and other Vannivaru often acted as autocrats and tyrants. This freedom may have contributed to many instances of their heavy-handed treatment of villagers. In such situations, villagers had no recourse or luxury to reach the King like those in Kandyan highlands, due in part to the distance and King's lack of interest or perhaps knowledge of the core customs of the people in this outer district. As Ievers (1899) records, in early 1800s, there are records of times when "People (of Nuwarakalaviya) seem to have been harassed by the tyranny and extortion of the Nuwarawawe Chief, who was the *Vanni Unnehe* and practically hereditary Governor of the Vanni" (p. 49)." As will be discussed later, the villagers chose to abandon their villages and moved closer to Vavuniya in the Northern Province, then under the British control.

A more recent comment of representative and traditional nature of these Chiefs was given little over four decades ago by one of the last members of the descendants of the Nuwarakalaviya Vanniya aristocracy, the avuncular parliamentarian E. L. B. Hurulle of Hurulle walawwa in Morakewa in the eastern part of Nuwarakalaviya. Following the abolishment of aristocratic titles in 1938, Hurulle had a short stint as a DRO. Finally, in 1956, he entered politics to represent Horowpothana constituency in the eastern part of the North Central Province. Brow (1996) writes of a speech given by Hurulle in January 1980 as the MP of Horowpothana to the residents of Samādhigama near Kukulawa on opening of the village built under Prime Minister Premadasa's *Udāgama* (Village Awakening) project on the boundary of the MP's constituency. Hurulle said:

> Morakewa (seat of his ancestors' who were *Vanniyars* of the region)
> has long been a center of the people of Kukulawa and other villages
> in the district. For centuries, it has provided them with shelter,
> comfort, and refuge. My ancestors knew these people well. (p.104)

Experience shows us that few decades after Sri Lanka received independence, politics already had begun a downward arc, but Hurulle was an exception. Few weeks after his death, an appreciation in the Sunday Times (May 3, 2009) read: "Cheap politics was never to his liking." [142]

The War of 1818 was a turning point in the power structure of the Kandyan Chiefs and their relationship with the British. The wartime activities brought to light the patriotic fervor of many Chiefs. But there were exceptions whose subservience to the colonial government was notable. Old *Dissava* Titles were abolished in 1818 which took away superior status enjoyed by the Chieftains. But those who pledged allegiance were allowed to keep their titles nominally in Nuwarakalaviya until 1834 when Talgahagoda, its last 'Kandyan' *Dissava*, resigned due to health reasons. Yet, nothing much happened in the province concerning its isolation.

After the British 'suppressed' the *Dissava* title, in its place they appointed Nuwarawawe Mudiyanse (Moodianse) as *Maha Vanni Unnehe* with a salary.[143] This

---

[142] Cited in Brow, 1996, 104.

[143] Ievers, 1899, p. 66.

can be regarded as the first time in Maha Vanni Bandarawaliya, the Order of Chieftains of the Nuwarakalaviya region was appointed formally by the Head of the State and remunerated. What is notable here is that this decision of the British was based on the doctrine of laws, not customs or traditions; written, but not verbally pronounced at the pleasure of one man – the King; and ratified by formal administrative process, a process unknown hitherto, at least in Nuwarakalaviya. And it was certified to last intact until changed in the future by the Governor as necessitated by established legal formulas.

Following the Colebrooke-Cameron Commission recommendations in 1832 to abolish the *Rājakāriya* custom in Sri Lanka, the old *Gam Sabhā* traditions also went into oblivion but the lineage of Chiefs continued under the scrutiny and patronage of the Colonial government which nevertheless showed no perceptible interest for the continuation of the Rata Sabhāwa tradition, among other traditions of Nuwarakalaviya life. The Colonial government must have been content that the Chiefs in Nuwarakalaviya did not engender any threats to their administration. With the recommendations of the same Commission, Nuwarakalaviya and Tamankaduwa *Dissavani*s were transferred further north to be administered from Jaffna, little over 300 kilometers north of Kandy.

ISOLATED PROVINCE, BUT IN CONTROL. Isolation, seen as separate, and enjoying unusual freedom from customary royal overview in distant regions in the country have been an accepted fact in the past. P. Arunachalam in 1910 called *Dissavani*s as parts of Commonwealth or Confederation. He noted that:

> Even before the invasion of Ceylon by the European powers, the Kandyan provinces did not represent a well-defined area. The village (s. *gama*) was not only a geographical, but also a social, ecclesiastical, and political unit. An association of several villages formed a Korale, two or more Korales formed a Hatpattuwa, an association of Hatpattu. These Dissavonies formed the Kandyan provinces – a Commonwealth – the head of which was the Kandyan King. It was not uncommon for some Hatpattu or Dissavonies to break loose from the Commonwealth and set up independent principalities, so that the Kandyan provinces expanded and contracted as the association of villages joined the confederacy or cut themselves away, according to events. The looseness of the tie between the villages and Dissavonies and the constitution (of Kandyan Kingdom) will account perhaps for the difficulty of fixing the limits of the Kandyan provinces at this date [*sic*]. (pp. 103-123)

The definition of Hatpattuwa referred to above needs clarification as it is not in alignment with historical evidence. Two or more Kōrales made a division, a *Pattuwa* (pl. *Pattu*) of which there were seven in Nuwarakalaviya in the 19th century. These seven *Pattu* together made the Vanni Hatpattuwa, the Nuwarakalaviya proper. Thus, the *Vanniya* (Vanniyar) was formerly addressed as Hat Pattu Maha Vanni Mudiyanse. See also Figures 3, 4 and Ievers, 1899, pp. 2 and 79-84 for a breakdown of all manner of divisions in Nuwarakalaviya.

The consequence of the cumulative result of this state of being a 'commonwealths' was the Chiefs – Vanni Bandara and *Ratemahatvaru* – in these isolated areas getting used to regard their territories as autonomous republics with little control or political supervision from the King.[144] Ralph Pieris (1956) believed these Chiefs enjoyed near "sovereign power" in the remote districts.

> Even under the Kings of Kandy it may be said [...] that the degree of State control over a given region was in inverse ratio to its distance from the capital, and at one extreme certain northerly villages of the kingdom have been described as autonomous republics, subject to little control by royal officials. (p. 233)

If I were to call it a diarchy state, I am not far off, for de Butts (1841) said the Maha Vanniyās administered the outlier provinces like "lords paramount" (p. 157). Over 350 years ago too, Knox referred to Maha Vanniyā as "Prince," suggesting the province he headed as extraordinary at the highest level and independent. Knox believed King's authority extended up to *CorundaWy River* (Kanadarāwa Oya?),[145] 15 kilometers north of Anuradhapura. But Maha Vanniyā as High Sheriff having a *nindagama* in Kaluwila, 9 kilometers south of the city makes a good reason to think how certain or knowledgeable was the sailor about the boundary lines this far north from Kandy where he lived his entire captivity. Writing about Pul Eliya village located between Anuradhapura and Mannar, Leach called the *Dissavaru* and Vanni Bandaras as "independent princes," and during Dutch time, if a *Vanniyā* "ever deferred to someone, it was probably to the Dutch garrison" on the coast northwest of Anuradhapura.[146] Knox wrote that Coilat Wannea was independent from the King and the Dutch, but paid tributaries to them. Inhabitants of Anuradhapura (*Anaroghurro*) "are neither under the King nor the Dutch [...] but are under the prince of their own [*sic*]" (p. 157). Once when King sent his army against the Dutch (probably to Mannar on the Northwest coast), "this prince let them pass thro his

----

[144] Knox (1681, 1995) wrote that Kandy King and Malabar princes in the Vanni exchanged letters (p. 175). This connotes the formality and diplomatic nature of their relationship, a contrast Knox noticed in *Dissavaru* of the Kandyan provinces. Such protocols were common in the Indian subcontinent and no doubt rulers in Sri Lanka, too, were aware of them. Tamil documents found in the palace in Kandy after British invasion and now in the Sri Lankan Government Archives show discussions of protocol of ambassadorial conduct while visiting Arcot near Vellore, about 100 kilometers from Chennai in South India. Discussions involved acceptable etiquette in the respective courts and even suggestions that those ambassadors who would not adhere to protocol may not be received in courts (cited in Sivasundaram, 2013, p. 37). S. Rasanayagam translated these documents in 1937.

[145] Knox, 1681, 1995, p. 175.

[146] Leach, 1968, p. 19. There have been other reasons and times how some regions became principalities. Certain parts of Kotte kingdom became autonomous principalities when King Vira Parakramabahu VIII (1477-1489 AD) appointed his brothers as *rajas* or prince regents to administer some areas to prevent the kingdom becoming fissiparous if they got unhappy (De Silva, K. M. D., 1981, p. 98). In the end, the kingdom became weaker, and these princes transformed to rule these areas as separate principalities. The story depicted in *Vijayaba Kollaya* (Robbery of Vijayaba, W. A. De Silva, 1938) took place in 1521. Kotte King Vijayabahu VI was assassinated by his sons and partitioned the kingdom as principalities (De Silva, K. M. D., 1981, p. 99).

country [sic]" (p. 175). Ukkubanda Karunananda too thinks *Vanniyas* were independent rulers.[147]

What this means is that anyone, even the King as in this case, could not send his troops through Nuwarakalaviya without a pass from its ruler, the Maha Vanniyā, who exercised an exclusive potency that placed him above *Dissava* or *Adikārama* in Kandyan highlands. In Kandyan kingdom, a Chief would deny King's troop movement through his district or *Kōrale* only at the risk of King's reprisal – certain death by beheading.

British were aware of the attempts by the Nayakkar Kings in Kandy to bring Nuwarakalaviya under their control as far back in the 18th century. At the end of the 1818 rebellion, the Governor by Proclamation of November 21st, 1818, declared that after the "Kandyan Chiefs prayed the assistance of the British Government for their relief and by a solemn act declared the late King as deposed, [...] and by the same solemn act ceded (Kandyan Provinces) to the dominion of British Sovereign [...]." Governor also proclaimed that all lands belonging to the "Chiefs whose loyalty and adherence to the lawful government merits favor" and exempted them from taxes.[148] The list of Chiefs published in this Proclamation contains only those living in Kandy and bordering districts, but none in Nuwarakalaviya or Tamankaduwa, evidence that at this early stage of occupation, the British had no immediate interest in the Nuwarakalaviya and Tamankaduwa *Dissavani*s, leaving them alone to maintain their own affairs as they have been doing before, a tacit acceptance of their extraordinary princely and sovereign standing! With all their might of conquering and even years after the fall of Kandy, Acting Governor Campbell was still complaining of the lack of connection between the British government and its subjects in the Nuwarakalaviya.[149]

It is worth noting that records are scarce that the King in Kandy ever interfered or participated in the inner workings of the Nuwarakalaviya including appointment of Maha Vanniyā or Chiefs and the *Atamasthānādhipathi* (*Anunāyake*), the Chief Priest of Eight Holy Places Anuradhapura that includes Sri Maha Bodhi. It is a sacerdotal title believed to go back to the times of Ven. Valivita Saranankara in mid-18th century during the reign of King Kirthi Sri Raja Singhe.[150] Unlike the Kandyan Chiefs, no *Vanniya* had a house in Kandy. Conversely, no Chief in Kandy bothered, or the King ever wanted him to have a house in Nuwarakalaviya even after being appointed as *Dissava*.

Sujith Sivasundaram (2013) finds "an eclectic and independent tradition of cultural identity flourished in the region where Anuradhapura lay (p. 138)." And the Kandy King had accepted this uniqueness, but seems to have retained a certain proprietary relationship, implied at that, with the Nuwarakalaviya people, including their Chiefs. To have such a reach was good politics for the King to show his might before his subjects in Kandy. There is folklore that King Rajadhi Raja Singhe (1782-1798) once imprisoned Maha Vanniyā for 12 years for failure to pay *dākum* and

---

147 Karunananda, 2009, p. 18.
148 *Legal Enactments of Ceylon*, 1875, pp. 61-62.
149 Sivasundaram, 2013, p. 148.
150 Karunananda, 1993, pp. 137-156.

certainly to show his might. It is also possible this could have been a misunderstood diplomatic row that went out-of-control rather than a regnal imposition upon a subject. This is still a common behavior trait of Heads of State. Rather than maintaining a relationship akin to a diplomatic or a conglomeration to fight off a conflict with a common enemy – the colonial powers – the King knowing that the Chiefs in this remote country did not have an organized army, acted unilaterally forcing his way to subdue a lesser potent provincial lord, a situation we can now call an invasion.

With these inconveniences in mind, knowing the unpredictability of Kandyan Kings, and being cognizant with the memory of the glories of Anuradhapura royal model which the King tried to articulate, Maha Vanniyā turned to maintain with him a cordial relationship. By this, he could also retain King's good grace, though tangential, to administer the province with minimal intrusion. He even had his own court system, the Rata Sabhāwa! For the Kandyan Court, Nuwarakalaviya was neglected back-country which may be why, tellingly, its representation was not considered needed in annual events like Perahera.[151] In King's inner thoughts Nuwarakalaviya was still a distant in all aspects, not just in leagues. Another example of his hands-off policy is the absence of prisons maintained by him in Nuwarakalaviya while surfeit of prisons - 17 of them – dotted across his kingdom, including Tamankaduwa.[152]

Fig. 10. Ulagalla Walawwa c 1950. Photo: Sanath Panabokke.

Soon after Kandy fell to British, the Chiefs of Nuwarakalaviya got busy revamping their relationship with the new lords of the land. Nuwarakalaviya *Vannivaru* must have had a busy four weeks since the signing of the Convention. Within days after the Kandyan Convention was formally ratified[153] news reached

---

[151] Bell, 1904, p. 126; Pieris, R., 1956, p. 250 n57.

[152] D'Oyly, 1929, p. 59.

[153] Governor Brownrigg first read the Proclamation of Kandyan Treaty on March 2, 1815, in Kandy, but the last two Dissavaru, Ehelepola Adikaram and Galagoda Dissava of Nuwarakalaviya, signed the document only on March 18, 1815, making ratification final.

Anuradhapura. On March 15, 1815, the Collector in Mannar, the predecessor of the Government Agent, wrote, possibly to D'Oyly, The Resident Officer and the Accredited Agent of the British Government in Kandy, that Suriyakula Kumarasinghe Vanniya of Nuwarawawe came to meet him two days earlier asking for protection from possible reprisal from the King or his supporters, and to affirm how happy he was for the changes taking place (in Kandy).[154] I believe Maha Vanniyā must have been thinking of this visit as nothing more than a diplomatic strategy from a head of a country to another requesting assistance and protection.

No sooner three months have passed than the evidence of *Maha Vanniya*'s questionable allegiance or cordiality to the new masters of Sri Lanka emerged. According to an incident recorded in a letter to D'Oyly by the Collector of Mannar on June 26, 1815, Kumarasinghe Vanniya's agents at Vilachchiya gravets, detained Wapoe Vidāne of Udunuwara. He was travelling with a passport issued by D'Oyly in Kandy. The agents in the gravets then seized Vidāne's cattle (*tawalama*) and merchandise. After Vidāne returned to Mannar and reported the incident, the Collector sent a "friendly *ola* letter requesting Kumarasinghe Vanniya to restore the merchandise and cattle [...] and allow him to proceed to Mannar."[155] This is an singular show of power by Maha Vanniyā. He was still employing his agents to control the land pass points in Nuwarakalaviya as a lord would do while British were well into the third month of their rule in Kandy and its fringe provinces.

D'Oyly wrote that on April 20th, 1815, elder Nuwarawawe Mudiyanse also known as Bulankulame Vanniya, was sending an advance messenger to Kandy to inform the Resident that he (Bulankulame) was coming to see him. Bulankulame Vanniya arrived on the following day and discussed the release of his half-brother Nuwarawawe Kuda Mudiyanse who had been imprisoned by the King.[156] Nuwarawawe Mudiyanse, accompanied by *Dissava* of Nuwarakalaviya, met D'Oyly and told him that he has no means to live or even temporary accommodation in Kandy, and requested permission to return to his "country." He further requested that the Nuwarawave Pattuwa be divided between the two half-brothers.[157]

LAND AND EVOLUTION OF WALAWWA. Diverse house designs reflect the cultural stratification of a society. They reflect the community rank they are attached to. It supported the living style of a people. The residence of a Chief was a walawwa. This moniker attached to the house of a Chief or its 'courthouse' built in the premises, shows attributes of the culture of a people.

---

[154] From the records of Mannar Kachcheri dated March 15, 1815 (by Collector to John D'Oyly), reproduced in Ievers, p. 44.

[155] Mannar Collector's letter reproduced in Ievers, 1899, p.44.

[156] According to a Gannoruwe Tikiri Gammahe (*Gamarāla*), he and Nuwarawawe (Kuda) Mudiyanse were imprisoned in Molligoda Walawwa c 1814 or around the time Kandy fell to the British. When English came to Amunupura in the outskirts of Kandy, they sent Kuda Mudiyanse to Poddalgoda (Gammahe's statement in 1819, cited by Lawrie, 1896, Vol. 1 p. 278.) Thus, it is possible Nuwarawawe Mudiyanse was still at Poddalgoda when his elder brother Bulankume Vanniya arrived in Kandy in April 21st 1815.

[157] D'Oyly, 1917, p. 264-265. See also Ievers, 1899, p. 43, regarding District Court case No. 156 of 1859 involving proprietary rights between the two branches of the Suriyakumara family – Bulankulam [*sic*] and Nuwarawawe.

When his children got married and moved out, whether they held any office or not, the new houses they occupied too were called a walawwa, irrespective of its location or the size. My discussion does not involve the houses of the adult children of Chiefs who have not become Chiefs yet.

M.N.R. Wijetunge (2012) quoted A. Rapoport to summarize the aforementioned traits of a house.

> The house is an institution, not just a structure, created for a complex set of purposes. Because building a house is a cultural phenomenon, its form and organization are greatly influenced by the cultural milieu to which it belongs [...]. (p. 39)

Thus, as can be expected, house designs were disparate according to the people's needs and their standing in society. Before the 'coffee table' housing designs that came in the second half of the 20th century, homes of elites in Sri Lanka built in the 19th and early 20th century show how they became expressive of the association of the social strata they belonged to.

Fig. 11. Bulankulame Old Walawwa with stone steps and remains of *korawak gal* or *mura gal* (Guard Stones). Photo: Ravana (Ravi) Wijeyeratne.

Adobes of commoners and nobility in Nuwarakalaviya have evolved over time during Anuradhapura period until the province was abandoned. Even after that, commoner homes in the province did not leave evidence of structural remnants because they were built with poor materials not strong enough to withstand diverse forces for long-term survival. At best, only barely noticeable mounds of housing compounds can be seen just below the tank bund where old village, now covered in brushwood, stood.[158] Therefore, trying to give a description of these houses even on a basic level is futile. But fortunately, traces of palaces, some homes of the elite, and monasteries survived rigors of time. Architects and civil engineers attribute this solely because they were built mostly with stone or well-baked brick and tile, showcasing the capability of the builder and potency of the owner.

As proof, there are many ruined buildings, mainly their stone skeletons still standing in Anuradhapura and Polonnaruwa and other corners of Nuwarakalaviya,

---

[158] Tillakaratne, 2013, p. xvii.

a millennia after they were abandoned. The palace of King Parakramabahu in Polonnaruwa, the monastery house on the banks of Kaludiya Pokuna (Black-Water Pond) in Mihintale and the Lovamahapaya (Brazen Palace) near the Sacred Bodhi Tree are good examples. Their thick walls were raised from sturdy foundations made with multiple layers of brick and stone. These walls were reinforced with stone pillars with rough-cut edges, built into them intermittently in harmony with their architectural designs. Pillars that were not built into the walls but visible were square- or octangular-shape, and polished. Rarely do we find cylindrical or fluted stone pillars. The roof was covered with flat tiles, often painted with blue, green, or yellow colors. Door and window frames were made with meticulously fashioned stone pillars that are often dove-tailed in place. From the half-circular linear marks found cut across the stone sills of some ancient doorways, it appears the door panels must have been built with thick wood and their bottom must have been lined with strips of metallic or granite strips or edgings. A few stone steps led to the door or the front verandah of the building. These steps were adorned with two balustrades of *korawak gal* (arty stone railings) or figures of lions, dragons, snakes, or gargoyle human figures on both sides, chiseled with their nautilus-like tongues spiraling out depicting protection and lively welcome. Often, at the base of the steps was a moonstone exquisitely decorated with animal and floral designs or a flat semicircular and polished stone slab.[159]

Fig. 12. Nuwarawawe Walawwa. Photo: Ravana (Ravi) Wijeyeratne.

A crude but permanent replica of this entryway design built in the mid-19th century is the doorstep to the Madukanda Maha Walawwa (Figs. 17, 51) near Vavuniya in the northern boundary of Nuwarakalaviya. The house is still occupied. An early version of the Bulankulame walawwa had stone steps, half walls, *korawak* stones and *mura gal* (guard stones) replicating ancient architecture. In Hurulle

---

[159] Major portions of this description (translated by me) are attributed to Charles. E. Godakumbura, 1960, Anuradhapura Yugaye Purawasthu in *Sahitya: Three Monthly Magazine*. p. 90.

Walawwa, the walls exposed after the devastating fire (Appendix E) were built with two-feet thick walls.[160]

In Kandyan times, even with the honor of being a leader appointed by the King in charge of different regions across the country, Chiefs continued to live in their ancestral homes in and around the cities of Kandy or Matale. This was done no doubt by King's design. This way he believed a *Dissava* would not attempt any Machiavellian maneuvers to undermine his authority with conspiratorial schemes in the cover of distance between his country home and the palace.

Conversely, in Nuwarakalaviya, *Maha Vanni Unnehe*, *Ratemahatvaru* (Mudiyansevaru) of Nuwarakalaviya – Nuwarawawe Bulankulame, Hurulle of Morakewa), Ulagalla (Nikawewa),[161] Tamarawewa, and a passel of *Kōrala*s and lesser officials maintained homes only in their respective districts enabling them to exercise direct and   extensive power enjoying independence as described earlier. King also neglected or not bothered to appoint a person with Nuwarakalaviya roots for *Dissava* or *Adikārama* title anywhere in the kingdom for fear of the Chiefs embracing independence from close royal oversight. Only the upcountry Radala families with centuries old roots in Kandy or surrounding districts received that honor – *Dissava* title of Nuwarakalaviya, which after considering the level of his involvement in the province, I liken to a sinecure – receiving perks without performing any tangible tasks in the province. With Nuwarakalaviya Chiefs not having residences in Kandy, it is easy to chart the absence of evidence of their involvement representing the province in the affairs of the Temple of the Tooth Relic or not walking with Kandyan Chiefs in the annual Perahera.

The King understood, implicitly, that the districts under the Nuwarakalaviya Chiefs' control were remote and had a loose affiliation to the Court. The threat level from them was nonexistent, mostly due to thinned out population base. Nearly half a century later, in 1852, though not yet a decadal exercise of the government,[162] the census showed population in the province was still sparse, 3.7 persons per square mile. According to 1881 census data, the population ratio between North Central Province and Central Province stood at 1:6. Provided the circumstances involving population dynamics remained unchanged during Kandyan times, retrogression of the population numbers should show this ratio to have been constant during the last decades of the Kings' times as well.   With such trying factors, Chiefs in Nuwarakalaviya were not able to muster a rag tag group of fighters and march to threaten Kandy.

On the other hand, during the last King's reign, whenever a *Dissava* left Kandy for his country home, the King expected his family to remain in the city.[163] Some called it holding the family hostage. When Chief Ehelepola defected to British, his wife and children stayed in Kandy and soon became hostages in their own home. In a betrayal heard across the country, Ehelepola refused to return. He stayed in

---

[160] See Lokubanda Tillakaratne, Hurulle Walawwa: A Piece of History Through the Ashes of Destruction. In *Sunday Times*, October 03, 2010.

[161] Known as *Ulagalle Nuwara* in *Three Sinhale Kada-Im Potha* (Abeyawaradana, p. 213).

[162] Census taking in Sri Lankan was started in 1871.

[163] Ievers, 1899, p. 59.

Colombo to help the British plan to take Kandy. History has recorded the sad end this cowardly Chief brought to his family.[164]

Except for the few that were demolished, the walawwas of Kandyan Chiefs located in the city of Kandy have all been converted to diverse purposes now. For instance, Giragama walawwa on Yatinuwara Veediya (Brownrigg Street during British times, and Daskara Veediya in Kings' times) was converted to retail stores; Ehelepola walawwa on Raja Veediya (King's Street) was the remand prison until 2013, and Dunuwila Walawwa is now the Kandy Municipal Council Complex. Galagoda Dissava, once the *Dissava* of Nuwarakalaviya lived in Patha Hewaheta, a division some 20 kilometers east from the palace. Another of Galagoda clan, Walapone Dissāva, had his house on Swarnakalyana Veediya until it was demolished after British took over the city. But their country houses in the respective districts remained open for Rata Sabhāwa or *Gam Sabe* gatherings. Contrary to the above description, most houses of Nuwarakalaviya Chiefs are still occupied or in the possession of their descendants. Exceptions are the Ulagalla walawwa close to Tirappane off A9 highway, and the Hurulle's Morakewa residence discussed before. The former was converted to a resort after last owner died without issue, and the latter was destroyed by hooligans with political ideologies.

Where and how Rata Sabhā and other traditional hearings or Sabhā were held in this early style of the housing compounds is not well understood. But a review of the architectural designs of those early walawwa complexes in general gives us an idea of the spatial characteristics of them.

Before the advent of the Victorian architecture in Sri Lanka beginning in early British colonial administration, the homes of Chiefs, despite being called walawwa, were not as outlandish as the structures built starting from the mid-19th century. These early houses of the Chiefs had mud walls, mud floors, and roofs thatched with straw. Tennent (1860) wrote that the "buildings encircle a courtyard round which covered verandah supported on pillars affords communication with several apartments." The rooms of these houses were built with "so little idea of domestic comfort or refinement [...] that the largest of these chambers are little dingy dens from ten to twelve feet square, each lighted by a single window, or rather a hole, the area of which does not exceed a square foot"(Vol. II, p. 427). The house was

---

[164] In hindsight, Ehelepola seems to be not only a perfidious but an idiosyncratic individual. Written accounts reveal he was accused of double murder while Dissava at Sabaragamuwa; As soon as the British arrested the King, Ehelepola asked D'Oyly to give him King's black horse; Later as the King was detained in Colombo, Ehelepola struck one of the royal physicians in the palace. At the inquiry held in the Audience Hall, the Chiefs hearing the case declared that no one could punish the palace servants except the King (CGA 23/2 cited in Ralph Pieris, 1956, p. 153 n43). On the day after ratifying the Kandyan Convention by the British, Ehelepola asked the Chiefs to kneel before the Governor in the Audience Hall (See page 87). While banished to Mauritius (Isle of France), he sent a letter to Sri Lanka in response to a suit brought against him by a Thamby Muhandiram of Kandy alleging Ehelepola owed him money. Also demanding money owed by him was a son of a *Rate Lēkam* and a Walandure Mohottala. After Ehelepola died in 1829, his estate was sued by Thambi Kundu Muhandiram of Borawa Veediya in Kandy demanding 18,688 rixdollars Ehelepola's brother owed to him (Lawrie, 1896, Vol. I, pp. 204-205). In fairness to Ehelepola, however, it is also possible that some individuals may have tried to take advantage of his sad predicament not being able to confront the accusers in person.

spacious, had multiple granaries in the compound. It was usual for the house or the whole compound to be surrounded by a moat and breastwork to deter wild elephants from damaging coconut and fruit trees.[165]

Usually, a wide and colonnaded corridor bordered the ubiquitous inner courtyard used for house chores like drying grain and other food items, and no doubt cloth-lines. According to Bulankulame family Facebook page, the old house (Fig. 11) in Bulankulame which is demolished now, is over 400 years old. The photo shows the loosened stone steps flanked by *korawak* stones, the steps, and the guard stones - *mura gal*. The house had 17 *Meda Midula* (inner courtyards). All the extended family lived in this house. Kobbekaduwa Maha Walawwa close to Kandy dating back to c 1720 (Fig. 13) has three court yards, three millstones, a shrine room, and a threshing floor (*kamatha*). The roof was covered with flat clay tiles until the 1960s.

Fig. 13. Kobbekaduwa Maha Walawwa c 1720 in Kandyan highlands.
Photo: Ananda Markalanda.

Some of the material to build the Chief's house was supplied by the villagers in his District. Residents of *nindagam* belonging to Paldeniya Walawwa of Ehelepola clan and another of their residences in Matale district had to supply 100 bundles of straw (*piduru katta*) yearly to thatch the walawwa roof. Villagers also burnished the floor and walls of the walawwa three times a year with cow dung.[166]

In *Living In Sri Lanka* (2006), Turtle Bunbury, the great-great-grandson of R. W. Ievers, the Government Agent of Anuradhapura during 1890-1893, introduced a turn of the century Sri Lankan manor house in this manner:

> A sleek black gate off [...] leads to a driveway of beautiful Riverstone, handpicked from the [...] Ganga; to the right, a grass lawn rolls towards the white colonial house. A verandah runs around the front of the house, its polished cement floor painted

---

[165] Davy, 1821, 2006, p. 473.
[166] Lawrie, 1898, Vol. II, p. 683.

egg white. Teak doorways from the verandah lead into the principal drawing room. Four sofas run back-to-back on teakwood floorboards down the center of the room. A large, gilded mirror magnifies the size of the room, reflecting a pretty canvas of a boat adrift on a lily pond. Glass bowls on glass top tables contain candles and flower petals. To the rear of the room two full size wooden sculptures stand sentry beside the doors leading into the dining area. Every piece has been meticulously placed to retain the ambiance of informality. [...] The exterior extends the confidence of the British Ceylon with its classical horseshoe arches and imperial balcony [*sic*]. (p. 48)

This house served multiple purposes. Regardless of the design and material that went into building it, most Chiefs' houses had ample rooms to do business of the people. It occupied a large compound, and the Chief could now accommodate the villagers who came to meet him. His family kept a measured distance from official activities by keeping the residential area out of bounds to the visitors.

Two living examples of former courthouses in a walawwa of a Kandyan Chief are found in Maduwanwela in Sabaragamuwa province and Madukanda (in Northern province, respectively. The former had the courthouse in a specially designed room in the walawwa, and the latter, in the garden (Fig. 6), free-standing next to the main house. This square-shaped structure, the courthouse, and called *Atapattu Maduwa* (*Maha Maduwa* when the Chief was present) was used to facilitate Rata Sabhā assembly in walawwa compound.[167] It was a half-walled large room with a spacious verandah, often as wide as 10-feet, running on the flanks and the front of the room. Villagers watched the proceedings standing on this verandah.

Court supplies and knick-knacks were stored in an attached back room. It was a sort of storeroom. While playing hide-and-seek in the *walawwatta* (garden), Septuagenarian Nanda Kumari Mahadivulwewa Wijeratne, granddaughter of Kapuruhami Ratemahattayā remembers seeing items like crumpled flags, few dusty *sesath* and some bundles of paper in the back room. *Sesath* (Fig. 7) were ornamental fans or hand-held disc-like parasol with colorful motifs geometrically weaved and fastened at the end of a pole to hold beside a dignitary as a sun shield. An umbrella called *wadana talatta,* also called *talatu* of treated and decorated frond of a palm tree, and *āyuda* (weaponry) were also stored in this room. Wadana Talatta can be folded horizontally when not in use. If the Chief had been granted a royal warrant to use a *dōlāwa* (palanquin) and its accessories – *moottuwa* umbrella made of the highest honor bestowed on a person of non-regnal lineage – also was kept here.

We have no information whether *Atapattu Maduwa* was also decorated as done for a *Maduwa* in a village when conducting a Sabhāwa. *Atapattu Maduwa* was also the record room to store *lēkam miti* (s. *mitiya*) and Chief's *kodi* (flags). On orders of the *Ratemahattayā,* offenders were imprisoned in the room attached to the courthouse or punished with sticks.[168]It got this name because the Atapattu people – bodyguards of the Chief (*Atapattukārayō*) provided security to the walawwa

---

[167] D'Oyly, 1929, pp. 8 & 14.

[168] Vimalananda, 1963, p. 221.

compound. They also provided logistical assistance during the Sabhā sessions, helped in tasks like messenger services for the Chief – carrying orders to the villagers, summon the people to attend judicial proceedings in the walawwa and performing sundry services in the compound. When a land dispute was decided in the *Atapattu Maduwa, Atapattukārayō* went to the village and announced it.

Starting from the second half of the 19th century, some Chiefs began to expand their horizons, literally. They began to travel abroad, a development unheard of in Sri Lanka until that time. Their itineraries included visits to opulent estates of ruling families in some Indian and Europe provinces. The Chiefs were awed to see the architecture of these princely houses and took note to emulate them after returning home. Soon, hybridizing the new stately houses with European and Indian styles began in haste. Importing architectural styles, construction material and furniture to appoint their homes became a fashionable thing. Thugs burned the Hurulle walawwa and razed it to ground in 1988 during the insurgency unleashed by rebellious groups. Themiya L. B. Hurulle told me that all historical documents and priceless heirlooms went in flames erasing the history of his family which began with the arrival of *Ayyanār deyyo* as found in the 19-century folklore of Nikawewa family. This deity is believed to have arrived at a time before the arrival of the Sacred Bodhi Tree. See also Appendix - E.

In 2009, on the debris field of the burned out Hurulle walawwa at Morakewa in Horowpothana, this writer saw scattered fragments of roof tiles with letters "India" and "1865" etched on them. Some evidence also showed the house had gone through periodic refurbishment.

Chiefs in Nuwarakalaviya, too, did not have to sweat out for material, especially timber since extensive stretches of virgin forest, some belonging to the Crown, were at their disposal freely. Timber for houses in Kandy and Matale area too was in plenty in the lands that were owned freely by the Chiefs. These lands probably were inherited centuries before Kandyan Kings were granting villages to Chiefs by *Sannas*. As found in Nuwarakalaviya folklore, the deity who protected these forests was *Ayyanār*, claimed primogenitor of some Chiefly lineage in Nuwarakalaviya as seen in later pages. Once I was fortunate to view a *Sannasa* by the King of Kandy in 1769, probably Kirti Sri Raja Singhe (1747-1782), granting villages. majority of them Northeast of Mihintale to a Chief in Nuwarakalaviya.[169]

Folklore is abundant with stories on large stretches of land, especially the 84,000-acre area belonging to Maduwanwela Dissava in Sabaragamuwa province. He used its resources for his needs, particularly to build his house and often to round-up wild elephants into kraals. The legendary tusker who lost his life after valiant resistance while trapped in the Panamure kraal in Dissava's lands is a heartbreaking story.

The Kandyan aristocracy, even while living in their often-unassuming adobes, occupied a larger and well entrenched sphere of visibility. They owned land grants and recognition earned as a reward for serving the royalty for centuries. Their counterparts in the Maritime provinces were the few families with titled lineage going back beyond the Portuguese times.

---

[169] The Chief's family requested anonymity.

Fig. 14. Hurulle of Morakewa Walawwa, in Horowpothana c 1988. The handwritten caption on the photo says, "built by Henerath Bandara Hurulle *Ratemahattayā* in 1902)." Photo: Themiya L. B. Hurulle.

These trends coincided with social transformation that was underway in the Maritime Provinces as stated earlier. However, the Maritime ranks of Chiefs envied the visibility enjoyed by their Kandyan brotherhood. One exceptional difference was that in Maritime Provinces some nobles, already well-provided with lavish wealth by Kotte Kings, Portuguese, Dutch and the British rulers were busy with their florid literary contributions. It raised their standing in the country. Sandwiched between these two classes were the new bourgeois in coastal provinces that gained wealth by capitalist economic policies of the Dutch and the British, especially the arrack renting business that began in the late 18th and early 19th centuries, first in the areas under colonial control and later in the Maritime Provinces at large.[170] These rich liquor franchisees were *rainda ralas* and became large landowners.

---

[170] British sold large swaths of land freely to both Sri Lankans and Europeans. During 1833-1843, 3456 lots with of 265,535 acres were involved in such sales. In 1840, among the Europeans who bought forest lands in the valleys of Ambagamuwa, Dikoya, Bogawantalawa and Maskeliya were Supreme Court Justice Carr with Capt. Skinner (822 ac), Gov. Steward Mackenzie (822 ac), Acting Colonial Secretary George Turnour (2217 ac), Surveyor General F.B. Norris with others (722 ac), and Assistant Colonial Secretary and Government Agent in Kandy P.E. Woodhouse (2135 ac). It

During the times of Portuguese, any grantee of a title with villages was called *rāla* – lord. But the *rainda rālas* were not titled. They held an unequal standing with the established aristocracy. Soon the post-Dutch period *rainda rālas* realized the wealth alone did not bring them same social recognition enjoyed by the Radala class in Kandyan highlands and its coastal counterparts. They wished for recognition and admiration already enjoyed by the two existing nobility fraternities titled since Kotte Kings' and the Portuguese times. Even with the success of economic gains overflowing around them, these *rainda rālas* still pined for the "manners and status of the Kandyan aristocracy."

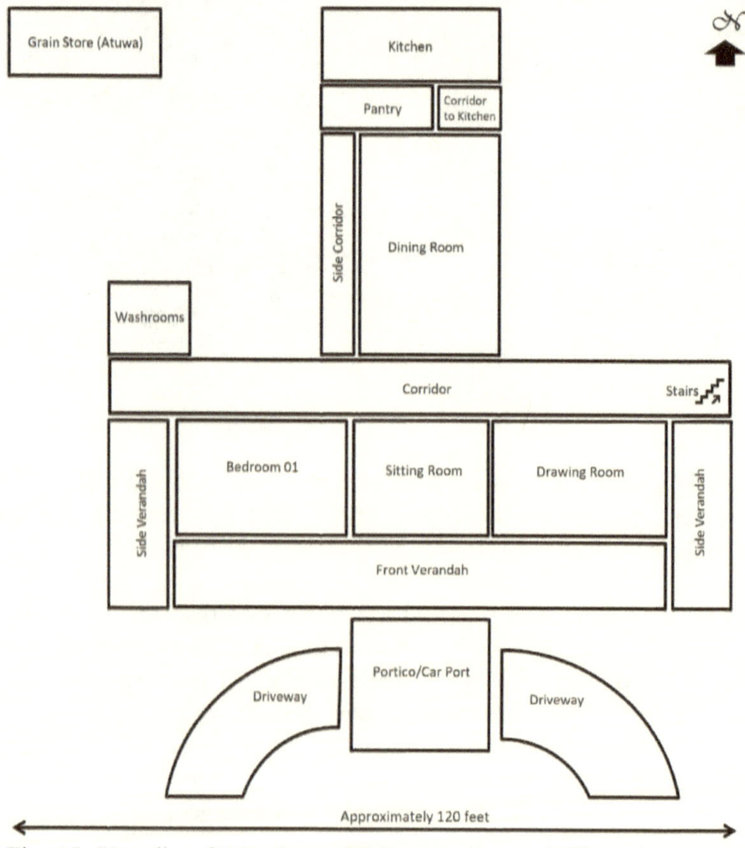

Fig. 15. Hurulle of Morakewa Walawwa. Ground Floor. Not to Scale. Themiya L. B. Hurulle. Redrawn by Niranjala Tillakaratne.

Thus came the need to consolidate, or mimic the visible and tangible characteristics – the livery and the size and grandeur – associated with a Kandyan *walawwa* model that separated the old Sinhala aristocracy from the wealthy trader-cum-landowner class in the Maritime Provinces. To mollify this gap, the coastal

___

was revealed later, they had prior knowledge of a road planned from Colombo to this valley (Lawrie, 1896, Vol. 1, p. 35). *Rainda rālas* also got into the fray. Some utilized them heavily to expand the coffee industry (Kumari Jayawardena, 2003, *Nobodies to Somebodies...* p. 141); John Stewart, Hansard, *Island of Ceylon*, May 27, 1830, Column 1159.

region began to broadcast luxury and status with manor houses that were truly architectural gems. In this regard Kumari Jayawardena (2003) wrote:

> [...] the new-rich renters, having made a considerable accumulation of capital, gave up their position as liquor merchants for the more 'honourable' designation of landowners. With a change in status came a change in residence. There was no better address than a walawwa (manor house) which went with landownership, an urban mansion with a fancy name [*sic*]. (p. 139)

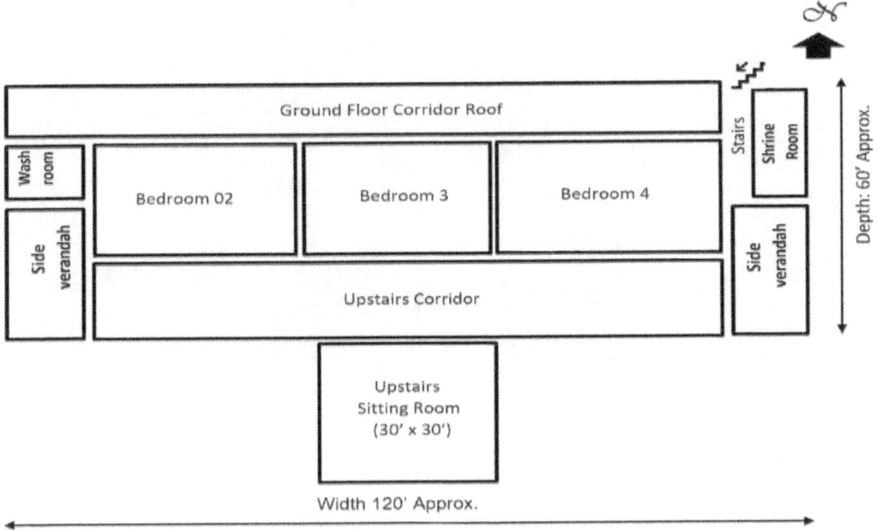

Fig. 16. Hurulle of Morakewa Walawwa. Upstairs. Not to Scale. Themiya L. B. Hurulle. Redrawn by Niranjala Tillakaratne

With a tint of self-conceit, these landowners often were excessively proud of their homes. For example, the owner of the 'Tintagel,' in a fashionable residential district in Colombo and later bought by Solomon Dias Bandaranayake, a Chief in Maritime Provinces wrote this:

> This contrivance was copied from the Hope de Paris, Seville. Unlike most big buildings in Colombo which were dark in the centre, this house was flooded with light. For the front verandah and the steps, I procured marble from North India, like that used by the Moguls in Agram ... [*sic*]. (p. 169)

Fig. 17. Madukanda Maha Walawwa. Photo: Niranjala Tillakaratne.

Fig. 18. Alittane Kōrale Walawwa, Tirappane.
Photo: Anula Kumarihamy Herath.

Fig. 19. Home of Maradankalla Wannihami Seneviratne, *Arachirāla* No. 23 Kandu Tulana (Elimeda).[171] Photo: K.B. Senevirathna.

---

[171] After opening the Post Office in the village in 1956, he graciously hosted it in his house for four years as a public service until the postmaster found an alternate building.

5. CRIMES, VIOLATIONS AND PUNISHMENTS

*a*s in any system of 'rule' at any time in history, in the absence of written laws, a plethora of customs or traditions took the role of regulating activities of people. Amongst these activities were diverse instances considered by the community as crimes or breaches or antisocial. Some breaches or crimes were unusual and unacceptable outright in comparison to today's standards. In response to the breaches of all levels, Michel Foucault (1977, 1995) wrote: "…A corpus of knowledge, techniques, and scientific discourse is formed and becomes entangled with the practice of the power to punish" the transgressors (p.23).

Véválketiya inscription (c 10th century AD) also gives a fair description of acts regarded as crimes in ancient Sri Lanka. In folklore or written accounts, preponderance of instances of capital punishment particularly, and varied forms of other not so palpable punishments show absence of any pattern of adherence to a standard principle and practice. In medieval, Kandyan, and early colonial times, the rulers punished their subjects with staggering cruelty without any contrition or afterthought. King could impose the same punishment on everyone who was within hearing distance of a crime regardless of the degree of their involvement. For example, in his mind, Ehelepola Dissava's wife and children were *particepes criminis* — partners in crime, so equally guilty of what Dissava who escaped to British territory was accused of. In a country with no written laws in Kandyan times, if a person did not behave in a manner accepted by any prevailing customs or norms, the punishment imposed was at the whim of the King who rarely displayed prudent charity towards his subjects. If there were written words, their power carried burden and authority which cogently elicited equity forcing the King to pause to act rationally and in a uniform manner.

Also remarkable was the absence of principles of justice. As discussed earlier, the result of not having written codes defining crimes was that punishments were not laid out horizontally in public in Sri Lanka. This interpretation fits into the ways of punishment levied by the Kings in Sri Lanka and their subaltern institutions like Rata Sabhāwa or *Gam Sabe* regardless of how *dharmista* (judicious) some of them were purported to be. But it appears the knowledge and the techniques did not stay uniform and textualized but changed often in accord with the whim of the rulers, or the majority. In King's time, purportedly, knowledge of all things about the crime was the privilege retained by those who 'prosecuted' the perpetrator. Therefore, there was no acceptable and proper way to defend the accused.

However, only a few crimes or violations and punishments described in the following pages came under the purview of the Rata Sabhāwa. They will be discussed later when and as relevant.

The essence of the Rata Sabhāwa was that villager in Nuwarakalaviya was aware and satisfied with his own safe and reliable system of judiciary, managed, and maintained by *kāriyakarawannō* – officials chosen from among their peers and overseen by the *Ratemahatvaru*. The villagers knew Rata Sabhāwa was unlike the dreaded and pendulous judicial system imposed and overseen by the King in Kandy and his condescending Chiefs. The villagers had reason to be happy as there was no record of an instance when the Maha Vanniyā ordered capital punishment on his subjects. Nor there is any report that the Kandy King extended his authority to Nuwarakalaviya to implement capital punishment on commoners. One reason for this can be attributed to the insulated state of the district by remaining isolated from the rest of the country as outlined earlier. Such muted attention went off the track if anyone roused King's ire. A case in point is the once arrest and imprisonment of Maha Vanniya for 12 years by Rajadhi Raja Singhe (1782-1798).

According to folklore quoted by R. K. Tillakarathne Mohottāla, when King Buwanekabahu V (1358 or 1558?) summoned the Vanni Bandaravaru and advised them about laws and customs, he also discussed all forms of punishments but death (See page 110).[1] This suggests the that the *mulādānivaru* believed they also had a royal decree to conduct their business.

While a broader description of crimes and violations will follow in this chapter, we will start with acts designated or generally accepted as crimes in the early 19th century. Before his death in 1824, John D'Oyly compiled a description of punishable acts existed in the Kandyan country in early 19th century. Not surprisingly, but obviously in D'Oyly's estimation, treason was significant than all other crimes and was placed on the top of the list as reproduced (partially) below: Treason, homicide, maiming, robbery (highway and other), burglary, arson, sacrilege, forgery and false coining, adultery, rape, assaults and quarrels, manufacture of arrack and toddy, gambling, elephant slaughter, hunting and killing animals, *huniyam* (sorcery, charms, or voodoo), slander affecting caste, murder of children, and suicide. In the case of suicide, punishment was levied against the living person who was imputed by the dead person to be responsible for her or his death.

There were also financial crimes. Misappropriation of treasury funds was a heinous crime. When lending money, the prescribed interest rate that could be charged was no more than 20% by Moor traders and 50% for Sinhalese traders. Any number more than that was considered usury. Even in the middle of the 19th century Thomas Berwick, District Judge in Kandy found that in Kandyan Districts 40% of major issues were of crimes of cupidity.[2] Molestation, persecution, slaying of parents, teachers, monks, offences against the King, cutting or defacing aniconic objects like religious paintings, plundering of property belonging to Buddha or the gods, plundering of villages, and highway robbery were crimes of major consequence to the offender.

Practice of witchcraft – dealing with evil spirits, was regarded as a punishable act. Witchcraft in Sri Lanka consisted of *bandana* (spells of malevolent restrictions) and any visual or physical attempts to threaten and cause fear to another person using spirits and other nether-worldly connivances. If the person did witchcraft against the King, punishment was death.[3] There were instances when a person suspected of practicing *huniyam* against another was brought before a Rata Sabhāwa.

---

[1] Hettiarachchi, D. E., ed. 1979, p.19.

[2] Sourced from Ferguson, A.M. 1868, p. 139.

[3] Vimalananda, 1963, p. 430.

In some areas of Nuwarakalaviya, Rata Sabhā must have been busy with sorcerers: J.P. Lewis quotes an unnamed official in Vavuniya district in 1895 who found that sorcery was common in the region. For instance, he once found a man in possession of 900 palm-leaf strips with written charms to be used as needed![4] Those who practiced *vas kavi* (versified spells) also came before the Sabhāwa.

In Dutch or British areas, not paying toll while crossing a river, passing a red lantern on a bridge without showing the contents of the bullock cart and other trivial pursuits were declared as breaches. In the Kandyan provinces including Nuwarakalaviya, a major theme of management of crime and punishment was that the acts and intransigent behavior of people identified as antisocial manifestations were understood as deep-rooted in their customs and traditions. But some may have been routine acts under the traditions and customs of villagers. In the colonial ways, tradition and custom had little to do with defining lawful or unlawful living. Particularly during the British period in Sri Lanka, definitions of crimes and breaches, rules, and punishments applied to them were published by gubernatorial edicts that were later concurred by the metropolitan England. Some of the crimes – evaporating sea water for salt without authorization – was something unthinkable under the Nuwarakalaviya traditions and customs.

ELLIOT AND BERWICK CRIME STUDIES. Queen's Advocate Edward Elliot, the Assistant Government Agent at Matara, and Thomas Berwick, District Judge in Kandy in mid-19th century were two pioneers who made perhaps the earliest known efforts to quantify and examine the litigation and crime data in Sri Lanka. These studies covered the periods between 1861-1862 and 1861-1864, respectively.[5] During this time Nuwarakalaviya was still a part of the Northern Province. Therefore, the statistical information presented in the two studies for the Northern Province includes Nuwarakalaviya as well.

Elliot tried a philosophical classification of crimes. He grouped them as:
- Ferocity and Malice (From Murder to Simple Robbery). Common weapon used for bodily harm was "catty" or *atkátta* (arched hatchet).
- Cupidity and Temptation (Forgery).
- Cattle Stealing and Coining.
- Crimes of Lust.
- Evil Speaking (Perjury and Cases of Libel).

Other than *tawalam* , carting and boating were the only other reliable mode of movement of goods until the train services between Colombo and Kandy started in 1867. Therefore, crimes against property, chiefly directed at cartmen and boatmen were rampant in the mid-19th century. A memo by Ceylon Railway Company states that prior to railroads, in 1847, there were 79000 cart trips between Colombo and Kandy. There were about 5000 carts licensed in Sri Lanka at the time.[6] These numbers were so astounding, that with the weather conditions making the roads

---

[4] Lewis., J.P., 1895b, pp. 176-185.

[5] For a detailed review of their statistical work on crime, see *Ceylon Directory:* A.M. Ferguson (1868), Observer Press, Colombo.

[6] Munasinghe, Indrani, 1972, *The Development and History of Transportation of in Ceylon...* p. 154.

depressive, the cart trips were understandably slow and tedious that would make them easy targets for criminals.

These carts were called bandys with arched roof and walls made of Cadjan. The roof extended on either side like awnings to provide shade for the carter. These carts also carried people. Once Governor Barnes rode a bandy on Colombo-Kandy Road with a visitor from India. This information gives an idea about commonality of cart-travel at the time and the extent of opportunities it gave thieves to be resourceful. Under these conditions, ulterior minds with cupidity lurking on the lonely stretches of 115 kilometers of dirt road between Colombo and Kandy snatching off some of the goods and proceeds from the carters was not implausible to think.

Historical accounts of the legend of 19th century highway robber Saradiel (1832-1864), illustrate the danger *tawalam*, carters and other forms of transportations faced on Kandy-Colombo Road and the convenience this busy traffic provided to highwaymen in the mid-19th century. As the railroads extended beyond each mile,[7] burden of cart loads shifted to rail cars. As volumes of goods took to railway, property crimes on cart roads began to take a dip, as the opportunist robbers could not catch up with the speed of the growth of railway infrastructure.

Elliot and Berwick studies also attempted to show a correlation between arrack taverns and crime rates in the provinces. With liquor licensing spreading across Central Province, consumption of arrack there became prevalent. An arrack tavern in the Northern Province was rented for £8 while in Central Province it was extraordinarily high at £1330. Between 1862 and 1864, rental income collected by the government from arrack taverns in Central Province changed from £38710 to £43984, an increase of £5274. For the same period, in the North Province, the corresponding increase was from £1087 to 1137, a difference of just £52. At a quick glance, this disparity of income from tavern rentals in the two provinces reflects the difference in demand for consumption.

The consequential anti-social behavior patterns of people under inebriety eventually reflected in the number of cases brought before the supreme courts in the two provinces. According to A.M. Ferguson (1868) in *Ceylon Directory* (1866-68), between 1862 and 1864, cases before the Supreme Court in the North Province rose from 29 to 30. The corresponding figure for the Central Province was a rise from 56 to 147![8] This information is incompatible with the population numbers in the two provinces – Central and Northern – taken few years after the study. According to the 1871 Census Data for the island, the population in Kandy District was 258,432 and in Jaffna District, it was 246,185! Almost similar population volume but nearly 3 to 1 ratio of criminal case volume disparity as evident in the Supreme Court records corresponds to convenience of access to alcohol consumption, a universal reason for belligerent behavior of people. Citizens of Kandyan highlands seemed to embrace and prove this maxim!

In Kandy region, 60% of the crimes were Crimes Against Person.[9] Burglaries and violent robberies were 34% of the crimes. During the time of study, the same

---

[7] Ceylon Railway began laying tracks only in 1864.

[8] Ferguson, A.M., 1868, p. 136.

[9] Ferguson, A.M., 1868, p. 139.

number for England was 14%. The average number of prisoners per case in Central Province during the study period was 2.25. Also, three or more persons were involved in 25% of the crimes, while no less than 10% of the crimes were committed by gangs of 10 or more. Berwick found in that period 37% of the cases in Central Province involved Crimes of Malice and Personal Hurt while for the same period in Dickensian England, it was 10%, remarkably a low percentage. Not much information is available about the temporal ground conditions, especially in Sri Lanka and England to get an idea as to the essentials of methods of collection and computing data in the two countries.

The obvious and stark difference in the crime levels between the Northern and Central provinces show some of the cultural, geographic, and economic dynamics in play at the time as well. Central Province had a booming Coffee industry which gave a person an easy medium for property crimes. Easy access and high demand for arrack catalyzed its widespread consumption. The province was also well-travelled even through mountain passes, and an inebriated person's tendency for crime increased with such avenues.

PUNISHMENTS. To say the ancient punishments were cruel, atrocious, arbitrary, and unusual is a modest statement. Majority of the criminals faced certain death sentence for stealing something as trivial as a mango from the King's Garden.

As far back as a millennia ago, Panakaduwa inscription of Vijayabahu I (1055-1110 AD) found in Morawak Kōrale in Matara district lists the severity of the punishments in this order: 1. Verbal reprimand, 2. Fine, 3. Imprisonment, 4. Confiscation of property, and 5. Capital punishment.[10] R. K. Tillakarathne Mohottāla wrote that the king Buwanekabahu V (1358 or 1558?) summoned the Vanni Bandaras to advise them how to conduct Rata Sabhā and what punishments to be levied. He placed injunctions on commoners far and wide. He demanded that if a person is found guilty, shave half of the head or subject him to *detis vada* (32 kinds of ordeal)[11] or banish from the province (perhaps the *Varige?*).[12] Ralph Pieris (1956) wrote the Buwanekabahu's edict as found in the folklore as follows:

> *O! Royal Princes! You must not mix with other castes or families. Do not intermarry with other castes. Do not go bear bodied. Do not let them approach you. Do not allow canopies, carpets, beds, chairs, or appointments in high offices. Do not allow them to wear jackets, hats, sandals, or use umbrellas. If they wear them and use them, they should be seized and tried, the heads of those found guilty must be shaved on one side, their ears must be chopped off, etc., and banished from the country. If one in your class mixed with one of them, he should be fined, and you should neither eat nor drink with him but have him trounced and relegated to a lower caste. Have no more intercourse with his dependents. Have such under your control. Observe all these injunctions. Hold Sabhā to try such and punish them according to their crimes. Inquiry into questions raised by*

---

[10] Nicholas and Paranavitana, 1961, p. 260.

[11] Lawrie, 1898, Vol. II, p. 650, quotes a 'Five Ordeals – *Pas Vada'* in a *Sannas*a written in 1798 by Wijesinghe Wickrama Wahala Herat Mudiyanselage Maha Lekam Manikrala kōrāla of Nugaliyadda in Hewaheta.

[12] Hettiarachchi, D. E., ed. 1979, p. 19.

the subjects. Maintain the laws of the land, laws of the King, and the laws of morality. Collect the taxes justly without oppression (p. 251).

But by the early 1900s, Rata Sabhāwa had provided some degree of opportunity to present a defense by those who appeared before it with accusations. In the confines of Nuwarakalaviya, generally, Maha Vanniyā was the final arbiter. His Chiefs in the *Pattu*, and the smallest title holders in the village, i.e., *Vel Vidāne* or *gamarāla*, also imposed punishments. Obviously, graveness of the punishment imposed was proportional to the rank of the official and the extent of the misconduct. Punishments that came under the purview of Rata Sabhā for breaches of social norms and acts found to be incongruous with the community guidelines were treated with a more humane and gentler manner.

King often shirked punishing criminals if the circumstances fitted to his convenience. He tolerated antics of Jan Egbertus Thoen, the former Dutch gunner who was married to a Moor woman in Kandy.[13] He knew the gunner was a spy helping the British soldiers imprisoned in and around Kandy to communicate with John D'Oyly in Colombo. Thoen also helped the king by making gun powder and teaching others how to do it. At some point, the king imprisoned him in Badulla only to release him later. As the gunner was a big help, the king looked the other way. He once let Ehelepola Dissava go after he was accused of murder of two *Kōrālas* in Sabaragamuwa.[14] An angry Dissava was a liability for the King.

As punishments were not clarified by writing, they remained just practices — some may have existed for a long time, some spontaneous and amorphous. Often, they were *lex talionis*, eye-for-an-eye-type retributive acts. In the absence of a written law, punishment could be decided as comeuppance, one that he deserved, but not as something broadly regarded as acceptable by all where written codes and statutes guided the process.

Infringements like adultery were subjected to less brutal punishment, but emotionally draining. The lengthy duration the judicial process lasted made it a potent and deterrent sight and equally effective in the eyes of the spectators. In some early American Colonies, for example, Puritanical laws required the magistrates to order a convicted adulterer to wear a scarlet letter *'A'* across her bosom for the rest of her life (Fig. 20).

After starting to administer justice in Kandyan provinces with the guidance of British laws written for the island, the British endured for a while a modicum of caste differences for punishment methods. In the heels of the ratification of the Kandyan Convention, Colonial government used caste for their expediency. During the Kandyan Commissioner's time, for example, after a case was decided, caste seemed to have been taken into consideration in choosing the punishment method. The British were able to do so as seen from the following language in the stipulations of the Article 4 of the Kandyan Treaty which required honoring caste traditions. [...] saving to the Adikars, Dissaves, *Mohottālas*, Coraals, Vidaans and all the other chiefs [...] the rights, privileges, and power of their respective offices and to all class of

---

[13] D'Oyly, 1917, p. 117.
[14] D'Oyly, 1917, p. 34.

peoples the safety of their persons [...] *according to the laws, institutions and customs established and in force amongst them* [*sic*] (italics by author).

Fig. 20. *Hester Prynne on the Pillory Stand.* Punished for adultery. The scarlet letter '*A*' is sewn to the dress across her bosom. Mary Hallock Foote in *Scarlet Letter* by Nathaniel Hawthorne (1878).

In Sri Lanka, as in most countries, up to the 18th and 19th centuries, punishing criminals was a public spectacle.[15] A convicted person was hanged in the village where he committed the crime. Judging from scattered places where the King hung people, it appears that there was no one fixed place, e.g., a cemetery, public square, or a prison compound, to carry out this punishment. Often, the reason behind this was not only the level of severity of the crime and its social impact, but the visual effect (of the execution) it delivered to forewarn any would-be violators in the populace. Those who were responsible for imposing the sentence thought the visual effect of the punishment was an exigent element to keep the people in a submissive state. Foucault (1977, 1995) wrote this as "an expression of infinite vengeance" (p. 57). Such a theme made it more necessary to infuse novelty and cruelty into the method of perfecting it. Not having written laws of conduct and punishments dovetailed with this practice. These were dark ages: no books to read, no schools, no formal exercises to teach about wrongs and rights. So, the public square was the school and the courthouse!

---

[15] Although a fictionalized story, see Alexander Dumas' *Count of Monty Cristo*, (1844, 2003), pp. 137-143 for the gripping description of an execution of a guilty person in the city square in Rome and city dweller who flocked around to see the event.

At the time of the public execution of Ehelepola Kumarihamy and her children in the palace square, whole city of Kandy was present to witness it. It is not known whether King ordered citizens to come. But he selected the place of execution of the children near his palace and Kumarihamy's at the Bogambara Weva in the center of the city. His intention for the choice of location was clear: to be seen by "people whose real and immediate presence was required for the performance (p. 57)." It is certain they would dare not boycott the spectacle for fear of the King's wrath. Either way, his intentions to warn the traitorous designs of his subjects served the purpose.[16] If he wanted to broadcast the spectacle, he would order a convict to be dragged, dead or alive, miles along the road to be seen by people.

CAPITAL PUNISHMENT. In Kandyan times, only the King could sentence someone to die.[17] The *Ars Moriendi* – Art of Dying – was an inconsequential concept to him. In instances of capital punishment, he imposed death by hanging for lower caste and ordinary persons while those of Radala caste, and held titles above *Mohottāla* and their close relatives were beheaded as they knelt and prostrated or rested the head on a log. It is believed to be most honorable way to die when receiving capital punishment.[18] An eyewitness accounts of the beheading of Keppetipola Dissava in 1818 was given by his friend Henry Marshall.[19] Prisoner of War Keppetipola faced death with dignity. On the contrary, Keppetipola's colleague Madugalle who was beheaded at the same time, had hard time controlling himself unable to face the punishment. 'Prisoners of War' was not in the vernacular then. When the British decapitated Keppetipola and Madugalle, the rules of punishment were set to medieval times.

Death sentence was also carried out by piercing the body by nudging an elephant to ram its tusks through the torso of the condemned. For this purpose, a conical casing with sharp end was fastened at the end of the tusks.[20] Ordering an elephant to tread over the convict was another method employed to carry out capital punishment. Elephant had been a capital asset of the crown in the Indian subcontinent since pre-Christian times. In Sri Lanka too, the same tradition prevailed. Therefore, killing an elephant itself was punishable with death.

King had no compunction imposing death penalty even to his Chiefs. Even under day-to-day affairs, working for the King was equivalent to walking on a minefield. Pilimatalawa Adikarama, most senior Chief at the time and the Dissava of Nuwarakalaviya in 1802, was beheaded by the King of Kandy in 1812. Upon conviction, a lower caste person was also given corporal punishment for the same offence.[21] When Petigammana Muhandiram stole the flag of Sabaragamuwa Province, King ordered him whipped to death. Then his body was dragged to

---

[16] Tillakaratne, Lokubanda 2022, Drowning of Ehelepola Kumarihamy. *Ceylon Today, Nov. 25, 2022.*

[17] Jonville, Mons, 1948, pp. 1-21.

[18] Pridham, 1849, p. 218.

[19] Marshall, 1846, 1954, *Ceylon,* p. 217.

[20] James Cordiner, 1807, *Description of Ceylon* Vol. 1, p. 246.

[21] Kulasekara, K.M.P., 1984, 2018,). *British Administration in the Kandyan Provinces* ... (Unpublished Doctoral Dissertation). p. 208.

Gannoruwa, about 4 miles from the palace, and hung for public display. There was an instance of death by hanging at a place called Hunukotuwa close to Gannoruwa.[22]

Execution methods were varied and no different than what Foucault wrote about in France centuries ago.[23] It was not "one death per condemned man," but "long and consequently cruel" method of execution. An example for this in Sri Lanka is the case of Halangoda Mohottāla. In 1803, King of Kandy who had been in retreat in Hanguranketa after the British stormed Kandy ordered to cut Mohottāla into pieces after accusing him of joining the English at Fort Macowall in Higgolla, Matale.[24]

Albeit the women were punished in the royal storehouse during the Kandyan times, the severity of the offence often determined the locations to carry out the punishment. Sometimes, women were drowned by tying a rock around the neck or putting her into a sack and throwing into water. The sad saga of suffering of Ehelepola Kumarihamy and her four children as city folks stood watching is like what Foucault called "the theatrical representation of pain." Such punishments often came very close to harmfully affecting public welfare and health. The case of Ehelepola Kumarihamy's death by drowning by order of the King in Bogambara Weva is a prime example. As a side note, Obeyesekere (2017) suggests that this drowning could have taken place not at Bogambara, but at Boraweva, a small pond existed then in the North-West side of the city (p. 208).[25] But the unintended light his untested hypothesis provokes us to discuss an important aspect of public health concerns Kandyans faced and solutions they adopted, then and even up to the middle of the 20th century (See Appendix H).

Another atrocious punishment method was impaling (Fig. 21). It was a method popular not just in Sri Lanka but in India, too. An undated ceiling painting in a temple in Avudaiyarkoil in Tamil Nadu shows men impaled on a row of standing daises.[26] During capital punishment of a convict, either in public square or while being taken on the street, he was subjected to torture and ridicule as his body parts were cut off one by one causing a slow and an agonizing death.[27]

CRIMES AGAINST THE KING. No one escaped to live a day if caught or suspected of a crime, or a breach against the King. These crimes drew his anger and brought unimaginable punishments upon the suspect. As far back as the Portuguese times (16th century), anyone caught forging the King's "Sri" signature was punished with death.[28] Touching any part of his body was considered a sacrilege. Naturally, the King would not allow someone even to see his bare body. Sivasundaram quotes the diary of Dutch Dr. Danielsz who visited King Narendra Singhe (1707-1739) of

---

[22] Vimalananda, 1963, p. 316A.

[23] Foucault, 1977, 1995, p. 12.

[24] Lawrie, 1896, Vol. I, p. 311.

[25] Also see Tillakaratne, Lokubanda. (2022, November 24). Drowning of Ehelepola Kumarihamy. *Ceylon Today*. The North-West end of the present-day D.S. Senanayake Street was named Borawe Vidiya in the 1815 map of Kandy by T.B. Keppetipola.

[26] P. Jeganathan (Personal communication, Thanjavur, Tamil Nadu, January 05, 2021.

[27] This is a practice existed in some countries in Medieval Ages. With the prism of cultural and religious influence, it is difficult to imagine a Kandyan crowd cheering the death march of a prisoner.

[28] Pieris, P.E. 1920, *Ceylon and the Portuguese 1508-1658*, p. 128.

Kandy to treat his illness. The King would not allow the doctor to see his bear body to save the ailing limb![29]

Fig. 21. *One impaled on a stake.* Seventeen-century illustration. From Robert Knox (1681, 1995).

Often, punishments were invented and manufactured for 'crimes' that were interpreted by the King as impinging on his godly person. Kings often showed wily ways or found bizarre and unbelievable ways to punish people. In 17th century when he wanted to find how his attendants would react to a critical situation, or simply to check on them, the King (Raja Singhe II) feigned death by drowning while swimming. Two young attendants jumped in quickly and pulled the King out of the water to safety. Later he summoned the two men to the palace and imposed death penalty on them for "daring to touch his person."[30] Entering the palace with a weapon, seated on the road while King passed by, and behaving inappropriately in the presence of him, all resulted in death penalty imposed on the spot. Usually, the King either invented or decided upon a punishment as he wished.[31]

The crime of regicide was unheard of in Sri Lanka in the 18th and 19th centuries. But in the Kotte period, there had been an in-family fight in the Court resulting in regicide by a family member. King Vijayabahu VI in the famed *Vijayaba Kollaya* was killed in 1521 by an assassin hired by the King's three sons

---

[29] SLNA Lot 1/3289, Diary of Dr. Danielsz's trip to Kandy to treat and cure the King, cited in Sivasundaram, 2013, p. 250.
[30] Knox, 1681, 1995, p. 46.
[31] Wimalakeerthi, 1955, p. 94.

Buwanekabahu, Mayadunne and Raigam Bandara from his first wife, to seize power in Kotte.[32] In most countries, when similar crimes were committed, undoubtedly, they were universally extraordinary events, and to quote Michel Foucault, the punishment levied was "an expression of infinite vengeance." A full measure of infinity of punishment was on display in 16th century when the assassin of prince William of Orange in Netherlands was tortured for 18 days.[33] Before the assassin was finally strangled to death, he had gone through all manner of cruelty some that were invented as the punishment progressed.

Capital punishment methods of Sri Lanka's colonial powers were no different. For crimes far less severe than murder, they imposed sentences with unimaginable brutality which can only be described as retributive and repulsive. When Portuguese caught native boatmen off shore in Negombo some swimming in the night taking missives (*kāda path* – palm leaf strips from the King) to Dutch ships anchored off the coast, they stuffed captive's mouths with gun powder and set them on fire.[34] After Dutch became the rulers in Sri Lanka, their penal law and how justice was served had serious irregularities. There was no mechanism to defend an accused. A person could be sentenced to death with as little as a confession from him obtained mostly by torture. As seen from the multiple techniques used to execute a convicted person, a standard method was a rarity. None was required because the colonial mindset was set upon the native people as uncivilized creatures inhabiting a distant island. But back home in the metropolitan Europe, punishment methods they had witnessed were far worse than vicious.[35]

During the Dutch reign in Sri Lanka, a Chetty was sentenced to death by hanging for an offence what would be regarded today as minor. His body was to be dumped into a sack and thrown into the sea. However, later the sentence was commuted, and he was flogged and banished from the city. A woman named Joana was found guilty of stealing a slave and was strangled to death, cut in half, and left to be devoured by birds.[36]

When the British began their rule, their capital punishment method was not a bit different from the Kandy King's or the other colonial powers who preceded them. Ceylon Gazette of Oct. 31, 1819, described in most nauseating terms the execution of Ellepola Maha Nilame in Bogambara in the southeast area of the city. British continued capital punishment until the end of their rule in Sri Lanka.

For each execution held at the Bogambara prison in Kandy in the turn of the 20th century, a priest stood preaching at the foot of the steps of the gallows while the activities atop the scaffold continued. Assistant Government Agent was also present in the prison for the occasion.[37] There is no instance on record where Buddhist monks being present while the convict was beheaded or hung. Usually,

---

[32] Pieris, P.E., 1920, p. 44.

[33] Foucault, 1995, 1997, p. 54, quoting Seigneur de Brantome, II, ed. 1722, 191-192.

[34] *Mukkara Hatana* (Mukkara War), 17th century palm leaf manuscript in Hugh Neville Collection, British Museum (Or. 6606 – 139), reproduced in M.D. Raghavan, *The Karava of Ceylon*, p. 178.

[35] See Michel Foucault's (1977, 1995) *Discipline & Punish: The Birth of the Prison,* for punishment methods existed in Europe up to 19th century.

[36] Pieris, P.E., 1918, 2018, p. 58.

[37] Leonard Woolf, 1961, *Growing: An Autobiography…* p. 167.

the convicts participated in religious services before taken to the place of beheading as in the case of Keppetipola who visited the Temple of Tooth Relic to conduct his own last rites.[38]

After the Rata Sabhāwa customs ended, stories fraught with sensationalism seemed to have flooded the folklore. An interesting item is the belief that Rata Sabhāwa had the authority to pass death sentence to a convict! T.B. Ekanayake Mohottāla of Kekirawa has countered this notion as nonsensical and pure fantasy.[39]

FINE. If the fine imposed was not paid, and if the convict is a titled person, his sword, cap or headdress, knife and shirt or jacket were removed from his person while he was kept in confinement. Even murders being exceedingly rare in villages in premodern times, if a murder suspect could not be found, the villagers were fined. But if the murder took place in the forest, they would be spared of any culpability. Occasionally, if one person in a village was convicted of a crime, everyone in the village was fined. Chiefs often imprisoned suspects and did not release them until the fine was paid in full. The fine was then retained by the Chief as a fee. Vimalananda tells that the fine was a main source of income of the *Vannihuru* and Kandyan Chiefs.[40] Although there were limitations to the amount of the fine a Chief could impose upon a convicted person, in frontier districts like Wellassa and Hath Kōrale, there were instances where fines larger than what was traditionally accepted were imposed arbitrarily. Fines imposed at Rata Sabhāwa will be discussed in later pages.

PARDONING. On occasions, the King pardoned prisoners, some even after they shirked public work duties. Once the Sabaragamuwa Dissava Ehelepola, with the pedigree connecting to a long line of Chiefs, was summoned to Kandy after having been accused of accessory to the double murder described earlier. It was also alleged that he killed or responsible for the death of Chief Elapatha Nilame of Sabaragamuwa and misappropriating property of his widow. Ehelepola reluctantly came to his house in Kandy and feigned ill fearing the King's wrath.[41] Hearing this, the King sent word to Ehelepola 'not to be afraid.'

Not just the Chiefs, but King often strategically released commoners condemned to death. In 1813, he recommended death sentence for five Malay men for escaping while working on the construction project in the Kandy Lake. He pardoned them, escorted them out to British controlled territory and with their families, with travel expenses of two Elephant Rupees for each. It could have been a strategic decision of the King. He did not want to irritate Malay men who were his drill instructors and some in training in Kandy preparing to defend expected attacks by the British.[42]

MUTILATION. A well-known and consequential mutilation is the one that was ordered by the King of Kandy on the suspected traders from Maritime Provinces who were found within the borders of Kandyan country in 1815. He accused the

---

[38] Marshall, 1846, 1954, p. 217.
[39] Hettiarachchi, D. E., ed. 1979, p. 21.
[40] Vimalananda, 1963, p. 335.
[41] D'Oyly, 1917, p. 3
[42] D'Oyly, 1917 p. 176.

traders as British spies. After they were captured, their noses, ears and hands were cut off as punishment upon the King's orders. The traders lumbered to Colombo with severed ears and hands and reported to the Governor the atrocity perpetrated on them. This action gave the British necessary pretext to begin the final assault on Kandy. The King also ordered cutting hand at the wrist for those who removed an *anabōla*, a broom made of twigs (Fig. 22).

Fig. 22. *Anabōla (Bol Atta, ekoliyama -* Broom of Twigs). Photo: Jananjaya Tillakaratne.

HUMILIATION & OSTRACISM. Both these punishments used in Kandyan country were effective, easy, and less atrocious. Forcing people to wear objects as symbols signifying the punishment fit for a convicted person separated him or her from others including acquaintances. It announces the guilt and tamps the spirit of the alleged wearer as he or she is subjected to insults and ridicule (Fig. 20). It also creates prolonged and deep mental pain and anguish in the culprit. Also, shaving the head of a women was regarded as a humiliation.

King did not spare his Chiefs and lesser officials from humiliation. He took away their titles or recalled them from a post with a simple gesture like snapping a finger. As far back as c 1910, Kapuruhami Madukanda Ratemahattayā (1948) with his first-hand experience of dealing with caste-related issues, particularly the humiliation and ostracism which followed the expulsion from a clan, wrote:

> To the simple-minded and unspoiled Kandyan who is much attached to his caste and clan, the mere idea of being cast out of it was a terror; therefore, hard and fast rules of the Rata Sabhāwa system were in no way considered to be a burden or hardship on him. (pp. 42-68)

Expulsion from *Varige* was an outright humiliation. Alternatively, ostracizing can also be a simple way of punishment.[43] But trying to explain the totality of ultimate humiliation Ehelepola Kumarihamy and her children received because of a

---

[43] Ryan, 1953, p. 251.

caste-related shame is a futile effort. Viciousness of the Kandy King in this sad episode notwithstanding, it highlights the cruelty and scale of socio-cultural shame of ostracism, humiliation, pressure of social norms and element of disgrace women faced centuries ago in Sri Lanka due to horrendous caste tenets.

The King ordered Kumarihamy and her children to be beheaded as part of the punishment for her husband's refusal to return to Kandy. Even Sri Lanka's fictitious yet bizarre and comical King Kekille would have loathed such an abhorrent act. But in Kandy was a real King, in real life and real people. To spare the lives of the children and hers, Kumarihamy was given the option of agreeing to be married to a Rodiya caste (the untouchables in Sri Lanka). Giving away in marriage to a person of Rodiya caste was the ultimate social disgrace at the time. It was an unthinkable proposition for her. Unwilling to defame the honor of her husband and family, she opted for death to herself and the children. Meanwhile, her husband Ehelepola Dissava was in Colombo under the protection of the British and dreaming of a future as the King. His detestable and cowardly act set a course with no return. Finally, on the day of execution, not a breath of air moved in Kandy, and the blue hills around it chocked up hearing the heart-breaking cries of Kumarihamy and her children facing a viciousness unimaginable, perpetrated by a heartless King and an appalling caste modality (See Appendix I). If only!

Those who slaughter cattle were punished by suspending a string of red flowers and bones, usually of the same animal killed by the accused, and humiliated by parading on the streets as he announced the nature of his crime. In the first half of the 20th century, this practice continued sporadically in rural areas, but by then it was not in the books as a legalized form of punishment, simply a way of shaming in public, humiliate, and stigmatize, often taken as an impromptu action by the investigating officer in the crime scene.[44]

CURSING. This was also a form of punishment imposed on certain occasions. A good example of what constituted a curse is found in the language in *Sannas* or deeds executed in Kandyan times. The *Sannasa* contains description of a potential punishment by cursing upon the individual in the event he or she violates the stipulations therein. Lawrie (1896) reproduced a deed given by Pilimatalawa Dissava in 1766 to Parana Vihare of Asgiriya temple in Kandy. In the deed, cursing was stipulated as a form of punishment for anyone infringing upon its contents and purpose!

> [...] Anyone taking back forcibly what was given (by Pilimatalawa
> Dissava), or others, will be born a worm, and undergo the sufferings
> for 60000 years. Anyone making use of even a blade of grass, a stick
> of firewood, a flower, or a fruit out of Vihare property, will be born
> a *pretaya,* evil ancestral spirit. (p. 73)

Sometimes a *Sannasa* might have a parable and a wish, not a curse. In Kadirana Sannasa (1517), King Vijayabahu VI has the following text immediately after the name of the Perumal (scribe of the *Sannasa*): "Good men do not eat rice left in charity by good men; dogs eat such rice, and although they may vomit, they eat again.

---

[44] Tillakaratne, *Ceylon Today* July 13, 2020.

Like them (the good men) if ye protect this grant given by good men, O good men!
You will acquire merit in both the worlds [*sic*]!"[45]

FLOGGING. Some convicted men were flogged with various implements like
cane, whip, broom, or just spanking with the outstretched palm. In Kotte period
the convict was tied to a wooden post known as *Kamba Kanuwa* and whipped.[46]
Flogging, often called knouting, was done with an implement called cat-o'-nine-tail
or a regular whip. This was used by the British in 19th century Sri Lanka. It is a
paraphernalia of nine leather strands, braided, each about 75cm long, attached
together to a handle on one end. The handle takes about half of the full length of
the gadget (Fig. 23).

Leonard Woolf (1961), a British Civil Servant in Sri Lanka, wrote of the
executions and flogging practiced by British colonial prison wardens in the 19th
century as "a horrifying experience, and the more I had to witness, the more horrible
I found them. [...] flogging (whipping) a man with the 9-thread was the most
disgusting and barbarous thing I have ever seen – it is worse than a hanging" (p.
166).

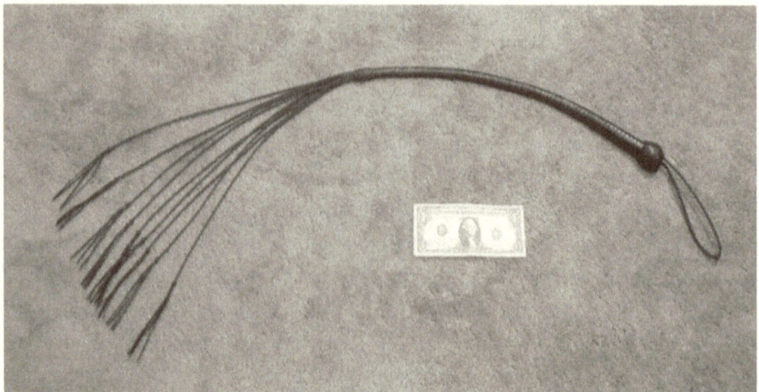

Fig. 23. Cat-o'-nine-tail, multi-tailed whip used by British in Sri Lanka
in the 19th Century. Photo: Wikimedia Commons

British colonial administration punished persons who simply refused to
participate their public health programs. After vaccination was introduced to Sri
Lanka in 1802, doctors went around vaccinating people. In 1819, near Kurunegala,
a man named Ambakiriya got 100 lashes in public for refusing vaccination for
smallpox and assaulting the army doctor and his assistant who tried to force-
vaccinate him.[47] He received 12 months imprisonment as well.[48]

In the past in Sri Lanka, a person convicted of a major crime was paraded
through the city streets while being flogged as drummers walked in front playing the

<hr>

[45] De Zoysa, Luis, 1873, *JRAS*, Part I, pp. 75-79.
[46] John M. Senaveratne, 1914, The Date of Buddha's Death, *JRAS (Ceylon)*, Vol. 23, No. 67, pp.
141-273. In Nuwarakalaviya, *kambas karanawa* is spanking someone, particularly a misbehaving
child or a teen by tying to a tree.
[47] Bennett, Michael, 2020, *War Against Smallpox: Edward Jenner and the Global Spread of Vaccinatioin.* p.
244.
[48] Sivasundaram, 2013, p. 274.

beat "*pita potta una potta wenaturu*" ("until the back skin come off like a split bamboo") as the popular saying goes. In cases of assault, and men of inferior castes who disrespect the Chiefs and Headmen, the punishment was *Atulpaagaseema* (slapping on the back with hand, another form of *kambas karanawa*). [49] A Buddhist monk or a superior caste individual was fined but not flogged.

Fig. 24. Manner of extorting the fine by bearing a heavy rock on the back. Seventeenth century illustration in Robert Knox (1681, 1995).

CONFINEMENT, DETENTION, OR IMPRISONMENT. This may be as simple as just drawing a circle around the person on the sand until he pays the fine. This practice was called *Wálákma* (restrain). [50] Rata Sabhāwa or *Gam Sabe* used this punishment method widely after a session. Officials drew a circle in the sand around the convicted person and asked him to stand inside, signifying imprisonment, until he or his family paid the fine. Manner of confinement during and after Rata Sabhāwa sessions will be discussed in later pages. Locking in a room or restraining in a *Dandu Kanda* (pillory) is another punishment practiced in Kandyan times. The pillory is a contraption of two wooden shafts with grooves cut in them to entrap the prisoner by neck, legs, or hands.

Another harsh confinement method imposed on a guilty person was to make him stand in the sun with a rock placed on his back. A 17th century illustration in Robert Knox's *Historical Relations* (1681, 1995) shows a man half-stooping with a rock on his shoulder while the official, probably who levied the punishment, stands arms

---

[49] Ekanayake, A. de Silva, 1876. On the form of Government under the Native Sovereigns of Ceylon. *JRAS (Great Britain and Ireland), New Series*, Vol. 8, No.2, pp. 297-304.
[50] D'Oyly, 1929, p. 26.

akimbo by the man (Fig. 24). During the Kotte kingdom period, instead of a rock, a basket of sand was placed on the back of the convict.[51]

Commoners were imprisoned in *Maha Hirage* (King's Prison). But Chiefs were imprisoned in Katupulle villages near Kandy. These were occupied by Chiefs' attendants. Confinement was a great insult. Kandyan rulers' treatment of incarcerated villagers was inhumane. Commoner prisoners were not provided food. Instead, they had to go out on the street and beg for food.[52] In the mid-17th century Sri Lanka, prisoners in chains were used to sweep the streets about the palace.[53]

Dutch did not bother to incarcerate convicted persons. They opted to create chain-gang-type companies of prisoners to work on their building projects. Forts of the colonists could not have been built only with the labors of European soldiers.

There is no record of a prison in Nuwarakalaviya used by the King of Kandy. Only Tamankaduwa had a penal station during Kandyan King's time, no doubt to detain prisoners banished to this district as it was designated as an insalubrious area.[54] The *kadawat* were also used to hold people until they paid due taxes or caught trying to enter or exit the Kings' country without proper documents akin to passports. Not much information exists about punishment methods in these prisons or holding locations.

DIVI **(OATHS).** Oaths (*divi*, s. *diviya*) are forms of asseverations (solemn declarations) or imprecations (self-imposed curses) practiced as an alternative to appearing before a Rata Sabhāwa or other forms of hearings. With the way its outcome was recognized by the community, it can also be regarded as a 'document of declaration.'

Resorting to such an option was a quaint way of solving conflicts and validate a fact in rural Sri Lanka. After an oath, its completion was recorded in a document called a *divi sittu*. A person subjecting himself to a *divi* does it to prove his point — proof of ownership or whether he is telling the truth. The belief is that at an oath taking, if a person perjures, he would be punished during this life or at a future birth. In Anuradhapura area, a *diviya* can take place under the Sacred Bodhi Tree, any Bodhi Tree in the village, Jetawanārāma stupa, Temples at Vijithapura, Minneriya, or Hurulu Dévale, also called Hurulu Wāsala. Some locations where such oaths were taken in Kings' times are still identified with the name to show their past association with the custom. An example is the present day *Divurum Bodhiya* temple, about four kilometers from Kandy in Ampitiya on Kandy-Talatu Oya Road where oaths by hot oil were performed under the Bodhi Tree in the temple.

In Nuwarakalaviya and Tamankaduwa regions, following are diverse types of oaths[55] taken:

Tel Diviya (Ordeal by Oil) — Immersing the hand into a container of boiling oil. The pain and damage this practice can cause warrants the order for it coming from a very higher source, i.e., the *Adikārama*, the Chief Minister. A strip of palm leaf was

---

[51] Senaveratne, 1914, pp. 141-273.

[52] Vimalananda, 1963, p. 316B.

[53] Knox, 1681, 1995, p. 40.

[54] Ievers, p. 63.

[55] This description of oaths was sourced from Ievers, 1899, p. 108. Also see Vimalananda, 1963, p. 319, and Hettiarachchi, D. E., ed. 2019, p. 42.

tied around the writs of oath takers readying for this oath. He cannot use the hand for any purpose until the oil is brought to a boiling point in the container and ready for dipping in it.

Dharmayata Ata Gasa Divireema	Taking the oath by placing the hand on a religious book.
Wee Diviya	Swearing on rice. Also called *Karal Diviya,* using a bunch of rice panicles to settle a dispute involving a rice field.
Hee Ket Diviya	Another method to resolve a conflict between two individuals about a paddy field.
Polawata Ata Gasā Divireema	Touching the earth and taking the oath.
Irata Ata Gasā Divireema	Swearing by looking at the sun.
Oluwata Ata Gasa Divireema	This is a common practice in some villages in Nuwarakalaviya.
Weli Uda Damā Divireema	Swearing by throwing up a hand of sand.
Tirasarayen Divireema	Swearing before the Buddha statue.
Pan Divireema	Taking oath with reed (*pan*). A hand of reed is spread on the field which is the subject of dispute. The person claiming ownership of the plot of land picks up the reed first.
Káta Sākki, Káta Allanawā	Touching a pebble on the hand of a *Mohottāla* or an authorized person to assert or deny a fact.
Dina Pála	Custom to tie three knots on a piece of cloth hung on a public place as a notice to villagers to assemble for a swearing.
Keta Padi Alleema	Some Rata Sabhā in Nuwarakalaviya practiced a punishment method like a promise or an oath. After a minor dispute between two villagers, instead of a cash fine or any other punishment, the accused party was asked to touch a *hee kāta* (clump of soil from a field ridge in a paddy). Sometimes a *mulādäniya* would ask the respondent to touch another object like *killote* (brass chunam vial) or his walking stick.[56]

PRISONERS IN PUBLIC WORK PROJECTS. People who shirked public work assignments, particularly the road construction and irrigation related work, went to jail. These prisoners were also ordered to labor in quarries as punishment. Between 1827 and 1830, labor of 27125 man-days were supplied for the construction of the wooden arch bridge across Mahaweli river at Peradeniya.[57] This project consumed 1039 days and 150 convicts working each day and rising to 1000 towards the end of it.[58] In 1839, 4197 labor-days were used for publi c works by prisoners. In Kalutara district too, in 1810, prisoners were used for road building projects. These prisoners were compensated for their labor. In 1840, however, Governor James Mackenzie

---

56 Hettiarachchi, D. E., ed. 1979, 2019, p. 49.
57 Munasinghe, 1972, p. 133; p. 83.
58 Sivasundaram, 2013, p.237.

abolished the policy of using prisoners for public work projects.[59] But, in the last decades of the 19th century, prisoners were back in public work projects. They were in restoration of masonry work in excavations at archaeological sites like top of the Abhayagiri stupa in Anuradhapura.[60]

Utilizing people in public work projects in different shades of confinement existed in colonial times. In what Nila Wickramasinghe phrased as the Chilaw Experiment, in early decades of British rule in Sri Lanka, Coviar, Nalavar and Pallar caste people enslaved in higher caste homes in Jaffna were offered freedom by the government in exchange for labor in public work projects, particularly on canals between Negombo and Chilaw on the western seaboard. These slaves were purchased from their owners by the Government Agent at a set price. With documents provided as proof by the Jaffna Collector (Government Agent) they came to Chilaw to be housed and fed to do hard labor, usually for a period of one year. The manumission certificates were retained by the Collector to be awarded to slave upon their return after the work assignment. Agency of this policy guaranteed the slaves returned to Jaffna to begin life as free men. But some stayed in the western coastal areas.[61]

BANISHMENT. Convicts were sent to live in villages that were appointed as insalubrious due to serious diseases like fever that could be contagious. There were 13 such villages in Hath Kōrale, Uva, Bintenna, Matale, Walapone and Dumbara areas.[62] Expulsion to a *Rodi* village was the punishment imposed on those who participated in incest or accused of eating beef. Except for the early 19th century British who sent shiploads of Kandyan prisoners to Mauritius island and the last King to Vellore in India, there is no report of banishment of people to other countries by Sri Lankan rulers.[63]

EXPULSION FROM VARIGA. In Nuwarakalaviya, a villager's expulsion from the variga by a Rata Sabhāwa for the misfortune of getting caught in a serious caste or variga violation had been the norm in the past. If few such families found themselves expelled from their variga, its unintended consequence was that they formed a village of their own in a new location. It can then become a 'village of one caste.' However, this scenario does not look universal. Brow (1996) noted it was difficult to assume that villagers always subordinated pursuit of their individual interests to the discipline of communal norms.[64]

BIZARRE PUNISHMENTS. In instances of adultery, social norms allowed the injured husband to beat the aggressor.[65] Wrapping non-poisonous snakes around the body of the convicted person, *tovil tahanam* (a common form of prohibitions in Rata Sabhāwa customs), pulling out the tongue, and burning around the waist

---

[59] Munasinghe, 1972, pp. 83-84.

[60] Ferguson, J. 1893, p. 360.

[61] Wickramasinghe, Nira, 2020, p. 126.

[62] Vimalananda, 1963, p. 316A.

[63] On the reverse, Sri Lanka had been the receiving end of banished prisoners, including royalty from neighboring countries. See Ronit Ricci (*Banishment and Belonging*, 2019) for a study of relocation of Malay and Javanese royalty and elites to Sri Lanka (Serendib) by Dutch colonists in 18th-century.

[64] Brow, 1996, p. 55.

[65] Pridham, 1849, p. 218.

(branding?) are some other forms of unusual punishments. Description of *tovil tahanama* will come in the coming pages.

There was a time the husband was allowed to kill the wife who was caught in the act of adultery.[66] After the fall of Kandy, these punishments were abolished by the colonial government.[67] Then they introduced the forms of punishment imported from England that were no different than what were in practice locally. As Assistant Government Agent in Kandy, Leonard Woolf (1961) was required to be present in some instances to give signal to commence the punishment at Bogambara prison in late 19th century. He wrote, "[…] our criminal law was both uncivilized and stupidly inefficient as a method of punishing or deterring crime" (p. 169).

Fig. 25. *The Supreme Court on the Judicature of Ceylon*, c.1818-19. Jury Box at right of the judge. James Stephanoff (1787-1874) at Yale Center for British Art.

COLONIAL COURTS AND JUSTICE. After the British took full control of the island, they found five systems of municipal common laws in force. They were: 1) Roman Dutch Law; 2) Thesewalame Law (for Malabars, including Tamils – inhabitants of Jaffna); 3) Mussalmans Law for Muslims; 4) Mukkuwas Law in Batticaloa, and 5) Kandyan Law.[68] Shirani Bandaranayake is of the view that not much evidence exists about the manner of Portuguese and Dutch local government legal systems,[69] nor information how they interacted with native institutions. But Portuguese reached an inflection point in their administration of the colony when the native King Dharmapala (1551-1597) died. To sort out the affairs of the country,

---

[66] Pieris, P E, 1920, p. 43.

[67] Hettiarachchi, D. E., ed. 1979, p. 26.

[68] Pereira, James Cecil Walter, 1899, Sources of our Laws. *The Ceylon Law Review*, Vol.1 No.1, pp. 5-8.

[69] Bandaranayake, 1986, p. 43.

after the two-day Malvana Convention held late that year with local representatives from each *Kōrale*, it was agreed that the Portuguese officials would guarantee on behalf of the King of Portugal that the "laws and customs of the Sinhalese should be maintained inviolate forever."[70]

As it turned out, they did not honor this agreement fully. But it is fair to assume, however, that on occasions colonists' laws must have functioned on the island with a degree of understanding, as needed often, allowing local traditions to coexist to prevent native displeasure. Yasmine Gooneratne (1970) put forward another view. Although 'they did not set out to destroy systems of established administration,' even with the promise of maintaining laws and customs forever, as pointed out, Portuguese 'systematically manipulated the native institutions to serve their commercial and private gains (116-123).

Dutch who overpowered Portuguese in Sri Lanka abandoned *Gam Sabhāwa* tradition and adopted conducting judicial functions with certain concessions in line with their own legal system. They set up country courts system called *Landraaden* (Land Court) in the coastal areas to reduce the burden of *Dissavaru*. One such court was held in Matara district,[71] and this court may have been in existence since 1661[72] while another was established in Batticaloa.[73] The Landraaden made available an arena for cross-cultural encounters: victims, perpetrators of the crime, and witnesses from all segments (cross-caste?) of society. Dutch and native elites were judges, and local advisors, translators (and interpreters?) helped them.[74]

Governor Falck Willem (1765-85) had asked the *Vanniyār* (Wannia) and Mukkuwa Chiefs of Puttalama to prepare 'a statement of their customs,' to familiarize with the native ways. He also directed the Chiefs in Batticaloa, similar to *Vanniyār*s of Nuwarakalaviya, to administer justice through Landraad in accordance with Sinhalese practice.[75] In Colombo, the Landraad consisted of a *Fiscaal* (the Vice President), *Tombohouder* (Keeper of Register of Land), *Eerste Landmeter* (Surveyor), and *Kapitein der Mahabadde* (Superintendent the Cinnamon Department). These officials were all Europeans. To them joined a Dissāva, the Maha Mudliyar of the Governor's Gate, and Atapattu Mudliyar or Mudliyar of Dissāva, all being natives and permanent members supported from time to time by lower officials.

The Dutch also had inferior courts called *Civiele Raad* (Civil Courts) and *Stads Raad* (Town Courts). They had no jurisdiction over criminal matters. They kept records of the proceedings and were called 'courts of records.' Such a mix of native and Dutch officials working together in a Landraad tribunal was a marked difference from the makeup of Rata Sabhāwa practiced in Nuwarakalaviya.

Landraads continued in Maritime Province even after British took over it in 1796. But by proclamation on August 20, 1801, Governor North abolished them in

---

[70] Pieris, P.E. 1920, p. 139.

[71] Liyanage, Jagath Premasiri, 2008, *Matara Wansaya* Vol. I, p. 330.

[72] T. Nadaraja, 1972, *The Legal System of Ceylon in Its Historical Setting* p. 7.

[73] Pieris, P.E., 1918, 2018, p. 124.

[74] Schrikker, Alicia and Ekama, Kate J., 2017, Through the Lens of Slavery… *Sri Lanka at the Crossroads of History*, eds. Biedermann, Zoltan and Strathern, p. 186.

[75] Pieris, P.E., 1918, 2018, p. 124.

Galle and Jaffna. Then on November 10, 1802, all Landraads were abolished, and their functions were merged with the colonial Civil Courts system.[76]

The Dutch decided the law practiced in the land must be their own, but the native officials like *mudaliyar* and similar titled persons could provide guidance on local customs to the European members of the court. Mudaliyar and other officials like *vidāne* and *Kōrāla,* had authority to decide minor disputes of natives. These officials seem to have not kept any records in Galle and Jaffna.

Fig. 26. Details of the jury box in *The Supreme Court on the Judicature of Ceylon.* Interpreter (*Tholka Mudaliyar*) is standing with folded hands facing the jury. James Stephanoff, 1787 -1874, at Yale Center for British Art.

Few decades later, in the Maritime Provinces, the British were in control with their laws in full force, and even conducting trials by jury (Fig. 26). Under the Ordinance 19 of 1844, government agents had to prepare for this a list of qualified jurors whose only disqualification from serving was "not being of sufficient intelligence and respectability and proficiency in English, Sinhalese and Tamil."[77] Decades earlier, as slavery was still prevalent across the island, Alexander Johnston, Chief Justice of Ceylon (1811-1819) encouraged juries to display their high moral values by voluntary emancipation of the newborn children of their slaves.[78]

In the early decades of British control, fearing a flare up of hidden embers of national sentiments, the administration moved to allow Kandyans and their Chieftains to continue enjoying extant customs and traditions in the provinces. From the manner the British colonial administration allowed this to happen along with their own laws, it is plausible they took note of what worked, and what did not for the erstwhile colonizers they replaced. From the beginning, the British hoped the indigenous institutions implied in the Treaty Article 4 of the Kandyan Convention, and acting as a counterbalance to their own would enhance the new

---

[76] Turner, L. J. B., 1919, The Civil Government of the Maritime Provinces… *Ceylon Antiquary and Literary Register,* Vol. IV Part III January 1919, 123-134.

[77] Ferguson, A.M. 1868, P. 59.

[78] Wickramasinghe, Nira, 2020, *Slave in a Palanquin,* p. 107.

Western-oriented judicial philosophy to prosper. Justice Johnston believed in the ability of the natives to sort out their disputes with understanding of fairness and reason. Within weeks after the British completed securing power in Kandyan and Maritime Provinces, D'Oyly began getting involved directly in disputes that had been unresolved up to his time, or issues that developed anew among the Chiefs and other subaltern officers. As the institutions, including the court system for the provinces sanctioned by the Governor got down to business, D'Oyly became the coordinating arm of the government in Kandy.

British court system had been in operation in full steam successfully in Maritime Provinces since 1796. To show interest for and acknowledgment of the native traditions and customs, and for concerns that citizens, particularly the elites, would be displeased if the colonial law might interfere with their age-old customs, the British Governors often overruled statutes in various Charters of Justice in force in the early 19th century. Nira Wickramasinghe (2020) cites a case in 1818 when a Judge ruled against a Mudliyar of Durava caste who beat a laborer for deserting work. But Governor Robert Brownrigg (1812-1820) stepped "in fear of subverting the social order" and enforced Regulation 5 of 1818 which allowed headmen to arrest and employ laborers who went against caste obligations. In another instance, the Governor suspended Clause LXXXII of Charter of Justice of 1801 "on the basis of respect for tradition." Clause LXXXII required justices and peace officers and similar officials to abide by the laws and the Supreme Court of Judicature on the island as a Magistrate would do in England (p. 185).

When the colonial courts in Kandyan country opened doors, the residents soon became aware of its novelty, straightforwardness, and consistent manner judges dispensed justice. Now, the citizens had a guaranteed and uniform system of justice to seek help. The result of this new phenomenon was that the court system got inundated with all manner of litigations brought by the people. Disputes, some which had been unresolved for decades or generations, found a ray of hope before the new courts. But to decide upon them, the courts needed more than just oral presentations that were the trademark of the old *Gam Sabe* in Kandy highlands or the Rasa Sabhāwa in Nuwarakalaviya. That was when the economy of traditional documents in use at that time – *Sannas* and *ola* books written on palm leaves or copper strips – found their niche.

The British judges were quite comfortable using them as evidentiary documents. Practically in every other page in the *Gazetteer* of A. C. Lawrie are hundreds of *Sannas* reproduced, some in extraordinary detail, some that had been scribed as far back as few centuries earlier. These *Sannas* were entered into record as evidence in cases involving land disputes, succession of property including slaves, and *rājakāriya* obligations to temples, all brought by parties seeking resolution by the new phenomenon – the colonial courts.

But contrary to what citizens believed, dispensing justice by the British in 19th century Sri Lanka just as their predecessors was not without shortcomings. Nor there is much written about it. Save for folklore and few records by native writers, British penchant for judicial improprieties had not been given full disclosure by writers in the 19th century because they were mostly British or natives acquiescent to their colonial masters.

Meanwhile, the colonial administration slowly and surely began to tighten their grip on the population. Three decades between the two rebellions – Uva of 1818 and Matale of 1848 – the people suffered through many injustices, not a bit different from what their ancestors few generations ago experienced at the hands of other European colonizing powers. Their dual exigencies, i.e., traditional institutions of the natives and western legal concepts failed to protect them as seen from the trying times of 1818 and 1848. Governor Torrington crushed the Matale rebellion with such force and unforgiving tyranny, no one in the island took arms against the British, even remotely resembling a rebellion for the next 100 years!

In as much as the cruelties ordered by Governor Torrington (1847 – 1850) to crush Matale revolt were of such vicious nature, some colonial writers did not have the heart to write about it. Some conveniently went along with the administration and kept the truth in the dark allowing the Governor's whims to foster. For fear of finding themselves on the wrong side of the Governor's rule, native writers too were not willing to take a chance by reporting about brutal control of the people.

But when the news of Torrington's vindictive rule sifted across the oceans to American soil, writers there did not hesitate to write about the truth. In 1851, Thomas Prentice Kettell) reported in *United States Magazine and Democratic Review* under the title, *English in Ceylon,* about crushing the rebellion. He called Governor's policy as 'Ceylon Tragedy.' He continued:

> The period embraced between the years 1819 and 1846, was not remarkable for any extraordinary occurrences in Ceylon; suffice it to say, that the history of the island during this interval, is made up of patient suffering and distress on the part of the natives, and of heartless tyranny and exaction on the part of their foreign rulers. …Courts martial, composed of subaltern officers, ignorant of the language of the country, tried, convicted, sentenced, and put to instant death, hundreds of the innocent inhabitants; and this, not only in violation of all law, human and divine, but in utter contempt of the 7th article of the treaty (Kandyan Convention of 1815), to which we have already referred, which stipulates that no sentence of death can be carried into execution against any inhabitant, except by the written warrant of the British Governor or Lieutenant Governor for the time being. (pp. 409-412)

In a letter by T.A. Drought, commandant of Kandy to a fellow officer who was sitting as the judge in the Court Marshal of 1848 Matale Rebellion mirrored the thinking of the British administration in Sri Lanka across globe at that time. A portion of the *English in Ceylon* feature article written by the American reproduced above[79] was read at the House of Commons by Mr. H. Baillies, MP for Inverness-shire:

---

[79] Baillies, H. MP. *Hansard,* Ceylon, May 27, 1851, Columns 20-26.

Much has been said of the magnanimity of the British soldier. Let the following letters, addressed by the Commandant of Kandy, to the presiding officer of one of the Court martial (in Matale) hounding him on in his bloody career, serve as a specimen:

'My dear Watson: You are getting on swimmingly. Impress on the Court that there is no necessity for taking down the evidence in detail; so, they are satisfied with the guilt or innocence of the individual, that is sufficient for them to find and sentence. This is the law and the mode.

Yours, T.A. Drought, Lieut. Col. Commanding. August 16, 1848.'

(Columns 20-26)

On orders of the same commanding officer, Capt. Bird holding a Court-Marshall in Kurunegala caused a man shot within half an hour after the trial (Column 22-23). The Hansard of 1851 also records snippet of injustices Col. Drought brought upon suspects in 1849 including Dullawe, the 1818 Dissava of Nuwarakalaviya. When Dullawe died in 1849, H. Baillies, MP, recorded that he was the "the last of the Chieftains alive who had surrendered Kandyan Kingdom to British." By the British government's own accounts, he was wrongly accused by Drought as having supported the 1848 rebellion. The MP, debating in the House, told that: "[…] There was not a particle of evidence to show that he (Dullawe) related to the outbreak." While Dullawe was imprisoned waiting for the trial, his house in Udasiya Pattuwa, Matale was plundered by British soldiers and their servants. Finally, his properties were auctioned off while he was still a prisoner of the government.[80]

These cruelties of the law and order of the British in Sri Lanka were not accidents or co-incidents. At the same time when the Empire was in full force forcing genocide of the Tasmanian and Australian indigenous peoples, and two years after MP Baily made his comments about Sri Lanka, in 1853 British novelist Charles Dickens, supporter of the British policy of genocide in Tasmania wrote:

[…] if we have anything to learn from the Noble Savage (indigenous Tasmanians) it is what to avoid. His virtues are a fable; his happiness is a delusion; his nobility is nonsense… and the world will be all the better when his place knows him no more. (p. 337).

When the British expanded the court system decades after fall of Kandy, the Nuwarakalaviya was still sorting out their conflicts through the good old Rata Sabhāwa. In early 1833, Governor Horton proposed to have an Assistant Government Agent in Anuradhapura whose duty involved working as the magistrate as well. Governor took this step after acknowledging difficulty Nuwarakalaviya citizens had to seek justice from the British Courts. They had to travel fifty to one hundred miles to file a case, possibly south to Kurunegala or north to Jaffna.[81]

PRACTICALITIES AND DIFFICULTIES UNDER RATA SABHĀWA. As time passed, while circumstances slowly began to confront the realities of the people in

---

[80] Baillies, H. MP. *Hansard*, Ceylon, May 27, 1851, Column 27.
[81] Governor Horton's letter in Jan 14, 1833, to Colonial Secretary, cited in Sivasundaram, 2013, p. 156.

the new colony, British judiciary also began to slip off its promises it kept with the proviso of the Kandyan Convention. Albeit the British agreed to continue with the 'Traditional administrative system,' citizens soon found, K. M. De Silva (1981) wrote, that the "traditional system was not unreservedly guaranteed, and the British retained the right and power to introduce changes as and when they deemed fit" (p.259).

In the context of cultural and simplest forms of judicial practices, particularly in the Nuwarakalaviya, no decision of the British colonial government, even if it came late in their time in Sri Lanka, was more consequential than the abolishment of the nobility, and subsequently the Rata Sabhāwa. The region lost centuries old practices and was exposed to new systems for dealing with minor conflicts and norms that they needed adapting to. Communities found themselves drifting after moorings of old customs and traditions came loose as the Chiefs were suddenly forced out of the scene. Now, instead of his own village or one nearby, a villager had to go to the court in the city often as far as 50 to 100 miles away to deal with a minor conflict. There is no doubt it must have taken a few decades for communities to forget the good old systems even after they had been in the rearview mirror for some time.

However, Rata Sabhāwa idea refused to die and shimmered in the hearts of the people. There is no doubt, the need to settle differences through less cumbersome means by casuists among them rather than outsiders who often did not even speak their language remained a priority among villagers. So, the allure of Rata Sabhāwa remained undiminished as illustrated by reports of few sessions convened in 1945, a decade after the tradition relapsed into twilight. Again, sometime in the early 1950s the last known Rata Sabhāwa, a fitting finale, was held in an inconspicuous village, after which traditions, customs, and the institution, all evanesced into history.

One of the most notable outcomes of the death of the Rata Sabhāwa system was the loss of simplicity of conflict resolution. For the old-timers the change must have been hard to adapt to. Having to come before a foreign system to resolve their ingrown issues was a culture shock to them in many ways. In rural Nuwarakalaviya, lawyering was not heard of. The villagers could not understand the laws, much less speak the language it was written in. It was a much worse situation than their unwritten but well-trodden ways through customs and traditions. De Silva (1981) writes "Unfamiliar formalities and technicalities were enforced in an alien language, while traditional institutions like *Gam Sabhā* and traditional laws and customs were devalued" (p. 260).

They were asked then to sit through and participate in the proceedings through an intermediary – the all-powerful interpreter or *tholka mudaliyar*, a job became so visible and considered distinguished, they began to be considered equal in stature to the *Ratemahatvaru* in Kandyan districts, or Mudliyars in Maritime Provinces. I have been summoned few times to interpret in cases involving Sri Lankans in foreign courts and understand the intricacies of two languages trying to say the same thing without missing the essence of conversation as small and simple as the meaning of a momentary pause.

Observers have noted that early interpreting and translating attempts had encountered difficulties. These early interpreters faced problems with the local dialects, while later translators and interpreters showed difficulties with English and even customs characteristic to the region. Often, this problem resulted in grim and devastating consequences in our history as evinced from the "mishandling" of the 1848 Kandyan Rebellion due to a deficit of language proficiency. Phillip Anstruther, the Colonial Secretary of the island (1830-1840) commenting on the lack of communication between officials and locals stated that "there is a complete curtain drawn in Ceylon between the government and the governed; no person concerned with government understands the language [of the people]" (Select Committee Report, 1850: 344).[82] Knowing how a native interpreter can easily misinterpret what he heard or his unfamiliarity of ways, slangs, and language in distant villages, it is not hyperbolic even to suggest that often justice did not flow through fairly and smoothly for villagers in colonial courts.

Directing conflictive issues between parties to a larger and complex matrix of bureaucracy of the government with laws of a distant Empire resulted in villagers' reluctance to seek help leaving the bothering question to ferment into unpalatable consequences. In this regard, the end of Chieftains tradition was an extraordinary development, not least because it ended the centuries old fraternity of nobility, but it forced the villagers to face their societal travails without an alternate judicature which could have continued to function tuned with their ways and means. In summation, closure of Rata Sabhāwa was no doubt an unappetizing reality the villagers had to face.

In the Maritime Districts, the Dutch neither endorsed nor sanctioned private or separate judicial proceedings in Mudliyar's homes for the natives. But Mudliyars also participated in Landraaden courts under the supervision of the Dutch officials. British continued somewhat similar judicial practices in these Districts. Therefore, it is not known whether walawwas in Maritime Provinces had courthouses like that found in the homes of the Kandyan Chiefs.

While Chiefs in Kandyan highlands, including Sabaragamuwa, held various forms of judicial proceedings in their homes, whether such proceedings were like Rata Sabhāwa of Nuwarakalaviya is not known. In 2018, when I was standing on the 4-meter-wide corridor encompassing the half-walled airy seating chamber of the courthouse in Kuda Walawwa compound at Madukanda near Vavuniya, it was not lost on me of a time a century ago when the weary and tense multitude gathered here to watch how rural justice delivered its promise to their peers (Fig. 6).

TRADITIONAL KNOWLEDGE AND BREACHES. Particularly interesting is how Traditional Knowledge, also termed as indigenous or local knowledge of Nuwarakalaviya had embodied into the Rata Sabhāwa customs, some of which are understandably silent in *Niti Nighanduwa* (Pali: *Niti* – law, *Nighandu* – glossary, catalogue). According to Kapuruhami Madukanda Ratemahattayā and elders who contributed essays for the SSS, there are 25 instances considered as contraventions and subject to the purview of the Rata Sabhāwa which stands as a buffer to avert any detrimental impact on the stability of the order in a community.

Rata Sabhāwa imposes fines on a villager who shirks his responsibility to participate in common work projects like clearing irrigation ditches to fields or

---

[82] Qtd. in Sandagomi Coperehewa, 2011, Colonialism and Problems of Language Policy. *Sri Lanka Journal of Advanced Social Studies* Vol. 1 (1) Jan - June 2011, (27-52).

repair-work on the tank bund. Also embedded in Traditional Knowledge in Nuwarakalaviya is the awareness of the caste status of citizens of the Maritime Provinces who belonged to the *pāthayō* caste and subjected to marriage constraints as stipulated in variga conventions, a marked difference from the custom of the Kandyan highlands. It is important, *nota bene*, that unlike in villages across Nuwarakalaviya, many conventional caste descriptions elsewhere in Sri Lanka do not have residents of Maritime Provinces labelled as *pāthayō*.

Rata Sabhāwa also stepped in to resolve minor land disputes. If a villager demarcates a tract of forest by clearing an area as small as a threshing floor, *kamatha*, the tradition accords him the ownership around it unequivocally to expand as a full-sized chena or garden plot. In *atuhanparaveni* cases (*atu* – branch, twigs; *han* – mark, branding; *paraveni* – possession) where land under review was in possession of the owners for generations, their ancestors first having demarcated it by marking the boundaries as a chena or a paddy field, but no document to show for it, infinite wisdom and traditional knowledge of it's past by the old-timers in the village was sought for an unequivocal resolution. Having old-timers who may also be *mulādānivaru* in the Sabhāwa, and knowledgeable of the boundaries of or prior ownership and any other information about a land at issue was a helpful moderating element in the resolution process.

Other issues that came under the Rata Sabhāwa were *kula pali* (disgraceful acts), exogamous marriage, e.g., out-of-*Varige* person or marriage with a low-caste and involvement with a family or person who is under a *tahanama*. Also came under the Rata Sabhāwa laws were conducts considered not in accord with its procedures, regulations, breach of etiquette while Sabhāwa is in session and acts that brought disrepute not only on the Sabhāwa authority, but on the *Varige*. Furthermore, defamatory acts or utterings directed at a Rata Sabhā session or a participant, and when the Sabhāwa is not in session, disparaging acts or comments towards a community member, disgraceful act(s) with a variga member or a member of another *Varige*, false and malicious accusations directed at another, dishonorable acts, demeaning utterances, or calumnious statements are other breaches or acts that drew Rata Sabhāwa scrutiny. Kapuruhami Madukanda Ratemahattayā's description of Rata Sabhāwa in Chapter 14 will also elaborate these breaches further.

There were three minor infractions a person could be accused of committing while Rata Sabhāwa is in session.

    a. *Ath veradi* – An inadvertent or accidental violation due to ignorance (fine imposed: 2½ -7½ Ridi).

    b. *Kata veradi* – Inadvertent utterances that are improper or imprudent and have the potential to lead to interruptions of the proceedings (fine imposed: 2½ -7½ Ridi).

    c. *Bat veradi* – Violations committed during the feast given to the officials and participants after the Rata Sabhāwa proceedings, and taking meals with someone who had been placed under a ban (*tahanama*) by a Rata Sabhāwa or by one of its officials (fine imposed: 7½ Ridi).

In addition to Rata Sabhāwa, there are also instances where feasts were held in the village for special occasions like weddings, receiving dignitaries, and religious or cultural events.[83] In these instances, too, there are etiquette related to the feast. If someone was found to have been wanting of convivial behavior and good mannerisms at the feast in the *Maduwa*, he is immediately tagged as one who breached etiquettes. He was then ordered to eat one more *bat ahura* (a fistful of rice) as the punishment. It then becomes an entertaining or amusing moment for all participating in the feast!

Under the Rasa Sabhāwa tradition, sorcery is a breach that is also punishable. As in many societies, in Sri Lanka too, use of sorcery and seeking assistance from supernatural and mythological pantheon for their purported powers for healing have been a tradition for millennia. In the same way, there are those who use rituals to direct maleficent thoughts and acts to evoke harm to others. These rituals are called *huniyam*. In the time of Rata Sabhāwa, *huniyam* were a concern to villagers.[84] It drew scorn, fear, and displeasure of the community. Usually, when a villager shows signs of psychological problems or becomes behaviorally unstable without no apparent reason, others who are around him begin to suspect that a sorcerer must be at work unleashing supernatural and maleficent forces against their relative. Even in late 20th century, if things did not go well for a villager, he may rush to place the blame on a *huniyam* act conducted by a fellow villager.

Immediately, incantations to deities begin to implore undoing of the bewitchment. This is done by placing a hand of betel leaves (*bulat dáhána*) with chunam, some sweets (*kávili dáhána*), cut half of a lemon (*dehi kapeema*) - all or fragments of them, in a votive tray and ensconced in a half open box of slivered and weaved young coconut fronds. This box is placed on a stand of four sticks (*pideniya*). When found near a house of a person, this ominous sight draws fear and suspicion that an enchanter had performed a *huniyam* spell there. If someone is certain that he has nothing do with these objects but experiencing difficulties with sicknesses or any losses, immediate concern is that someone had directed maleficent thoughts and energy towards him by performing an evil act. He then seeks help. He approaches the Rata Sabhāwa to investigate to find those responsible.

Since the time of Kings Narendra Singhe (1707–1739) and Kirti Sri Raja Singhe (1750-1782), sorcerers have been punished with death.[85] In Nuwarakalaviya, anthropologist Brow in 1983 found villagers in Kukulawa and nearby Samādhigama, bound by kinship connections, were still believing in sorcery. In 1980, over the disagreement with the distribution of houses in the newly built Samādhigama under the village awakening program, they nearly began fistfights accusing maleficent acts and sorcery against each other.

---

[83] *Kiribandi Pujāwa* in Walimapothana near Horowpothana, *Gambádi Rājakāriya* in Kukulawa near Kahatagasdigiliya, Hururuwawe Dewale (Wāsala) Perahera are such local events where people come to feast.

[84] Ievers, 1899 qtd. in Pieris, Ralph, 1956 p. 255; Kapuruhami, 1948 p. 45. In folklore of Nuwarakalaviya and Hath Korale, *Huniyam* yaka or devatava is a formidable demon. He is the son of Susiri, Queen of Sagalpura in Madurata (India). He rides a horse and has six apparitions: 1. Kela (cala) Oddisa (demon of incurable diseases; 2. Naga Oddisa (demon of serpents); 3. Kumara Oddisa (demon of price); 4. Demala Oddisa (Tamil demon); 5. Gopalu Oddisa (demon of cattle) and 6. Raja Oddisa (royal demon) (Dandiris de Silva Gooneratne (1865) *JRAS* Vol. 4, No. 13, pp. 1-118

[85] *Niti Nighanduwa,* 1880 p. xxxii.

6. OF CASTE DYNAMICS AND *GAM BÁNDEEMA*

*A*lthough began as casteless bands, as time passed, humans realized they needed barriers between them to sort out differences and demands for survival. To achieve this goal, boundary lines between groups were carved out. Then within the bands, caste inched in as a tool of necessity. These were the main imperatives of the spread of human societies. By the time Rata Sabhāwa came around, its practices involved more of a state of guarantee of peace in the communities. Caste practices played a major role in achieving this goal. We must abide by the historical perspective under which it operated. But attempting to practice it now is an oddity.

The people who were part of this system, regardless of the locality, did not understand any other way as caste was ingrained in their social conscience after millennia of division and existence. But such a 'state of existence' was achieved at a great price. In 2023, Pulitzer Prize winner Isabel Wilkerson wrote:

> "[…] Caste system relies on strife and inequality to sustain itself. It programs people to believe they have no stake in the well-being of those they have been told are beneath them, those they are told are unworthy, undeserving. It makes for a less magnanimous society, a built-in us verses them distance between groups. Because of the caste system, we more readily turn against one another. Because of caste, we insufficiently protect one another. (34-40)

People were hardly aware of the theoretical nuances of caste as we see it now. Their objective was to adjust to the extant medium of civic polity and make it through one way or another, so the group's co-existence with other groups was safeguarded and guaranteed. It was essential for groups to be mindful of the manner of participation in cultural and social activities, including marriage and kinship rapport between villagers that were all subjects of Rata Sabhāwa concept and caste norms.

In Nuwarakalaviya, a village was a community of homogenous people guided by kinship, caste, and the locality.[1] Caste upheld the social organization passed down through oral traditions, and one that embraced its tangible protocols like interactions within a community and between communities.[2] Rata Sabhāwa functioned as the poster board to run these protocols as observed and designed by tradition.

Strict *Maduwé Chārithra* (customs of the meeting hall) practiced in the Rata Sabhāwa in Nuwarakalaviya and Kandyan areas in the first decades of 19th century[3,4] were guided by social hierarchy protocols described by Kapuruhami Madukanda Ratemahattayā in 1948. These customs include the seating protocol: number of

---

NOTES

[1] Brow, 1996, p. 50.

[2] For description of caste relations existed in early 20th century Sri Lanka, see Bryce Ryan, 1953 *Caste in Modern Ceylon: The Sinhalese System in Transition.* New Jersey: Rutgers University Press.

[3] John Davy, 1821, 2006, p. 167.

[4] D'Oyly, 1917, p. 49.

rolled out reed mats, number of linen sheets laid out on them, and dining protocols: sheets of banana leaves placed to serve food at the feast according to the rank and caste of the person and so forth. There are other nuances that I will discuss later.

In 19th century, there had been instances where Rata Sabhāwa in Nuwarakalaviya showed diametrical ways regarding caste neutrality. Once Bulankulame *Ratemahattayā* who held no employment in the colonial administration at the time was at ease ordering a government official to execute a decision reached against a person by a *mulādāniya.* He was simply acting based on what he believed was the authority vested in him with caste norms at the time. After becoming aware of *Ratemahattayā*'s unorthodox request and thinking that such efforts of *walawwa* officials might become a problem for government officials who were intended to be caste neutral, the Assistant Government Agent advised them to disregard the orders of such "pseudo-officials."[5]

On the other hand, in instances of caste-related issues, especially the improper relationships between high-caste women and low-caste men that had the potential to shake social foundations, the Assistant Government Agent referred them to the *Ratemahattayā* of Nuwara Gam Palatha who settled the conflict after a hearing at a Rata Sabhāwa, and the families involved were 'rehabilitated.'[6] Therefore, It is reasonable to suggest the existence of a state of amicable relationship of sharing concerns between the provincial colonial machinery and the native institutions when a caste conflict threatened to pollute the peace of a community. In the same way, the colonial government was bent on upholding its own laws, so did the Nuwarakalaviya institutions practicing their caste customs. Such vicissitudes in the practice of laws and customs during Sri Lanka's colonial days are not unusual. In 1906, even the Supreme Court Justice J. Middleton noted that Ceylon as a "polygynous country with diverse systems of laws...."[7]

***GAM BÁNDEEMA* AND WATER-DEPENDENT CASTE LOCALIZATION.** From ancient times, a community of people coalesced in so many ways as a unit to identify it as a village. Each village retained certain characteristics that represented their make-up based on cultural, economic, and political affiliations. If forced relocation e.g., resettlement programs of the government were the reason for the start of a community, such a village may look diverse in caste norms because its members came from diverse backgrounds. I will describe a few such instances in later pages.

During a time when caste system was the bobbin which helped make colors of the social fabric, if groups of multi-caste and multi-variga families got together to build a tank and a village below it, the clash of traditions and customs were sure to influence the web of social interactions and even threaten the stability of the community. To avoid such unhelpful certainties, several villages of similar caste identity opted to join as a *Varige.* It was a convenient and good social investment

---

5 Diary of Government Agent, Nuwarakalaviya, Oct. 6, 1862; SLNA 41/245 cited in Karunananda, U. B., 1990, *Nuwarakalaviya 1815-1900*, p. 46.

6 Ievers, 1899, p. 93.

7 Jayewardene, H.D.1907, 1951, in Cassim et al. v. Dingihamy et al. (1906), NLR Vol. 9, p. 274.

for the residents. Then a *varige* acted like a conglomeration of small republics with enhanced visibility and influence among communities.

Caste helped every village to maintain an association and character in varying degrees with the neighboring villages.[8] This is evident from the demographic construction and distribution of villages during last quarter of the 19th century in North Central Province. In 1873, at the time of its creation as a new province carved out of the Northern Province, the North Central Province consisted of 1061 villages. Soon a remarkable characteristic came to light. Among the villages in the new province, only 9 were occupied by residents with multi-caste origin![9] A century later, during his field research in 1983 in Kukulawa village, about 15 kilometers east of Anuradhapura, anthropologist Brow also found that this situation – unitary caste in a village – had not changed much as underlying cultural currents that shaped communities a century ago still found space in the village to maintain a unitary identity.[10]

Large reservoirs like Kalaweva, anchored clusters of old but homogeneous villages, each occupied by a different caste, only connected by its arterial irrigation canals. The Mahaweli Diversion Project, which began in 1970, seemed to tweak this state by developing new areas as communities often bordering existing villages. These new communities have shown lesser caste sensitivity following the influx of people with diverse cultural and caste backgrounds.

In the Dry Zone particularly, existing villages must have been started from ground up during one time or another by few families or individuals who were naturally closely related or of the same caste or shared common interests with potential for building future kinships. A group of families can descend upon a dilapidated or abandoned small irrigation tank in the jungle, or an unmolested and mostly ephemeral stream with potential for damming. Such locations were not hard to find. Quoting 1982 Survey Department maps, C.R. Panabokke reported that there were 15373 village tanks and 7753 of them were abandoned. In the North Central Province alone, there were 4017 tanks and 1922 of them had been left fallow.[11]

The families then start building the irrigation infrastructure and the dwelling compound – basic hovels (*karal ge*), first near it or below the bund to be restored.[12] By sharing the labor for building the community, they earn capital to share water rights from the tank[13] and space to carve-out their share of the plots to grow rice and build a home garden. This commonality was the notion that made the *gambándeema* (building a village from ground up) possible.[14] As time passes,

---

[8] Nandadeva Wijesekera, 1990, *The Sinhalese,* p. 224.

[9] Ievers, 1899, p. 90.

[10] Brow, 1996, p. 12.

[11] Panabokke, C.R. (2002). *Evolution, Present Status and Issues Concerning Small Tank System in Sri Lanka.* Colombo: IWMI, *p.* 5.

[12] Personally, I know a derelict tank once, Mugappalliya, about 15 hectares in area, three kilometers above Maradankalla near Mihintale. This tank was restored in early1970s by few families from Maradankalla and aswaddumized below the bund as a collective of paddy fields after building houses alongside it.

[13] Leach, 1961, p. 23.

[14] Codrington, 1938, pp. 62-65.

descendants of these pioneers too naturally inherit rights to shared ownership of the tank, the village, capital it built and other resources around it. Families are of the same *Varige* and caste. Those with similar characteristics were allowed to establish kinships or friendships as time wore on. I call this 'water-dependent caste localization' or a 'one caste – one village' model.

In instances where those who were expelled from the *Varige* by the Rata Sabhāwa after failing to get its decision changed, they could also move out and align either with others ready to welcome them, or others who had gone through similar experience. They stay and participate in building the new community. With new geographical boundaries, now they are considered outside of the former variga or caste jurisdiction and free to build their new identity. Over time, this community multiplies and even expands out to other areas as members of a subgroup or attach to other villages that have similar variga identities or the old *Varige* which has faded memory of the previous break-up.

On rare occasions, they may represent themselves as a subcaste[15] within a *Varige*. The families would multiply, and members spill over to other locations to the extent that after a few generations, they lose traces of their primogenitary roots altogether and become a *Variga* of their own. But their collective memory becomes their folkloric history and as Brow (1996) found, their "communalization is further strengthened by the conviction that what ties (the) group of people together is not just a shared past but a common origin" (p. 21), which supports the claim that they once belonged to the same caste and practiced similar traditions and cultural norms.

Nira Wickramasinghe (2020) found multiple instances of how a group of people discards its former identity and merge into the larger society as a new people. It may not have all the ingredients like that of the expulsion from a *Varige* but show other interesting parallels. She studied the transformation of slaves who after separating from their bonded state and 'becoming another' completely, particularly in early years of British administration in Sri Lanka. [16]

VILLAGE BUILDING BY RESETTLEMENT. This happened in multiple and distinct ways. They are: the most recent effort of model village program called Udāgama begun after 1970; a community chena gradually transforming into a permanent settlement after few seasons of crop production; population overflow from the old *gammedda* (core village compound) triggered by wanting to acquire larger plots of land; easy road access (called *maha pāra* or *pin pāra*) bordering the old village; a villager finds an ephemeral stream through a low-lying section in the landscape with potential to develop as a small tank; often the government demarcating a section of a footpath, cart road, or *pin pāra* running through a lone tract of forest; and providing funds to a few chosen villagers for the partial cost for building their houses and garden plots, a program known in vernacular as 'Projects' (*Viyāpara*). This new community may get their own name and if possible, share water with a nearby village, or topography permitting, build their own tank or get connected to an anchor reservoir for water and land.

---

[15] Ryan 1953, p. 13.
[16] Wickramasinghe, 2020, pp. 195, 196.

Olagama, an uninhabited village with a functioning tank may draw residents from the nearby village which owns it to build homes when its population pressure of the latter becomes unsustainable. These two villages have now become a homogenous community.

Most prominent and observable way villages were built were the irrigation colonization programs by the government launched throughout the 20th century. Peasant families from old villages near and far from the proposed colonization area were selected and brought in as potential residents for settlements that would be developed as caste-blind model communities. The primary livelihood of the new settlers was agriculture, mainly rice farming. Governments hoped these steps would boost food production which in turn improved the revenue base of the government and the villages themselves.

One of the earliest attempts to build irrigation canals for new communities in modern Sri Lanka is Uma-Ela in Uva Province by Governor Henry Ward in 1858.[17] Other major irrigation projects like Huruluwewa, Mahakanadarāwa, Senenayake Samudra, Kalaweva, Minneriya, Rajangana and Padaviya, not necessarily in that order, are models of such new communities established over the years in Eastern and North Central Provinces.

Sri Lankan administrations that came into power after independence from British expanded colonization programs covering more areas. By 1951, there were over 9800 families settled in 24 colonization projects completed or on the way to completion in the Dry Zone.[18] These expedited and sprawling agriculture and irrigation development programs created opportunities for influx of populations with diverse cultural backgrounds into areas that were once uninhabited.[19]

Simultaneously, with the building or restoration of the agricultural and irrigation infrastructure, the government also built houses nearby or along the canals for the new residents who would occupy the project area. In the early phases of these resettlement programs, houses came with somewhat large garden plots as much as 2.5-acres to entice potential candidates[20] to the area hitherto regarded as rampant with diseases like malaria. In later resettlement programs, acreage given to settlers was smaller than the earlier programs. The forest areas under the reservoirs and canals were demarcated to develop into tracts of rice fields. Along with the houses and their garden plots, 6 acres for paddies were bequeathed to each family who will become a shareholder while at the same time providing labor for the development of the new agricultural venture. Running water and electricity became additional incentives for colonization projects that came decades later. First of such

---

[17] White, Herbert (1893), p. 68. *Manual of the Province of Uva*. Colombo.

[18] Farmer, B. H., 1952, Colonization of the Dry Zone of Ceylon. *Journal of the Royal Society of Arts* (JRSA). Vol. 100 No. 4876, June 1952, (547-564).

[19] Soon after independence, as Sri Lanka began to get bogged down in accusatory and divisionary politics on ethnic lines, some began to call the irrigation colonization programs as ethnic expansionist and divisionary projects.

[20] In addition to the peasant resettlement schemes, the government also introduced a Middle-Class Colonization scheme in which the Middle Class (usually well-to-do citizens and former Chiefs in retirement) were granted comparatively large lots of crown land (15 acres of highlands and 10 acres of paddy lands intended for increased crop output) (Farmer, 1952, *JRSA* No. 4876, pp. 547-564; D.B. Diwakara Mahadivulwewa (Personal communication, Nov. 21, 2021).

programs was started in Minneriya in 1902 but had to be abandoned due to insalubrious conditions that were also one of the staple drawbacks in these regions for centuries.

As the new community was made up of a motley group of residents, they were strangers to each other in the beginning, diverse in caste, variga and kinship affinities. Except for the irrigation canal, there was no common denominator that tied them together like in traditional villages where social institutions like Rata Sabhāwa or Variga Sabhāwa and the tank were essential parts of their makeup. In the same way, they obviously did not have community leaders like the *mulādānivaru* in old Nuwarakalaviya villages. There was no need for a *gamarāla* here as irrigation, social and welfare-related needs of the new community were the task of Irrigation Department. Resolving the said issues and quotidian conflicts of the settlers became the role of the career government employees who in the early years treated political neutrality as an inviolable duty. Yuval Noah Harari called a similar situation as an "imagined community" where in the beginning people don't know each other but as time passes begin to think they know each other.[21] Over time they begin community relationships.

A few generations later, these communities acquired their own identities, drew in others of diverse social and cultural backgrounds prospecting in commercial and land opportunities. Unlike the homogeneity found in a traditional village, which often claimed their origin with the *gam bándeema* tradition generations ago, inflow to the new communities of people of varied backdrops and interests made them 'melting pots' of demographic and cultural vagaries. Before long, these pluralist communities emerged with their own identity, acquired names, some just numbers e.g., Tract A, Tract B, Left or Right Bund, Left of Right Canal or simply the Colony, and formed new social and kinship affiliations. This then transformed them to a community with diverse characteristics far removed and often different from the old places they came from.[22] In short, they became villages gradually creating their own social order and culture while individual families tried at every turn to retain some elements of their old traditions intact as much as possible.

Some practices old villagers considered important for survival as a group became unworkable in the new communities. A telling example is the *bethma* custom related to paddy fields. It was an indispensable survival exercise of water economy for the farmers in the old days in the village. When the small irrigation tank did not receive enough water in the beginning of a season to cultivate the whole tract of field, each villager agreed to cultivate only a half of his tract and leave the other half fallow. Reducing the cultivating area by half, watering need also became half, and everyone was assured of some safe crops return better than what would have been expected had water demand remained higher with less water. But on the other hand, in the case of large irrigation schemes, even if the farmers by order of the Irrigation department agreed to cultivate half of each tract, loss of water flowing through the vast network of clay ditches, often extending for miles, would make it a moot alternative.

---

[21] Harari, Yuval Noah, 2015, p. 362.
[22] Farmer, 1952, *JRSA*, No. 4876, pp. 547-564.

Success of irrigation colonization programs earlier gave impetus for similar concept of community building to stir up later in the 20th century. One such instance is the *Udāgama* concept (Village Awakening Program) of the late 1970s mentioned earlier. Udāgama village conception is designed as resettlement of low-income families selected from neighboring villages. It was not a colonization scheme per se. Its purpose was to build houses close to each other with modern luxuries and called it a village, but not necessarily like the newly built irrigation colonization programs. Udāgama model was in existence through mid-90s, in smaller scale but with a lofty profile as it was the brainchild of the housing minister, later the President, R. Premadasa. With his untimely death in 1993,[23] the Udāgama concept lost its patron and became defunct. This was one modern watershed moment compatible with the different versions of *gam bándeema*, the practice described earlier.

But review of the totality of the Udāgama program through the years show that no long-term plans were in the drawing board for the new villagers after they moved in, suggesting that the whole project had markings of a concept designed to gain political capital and advantage. Residents in neighboring villages of the Udāgama program too noted this. A telling example is the observation of a villager named Wannihami in neighboring Kukulawa made in 1983, three years after one such Udāgama village in the Horowpothana electorate was built. He remarked to Brow (1996) that "Samādhigama …was not even a village. It has no tank, no paddy fields, no land" (p. 154). Samādhigama area was represented in the parliament by E. L. B. Hurulle, a senior Minister of the government and the scion of nearby Hurulle of Morakewa family which had helped maintain Rata Sabhāwa tradition in the area until 1938.

Immediately after Samādhigama was established, bureaucratic confusion, errors and improprieties in principles planted seeds for estranged relationships between hitherto peaceful neighboring communities that felt they were shortchanged during the house distribution process.[24] For example, residents of neighboring Kukulawa accused the Samādhigama residents who were also their kinsmen as receiving new houses because of their membership in the local branch of the United National Party (UNP) which was in power at the time. As it turned out, of the 60 houses built in Samādhigama, most of the families receiving keys to them turned out to be members of the UNP!

Thus, Udāgama concept also became a victim of party politics characterized by creating divisions among communities, even close relatives, and having no mechanism to work out such situations. The conflicts were rancorous so much so, some in Kukulawa even thought of severing all *variga* relationships with Samādhigama. Kukulawa supposedly belonged to the so-called Vedda *Varige*.[25] Some in the two communities stopped going to funerals of each other and hurled

---

[23] President Premadasa was killed by a suicide bomber of the Liberation Tigers of Tamil Elam (LTTE) terrorist group in 1993.

[24] For description of the protocol for selection of residents for distribution of 60 new houses built in Samādhigama, a community built under the Udāgama concept, see James Brow (1996), *Demons and Development: The Struggle for Community in a Sri Lankan Village.*

[25] Calling these villages as 'Vedda Villages' is a mistaken and misrepresentative idea. See page 52 for comparison of these villages and the traditional Vedda villages in Uva Province.

accusations back and forth. Some residents of Samādhigama even began to go into trances and alleged that their misfortunes were the result of sorcery carried out by their kinsmen in Kukulawa. But as time passed, bruised egos and sentiments in Samādhigama and Kukulawa healed. After a while, the two communities resumed variga and kinship affiliations as their ancestors have done for generations.

For new villages under the irrigation colonization or the Udāgama concept, there was no institution existing or created by the villagers or the government to address in-house instances of conflicts between its new residents. There was no Rata Sabhāwa to offer help, for it had ceased to function some decades ago. The only way to resolve conflicts in these communities was through existing government instruments like courts, *Sama Mandala* (Peace Councils), or the hard proposition – changing the government at the next election!

A collection of forest plots cleared as a communal chena could also become a village few years later. Firstly, few villagers get together and walk to a virgin forest and demarcate boundaries and clear it for chena plots.[26] They build a small watch hut, sow millet, and after the first-year harvesting was over, continue in the second year and if satisfied, for a third year. As years pass, the small watch hut gets additional floor area. Residents may plant fruit trees and before long, the chena collective begins to look like a nascent village. The owners of the plots might dig a well and even dam a small ephemeral stream nearby to make a pond. When they add few paddies below to work using water from the pond, it now looks like a prototype of a small village. Every year the community makes repairs and makes the dam bigger and longer. In a few years, the pond acquires the characteristics of a typical village tank.

ONE VILLAGE, ONE CASTE; MANY CASTES IN ONE VILLAGE: Contrasting dynamics in placement of castes in a locality appear in Kandyan highlands and Nuwarakalaviya. People who were under some form of service tenure obligations occupied most of the villages/communities during Kandyan times. These villages were of three primary types: *gabadamam* (or *muttetugam*) of the King; *viharagam* of the temples & *dévāla* – houses of deities; and *nindagam* of the Chiefs. In the Kandyan highlands with one King, and a high number of Chiefs than in Nuwarakalaviya, the number of villages with tenurial obligations was also higher. As caste principals were based on the nature of the work or professional services[27] villagers provided to the King, the Chiefs, and individuals of higher standing, it was natural, at least in Nuwarakalaviya, for residents of one caste to remain clustered in one village fed by one water source, its irrigation tank. This water source most likely could have been built centuries ago under the *gam bándeema* concept by primogeniture with similar social characteristics. Their descendants continued to live in the village, and it provided them with a singular identity. These villages had vast stretches of land to

---

[26] See Leach (1961, 1968), pp. 292 & 294 for illustrations of two types of Chena: Keta Héna (*Iriwili Héna*) and Wheel Chena (*Mul Keta Héna*) in Nuwarakalaviya.

[27] Some of these categories are: 1. *Uliyamkarayo* – provide menial service to the Chiefs; 2. *Nilakarayo* – cultivate Chiefs' *Nila Kumburu* (fields) and give part of the crops to him; 3. *Hewapannehe* – provide honorable soldierly services to the Chiefs; 4 *Vatukarayo* – cultivate Chiefs' gardens; 5. *Asvaddumkarayo* – develop Chiefs' waste lands into cultivation; and 6. Others who are supposed to provide token services and homage to the Chiefs (Codrington, 1938, p. 25).

carve out their boundaries and expand as needed with their own stationary water source within. But they were far in between and there was less probability for service tenure obligations due to thin Chieftain base and few temples that require such services. The identity and the population constitution of those villages that provided some form of service tenure showed a near caste-homogenous population.

On the other hand, in Kandyan highlands, there are no system of tanks like what we find in the dry zone. The livelihood of villagers in this region depended on nature's offerings like slopes, ridges, valleys, and most importantly, the perennial streams that cut through their villages which usually determined their boundaries and sometimes their names. For example, the stream Talatu Oya cuts through the small town with the same name before it debouches to upper reaches of the Victoria Reservoir, east of Kandy on Mahaweli river. Different caste members serving the same overlord or same caste members serving different overlords had to share the water source like the stream that flows through Talatu Oya town. Therefore, they could not carve out their own caste-themed precinct, like a village in Nuwarakalaviya, but were bound to the common denominator, the aforesaid stream which provided a community opportunity to maintain a shared identity on its banks, but different and individual social and caste affiliations. This commonality determined the character and identity down to the individual residential plot.[28] So, for all residents in villages like these in the hill country, caste considerations perforce became secondary when choosing a place to live.

As a resident in a village with a neighboring village of a different caste in Nuwarakalaviya, I have drawn on my personal experience to observe the situations described above. We do not have natural barriers like hills and valleys to separate us for day-to-day life's activities. Both villages shared a common ephemeral stream that fed their irrigation tanks in the same river valley. In our village, the next-door neighbor did not claim a different caste identity from the other. All residents in the neighboring village also were of a homogenous lot. Although at our weddings or at other events, out of caste people were not invited, the ubiquitous presence of *henayā*, the washerman, was an exception. He provided *viyan* (ceiling awnings) to decorate the room or the *maduwa* where celebration was to be held, and certain items and some services as required by tradition. Contacts between residents in these two neighboring villages continued within the boundaries of caste definition. But even with different water sources, these two villages still shared a peculiar identity aided by the geomorphological feature, the Tank Cascade System – a chain of tanks linked together sharing water fed by the same river in the valley.[29] This fact made the

---

[28] Nugaliyadda in Patha Hewaheta, east of Kandy is an example of one such village. In the administrative boundaries of this village live families that claim affiliation to nine castes. Thus, it is called a *Nava Kula Gama* (village of nine castes). Its history spans many centuries and has descendants of people who held service tenure for the King, the Temple of the Tooth Relic, the temple in the neighboring village of Sagama, and participated in the Kandyan War of 1818. This mix of people lived on the banks of the Nugaliyadda Oya (stream) and shared its water rights for irrigation and personal use. In caste terms, they remain isolated as ever but live in the same village and share its main water source. L. B. S. Wickramasinghe (1927-2021) resident of this village told me that there had been no intermarriages between castes here as far as he can remember (personal interview, Dec 15, 2017).

[29] Madduma Bandara, 1985, pp. 99-113.

homogeneity of a village in Nuwarakalaviya more pronounced but contrasting than that of a village in Kandyan highlands.

As for interaction between villages, a resident from a lower caste village may approach a neighboring village of a different caste affiliation and ask for permission from a landowner to work a plot of land on *ande* (Sans. *ardha* – half) terms. Or, in the reverse, a higher caste landowner in a neighboring village who could not work his lands for any reason may approach a resident in a low caste village and offer his land to work on *ande* terms. In both instances, the essential customs governing this relationship including *ande* terms remain caste-free.

ABANDONMENT OF VILLAGES: Families moved out of their village to make a new homogenous community due to poverty, epidemics like malaria and cholera or harassment and annoyance from Chiefs overseeing the village. Instances of Chiefs abdicating *noblesse oblige* – responsibility to act generously and kindly toward commoners, are many. Scores of colonial writers have found the demeanor of Chiefs to be wanting. Schrikker (2007) wrote that in 1789, Thomas Nagel, a Dutch army officer who leased remote parts of north-east Sri Lanka from the Dutch government called the *Vanniyars* in the area as "tyrannical headmen who ruled their people arbitrarily without proper laws" (p. 104). Not only *Vanniyars*, but Chiefs elsewhere too having egotistical demeanor is not new. Kandyan Chiefs often were party to alarming traits of arrogance and crime. As noted in early pages, written accounts have exposed an instance in 1810 of murder accusation referenced earlier against Ehelepola Adikārama of Sabaragamuwa. Later, when Elapatha *Ratemahattayā* of Sabaragamuwa died, Ehelepola Nilame (*Adikārama*) grabbed land and property inherited by Elapatha's widow.[30] British also reprimanded Ehelepola after he was found harassing the servants of the deposed King.

In the neighboring Nuwarakalaviya too, Maha Vanniyā, or Chiefs in general, often did not have good rapport with the villagers in the territory. Maha Vanniyā, for example, was known to punish even *Kōrala*s. He once kept *Kōrala* of Ittikulama in irons for nine months for invoking allegiance to the British and refusing to collect tax at a *Kadawata* belonging to Maha Vanniyā.[31]

There were incidents on record where residents in Nuwarakalaviya were unhappy with tyrannical Chiefs or pure poverty migrating out of the village or self-exiled to a new locality. Present day Madukanda village (Mandukkodai) in the outskirts of Vavuniya in the North Province is a village that drew such unhappy immigrants from Anuradhapura area. In 1810, 30 families packed up and left a village near Anuradhapura for Madukanda alleging harassment from the Nuwarawawe Maha Vanniyā. The migrants' destination was an attractive location near Vavuniya known for its folklore and archaeological finds.[32]

After settling there, the villagers applied for permission to restore the Iratperiyakulama irrigation tank near their settlement. It is not known whether the British granted their request. Although Madukanda village pioneers sought 'asylum' in the British Vanni, they seemed to be well-to-do villagers. After arriving, they

---

[30] D'Oyly, 1917, p. 135.
[31] Ievers 1899, p. 46.
[32] Lewis, J.P. 1891, Buddhist Ruins near Vavuniya. *IRAS*, Vol. 12, No. 42, pp. 111-112.

bought paddies and tanks in the area.[33] Their exilic life was enterprising. It is worth noting that in 1817, Madukanda had more people (153) than Vavuniya (99). Therefore, even in 1810, it must have been a pressing need for them to have a distinguished person as their Mudliyar, a title on a par with *Ratemahattayā* of Nuwarakalaviya, to represent their traditions and customs. J.P. Lewis, a Civil Servant in Northern Province in 1890s reports that the villagers submitted the name of Kiernainden (Kiri Naidé?) as their Mudliyar to George Turnour, the Collector of Vanni.[34] We cannot find any record that the colonial administration agreed with this request. But because a person named Kapuruhami holding *Ratemahattayā* title lived in the same village seven decades later is hardly a coincidence.

Elsewhere, in 1811, about 40 kilometers east of Anuradhapura, a group of about 100 villagers from Hurulu Pattuwa (Soorely), immigrated to Killakkumulai division in Mulative District in the Northeast due to poverty.[35] In mid-seventeenth century, a unit of arrow soldiers from 'Vedda villages' in Hurulu Pattuwa went to fight the Dutch on behalf of the Kandy King. Upon return, fearing the possibility of being called for a second tour of duty, they abandoned the village and disappeared into the jungle.[36] Even in 1813, Vanniya of Soorle Pattu (Hurulu Pattuwa) wrote an *ola* to the British Governor in Colombo expressing his desire to immigrate with his people to Catacolum Pattu (Kaddukulam Pattu) in north-east Sri Lanka.[37]

Diseases too caused inhabitants to desert a village.[38] If several deaths take place in a dwelling house in an isolated village in short intervals, residents quickly deserted it and moved to another village or established their own village in a different location.[39] Closer to Kandy, travelers have seen deserted villages. Once in mid-19th century, British billeted workers in a village near construction site of the bridge across Mahaweli river at Katugastota. When many workers perished after contracting plaguey malaria, all villagers and workers hastily abandoned it for fear of the disease.[40] On other instances, if the villagers cannot identify the disease but patients continue to die, they may ascribe it to supernatural and evil powers and moved out of the village.

Migration happened in reverse order as well – from Maritime Provinces to Kandyan provinces. In 1735, a contingent of about 1000 Chaliahs (cinnamon peelers) in Maritime Districts left the province to escape punishing and tyrannical working conditions under the Dutch in cinnamon industry. They built two villages in Hath Kōrale which was under the King of Kandy then.[41]

The other reason people may want to have the urge to move out was the lack of security and conveniences, and often the issues of the castes. A one-variga or caste construction of the village was advantageous to residents to maintain strong

---

[33] Lewis, J.P. 1895, 1993, *A Manual of the Vanni Districts*…p. 98.

[34] Lewis, J.P. 1895, 1993, p. 95.

[35] Lewis, J.P. 1895, 1993, pp. 94-95 n1.

[36] Knox, 1861, 1995, p. 62.

[37] D'Oyly, 1917, p. 179.

[38] During the period 1840-1867, Cholera broke out in Nuwarakalaviya 11 times, Ievers, 1899, p. 103.

[39] Perera, A, 1917. P. 13.

[40] Reginald Herber, 1828, *Narrative of Journey Through the Upper Provinces … 1824-1825*, p. 194.

[41] Marshall, 1846, p. 7n.

kinship relations, practice customs and traditions without hinderances and hassles. Understandably, a mix of residents with traditions and religious practices that do not conform to common interests or ways of a section of the population always means shaky relationships between the multitude in that community. Added to this conundrum is the understated situation where a caste, an ethnic or religious group may practice customs that may not be to the liking of or annoying to a neighbor. These migrants then joined a compatible *varige* or a Rata Sabhāwa and established kinships in the new community. Such demographic dynamics have now taken a new form: ethnicity, wealth, color of skin and language.

Although there are some who believe that some villages in Nuwarakalaviya were built by those who migrated from Kandyan country, there are no written accounts to substantiate these claims. This province was a region beset with diseases and droughts. It is highly unlikely a villager in the hill country would leave his verdant land rewarded with year-round water and lovely weather to come down to the unfamiliar dry province to live. There are, however, instances of some Kandyans sneaking out to Nuwarakalaviya after the War of 1818 to escape British persecution. Well-known examples are Keppetipola, Madugalla and Pilimatalawa who were hiding in Parawaha near Manewa, and Vilbave and the Pretender in Anuradhapura. These are rare instances. Meanwhile, in the border area between Nuwarakalaviya and Kandyan country, kinships could have blossomed between villages due to proximity to each other. However, only after the irrigation colonization programs started in the early 20th century, large scale migration of villagers to Nuwarakalaviya took place from other provinces under the sponsorship of the government to develop newly cleared irrigation lands.

7. LITERATURE HISTORY REVIEW

The Sri Lankan classic *Mahawansa* is one of the earliest chronicles, *inter alia*, that describes the organized administration of justice and traditions including the religion in ancient times. It is a collection of serialized metrical verses in Pali on a book of treated palm leaves about the history of the country starting from 3rd century BC, believed to have been authored by a Bhikkhu named Mahanama at Dighasanda Vihara. This book, along with *Deepawansa*, is the first to describe the region that later came to be known as Nuwarakalaviya. It tells the regnal and religious antiquity of the country, sometimes describing boundaries in cities and provinces, and instances and manner of appointment of officials to administer them. I will discuss the nature of the specific duties of these officials in coming pages.

MAHAWANSA AUTHENTICITY. *Mahawansa* class of chronicles, e.g., *Deepawansa*, *Chūlawansa* and *Rājāvaliya* are records of firsthand information etched in the cognizance of a people as their history based on eye-witness accounts and folklore. Thus, this book is not a fiction or imagination of an erudite monk as some skeptics have argued. Its contents include archaeology, tales of legends, politics, and local administration methods and anecdotes of the country from North to South and across India. Written accounts of evidence of Mahawansa authenticity have been found in India.

Physical evidence for accuracy and authenticity of *Mahawansa* was found millennia after it was written. In 1851, Major Alexander Cunningham during his excavations of two Topes (stupa) in Sonari and Sanchi in India discovered multiple reliquaries with calcified human remains. In the lid of one was written in Brahmi script two names: *Sapurisasa Majhimasa Kodiniputasa*, i.e., (the relics) of the worthy Mahjjhima, son of Kodini; *Sapurisasa Kassapagotta*, and the bottom of reliquary was written *Sapurisasa Haratai-putasa*. On the lid of another reliquary was written *Suparisasa Mogaliputasa* who convened the Third Sangayanawa (Third Buddhist Synod) which decided to send Buddhist missionaries across Asia during Emperor Asoka reign. Interestingly, centuries before Cunningham's excavations, the *Mahawansa*, in its Chapter describing these missions, wrote the same names with regions they travelled as 'Monk Majjhima' and 'wise Majjhima' (sent) to Himalaya (Himawanta) and Thera Moggaliputra as the 'illuminator of the religion who brought the council to an end'. This points with certainty that names scribed on reliquaries calcified remains unearthed by Cunningham to be the same written in the Sri Lankan chronicle showing that the author of the chronicle had access to folklore, tales about true legends lived centuries earlier in India.[1,2] Wilhelm Geiger calls this find a 'striking confirmation' of authenticity of *Mahawansa.*

OTHER WRITINGS. Except for *Mahawansa*, *Deepawansa* and other volumes on ancient history and archaeological treasures, some mere remnants buried in jungles,

---

NOTES

[1] Cunningham, Major Alexander. 1854, pp. 119-120.

[2] Geiger (1912, 2003), XII.1 & 6.

there is very little written in pre-modern times in Sri Lanka in general or Nuwarakalaviya social order and customs, in particular.

After months at sea and while miles from the shore and sailing into the harbor European writers invariably saw the enchanting and paradisaical beauty of Sri Lanka's coast fringed with coconut trees and misty mountains in the distance. One such writer, Gordon Cumming (1892) travelled across Sri Lanka for two years and wrote about the illustrious beauty of the land with this admission: "I only wish it were possible for words to convey something of the charm of such surroundings, of majestic crags, clear streams, and fruit-bearing trees with varied cultivation [...]" (p. 277). She wrote these lines while staying in Alagalla near Kadugannawa in central Sri Lanka. Later she did not forget to write her honest observations and tremendous adulation about cities like Anuradhapura and Polonnaruwa. But she wrote little about the Nuwarakalaviya customs and traditions as her attention was for what was visible on first sight, remnants of ancient living popping up all the over the landscape in the province.

When we look back to the 19th century Sri Lanka, not all colonial writers were in awe with the customs and traditions of the living society they were in contact with on daily basis. Some recorded arcane ways in a smattering of words like "curious customs," "boycott," referring to the ban (*tahanama*) a punishment meted out by Rata Sabhāwa.[3] Thomas Nagel to whom the Dutch outsourced the administration of Vanni districts centered around Mullativu area along the northeastern seaboard in the late 18th century was not kinder. Schrikker (2007) quotes him: "The people of the Vanni are the most primitive kind, on the most natural and basic stage of human development and are much in need of Company rule to be civilized" (p. 105). Meanwhile, some writers spent a lifetime learning about the country by combing and excavating sites built by its ancient people and write detailed volumes authoritatively.

It is important to note here that while these writers loved and enjoyed the beauty of the country, some of them did the unthinkable by removing national or cultural treasures, and even body parts of people from the colony to Britain. They carried off the last King's throne to England. They auctioned off the valuables of the palace. Reputed writer Henry Marshall desecrated the body of his supposed friend Keppetipola. After the latter was beheaded by the British, Marshall took the severed head to Phrenological society of Edinburgh in Scotland which was promoting ways to differentiate races with the size of their skull measurements. Such 'studies' were commonly practiced by British scientists in the colonies back then. When William Lanne, often called King of Tasmania and believed to be the last full-blooded indigenous person in the country died in 1869, his body was secretly exhumed, decapitated, and dismembered by a surgeon named William Crawther who later became the Prime Minister of the colony. He used Lanne's body parts, including the head for research. This was, as the noted Australian historian Helen Macdonald wrote in 2005, to find "the improvement that takes place in the lower race when subjected to the effects of education and civilization"[4]. British

---

[3] Ievers, 1899, p. 93.

[4] Quoted in Lawson, Tom, 2014, *The Last Man: A British Genocide in Tasmania*, p. 167.

Phrenology is the now disgraced science that worked to determine the intelligence and superiority of one race over another.

Sans Marshall's questionable act, most other tales left by writers reflect the learning interests of those few that stressed directing light on the unknown country and their love and admiration of its past. Young Europeans in their early twenties, just landed in this country as enthusiastic amateurs too noted this trend. In the beginning, they were lost trying to understand what they were seeing and hearing. But gradually they amassed their information which turned out to be priceless to later scholars and enthusiasts of history and culture. Upon arrival on the island, whether they were just privates in the army or blue-blooded civil servants, these young passionate colonial officials found a country rich with history longing to be written about. Twentieth century celebrated writer J.R. Toussaint (1934) wrote:

> In the early days of British rule, the field for original research was wider and richer than it is at present, and its investigation called for more sustained effort. There was however no lack of qualified men ready to take up the work. These pioneers applied themselves to their task with an assiduity and thoroughness worthy of the highest praise, and there is very little now that is left for original research. In a general sense, all that remains for the research worker of the present day is to build on the foundation already laid, to fill up gaps, or to make minor corrections regarding ascertained facts. (p. 113)

Throughout their tenures, these vanguard corpora of writers, some even after returning home, continued to search sparse literature on the essence of the peoples they served in the colony. In doing so, they became purveyors of understanding the country, and encouraged a rarified fraternity of Sri Lankans to get interested in writing about the history of their motherland. At the same time, even with the primary goal of the colonial governments in early 19th century being the advancement of interests of the British Empire, they also introduced their print culture and instruments like intellectual societies – Royal Asiatic Society (RAS) for one, unequivocally accepted as the most important contribution to nascent literary historiography scene in Sri Lanka, and its renowned Journal, the communication medium of the colonial writing fraternities in the early going. Starting from the early decades of the 19th century, the RAS members with their eagerness, inquisitiveness and influence brought from home enriched the knowledge base on Sri Lankan history, culture, and natural sciences. But as happened throughout the centuries before, this new genre of native writers too was late or rather slow to make inroads to Nuwarakalaviya.

NUWARAKALAVIYA SILENT IN *SANDÉSA* POEMS. Absence of written descriptions or referencing about Nuwarakalaviya in Sri Lankan ballad genre known as *Sandésa Kāvya* (s. *Sandésaya*), messages in poems, few centuries prior to colonial times too is worthy of examination. Polyglot Buddhist monks like Ven. Totagamuwe Rahula or learned lay people like Alagiyawanna Mukavetti and few unknown authors wrote these masterpieces of poetry. The messages in poems were carried by the authors' chosen fictitious avian messengers to deities or important personalities in destinations across the country asking for a favor or sending felicitations. As Stephen C. Berkwitz (2017) writes:

Each messenger poem reconstructs a particular journey and distinctive geographical vision, which in turn represents a strong commitment to endowing local settings with the honour of being described in poetic verse [*sic*]. (p. 100)

Sandésa poetic culture blossomed in the 14th to early 15th centuries in Kotte and Sitawaka kingdoms. There were at least over dozen such ballads written during this period.[5] Their thematic preference showed no 'cosmopolitan' character but a 'local' disposition. It is particularly remarkable that out of the ten ballads, only one avian messenger bird was sent to the northern part of Sri Lanka. All others were asked by the poets to crisscross only the western and southern regions of the country. Some of these messengers flew to destinations separated by a few miles. The poets sent messenger birds from Kotte near Colombo to places as far as Saman Dévāle in the Sabaragamuwa province or from Devinuwara in southern Sri Lanka to Kotte.

I call these 'local' trips mainly for the familiarity the poets displayed about these areas and their relatively slim know-how about the distant and remote eastern seaboard or northern parts of the country to which they chose not to send the messengers. The poets took extraordinary efforts to articulate in superlative language telling the avian messenger to enjoy the dazzling beauty of the country, places of interest, major temples, Buddhist religious teaching centers (*piriven,* s. *pirivena*) and general description of the lives of its people on their designated flight path. These writings show the degree of writers' intimate conversancy with these areas.

On the other hand, when birds with missives crisscrossed the Western and Southern Sri Lanka, that time was the darkest in Nuwarakalaviya and the poets are silent about any reference to it, for, I believe, want of familiarity with this region. Convenience of travel to this province was prohibitive due to lack of roads. Permeated fear of diseases also contributed to many in the western and southern area to abandon or nothing to do with province.[6] This made Nuwarakalaviya a distant and an unknown realm to poets or any person living in southern half of the country. So, it is possible the composers of *Sandésa* poems living in areas stretching from Matara to Kotte had no ways to know the Northern and North Central interior of the country to write about. Thus, they could not describe it with a modicum of floridity, much less sending the imaginary messenger on a trip over Nuwarakalaviya with a memo as trivial as "Hello!"

Surprisingly, only messenger bird which diverged the traditional routes and flew to northern end of the country was the Kovula (Koel bird, a type of cuckoos) with *Kokila Sandéshaya* written by the Chief monk named Tillaka in a *pirivena* in

---

[5] These ballads are: *Tisara* Sandéshaya (Dedigama to Devinuwara); *Neelakobei* (Matara to Kataragama); *Savul* (Sitawaka to God Saman in Ratnapura); *Mayura* (Gampola to Kelaniya); *Parevi* (Jayawardenapura Kotte to Devinuwara); *Kokila (Paraputu)* (Devinuwara to Jaffna); *Selalihini* - Starling (Kotte to Kelaniya); *Gira* (Kotte to Totagamuwa Wijayaba Privena); *Hansa* (Kotte to Keragala Padmawati Pirivena); *Kaha Kurulu* (Hema Kurulu -Kotte to Kataragama), *Nāri-sath; Asta Nāri; Suwa* and *Diya Savul* Sandésaya in 1813. Partially sourced from Kusuma Karunaratne, 2008, Matara Era Literature and Literati. *Matara Wansaya* Vol. II, p. 23.

[6] Travelling in the country was most primitive at the time. Even after 150 years later, Robert Knox leaving Eladetta south of Kandy walked 26 days to reach Arippu near Mannar (Knox, 1681, 1995, p. 168).

Devinuwara c 1440-1446. The bird flew out from this city in southern tip of Sri Lanka to Jaffna (Yapa Patuna) on the northern tip with a felicitating message to Prince Sapumal who had established his base there after defeating the Jaffna ruler, Arya Chakravarthy. As the poet was knowledgeable of the cities and attractions along the western littoral only, he asked the Kokila bird to fly over the coastline – through Kelaniya, Wattala, Negombo, Chilaw, Mannar, and reaching the peninsula 13 days later.

Marine traffic was the only mode of communication between countries at that time. Ships sailing North and South and anchoring in harbors on the west coast of Sri Lanka were helpful to propagate information about cities up and down the coast, not just to writers, but ordinary people as well. During 1705 and 1706, 103 boats sailed between Colombo and Coromandel Coast in India (Point Calimere on eastern coast of India 30 nautical miles north of Point Pedro and Ganjam in Orissa up north).[7] Also hundreds of ships sailed from Malabar Coast in Southwest India as well. Writing about slave trade between Cape and Asian cities like Colombo and Batavia, Mbeki and van Rossum (2017) found people sharing and exchanging knowledge between the VOC workers on ships and in the settlements throughout Asia (pp. 95-116).

The author of the *Kokila Sandésaya* no doubt used this knowledge spread along the coastal cities to describe them and their people in his prose. Therefore, the poet's only option was to send the bird along the western coastline he had heard about, likely from sailors, merchants, and travelers. He also must have traveled along the coastal cities himself visiting other temples. Probably, this experience made it easy for him to describe coastal cities and harbors from Devinuwara to Jaffna. Nuwarakalaviya remained, therefore, a mystery to his erudition.

Ven. Kotagama Wachissara (1961) wrote that after Tamil invasions of Polonnaruwa, Kings brought brides from South India. During Kotte period too, Kings continued this tradition. This influenced popularization of the Indian dietic pantheon in the royal households.[8] Most poets in the Kotte period, being exemplary intellectuals of the day, took special attention to give lofty praise in their flowery ballads to Upulvan, Vibhisana, Nātha, Saman, Siva and many other minor Indian deistic pantheons which had taken a Sri Lankan hue and favorite of the royalty. But I was unable to find a praise quatrain fancying about Sri Maha Bodhi or revered religious monuments in Nuwarakalaviya authored by these writers. During this time, however, Pearl Fishery in the northwest was making waves and the poet who wrote *Kokila Sandéshaya* even made sure the Kokila bird sees women picking up dead pearl oysters (*Mutu Bello*) washed up on the beach close to Mantota (Mannar), sixty kilometers west of Anuradhapura as the crow flew. This was the closest a Sri Lankan writer in the 14th century got to Nuwarakalaviya!

Next to *Mahawansa, Deepawansa* and the Chinese traveler Faxian, Englishman Robert Knox, I propose, is the first writer to describe Nuwarakalaviya in extraordinary detail, occasionally down to the footprints on the sandy bed of Malwatu Oya, lifeline of the province trickling through Anuradhapura. Couple of

---

[7] Wickramasinghe, Nira, 2020, pp. 4 & 91.

[8] Kotagama Wachissara, 1961, *Valivita Saranankara*, p. 160.

centuries later, people living in the west coast, including the colonial powers, were still unfamiliar with the Nuwarakalaviya so much so, the Dutch Governor based in Arippu on the coast west of Anuradhapura showed how little he knew about the province when he asked Knox who had just passed Anuradhapura, the route to send spies to Kandy. Knox told the Governor that "people of Jaffnapatam," then under the Dutch, "have great correspondence with people of Nuwarakalaviya," a reference to accessibility of communication channels, albeit in medieval standards, to the province and interior of the country.[9] Although the Chiefs in Nuwarakalaviya were in some level of contact by sending elephant tusks to the colonials on the coast as annual *dákum* (tributes), Dutch knowledge of the province remained vague at best.

Several writers have argued that ancient Sri Lankan poets disregarded writing about people but created a genre of literary works known as *alankāra vādaya* – focused on narrative of style, flamboyance, and aesthetics. I cannot agree more with this assertion. As Martin Wickramasinghe has suggested once, poetry should be a commentary about the society.[10] Poets who wrote about ordinary people are the ordinary people whose creativity of dissecting the day-to-day life was obvious on every line in their poems, genre of which is known as *Jana Kavi* (Folk Poetry) which became popular in the 18th century and later. As the Kotte era writing fraternity faded away, Matara era (1750-1850 AD)[11] writers became the prominent literati in the country. But for the same reasons characteristic of the *Sandésa* poets, Matara era writers too showed little familiarity or interest in Nuwarakalaviya.

In the meantime, only a few Kandyan or Nuwarakalaviya Chiefs made tangible literary contributions of any kind. One among them is T.B. Panabokke, Rural Court President in Dumbara who was also related to Ulagalla clan in Nuwarakalaviya by marriage. But his writings (with collaborator C. J. R LeMesurier) were mainly on the Kandyan highlands that also contained many customs and traditions practiced in Nuwarakalaviya.

Perhaps the last contributor of significance in such work was Kapuruhami Madukanda Ratemahattayā in Northern province. Kapuruhami not only made space in the Royal Asiatic Society publications, but with his folk-poetry, he found audiences in most unlikely corners of Nuwarakalaviya. It was no coincidence when a teenager, I was once privileged to hear one of his poems sung by my mother sitting under a tree in our Kurahan (millet) chena near Mihintale. In these verses, an unknown poet wails the death of his wife Giranga during childbirth.

Only after I visited the Madukanda Maha Walawwa (Fig. 17, 51) near Vavuniya a half century later in 2016, its occupants told me their great-great-grandmother's name was Giranga and family elders had told them she died in 1901 giving birth to her child. Her first son became the last *Ratemahattayā* of Madukanda in 1930. While meeting with Kapuruhami Ratemahattayā's granddaughter Nanda Kumari Mahadivulwewa Wijeratne in Uhumiya near Kurunegala, she pulled out from a wood

---

[9] Knox, 1681, 1995, p. 172.

[10] Rajakaruna, Ariya, 1958, 1962, Martin Wickramasinghe Hā Parani Kāvya Sampradaya. *Sanskruthi – Tri Montly*, Vol. 6, No. 4, pp. 56-75.

[11] Kusuma Karunaratne, 2008, p. 16.

thaila pettiya (strongbox) a bundle of yellowed foolscap sheets filled with handwritten poems. Among them was the sheet containing four quatrains written by Nanda Kumari's grandfather bemoaning over the death of his wife Giranga who left behind two sons. One refers to the death of her two daughters as well.[12] Even in his most difficult hour, engaging in achingly beautiful poetry like these, he magnified his contributions to enrich folk culture as seen over a century later when villagers like my mother found them enjoyable and worthy of reciting and celebrating the richness of a literary gem.

While Portuguese, Dutch and the Kandy King concentrated to consolidate power and security in their areas of control, British had an expanded formula for the governance of the country after they secured the total dominion over it. Thus, we find British officials posted to these interior regions in the 19th century begin to get interested in this extraordinary country they were seeing. They made remarks in their missives to Colombo about Anuradhapura. The officials usually stayed in Nuwarakalaviya for no more than a year or two. And slowly they too began to author lengthy reports about the history, hydraulic-culture, and people in the province.

Except the serendipitous find of the ballad by Kapuruhami Ratemahattayā of Madukanda referenced above, I cannot find any other Chief or ordinary citizen in Nuwarakalaviya who contributed with such writings during this period. No natives in the province, including the descendants of former aristocrats, have been able to provide references or direct us to any written resources on the region. Nor do they provide us with any information about functions of their ancestors pertaining to Rata Sabhāwa or the unique culture of the people. It is possible whatever material they had kept in their garrets could not escape the injury of time. Therefore, it was a difficult task to line up material, particularly the written type about Rata Sabhāwa of Nuwarakalaviya for this book.[13]

In this regard, it is fair to say, Robert "Bob" Wilson Ievers (1850-1905) was one British Civil Servant who stood out (Fig. 27). In the last decade of the 19th century, he wrote the *Manual of North Central Province*, the only engagingly enthused account the historians agree as a remarkable contribution devoted to the region up to that time. This book was also one of the genres of exhaustive reports – *Manuals* – written by colonial civil servants in the second half of the 19th century focused on specific regions they served. This writing trend started when Governor Arthur Gordon (1883-1889) ordered every Assistant Government Agent to write a manual of his district. Impactful decisions like these must have pleased his aide-de-camp Maha Mudliyar, Chiefs and public at the time. We find a Hansard report of a petition

---

[12] *Saka visinoka dahas atasiya thevisi wana – waka aka pura theles lath ilmasa rivi dinana*
Neka guna pasindu woo Giranga nam angana – Pathara duk gewa maru muwata path una.
සක විසිනෙක දහස් අටසිය තෙව්සි වන - වක අග පුර තෙලෙස් ලත් ඉල් මස රිව් දිනෙන
ෙනක ගුණ පසිඳු වූ ගිරඟා නම් අගන - සසර දුක් ෙගවා මරුමුවට පත් උන
This is the 1st verse of a ballad known in Nuwarakalaviya as *Madukande Gedara Kavi* – Poems of Madukanda.

[13] A notable and a prominent ethnographer in the post-Rata Sabhāwa Nuwarakalaviya is Ranbanda Senevirathna. His poems, songs and legal compositions have entertained us in the second half of the 20th century. Since the middle of that century, however, literary landscape in Nuwarakalaviya has blossomed as seen from the works in science, humanities, and art put out by a wide array of writers living or having ancestral links to the region.

they sent around for signature requesting the extension of governor's tenure beyond 1889.[14] Ievers' *Manual* helped generations that came after him to get enlightened about the geography, history, folklore, economy, and politics of the province as it was coming out of obscurity. He also wrote the little-known *Anuradhapura Anthem* which appeared in *The Times of Ceylon* 1917 Christmas issue.[15] And he is the first to schematically illustrate the layout of a paddy field under the village tank in Nuwarakalaviya.[16] However, just as his colleagues before and after him, Ievers too failed to lift the veil over customs and traditions of the region, cornerstone of which was the Rata Sabhāwa.

But rich tapestry of fields of ancient monuments buried or hidden in forest in Nuwarakalaviya drew excitement from other colonial government officials stationed in the province as well. They took every opportunity to write volumes about their findings. Hugh Nevil, H. C. P. Bell, and A. O. Brodie are few remarkable Civil Servants who joined together with Ievers to Nuwarakalaviya fraternity of writer-scholars. While the Christian missionary influence is manifestly imbued in colonial hold in the island, these writers tirelessly continued to look and restore the past up to date with the present. They were digging into every corner of the landscape literally, listening to ordinary people, and turning dusty pages of palm-leaf books to record the living culture, religion, and political discourse of the ordinary people.

Also, I must not fail to mention the contribution of two Chiefs in Nuwarakalaviya. They were not known as poets but contributed to the discovery of ancient compositions. Eriyawe Dissava in Northwestern Province, which also practiced Rata Sabhāwa, was in possession of a *Vitti Potha* (Book of Incidents), a document believed to have been written in the 16th century. It was well-known in Northwestern and North Central provinces, and recorded traditional accounts of royal and important families, villages, and tanks. In 1889, he gave a copy of it to a British ethnologist and this copy is now in the British Museum.[17] Hugh Nevil mentions a poetry collection called *Kappiri Hatana* (Kaffir War) written in Nuwarakalaviya and was discovered in Tamarawewa, the seat of the Chief by the same name in Eastern Nuwarakalaviya.[18] It is likely this Chief was involved in finding this work, because naturally, the first contact an ethnology enthusiast makes in an isolated village is its Chief.

ORIENTALIST VIEW. In the biosphere where society lived for generations isolated in oceans of sylvan country, it was a far cry and miles away from the post-medieval Western legal concepts that ironically viewed the indigenous culture that guided the rural life in Sri Lanka as foreign or strange. For example, in 1789, a Dutch contractor who leased coastal area of Northeast under the Dutch East India Company wrote about the people in the area in most demeaning manner. He

---

[14] (https://api.parliament.uk/historic-hansard/commons/1889/apr/02/governor-of-ceylon).

[15] http://www.turtlebunbury.com/history/history_family/hist_family_ievers.htm. Sourced from Turtle Bunbury. Last accessed on April 9, 2020. All attempts to find the original source document *The Times of Ceylon* 1917 Christmas issue were not successful.

[16] Ievers, 1899, p. 172.

[17] Wickremasinghe, 1900, Para 74, P. 79

[18] Nevil, Hugh. 1869-1886. Sinhala Verse (Kavi). ed. P.E.P. Deraniyagala, *Ethnolgoy*. Vol. 3, 1955, Poem 783, p. 206.

believed that people in the area had no history, no memory of their ancient culture which existed before them.[19] Nearly a century later, Ievers who grasped Nuwarakalaviya customs with a clearer understanding like no other colonial civil servant before him called residents of the province as having "curious customs!"[20]

Fig. 27. Robert "Bob" Wilson Ievers (1850 – 1905)   Government Agent, North Central Province 1890-1893. Photo: Turtle Bunbury, great-great-grandson of R. W. Ievers.

But in 1888, he was able to experiment with the same people, and involved heavily in the development of the first ever conical pipes of earthenware and later concrete *horow keta* to operate the sluices in village tanks in Anuradhapura.[21] But the totality of Ievers' writings show that he was careful not to view the province and its people with a Eurocentric viewfinder which Edward Said described and compared with Eastern Orientalism profoundly in 1979.

It is known that colonial governments institutionalized some aspects of the Sri Lankan affairs to further their own interests. Rata Sabhāwa was not one of them. They found no reason to attempt rural judicial traditions as they suspected no direct benefits could be reaped by courting such arcane ways. Despite such doubts and skepticism of the colonial observers, the inconspicuous institutions like Rata Sabhāwa in Nuwarakalaviya, and *Gam Sabe* in Kandyan highlands did their job painstakingly. There is no doubt this had an influence and values instilled in the

---

[19] Alicia Schrikker, 2007, *Dutch and British Colonial Intervention in Sri Lanka 1780-1815*, p. 105.

[20] Ievers, 1899, p. 93.

[21] Ievers, 1899, p. 158.

people. Henry Marshall wrote that the "moral character of Highlanders [...] in carriage and behavior, the Kandyans are very grave and stately [...]."[22]

It was an uninformed response of the colonial officers in 18th and 19th centuries when they often suggested some native traditions and customs as "curious." Land Regent of the Dutch, Thomas Nigel Nagel mentioned earlier showed his poor understanding of the native people. He fits purely into the category of amateurs in the country. His description of Vanni residents nearly fits with some Western scholarly descriptions of non-European societies at that time. Schrikker (2007) quotes Nigel who wrote rather sarcastically: "The Laws of the Vanni were very short, because there were none, neither from tradition, nor written by their lord" (p. 106).

It laid bare the truth that some European writers were slow to grasp the uniqueness and full context of all things cultural and historical, not just in Sri Lanka but territories they colonized ranging from smallest like the few miles of the atoll Tarawa in the Pacific to a Subcontinent like India. Instead, often Eurocentric thinking of colonials helped them chart disparaging and dehumanizing comments about the natives they came in contact in faraway lands. Anthropologist Gananath Obeyesekere warned us to be suspicious of such historiographical observations because they appeared at "a time when critical scholarship in ethnography was virtually non-existent."[23] It is essential to remind ourselves that unlike Australia and Van Diemen's Land (Tasmania) in the beginning of the 19th century, colonists did not come to a *tabula rāsa* – a clean slate – in Sri Lanka. The country had a rock-solid civilization going back in two millennia, established customs and traditions accepted as its forms of 'law,' though, they were seen as different from Western ways and eyes, enough for the writers to discard the colony as irrelevant and primitive.

That said, except for rare references attributed to the likes of Ievers, allusions and scholarship on Rata Sabhāwa in pre- and post-colonial documents or unofficial writings as little as a paragraph are hard to find. One reason for this is that the configuration of Rata Sabhāwa in the national or regional discourse was not well known. But inclusion of popular parlance like *Govanadoru Utumanan Wahanse* (His Excellency the Governor) or *Kolamba Rajjuruwo* (King of Colombo) in invocatory incantations or closing addresses during Rata Sabhāwa proceedings can be called either a passing and inconsequential formulaic phrases or signs of political changes, particularly with Rata Sabhāwa traditions that had taken place in the country since the fall of Kandy. Rata Sabhāwa never had a mandate to report its workings and conclusions to the Governor or the King of England. Such requirements all ended up at the door of the Nuwarakalaviya Chiefs. However, by citing the highest authority of the land, Rata Sabhāwa found a way to emphasize its supremacy of social and cultural authority and legitimacy of the proceedings while recognizing the

---

[22] Marshall, Henry 1846, 1954, p. 14.

[23] Obeyesekere, Gananath, 1992, 1997, *The Apotheosis of Captain Cook...* p. 66.

presence of the country's new rulers who, though, were least aware of its existence.[24]

In this regard, the onset of political winds in the 19th century, and vicissitudes in Kandyan people's thinking about its direction is worth a look. Signing the Kandyan Treaty in 1815 left Sri Lankans with no alternative but the reality of turning their full allegiance to the English King. The observation of Sivasundaram (2013) is a good example to support this premise. It relates to the thematic changes in some literary genres that existed at the time regarding the change of ruling chemistry in the country. Three kinds of literary traditions: *astaka* (praise poems), *prasasti gee* (royal paeans) and *vamsa* (ancestry & history) which honored and praised Lankan royalty and the nobility during pre-British times suddenly began a metempsychosis, a transmigration, changing the pitch and the bulk to praise the colonial elites instead. These praise poems by Kandyan literati proved them flipping the acquiescence to the new masters in a speedy way.

Fig. 28. Mihintale Twin Rock Inscription Slabs of Mahinda IV (956-972 AD) on the mezzanine plaza on the hill. Photo: T.A.M.B. Tillakaratne.

British officers, some of them once double agents conspiring with the native nobility to topple the King, and later came to occupy the palace, were the recipients of praise from the native population with Astaka tradition and other ways. In these ballads the British officers were elevated to the 'solar caste' or heroes as 'lions' and included them in 'divine clans.' Sivasundaram quotes a palm leaf manuscript in the British Library, *Dathagotrapradipaya*, which described D'Oyly as a good man, 'fulfilling perfections to become a Buddha.' The poem *Jorgi Astaka* felicitated King George.[25] As described in plenty of other palm leaf manuscripts written after the fall of Kandy, high ranking British officers were described as the new Kings of the country. Such

---

[24] This is not unusual. Colonial times schoolbooks from kindergarten had poems and phrases praising the King or Queen of England and kids recited them in class. Special programs for King George's birthday were common in schools.

[25] Sivasundaram, 2013, pp. 6-7.

acquiescence from Sri Lankan literati to their colonial masters was not surprising. The authority that gripped these writers called for all of them to be in good grace of the new masters.

In this background, my attempt in this chapter is to elucidate literature to provide more clarity on attempts at writings on the law and record-keeping existed pertaining to Rata Sabhāwa and similar native institutions since the pre-Medieval Ages to the turn of the 20th century. I examine the evolution of commands burst out as laws 'from the Sri Mouth of the King,' and customs and traditions that have been highlighted in written form up to the time the Rata Sabhāwa fell by the wayside. It appears that none of these laws 'by the Sri Mouth' did shape or influence the operational practices of the Sabhāwa. They survived within the larger concept of customs that existed as loose rules on ways of doing things in the region. Having no guiding document to maintain authenticity and consistency of the practice, the Rata Sabhā weaved through disparate practicalities of oral traditions occasionally giving the Chiefs, if needed, carte blanche to improvise their role to conduct the proceedings and make final decisions.

RECORD TYPES AND WRITTEN VILLAGE BOUNDARIES. Native writers found multiple ways to record their thoughts. Rock inscriptions give us ideas about the social organization and executive structure existed in early Sri Lanka. In 1883, Edward Miller listed 172 rock inscriptions spread across the country. Some observers have listed 155 rock inscriptions in Nuwarakalaviya,[26] some carved as far back as 3rd century BC. Two highly noticeable rock inscriptions are Mihintale twin-slabs (Mahinda IV 956-972 AD) on the mezzanine plaza of the hill (Fig.28), and free-standing slab on the stone plaza of the Ruwanweli stupa at Anuradhapura.

In addition to rock surfaces, writings were on mediums like wall surfaces made of peculiar plaster. A remarkable example of laymen's writings etched on wall surfaces is found on the Mirror Wall in Sigiriya rock fortress near the southern boundary of Nuwarakalaviya. Once a General named Kitti of King Sena's army (9th Century) visited Sigiriya[27] and engraved the lines: *Seneviradun Vahaege… ae dáka agana sihivana hitini* […] *Sen Rajáli Kith* […] *rasa gaa li* – Honarable General (of the King's army) […] these golden ladies […] I am Kit (Kitti) who serves King Sena (Sena Rajali)."[28, 29]

During the reign of King Udaya I (797-801 AD) judgements were recorded for future reference and kept in the palace.[30] *Chulawansa* also notes of a Law Book written during Queen Kalyanawathi's reign (1202-1210 AD) but no further

---

[26] De Soyza, John Siriman., 1960, Rock Inscriptions of Anuradhapura Period. *Sahitya: Tri-Monthly Magazine.* p. 81.

[27] The fortress-like palace compound atop a 350-meter solid rock was built by patricidal King Kasyapa (477-495 AD). Scholars believe *Mahawansa* was written at Dighasanda Vihara (or Monastery) during the reign of King Dhatusena, father of Kasyapa.

[28] Priyanka, Benille, 2010, *Recently Deciphered Records from the Mirror Wall at Sigiriya,* verse 709, p. 635.

[29] Turtle Bunbury, the great-great-grandson of R. W. Ievers, the Government Agent of Anuradhapura in late 19th century, provided me an interesting anecdote. Ievers once admitted to his friend H. C. P. Bell, the archaeologist who did excavations in Sigiriya and other locations in Sri Lanka, that he etched his name on the Sigiriya Mirror Wall. Understandably, Bell was not happy what his friend did.

[30] *Chulawansa* 49.21, qtd. in Ariyapala, 1956, 1997, p. 124.

information is available on this work.[31] It mentions four *varnas* (colors) of social order.[32] This is not a color coding of some sort, but no doubt a reference to castes in the kingdom.

Mudliyar A. De Silva Ekanayake (1876) believed that in all probability, laws must have been written but waves of Indian invaders wantonly destroyed these records and libraries leaving the later Kings to rule the country with *lex non scripta* – law not written.[33] King Nissankamalla (1187-1196) seemed to have encouraged teachings of Brahminical legal concepts found in India. Although since no written law treatises were found, his penchant for inscriptions is clear. As described earlier, his courts of justice, *dharmadhikarana*, functioned like trial by jury. After the litigants presented their version of the case, a group of 'assessors' expressed their decision to the President of the tribunal who delivered the judgement.[34] King Nissankamalla is believed to have created a measure of distance known as *Nissanka Gauvva*, a distance equal to a league (3-4 miles) and installed pillars marking each *Gauvva* spot on the roadside.[35] On these pillars must have written instructions or edicts to his people.

D'Oyly found no written laws or any written record of judicial proceedings existed in Kandyan districts.[36] Henry Marshall (1846) believed the people of Kandyan kingdom were more interested in "administration of long-established customs than establishing laws" (p. 221). There is scarcely a better way to portray the deficit of written laws in ancient Sri Lanka, where over time, customs and traditions became Law, than Alfred Tennyson's words in *Aylmer's Field*:

> "… As we task ourselves
> To learn a language known but smatteringly
> In phrases here and there at random, toil'd
> Mastering the lawless science of our law,
> That codeless myriad of precedent,
> That wilderness of single instances,
> Thro' which a few, by wit or fortune led."

Villagers carved Boundaries of their communities, plots of land and *rata* (provinces) on trees in the form of symbols (e.g., stars, moon, sun, or geometric signs and such other). These practices in communities were essential parts of Rata Sabhāwa traditions. Because a boundary dispute is always likely to see a place in the Sabhāwa agenda. Boundary Books (*Kada-im Poth*) and Boundary Ballads, primarily written on palm leaves and only emerging in Gampola period (mid-14th to early 15th century) go beyond describing boundaries of localities and provinces. They also tell us demographic characteristics of some villages or provinces, and clips of the makeup of social order and traditions.

Types of records of boundaries and laws and customs were inscribed not just on the surface; they were passed on to later generations through oral traditions as well. Folktales of a culture may seem like just stories about a sagacious hare, wily

---

[31] *Chulawansa* 80.41, qtd. in Ariyapala, 1956, 1997, p. 124.

[32] Nicholas and Paranavitana, 1961, p. 260.

[33] Ekanayake, A. De Silva, 1876, pp. 297-304.

[34] Nicholas and Paranavitana, 1961, p. 259, 260.

[35] Nicholas and Paranavitana, 1961, p. 240.

[36] D'Oyly, 1833, 1835, pp. 235 & 236; Modder, 1899, 24-25.

jackal, or the wicked crocodile offering help to cross the river. In these stories, we give little thought to the most obvious elephant in the 'river': the river's path itself demarcating the boundaries of village communities and even provinces it had carved naturally and permanently along the banks. Such traditions, and of course boundaries, themselves based on just as today's written guidelines, no doubt must have gone through changes over centuries. Rata Sabhāwa functioned earnestly with whichever extant customs and geographical boundaries presented to it etched on trees or community memory and traditions defining its jurisdictions.

Just as Rata Sabhāwa attempted to maintain a moral code among the villagers, the role of Buddhist monks in writing religious discourse for mostly an illiterate multitude was a priceless service. Their writings touched historical aspects of social institutions in Sri Lanka.

Dutch Governor Iman Willem Falck (or Falk) questioned senior Buddhist monks on August 12, 1769, about ancient laws, and customs of the Kandyan country and King's authority for sentencing, including death penalty. Then he wrote down their replies. Bertolucci (1817) quoted the Governor:

> When a person has committed a capital offence [...] the custom is
> to have circumstances of the case inquired into by the people and
> by the 'Judicial Chiefs,' and to make a reference to the antient Book
> which contains ... what is, and what is not lawful [*sic*]. (p. 458)

The concept of 'Judicial Chiefs' stated here seems like a tribunal of people having preliminary role, at least on judicial matters drawing similarities with Rata Sabhāwa of the 19th and 20th century Nuwarakalaviya, *Gam Sabe* or similar bodies in Kandyan country. Ancient books the Chief Bhikkhu alludes here seem to be the genre of Buddhist texts (on palm leaf book form) or a broad term encompassing the oral traditions and folklore.

The *Mahawansa* describes how King Pandukābhaya (377-307 BC),[37] chose the seat of his kingdom at the place called Anuradhapura, the village built by his great uncle Anuradha. Afterwards, Pandukābhaya created four suburbs in this city. He also clearly demarcated boundaries of villages across the kingdom.

Centuries later, seven miles east of Anuradhapura, at Mihintale hill, two rock inscriptions of Mahinda IV (956-972 AD) sitting side by side in the mezzanine plaza on the way up to the Ambastala stupa on the hill-temple record functions and duties of both the monks and the laity, and punishments to be levied on those who eschew

---

[37] According to the *Mahawansa* and Nuwarakalaviya folklore, before ascending to the throne, and while on his way to war with his uncles, Pandukabhaya stayed three months near Kasa mountain (Kasa-Pabbata), to muscle up his army and stockpile supplies. He recruited 700 soldiers from the nearby village of Pana (present-day Tirappana near Kasa mountain?) north-east of Kahala-gama in Ulagalla Kōrale (Kahapathvilagama – Kasagama, 15 kilometers east of Anuradhapura) (*Mahawansa* n.d. 1912, ed. 2003, X.27 & Appendix C, p. 288). Kasagama is the birth village of my father, few kilometers from my own. Incidentally, two centuries later, King Dutugamunu also stayed at Kasa-pabbata for few months resting his troops and procuring supplies. He built there a tank and a village named Pajjotanagara (city of yellow flames) (*Mahawansa* XXV.50) and held water festivals before making the final thrust to war with Tamil King Elara at Anuradhapura. Wilhelm Geiger thinks having two Kings stopping by this mountain suggests the presence of a military road that ran North and South past it (*Mahawansa* Appendix C, p. 288).

maintenance duty on lands and edifices belonging to the Aet Wehera[38] temple and monastery in the complex (Fig. 28). Aet Wehera was a Buddhist temple under the patronage of Abhayagirivihara sect in Anuradhapura started around 1st century BC. The long inscriptions (each slab contains 58 lines) on two 3' x 6' rectangular stone slabs explicitly state that workmen who shirk duties at the temple or villages (belonging to temple) must be reprimanded by the 'whole priesthood,' and not by a single priest.[39] Although not purely a council of laity like Rata Sabhāwa or its precursors, 'the whole priesthood' in this inscription is evidence of a form of body of monks with some form of judicial authority or acted as a jury-like structure sanctioned by the King or the Buddhist clerical establishment, possibly by the cultural modalities existed in pre-medieval Sri Lanka.

The inscriptions also give us a glimpse of duties of slaves, priests, and grants or dues to the temple by villagers near and as far as Minneriya (80 kilometers to the Southeast), and fines to those who avoid their temple responsibilities. Even the monks were subjected to expulsion from the temple. In other words, could Aet Wehera stupa located on the highest spot on the hill complex implied that the name ascribed to it had no doubt enjoyed a commanding seat in the monastic administrative structure of this religious milieu? If the text on the stone slabs by itself is not convincing and descriptive enough, exquisite finish with raised molding-like edges and occupying a central spot on the 4-acre plaza where evidence of stone-based architecture of the ruined buildings spanning centuries spell out the attention and importance of the system of social and religious order of a time it passed on to ages.

LÉKAM MITI, SITTU (ORDERS) AND *VITTI POTH* OR *VITTI PATTARA.*

Descendants living in some walawwas told me that they are not aware of records like *lékam miti* or *sittu* in their storage area as the tribunals stopped functioning decades before most of them were born. Making the prospects of my task of finding such a document bleaker was the fact that some likely repositories of such records have been converted to other purposes like resorts,[40] bestowed to the *sasana* to be used by the Order of Monks as temples,[41] taken over by the government,[42] destroyed due to callous political and social unrest erupted in communities,[43] or simply faced inevitable hazards of time.[44] New alternatives for social order, particularly written laws, replaced the void.

---

[38] *Aet-* should read as *Anto* in Pali = *Inner,* thus an *Inner Temple* (Anuradha Seneviratna, 1994, *Ancient Anuradhapura,* p. 262.

[39] Muller, 1883, p. 116.

[40] Ulagalla walawwa, few miles off A-9 highway on Tirappane in Anuradhapura district, is now a tourist resort.

[41] Kuppiyawatte Sri Jayasekararamaya temple in Colombo (former Jayasekara walawwa); Dadalle Mahamudalindarama temple in Galle district (former Dadalla Rajapakse Maha Mudali Walawwa).

[42] Kandy Municiple Council (former Dunuwila Walawwa) and Kotalawala Defence Academy (former Kotalawala walawwa, and former Kandy remand prison (Ehelepola Walawwa).

[43] See Tillakaratne, Lokubanda, 2010, Hurulle Walawwa: A Piece of History Through Destruction. *Sunday Times,* October 03, 2010.

[44] The thatched and wattle and daubed old walawwa in Bulankulama is an example.

A *Sittu* can be a single or a few strips of palm leaves, while *Lékam Miti*, as the name suggests, was a 'bundle' of palm leaves denoting a volume of multiple single-page record(s) or single document of multiple leaves. They existed in the Portuguese time too, and during King Dharmapala's (1551-1597) reign, they were translated into the Portuguese language.

Fig. 29. A Palm Leaf Book Library. With
decorative wood covers in Habaraduwa
Katukurunde Purana Viharaya.
Photo: Subhani Sachintha Guruge.

Lékam miti were of several types: 1. *Kat Hal Lékam Miti* (pingo dues) 2. *Dissava Maha Lékam Potha* (list of villages belonging to the walawwa) 3. *Hee Lékam Miti* (cadastral records of ploughed lands) 4. *Dunukara Lékam Miti* (maintained by Department Heads for labor force records) 5. *Walawwe Lékam Miti* (Records of Walawwe activities & sessions, including Rata Sabhāwa) and 6. *Maligawe Lékam Miti* (Record of activities of Temple of the Tooth Relic).[45] Reference also has been made to a *Hatara Lekhana* (four registers) which is composed of 1. Tanag(h)al *Lékam Miti*, 2. *Dissa Lékam Miti*, 3. *Hee Lékam Miti*, and 4. *Dunukāra Lékam Miti*.[46] *Tanagal (tana hāl?) Lékam Miti* have been also called *Kat Hāl Lékam Miti*.[47] *Lékam miti* kept by *Vannihuru* were called *Vanni Lékam Miti*. As writing paper (*kadadāsi*) was not available for widespread use in Sri Lanka until first decades of 19th century,[48] Rata

<hr>

[45] Pieris, R. 1956, p. 119.

[46] Abeywardena, 1978, p. 24; Pieris, R., 1956, p. 119.

[47] Vimalananda, 1963. p. 406.

[48] One of the earliest references to the word *kadadāsi* appears in D'Oyly's *Diary* dated Sept. 25, 1810. While he communicated with Kandyan spies with letters written in ink (on *kadadāsi*), D'Oyly received letters from his spies only on ola scribed on strips of palm leaf, a good indicator that print

Sabhā decisions sent to the *Ratemahattayā* or Maha Vanniyā continued to be recorded on *Sittu*[49] or *Lékam miti* and likely kept in their possession. It is not known if they were really sent to appropriate departments of the palace in Kandy on a regular basis for the same reason: travel-related encumbrances.

Also used as written medium were palm leaf books called *puskola poth* (s. *potha*).[50] A *puskola potha* can contain hundreds of pages (Fig. 29, 30). Not just ballads or stories, native sciences and recipes for medicinal drugs and treatment methods were also recorded on *puskola* manuscripts. The *Bhesajju Nidhāne*, a comprehensive medical book written in c.1760 by Mudliyar Don Simon Tillekeratne in Matara consists of 400 pages.[51]Throughout the history in Sri Lanka, there are records of prescriptive messaging and attempts to describe how certain social establishments should function. Royal edicts, details of grants to individuals or institutions, personal comments, and creative writings are the usual contents of these works. These early ways of recording passed on through generations have shaped the late models of maintaining social order including Rata Sabhāwa in ways large and small.

Often, the King proclaimed his intentions and the boundaries of the precincts with not with a *'Sri Sannasa'* by his 'Sri Mouth.'[52] It is a verbal edict (Fig. 31, 32). After he made a proclamation, it can be written and attested by a Chief Minister or a secretary, often called *Sannas* Tiri(u) Warahan Perumal (or Tiruwarahan Perumal) or a person with a name suffixed with Perumal, an appellation we see on *Sannas* spanning couple of centuries after the end of first millennium.[53] Often this *Sannasa*

---

paper was not yet popular at the time. Precursor to *kadadāsi* was *káda path* (e.g., in *Mukkara Hatana*). Rather than carrying documents on paper which could point to a privileged or special relationship with the British or anyone in Maritime Districts and stirring interest during inspections at land border points, ordinary Kandyans preferred old methods of writing.

[49] Written decrees; Often called *wattoru*. See T. Vimalananda (1963), *Udarata Maha Keralla,* for a full description of types of documents, letters and certificates produced in 18th and 19th centuries in the Kandyan Kingdom.

[50] Strips of leaflets torn off the spines of Talipot palm fronds are first boiled, then treated by controlled drying. After etching letters on the dry leaf using a metal stylus, the surface is rubbed with carbon black for better contrast and readability. These strips are bound into a book by tying them with a cord sent through two holes made on both ends. Its front and back covers are usually two exquisitely carved or painted wood strips. Some exceptional books have pages with gilded edges and decorative borders.

[51] J. Attygalle, 1913, Medical Research of the Sinhalese by W.A. De Silva, *JRAS*, Vol. 23, No. 66, pp. 34-50.

[52] Davy (1821, 2006) wrote that a *Sannas*a with the words *Sri* or *Swasthi* (ශ්‍රී ස්ව) etched on the top or at a conspicuous place on the text symbolized that it was issued (and signed) by the King (p. 186), thus making it a regnal fiat not needing witnesses. Usually, as a practice, all other *Sannas* had names of the executor and few witnesses.

[53] From the time of Parakramabahu the Great (1153-1186) through the early decades of the 19th century in Sri Lanka, many scribes who were associated with producing royal *Sannas* seem to have the *Perumal,* a title as a prefix or suffix to their names. See H. C. P. Bell, 1904, *Report of the Kegalle District of the Province of Sabaragamuwa,* pp. 68-106 for a list of such *Sannas* written up to 1814. Some of these scribes were: *Gampola* **Perumal** (c 1302-1326); *Sannas Thiru warahan* **Peruma** (*labma – jïy, me.*) c 1436; *Wijaya Singhe Ekanayake Kappa* **Permul** c 1475; *Sannastiruwarahan Wickramasinghe Adhikari* **Perumal** (*wamha - me*) c 1478; *Sannas Tiruwarahan* **Perumalu(mha)** in Devundara Dévāle *Sannas*a, Vijayabahu VI, c 1516- ?; and *Sannasiwatte Wakelu* **Permal** c 1509 (in Lawrie, 1896, Vol. 1, p. 339). In Edward Muller, 1883, p. 141 a Sanhasmakuta Werun Wanspa **Perumal** wrote the

was then called a *Wadāla Panatin Sittu.*[54] They then became the tradition, and in the course of time it acquired 'legal status.'

An example of a *Sannasa* requiring no witnesses is the Sri Sannasa – edict of the King. No witnesses' name appear in a Sri *Sannasa* granted by the King Sri Wijaya Raja Singhe (1739-1747) (told in a family *Sannasa* in 1745) gifting villages to Ehelepola Mudiyannehe for his service representing the court as an ambassador cum *mangul kapuwa* (marriage arranger) to South India to bring princesses as King's consort "from Madura of the Solar dynasty with great effort and undergoing great troubles ...." (Lawrie, p. 200).

Sri *Sannas* are deeds of recognition, land grants or any other endowments bestowed by the King and signed by *Adikaramvaru.* Orders or Charters of the King, any high official or between individuals were etched as rock inscriptions or lithic grants (*gal Sannas*), *tudapoth* (also called *tudapatha* – royal decree or a deed written on palm leaf), *talpoth,* (palm leaf books of ordinary people), *Sannas* or *hannas* (documents or notes of action of Chieftains), *ola poth,*or *karepoth* (grant deed documents written for sale or purchase of a slave), copper or silver strips, *vitti patra* or *vitti poth* – description of events. Copper or silver *Sannas* were made in the *Abharana Pattale,* Smiths' Guild, which had four branches called *Hatara Pattale* spread across the country.[55]

Sannas written on one or multiple palm leaf pages, often called *lēkam miti* or *sittu,* and those etched on rock or wood surfaces were documents that became accepted as law encompassing the purpose it was written for. These purposes included grant deeds to property, titles to individuals, transfer of property, including transfer of slaves from one owner to another or their emancipation rewards and notes of appreciation.[56]

Also included in this category of written material were palm leaf books, *tuda poth* (also called *tudapath* where royal grants were written), and *handahan* (record of birth with owner's planetary charts etched on it). Since there was no concept or a 'law' of registration of births, marriages or deaths, there was no necessity for registers or volumes like parish registers to record such events. Unlike ecumenical houses of worship, producing and keeping birth or death records of their devotees was not the practice at the Buddhist temples.

Kadirana Sannasa of King Vijayabahu VI (1513-1521) probably on the day of the annular solar eclipse on June 19th, 1517 (*NASA Catalogue of Solar Eclipses*) but seen partially in Sri Lanka. The early 19th century poet scribe Gajaman Nona (Lady Gajaman), a descendent from a family of celebrated writers had her name suffixed as **Perumal**. Gajaman Nona was under the tutelage of Karatota Dhammarama, John O'Doyly's Sinhala teacher. When she died in 1814 (Gooneratne, Branden & Yasmine, 1999, p. 223) the third line of the dedicatory quatrain scribed on the *pandol* – ornamental gateway - built over her grave read: ...*Neka guna Dona Isabel* **Perumal** *Digeasa* - The virtuous Lady Dona Isabel Perumal (Gamage, H. H. 1988, p. 24, *Andare Saha Gajaman Nona.* Maradana: Indika Press). Gajaman Nona's niece Dona Francisca **Perumal** Abeysinghe was also a prolific poet in the Southern Province (Kathleen Jayawardena, 2008, *Matara Wansaya,* Vol. II p. 80).

[54] J. M. Perera, 1861, p. 134.

[55] They were: *Ran Kadu Pattale* (Sword makers), *Otunu Pattale* (Makers of Crown), *Sinhasana Pattale* (Makers of Throne), and *Sittaru Pattale* (Painters and Lapidarists) (D.C. Kandy 34396, cited in H. C. P. Bell, 1904, p. 91).

[56] Lawrie, p.1898, 764, 529.

Usually, the *situ* was a binding document (order). Only persons of authority had the power and privilege to write one. Having this power also established that the person had the authority to judge the matter specified in the document. Record keeping by Rata Sabhāwa by and large was not a very complex or lengthy process. After the sitting, sending the decision to *Ratemahattayā* or Dissāva written on a *sittu* or *lēkam mitiya*, also called *dada mudippuwa*, if it was a fine, was considered an adequate record of the proceedings. There was no practice of issuing a receipt after paying a fine. It is not known what mechanisms or practices, including storage methods, were used for such records. It is likely those who received a *Sittu* kept it in the family as seen from hundreds of *Sannas* and other documents produced decades later by litigants in colonial courts as shown by A. C. Lawrie in the *Gazetteer.*

Fig. 30. An open Palm Leaf Book. Note the binder threat holes.
Photo: Subhani Sachintha Guruge.

The complete inventory of recording similar practices in Kandy is also not known. But a *Sittu* was also used to record other decisions by Chiefs and given to the person who deserves the advantage – a winning situation. Thus, it was a deed, certificate, or acceptable statement confirming a fact. In 1859, Asgiriya Mahanayake Thero stated that writing a *Sittu* after a *Gam Sabhāwa* (in Kandy) proceedings was "not an old custom."[57] According to Kapuruhami Madukanda Ratemahattayā (1948), a century after the Kandy King was deposed, however, writing of a *Sittu* was found to be not in vogue.[58] But these recording habits seemed to have continued as seen from the diary entry I found maintained by former Alittane Kōrāla. One notation in it is about a dispute a between two villagers brought before the *Kōrāla* over crop damage by a herd of buffaloes belonging to the other (Appendix – G). Officials like *Arachirāla* or *Vel Vidāne* made records of their official activities in government-issued diaries. In addition to their day-to-day official activities, some notes were concerned with resolution of mundane disputes. My grandfather, *Vel Vidāne* of Manakkulama, had a 5'x5'x1' Diary and I remember him writing on them attentively after a gathering of a few villagers in his house (Fig. 37).

---

[57] Goonesekere, 1958, p. 142.
[58] Kapuruhami, 1948, p. 42-68.

The *Vitti Potha* stated earlier was common in North Central Province.[59] *Vitti Patraya* (Page of Incidents), is another form of document as shown in Mangalagama Sannasa (a village near 54th mile-post on Colombo-Kandy road) granted to a Mandalawalli Naidé Mulachariya (also known as Mangalagama handu naida in 1644 AD, believed to be by King Buwanekabahu VI of Kotte.[60]   From the year of its execution as stated in the *Sannasa*, scholars argue that it is possible it was given by King Raja Singhe II.   During the same period, there was another type of document called *Gam Vittiya* (land dispute incident).[61]

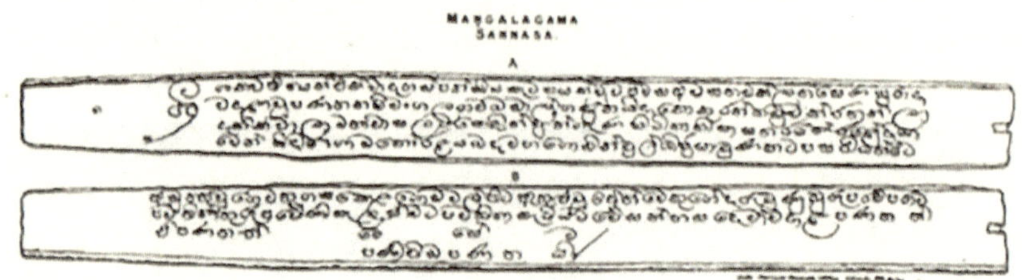

Fig. 31. Mangalagama Sri *Sannasa* (c 1644 AD). H. C. P. Bell, *Report on the Kegalle District.*

The colonial writers seem to have not taken into consideration or missed altogether the palm leaf book records people made on agreements or contracts of various nature. They became 'law' applicable to the parties specific to the incident. In a sense, they were binding instruments between two or more parties as seen from widespread use of them as evidence in 19th century court cases. Except in suspected forgery situations, they were honored by all. *Sittu* on palm leaf books contained all issues relating to land e.g., their sale, transfer, succession, or division. Lawrie showed this practice well in the 19th century as he made notes either by reproducing hundreds or making references to many as he found in court records.

WANTING OF PRINT TECHNOLOGY. Two main factors seem to have contributed to the paucity of existence of records. First is the non-existence of print technology in Sri Lanka during that time. The earliest known book in Sri Lanka was printed in 1708, most likely on paper imported by the Dutch; and the first book written in Sinhala letters, a prayer book, came out in 1737.[62] It should be noted this was the time when missionaries were busy recruiting candidates for conversion[63] and

---

[59] Wickremasinghe, 1900, Para 74, P. 79.

[60] Bell, H. C. P,1904, p. 98; Senaveratne, John M. 1914, p. 210.

[61] Senaveratne, John M. 1914, p. 211.

[62] Arangala, Ratnasiri, 2014, Keynote speech at the Godage Literary Award Ceremony, p. 2.

[63] In early British Sri Lanka, missionary expansion did not limit to religious booklets, or debates with monks. Using friendship of Sri Lankan literati to advance these goals happened in most unusual and unexpected ways. In 1818, when Chief Justice Alexander Johnston who introduced Trial by Jury to Sri Lanka was preparing to leave the island upon retirement, his 89-year-old friend Karatota Dhammarama Nayaka Unnanse came from Matara to Colombo to see him. Dhammarama Unnanse helped the Justice, D'Oyly host of colonial Civil Servants with language related issues. To the Justice he introduced two monks named Sree Guna Muni Ratana (27 yrs.) and Dhamma Rama (25 yrs.) [sic], cousins, who lived at Dodanduwa temple.   The young monks

distributing religious literature and setting up printing technology that they believed would augment their practice of aggressively debating Buddhist monks face to face to spark interest in Christianity among the devotees who came to the temples.[64] In 1814, Wesleyan Methodist Missionaries brought, among other things, their printing press, a box of ink, printing types and a box of printing paper.[65]

Paper and pencils were available to Kandyans only during the waning years of their kingdom.[66] But dearth of written volumes by native writers during that period may indicate that they preferred the old way of communication and record keeping. John D'Oyly's corps of native spies, usually a select group of well-placed individuals in the Kandyan society, sent him covert missives written on ordinary-looking palm leaves.[67]

However, it is interesting to note that little over a century before that, writing accessories seem to have been introduced by foreigners as gifts or novelties to the Kings and the elites in Sri Lanka. When the Dutch soldier Henricus van Bystervelt came to Hanguranketa in 1671 as an embassy of the Dutch government in Colombo, King Raja Singhe II presented him, among other gifts, a silver inkstand.[68] In 1707, Dutch Ambassador Gregorius Da Costa carried 4 books of small-sized writing paper to Kandy.[69] Although there is no widespread evidence of any document written with ink on paper by a Kandyan in the 17th century, objects like inkstands ornately crafted in brass or silver with glided edges and handles emulating artful figurines no doubt must have come to King's possession as a part of a gift or souvenir he received previously from a visitor. And having exclusive gifts like an inkstand shows he must have been aware of writing with ink. Obviously, such exclusive objects remained accessible only to the royalty and aristocratic class.

MULTIPLE COPIES OR DUPLICATES. Although the creativity flourished, due to lack of writing equipment and know-how to produce multiple copies of a document, Kandyans were left with the only alternative technological advancement they had for any occasion of writing: the stylus, and the treated palm leaf. Also, in cases of *Sannas*, it is not known whether multiple copies of them were made. But those who needed it most and had the urge and mindset found ways to duplicate the

---

wished to go to Britain to learn different religions. The Justice consented and after sailing home with them, charged the two to a Pastor Adam Clarke of Liverpool who agreed to host them. Two years later, they disrobed, and the pastor baptized them as Adam Sree Goona Muni Rathna [*sic*] and Alexander Dherma Rama [*sic*]. (*An Account of the Religious and Literary Life of Adam Clarke*, By a Member of His Family, 1833, London: T.S. Clarke, pp. 351-371). They obviously appear to have added Adam and Alexander, respectively, to honor their two British benefactors. After returning to Sri Lanka, they began working under the British after receiving titles as Muhandiram in Moratuwa and Galkissa, respectively (Sourced from Sivasundaram, 2013, p.111).

[64] For print culture of missionaries in early 19th century, see *Recollections of Ceylon* by Rev. James Selkirk (1844).

[65] Harvard, W.M. 1823, 2016, *A Narrative of Establishment and Progress of the Mission to Ceylon and India*, p. 136.

[66] Obeyesekere, 2017, p. 120.

[67] D'Oyly wrote about a letter sent by Warigama Atapattu Nilame to him on Jan. 13, 1812, on China Paper (1917 p. 79). By 1800, printed currency notes of 25, 50 and 100 Rix dollars were in circulation in Sri Lanka (Turner 1919, p 185).

[68] Pieris, P.E. 1918, p. 18.

[69] Abeysinghe, T.B.H., 1985/1986, pp. 1-40.

early palm leaf documents. Instances of forged *Sannas* have been known in a case brought to light at the Asgiriya Temple in 1832.[70] The British officials were able to make multiple copies of documents as the Government Press was already in operation. M. S. Crawford, Assistant Government Agent in Mannar sends a letter dated March 15, 1815, to O'Doyly in Kandy. Crawford mentions that he gave a copy of this letter to Suriyakula Kumarasinghe Vanniya as well. Crawford also gave the Vanniya 20 copies of Governor's Proclamation written in Sinhala[71] showing the efforts of British to prepare large number of hand-written copies of a document. In 1821, Chief Secretary's Office sent 300 copies of Regulation 8 of 1821 consisting of close to 1000 words to magistrates in Jaffna area to be read in Tamil about the emancipation of female slave children.[72] It is not known what duplication methods were made at this time.

The burdensome steps involved in the process of producing components of a palm leaf book was not a welcoming prospect if ever duplicates were needed. However, validating the majority of *Sannas* by multiple people who allowed their names to be written on the document as witnesses present at the time it was created seemed to have mitigated any potential adverse outcomes or questions for not having duplicates. What was important was for the grantee to keep the document safely in the family heirdom with multiple people named as witnesses.

Record keeping was a daunting task amid perpetual dangers a bundle of palm leaves can fall into. They were prone to irrevocable damage from nature. I did not have to look far out to experience this. My horoscope, *handahana,* was my pride because it was the first object that had my name scribed on it with floral letters certifying my presence at the time of my birth! It was a processed strip of palm leaf about a foot long. It had my biodata: date, time, and place of birth etc. After I started working in Kandy in 1969, my father put it in a metal trunk box for safety. One night, the word leaked out about a buffet of treats in a strong box. Alerted after hearing this sweet song, a colony of termites on a foraging tour across our front yard changed course and descended on the feast in a hurry. By morning, they had processed it into something akin to leopard skin. Black holes in yellowish background appeared where my heavenly charts and friendly planets had been. Thankfully, my date of birth was visible allowing me to navigate through bureaucratic maze later as I began to age. Although the pageantry of my birthday celebrations continues to date, I have no proof to show what the astrologer wrote as the planet I came from.

WILL OF THE KING. The second reason that a potential record keeping practice could not survive was the reality, at least in the legal literature field in the kingdom. Knox (1681,1995) said "there are no laws…" in Kandyan country to write about, "…but will of the King… But whatsoever came out of his mouth became the immutable law" (p. 101). In ancient Sri Lanka, King and the Priesthood were "the two fountains of law." Answers to most questions were determined by the

---

[70] Lawrie, 1896, p. 70.

[71] Ievers, 1899, p. 44.

[72] SLNA Lot 20/2016, CSO to Collector in Jaffna, April 18, 1821, cited in Nira Wickramasinghe, 2020, p. 133.

"pleasure and caprice of the King" (p. 215). The King's law basically was a road without mileposts – distance variable and no checks and balances to keep his whims reasoned. A written law, even if it was least likely, could not have survived long under the influence of the 'will of the King' which naturally changed at his pleasure or whim. So, even if a scribe wrote the law on a palm leaf book, before he put it on a shelf, it would become obsolete no sooner than the King changed his mind. It was the norm then that those customs, traditions, and folklore, though not written, passed down through generations as the 'law' remained embedded in the perception of the people as records until the next version about the matter came 'out of the King's mouth as his 'will.' So, the 'law' in Kandyan country remained in a state of fluidity.

ශ්‍රී ලංකේශ්වරවූ උතුම් අපගේ දෙවි සවාමි
දුරුවාණන් වහන්සේගේ අසදෘස
අතිගම්භිර වූ ශ්‍රී මහා කරුණා දිවස්
එලියේ මහිමතාවයෙන් වදාළාවූ පනත නම්
දොඩංවල විකුමසිංහ චන්ද්‍රසේකර කරුණාතිලක
සෙනෙවිරතන පණ්ඩිතමුදලියා උතුම් වූ මහා වා
ශලට සොඳ සිතින් දුක්ගැන සිටිනා නිසා [. . .] ෳ
[. . .]
ශක වෂ් එකුඩා දහස් සසිය අසූ හයට පැමිණි
තාරුණ නම් වූ මේ වස්යෙහි දුරුතු මශ අව
තෙළෙස් මත් නම් තීරිය ලත් සෙණසුරාඳ මේ
දවස මේ සන්හස දෙවා වදාල පනතත් එප
ණතත් මෙසේම පණිවුඩ පනතයි [sic] ෳ

'SRI - *The edict proclaimed and bestowed with the divine glow of kindness of our infinitely supreme, magnificent, and glorious Majesty of Sri LankaAs Dodanwala Wickramasinghe Chandrasekara Karunatilake Senevirathne, the pundit Mudaliya had been an extraordinary servant with devotion to the exalted Great Palace* ෳ
[. . .]
This decree so is the command and may it be known that this Sannasa was proclaimed and bestowed as thus on this. Saturday 21st in the month of Duruthu (January) in the Saka year of sixteen hundred eighty-six (Jan. 21st, 1764, AD)." ෳ

Fig. 32. A partial 'Sri' Sannasa on copper plate (12.5" x 2") believed to have been granted to a Dodanwala Senevirathna Panditha Mudliyar by King Kirti Sri Raja   Singhe on January 21, 1764. Don Martino de Zilva Wickremasinghe, 1900. English translation by the author.

But Gooneratne, Branden and Yasmine (1999) note, "the Chiefs had been the repositories of customary law: when the need arose to make a decision" the King consulted them for suggestions and assistance (p. 171). Chiefs' memories and experience in judicial affairs were the *stare decisis*, long standing precedents, settled law the King and citizens could depend on. Deficit of any legal guidance in written form also made the King and other authoritative persons to be surrounded by a constellation of flaws and shortcomings in social justice, often with chilling and bizarrely lack of sympathy and reason to make decisions pertaining to breach of social norms. Thus, due to lack of a central guiding primer of legal principles for implementation of law and maintaining conformity and consistency in keeping records of decisions, it is probable Rata Sabhāwa or *Gam Sabe* traditions were practiced often with disparate ways. Occasionally this gave the Chiefs the opportunity to make impromptu decisions as they deemed fit at a Sabhā. Robert Knox (1681, 1995) noted that when they faced a situation where they were ignorant or unsure of what their duties or what the relevant customs (laws) and procedures existed to resolve a problem, the inferior officers – *mulādānivaru/kāriyakarawannō* – who were in attendance did "teach and direct them how to act" (p. 50). Gooneratne B. & Y. (1999) think, though the Chiefs were the "repositories of customary law" handed down by word of mouth, they feared their jealously guarded power was in danger of erosion (p. 171). This may not totally explain the reason only a half dozen Kandyan Chiefs made attempts to write down customs and traditions as laws even after writing papers were introduced in early 19th century.

Under modern standards, want of a written code of law and procedure and a central document *à la* register or a registry to retain records of decisions made orally at Rata Sabhā or any other *sammuthi* were a major drawback of the rural judicial system in Nuwarakalaviya.

Even written *Sittu* as notices or memos sent to the Chief did not survive the vicissitudes and incertitude over the course of time. But what worked was that in those days, things agreed upon orally at discussions were honored, so much so, keeping a record or duplicate was found immaterial to uphold the central theme of the agreement. Such decisions or agreements were valid in perpetuity 'as long as the sun and the moon existed.' Found in many *Sannas*, such phrases may seem like a metaphor, but the underlying connotation was clear, nonetheless. The agreed upon decision even without a written record usually can become a form of duplicated or parallel version when it immerses itself in the folklore of the community. Over time, it can jump the community boundaries giving a wider exposure and acceptance.

Third-party writings too were non-existent and written material directly focused on Rata Sabhāwa was not available too. Undoubtedly, the reason for this was the lethargic interest or attention of anyone to study this tradition because it was not a legal institution that was directly under the Sinhala Kings, or afterwards, the colonial administrations. Many government agents told the Colebrooke Commission that they were unaware of the digests of D'Oyly, or Sawers and knowledge of local language was not essential for their work.[73]

---

[73] Sivasundaram, 2013, p. 131, citing SLNA Lot 19/103.

Secondly, in the eyes of the writers who had no personal stake in the actual concept, it was a practice only privy to the natives who used it to maintain their tribal and communal norms. Thirdly, the 'insalubrious' conditions in the region must have dampened the impetus for those sagacious few to learn and write assiduous notes about the culture and customs of the Nuwarakalaviya people. These customs were alien and of no concern, not just to them, but to many Sri Lankans, particularly in areas once ruled by the Kings of Kotte and the European colonists on the coastal regions.

The few who could write were on a path acquiring characteristics of a diaspora within their own country. Moreover, many European writers were in awe of Sri Lankan history. In general, it influenced the native writers too to concentrate more on history and folklore in Maritime Provinces and adjoining areas of Kandyan highlands. They missed again the post-medieval Sri Lankan interior in northern half and coastal regions in the East. Their writings included a plethora of material produced by prior native intellectuals on various subjects that were available mostly in Buddhist temples and occasionally in private collections. Immediately prior to the European arrival, the authors of *Sandésa* poems described earlier also showed their scarce know-how of Nuwarakalaviya. The only exception I can think of is Simon Casie Chitty (1834) whose research for his *Ceylon Gazetteer* took him further interior and across the country than any mid-19th century native writer. He was a brilliant native son, born and grew up in Puttalama area.

WRITERS WHO ADORED THE ISLAND. But the above description does not take away the extraordinary scholarly contribution of a community of colonial writers like John D'Oyly, Simon Sawers (1780-1849), A. O. Brodie, Robert "Bob" Wilson Ievers (1850 – 1905), H. C. P. Bell (1851 – 1937), H. W. Codrington (1879-1942) and Leonard Woolf (1880-1969), and many others who no doubt fell in love with the island. Woolf's classic novel *Village in the Jungle* (1913), even in fictionalized story, shows his deep understanding of the villagers' way of thinking, culture, and traditions. In *Growing* (1961), he wrote:

> I fell in love with the country, the people, and the way of life which
> were entirely different from everything in London and Cambridge
> […] I became completely immersed, not only in my work, but in
> the life of the people. The more remote that life was from my own,
> the more absorbed I became in it and the more I enjoyed it. (p.
> 180 & p. 225)

Ievers, Bell, and Brodie, adored Nuwarakalaviya and made extraordinary efforts to record its history, customs, and traditions. But as noted earlier, they simply missed or disregarded Rata Sabhāwa as an intrinsic institution in the region.

However quaint and visceral was his literary style, Robert Knox (1681, 1995) without doubt was the earliest to write down on paper in scholarly passion series of laws and customs practiced in pre-modern times in the Kandyan country. He still called the island a "strange and pagan Land" (Epistle Dedicatory in *Historical Relations*). Little he knew, his incisive observations would be a priceless treasury of facts for historians who later wrote about life on the island he lived for 20 years, four centuries ago as a prisoner of the Kandy King.

H. A. I. Goonetileke in the introduction to 1995 edition of *Historical Relation* notes:

> One must not fail to mention that contemporary anthropologists surveying the peasant locale and rural organization in the interior of Sri Lanka fall back on Knox's account as a periscope in their research(es) – while modern historians examining the tides of history in the medieval period of the island's story […] still depend on his relation as a guide and outline [*sic*]. (p. xv)

A little over a century later, even before the oft written about *Niti Nighanduwa* Bertolacci compiled an informal and unstructured short inventory of Kandyan laws, politics and social justice based on a question-and-answer session that took place on August 12, 1769, between the Dutch Governor Iman Willem Falck and an un-named and best-informed Kandyan Buddhist monk. The Governor asked 48 questions covering issues like King's coronation, his power to impose penalties, nature of judicial process, death penalty, succession of property inheritance, and a mélange of other topics on Kandyan ways. The monk talks about taking guidance from a book called *Niti Sasthra* (Science of Law), probably the literary work with the same name by Chanakya, an Indian philosopher who lived in in 300BC. The monk also refers to "*Tela Patta Jatakaya*" (story about a previous birth of Buddha), and the *Mahawansa*, a Chronicle Kings referred for precedents.[74] It is an interesting revelation of folklore during the early colonial times that highlighted the Sri Lankans' awareness of reference to the said *Sasthra* and Chronicle and snippets in them relating to their early laws and customs. And Falk's discussion took place six decades before British civil servant George Turnour found the copy of the commentary of the original palm leaf book of *Mahawansa* from Mulkirigala temple!

In early 1800s, Percival wrote praising Sri Lanka for its commercial and political importance. He called the island a "trading emporium.[75]" After their tenures were over, certain factions of the British citizenry in Sri Lanka, whether military or civil service, either opted to retire in the island to become merchants or take up other ventures or went back and forth between the home country and the colony to reap wealth of its burgeoning economy.[76]

COLONIAL INTEREST AND CONTRIBUTION. Portuguese occupation in Sri Lanka was a time more of destruction than progress. I quote Robert Percival's writings in 1803 about the Dutch who replaced the Portuguese:

> [...] the Dutch prevented their own people from publishing any observation which they might have made during their stay in the island... Few were anxious to inquire the history either of the country of the inhabitants...They concerned themselves with very little about the interior of the island [...] many (of them) resided on Ceylon for a considerable number of years without having ever been so much as a few leagues from the coast [*sic*]. (pp.1-2)

---

[74] Bertolacci, 1817, pp. 451- 477.
[75] Cited in Sivasundaram, 2013, p. 71.
[76] Sivasundaram, 2013, p. 84.

Furthermore, the Dutch had a different logic for why they did not consider the native laws relevant to their governing. In *Instructions from Governor-General and Council of India to Governor of Ceylon during 1656-1665*, Sophia Pieters (1908) finds the little regard the Dutch had for laws and customs in Sri Lanka:

> Because nearly all the lands in this jurisdiction are de-populated, abandoned, and laid waste, we have no need to follow any old laws, customs or practices of the Sinhalese in cultivating them, but may be guided by such regulations as may be made in the interests of the Company and for the welfare of the Island. (p. 17)

But the British had a different view about the island. From the beginning, they were convinced this was a special place. Therefore, they often chose to promote the utility of one native characteristic over another. It is no secret the colonists perpetuated such thinking purely for their own interests than anything else. But rural matters like Rata Sabhāwa were not in any of their schemes as seen from the absence of significant written material about it.

Meanwhile, another unrelated but emblematic reason the British utilized and encouraged the local writers in the early 19th century was to collect botanic specimens and writing about them while creating botanical gardens in the country. As found in the *Hansard* (1830), this is in conjunction with colonial government taking strides to capitulate forest resources of the country as a major part of its strategy to benefit the Crown. A letter dated December 27th, 1821, by Governor Edward Barnes to Earl Bathurst read in the House of Commons (*Hansard* on May 27, 1830) states:

> The culture is completely within the control of the Government, as every tree in the island, whether growing wild or in private grounds, or in the preserved gardens, equally belongs to it; so that, if it became an object to eradicate it partially or in toto, it is perfectly feasible, and within the unshackled power of the Government to do so. (Columns 1155-1162)

With this mindset, they embarked on soliciting help from locals who were prolific note-takers and illustrators. This botanic idea was also to mimic the homely atmosphere for their employees who were in the colony for years and oceans away from home. Creating gardens reminiscent of the likes of Kew in London must have been an urgency of the administration much more than their interest in the economy of botanic ideas of the colony. This thinking helped recruitment and retention of young men to serve in a distant island. Towards this goal, they needed to collect botanical specimens from across the island and recruited Sri Lankans for the task. They were scribes, and knowledgeable in collecting native plants.

The government acquired land to build botanical gardens, on occasions targeting blocks of land already owned by Kings and temples. An example of such a block of land existed bordering the Mahaweli river in Peradeniya near Kandy decades before the arrival of the British. It was a royal pleasure garden probably existed as far back as 1371.[77] In 1821, botanist Alexander Moon started planting

---

[77] Sivasundaram, 2013, p. 185, referring to a recent visitors' guide at the Peradeniya Botanical gardens.

coffee and cinnamon on experimental basis in this strategic block of land locked in a singular loop of the river. The government also created botanical gardens in Slave Island and Kalutara on the West Coast. There were proposals to create another garden in Pussellewa located between Nuwara Eliya and Peradeniya in the hill country, but the idea was abandoned later as a new garden was started at Hakgala near Nuwara Eliya in 1861. Colonists had Kew Gardens as a standard in creating these gardens.[78]

The most pioneering native they recruited for this endeavor was Harmanis de Alwis Seneviratna (d. June 10th, 1894), a writer and illustrator. In 1818 he joined Alexander Moon to compile the *Catalogue of the indigenous and exotic plants growing in Ceylon...* (1824) the first of its kind in the country. Though it was not necessarily a Linnaeus-type account, the *Catalogue* brought together a vast collection of plants and tabulated them in groups as they thought the best way to present the unique flora of the island. In the preface of the book, Moon mentions the liberal assistance he received from the government, but not a word about his indigenous collaborator.

Governor Barnes, however, was so impressed with the contribution of de Alwis Seneviratna, in 1831 he conferred upon the latter the native title of Muhandiram and promoted him as the Draftsman. Few months before his death in 1894, the British conferred him with the title of Mudliyar.[79] It is not surprising if one wonders how the government was interested in one sector of Sri Lanka, encouraged sharing and celebrate the efforts of pioneers like Moon and natives like De Alwis Seneviratna but not inspiring the writers to look for culture that was hidden deep in the rural areas few leagues from the coast.

WRITING NATIVE LAWS. After the British took full control of Kandyan kingdom in 1815, and crushing the Kandyan War that followed in 1818, they realized the significance of validation and acceptance of indigenous legal, religious, and social ways. They concluded that this fact ought to be a practical necessity for application of the British law in the Kandyan country. For this, they proposed to write a compendium of such native laws, traditions, and customs. Since few decades earlier, elsewhere in the British Empire, the potential benefits of acknowledging traditions of natives of colonies had been in consideration too. Warren Hastings, Governor of Bengal (1773-1785), took into consideration indigenous customs and traditions of the Subcontinent in formulating civil and criminal laws for the masses of India.[80]

As found in Cohen (1996), Hastings while addressing the Directors of East India Company in 1784 noted:

> Every accumulation of knowledge obtained by social communication with people [...] over whom we exercise dominion founded on the right of conquest is useful to the state

---

[78] Sourced from Sivasundaram, 2013, pp. 173-208.

[79] Trimen, Henry 1894, Obituary of Haramanis de Alwis Seneviratna. *The Journal of Botany, British and Foreign* 32(380), Aug. 1894, pp. 255-256; Sivasundaram, 2013, pp182-192.

[80] Dirks, Nicholas B., 2006, *The Scandal of Empire*, p. 209.

> [...] it attracts and conciliates distant affections; it lessens weight
> of the chain by which natives are held in subjugation [...]. (p.45)[81]

In this background, in the early decades of the 19th century, with the labors of colonial writers like John D'Oyly (c 1818-1824; 1835, 1929) and Simon Sawers, notes on Kandyan laws, 'fragmentary and imperfect,' came out nonetheless with immense value and significance to colonial administration. D'Oyly's *Sketch of the Constitution of the Kandyan Kingdom* was a remarkable achievement to coalesce as a manual of customs and traditions that were the 'laws' in Kandyan country at the turn of the 19th century. In 1831, the transcending manuscript *Sketch* (1835) was submitted posthumously to the Royal Asiatic Society (Great Britain and Ireland) by Sir Alexander Johnston, Chief Justice of Ceylon (1811-1819) who founded the Royal Asiatic Society and a colleague of D'Oyly. Introducing the manuscript to the Secretary of the Society in 1831, Johnston declared, rightly so, the authenticity of D'Oyly's effort wherein his thesis was compiled:

> [...] from the information of the principal officers of the former
> Kandyan government, who at the time had no motive to suppress
> the truth and were perfectly competent to give him an authentic
> account of all that related to the nature and the constitution of their
> former government [sic]. (pp. 191-252)

In 1835, it came out in the Transactions of the Journal in full. As D'Oyly, Simon Sawers too belongs to the ensemble of British writers, some in the Civil Service, who contributed mightily to the legal literature of the island. His *A Digest of Kandyan Law* is one of the standard and pioneer works on the subject.[82] Commissioner, and later the Revenue Commissioner in Kandy followed the D'Oyly's *Sketch* with his other Digest, *Memoranda of the Laws of Inhabitants*.[83] Sometime after 1860, Sawers' *Digest* was published by James Campbell of the Hultsdorf Press, as *Sawers' Digest of the Kandyan Laws with an Appendix Containing Orders of the Supreme Court in Cases Decided in Appeal Bearing on the Kandyan Laws from 1851 to 1860*. No publication date is given on the title page.

Around the same time, *Niti Nighanduwa* appeared in Sinhala. Some suggested it as a summary of unstructured recapitulation of laws that already existed in writing. But according to Thambiah (1989), its 'antecedent expressions' suggest that it 'finds its authority in Mahasammata.'[84] It may also have been written anonymously. Altogether, however, transmission of news of such work seems to have been very poor or hampered at the time as seen from comments of many Government Agents who said they were unaware of the emergence of works of D'Oyly's or Sawers'

---

[81] Hastings was impeached upon his return to England (acquitted later), but his name is etched in road names and schoolhouses in India, undoubtedly a show of appreciation by the Indians for his respect for their customs and traditions.

[82] Toussaint, J.R., 1934, pp. 113-143.

[83] In 1900, Ælian Ondaatje edited it as *Digest of Kandyan Law*.

[84] Thambiah, 1989, King Mahasammata. *Journal of the Anthropological Society of Oxford*, Vol. 20, No.2, pp. 101-122.

Digests. Matale Government Agent observed that he was not aware of a Digest has been made since the start of the British Government.[85]

No one can say for certainty whether Sawers was asked by the government to compile a volume of Kandyan laws. But his liberal views and enthusiasm in wanting to learn the Sinhala language and Kandyan customs and traditions are well known. Sir Charles Marshall, Justice of the Supreme Court of Sri Lanka rectified errors and imperfections of Sawers or D'Oyly's unpublished writings by reproducing material portions of them in his volume with judgements and decisions of the Supreme Court between 1833 – 1836.[86] A. C. Lawrie suggested that the *Niti Nighanduwa* and what Sawers compiled as *Digest of Kandyan Laws* have commonalities, thus could have been written by the same writer.[87]

But later in 1880, *Niti Nighanduwa* was translated by the duo of C. J. R. LeMesurier, a Civil Servant in the Colonial Secretary's office, and T. B. Panabokke, President of Dumbara Village Tribunal, a Rata Sabhāwa-type assembly but with legal recognition and obligations mandated in 1871 by the British. According to LeMesurier, the book was the result of a committee of Chieftains who assembled following the request of Sawers to compile a Code of Kandyan Laws. For this project, a monk at the Malwatte Temple aided as the Secretary. As of 1899, draft of this *manuscript* was in the custody of Wegodapola, the Basnayake Nilame of Pattini Dévāle. It was published as *Kandyan Laws or the Vocabulary of the Law as it existed in the Last Days of the Kandyan Kingdom.*[88]

Interestingly, Panabokke family with roots in and around Kandy, would later become part of the Rata Sabhāwa tradition in 19th century by happenstance. For the family lore on this, see Appendix B for a reading of an encounter with storybook ending one day in the waning decades of the 19th century.

Another extraordinary contribution to Kandyan Law literature was made by John Armour, who was first the Interpreter in Kandy in 1819 and later the District Judge in Hath Kōrale. He was known as a "Judicial Agent" in early British occupation in Sri Lanka. He published *Grammar of the Kandyan Law* in 1846. It was in the genre of *Niti Nighanduwa*. It is believed that native Chieftains could have provided him information for the volume.[89] *Colombo Observer* of March 10, 1845, wrote him as "confessedly the best authority in the island on the complicated system of unwritten Kandyan laws.[90] He is said to have learned Sinhala from D'Oyly's language teacher – Karatota Nayaka Terunnanse, also known as Karatota Dhammarama, initially at Matara Weragampitiya temple. Armour married a Kandyan lady, so his love to learn and write about the native laws was no surprise. In 1857, Kandyan laws, customs and traditions described in Armour's treatise have

---

[85] Sivasundaram, 2013, p. 131 citing SLNA Lot 19/103.

[86] Modder, 1899, p. 24-28.

[87] Jennings, 1952, p. 185-220.

[88] Frank Modder, 1899, Kandyan Law. The *Ceylon Law Review* 1(1), pp. 24-28.

[89] Armour's popularity among Kandyans seem to have been unmatched to any at the time. A native bard wrote a poetic encomium (*prasthi kavi*) called *John Armour Astaka* for him on a palm leaf book found in British Library, London under OR 6601 (11). Sourced from Sujit Sivasundaram, 2013, p. 7 n13.

[90] Lewis, 1913, *List of Inscriptions on Tombstones...* p. 436.

been used as precedents by the Assistant District Judge T. C. Power of the District Court in Kandy to deliver his judgement in case number 29890.[91]

Kandyans were subjected to their own laws and when these were silent, the Roman Dutch law governed them.[92] 'Kandyan Laws' here is a reference to extant traditions and customs that were being promulgated as written codes at the time. Thus, first attempt of the British administration was to use Kandyan laws to resolve issues in the province. Act number 5 of 1852 says that when no guidance is available under Kandyan law, the law in practice in the littoral can be used as an alternative. The impact of this cross-cultural mix between two legal traditions, Roman Dutch, and the indigenous social norms in the colony in the early years of the British administration, particularly on the interior country of Nuwarakalaviya, was not acutely perceptible. If the early writers collecting snippets for their legal theses tried a bit hard, they would have known that the legal systems of British, and Dutch before them, were daubs of paint on an artist's palette, while the rules, and procedures of the arcane Rata Sabhāwa, at least on their eyes, would be the painting depicting the cloudless blue sky – unknown and distant.

Several legal scholars then updated and copied some parts from the written volumes outlined earlier for their own treatises that included new case laws that came out of the Supreme Court. Only in 1883, by the Ordinance No. 2, *The Penal Code* of Sri Lanka, was introduced.[93] In the fine de siècle, Justice Lawrie compiled *Gazetteer of the Central Province*, in two-volumes in novel form and in extraordinary details of history, geography, demography and legal issues of the Central Province. He discusses mostly court records and the history of families, past transactions of property rights, succession, and various issues ensued between parties. The factual bases in these descriptions often go back in generations. Also reproduced In the *Gazetteer* were hundreds of *Sannas* in extenso. The *Gazetteer* laid out how villagers as litigants sought help from the colonial laws through the "newly minted court system." In the process, centuries old customs and traditions with lasting impact on individuals, their heirs and ancestors came to light.

KNOWLEDGE GAP. In the beginning, as English law began to extend its presence across the country, the colonial administrators seem to have generously used the Kandyan concepts discussed in the two law treatises stated above. But D'Oyly (1917) observed that either British or Kandyan, not all aristocrats were well conversant with these laws. He wrote:

> [...] Chief officers being principally chosen from the noble families, [...] they were persons of inactivity; and being inexperienced in affairs of the province... were frequently guided in judicial as well as other concerns by the provincial head men, or by those of their household [...]. (p. 234)

---

[91] Perera, Joseph Martinez, 1861, Armour's *Grammar of the Kandyan Law* p. 136.

[92] *Ceylon Directory*, 1868, p. 11.

[93] https://www.ilo.org/dyn/natlex/natlex4.detail?p_isn=67628&p_lang=en, last accessed on August 9, 2021.

Yet, collective efforts were extremely helpful to the colonial scholar-civil servants to build the legal compendiums to keep Kandyan laws relevant.[94] Chiefs in Nuwarakalaviya too had a fair knowledge of the Kandyan customs and the nuances through acquaintances and relatives. This allowed exchange of ideas conveniently, and "sharing of notes" to occur freely between them.

As illuminating as they could be with their extensive coverage, the surfeit of law volumes stated above hardly made any discernible references to the Rata Sabhāwa tradition. A couple of facts lend plausibility to how this could have happened. Up until the last decades of the 19th century, didactic training in Sri Lanka took place as one-on-one setting. It was composed of professions learned with hands-on experience in carpentry, astronomy, aesthetic activities, medicine, and agriculture, just to name a few. There was no formal primer for language training except a few books of prose. Whatever writings that existed were not in mass circulation. Among them, *Sidath Sangarawa* was perhaps the premier language training manual. It was first written in Elu, an early version of the Sinhala language. There were no schools to train even the few who could afford to hone their skills on textual creations, let alone delving on any legal skills.

During the Dutch times, often priests went to Siam (Thailand) to study.[95] But by 1870s, villagers realized the importance of education and joined the fray by going to the extent of even building schools voluntarily in their communities[96] and undertaking their upkeep and repairs. But it was not enough to reduce the gap in education availability and affordability for the masses.

Pirivena schools – traditional learning centers designed primarily to train novice monks to advance Buddhist religious learning – gave language and religion training which usually only the elitist class had access to. Senior monks conducted these schools at the temple premises. They did not focus on teaching students to view a subject with a sociological footing, an important ingredient needed if one tried to write about existing cultural traditions upon which social institutions like Rata Sabhāwa and *Gam Sabe* and even religious education center, *pirivena*, were founded.

With elitist power as their capital, native Chiefs had a deep understanding of how the cultural institutions functioned, not by formal training but by hands-on experience, while the common people remained subliterate in most didactic disciplines. As seen from essays contributed to the *Sinhala Sirith Sangrahaya*, knowledge of the 32 author-elders was not only broad, but long in traditions and folklore of the region. But not until colonial intellectuals and enthusiast of the land like Knox, D'Oyly, Sawers, Armour, Lawrie, Panabokke and few others provided cues and encouragement did more writers opened up the bowers of the indigenous laws and customs to present them in written form.

---

[94] I believe that except for Kapuruhami Madukanda Ratemahattayā of Madukanda near Vavuniya (*Rata Sabhāwa,* unpublished mansucrit written in Sinhala in c 1910 and published in English in 1948), and few decades earlier T.B. Panabokke, President of Dumbara in Kandy with C.J.R. LeMesurier (*Niti Nighanduwa*, 1880), and few Buddhist monks, very few Kandyan Chiefs had produced scholarly works of significance in the 19th century pertaining to traditions and customs of Kandyan provinces.

[95] Davy, 1821, p. 308.

[96] Fairfield, Edward, 1880, *The Colonial Office List for 1880...* p. 66.

Another reason for the lack of writings is the existence of a knowledge gap between Western and indigenous traditions. Potential writers who wanted to write about them could not reconcile this. For example, native Chiefs and officials who knew their institutions did not know even marginally the merits of other legal traditions and philosophies, particularly the ones that had been put into practice by the Europeans in the Maritime Provinces. Those pioneer Sri Lankans who came trained in Western legal traditions, on the other hand, did not have an in-depth understanding of the native traditions, particularly in the realms of conflict management and social order in remote areas that the Rata Sabhāwa was centered upon.

British often displayed doubt and even disdain on native institutions and traditions. Colonials who climbed Adam's Peak in the early 19th century wrote belittling comments on the faith, beliefs, and the folklore theme of Sri Pada. Some of these travelers were experts in historiography and ethnic meanings as they knew it but believed indigenous beliefs and customs and religion to be of not worthy of discourse. Evangelical missionary influence and the Europeans' general position that these distant islands were populated by Pagans and atheists may have had a part in this. After visiting the Adam's Peak, John Davy (1818), whose writings on Sri Lanka regarded as priceless by historians, wrote to his brother Humphry Davy a letter datelined Colombo, May 2nd, 1817, with clear tone of scorn:

> The object of their worship is strong example too of the lowness
> of their faith, and their amazing credulity; it was painful to see them
> on the summit of a mountain... forgetful of the God of Nature
> and prostrate before a thing deserving only contempt. (25-30)

Prominent people in the British Empire in the 19th century were known to harbor such demeaning views about people in their colonies. Referring to the indigenous people of Tasmania and Australia, Charles Dickens famously wrote in 1853: "His (Noble Savage) virtues are a fable; his happiness is a delusion; his nobility is nonsense..." With such peculiar and slanted approaches as ballast, it is plausible that some factions of colonial officials, as well as writers, were not interested in knowing about traditions like Rata Sabhāwa practiced across Nuwarakalaviya.

LANGUAGE TRAINING. Regarding language in colonies, British colonial administrations placed the 'Command of Language' as an important factor in their 'Language of Command.' Therefore, one of the major steps towards understanding the culture of the people in the colony by its administrators was the establishment of Colebrooke-Cameron Commission in 1832-1833. Some government agents told the Commission that local language was not needed for their work. The Commission recommended Europeans in Sri Lankan Civil Service must be competent in Sinhala or Malabar (Tamil) languages. Giving evidence before the Commission, George Turnour said that it is important public servants to communicate with people in their own language without the help of interpreters.[97]

Cohen (1996) wrote: "language (in India) as Command was not only a domestic or personal matter, but a matter of state" (p. 40). In Sri Lanka too, language training was slow to catch up. During 1833-1848, only two British Civil Servants had passed

---

[97] Sivasundaram, (2013) p. 131, citing SLNA Lot 19/106 Evidence of George Turner, Esq.

the language requirement.[98] In truth, in this background of disinterest and disinclination to learn the language of the natives they ruled, it is abundantly clear the European writers had little appetite for knowing or writing about the indigenous institutions. Except for occasional crossings through Nuwarakalaviya from the coastal areas to the interior on foot or other means, Western writers had never experienced the life in these remote provinces up close to develop an interest in them. Lack of interest on each other's systems too contributed to this knowledge gap. Had they known at least a semblance of other's legal traditions after gaining competency in its expressive medium, it would have inculcated a sense of eagerness for inquiry. The inevitable consequence of this was that there was neither interest for analytical thinking of these systems nor enthusiasm to put them in textual form.

This was not the first time a similar situation, but in different context, existed in Sri Lanka. It is worth noting that during the early struggles of the British to gain control of the island, they "lacked the knowledge essential for political control.[99]" Particularly, it was the topographic knowledge of the mountainous region of the country they lacked. This deficiency kept all three eager colonizers out of the Kandyan Kingdom for three centuries shielding them from learning the native ways.

But it is reasonable to suggest that regardless of this language divide of the colonizer and the colonized, customs in Kandyan highlands continued to shape Rata Sabhā traditions in Nuwarakalaviya. As found in the sources discussed heretofore, even after fall of the kingdom, both Rata Sabhāwa and the Kandyan customs progressed together with the evolving colonial laws and language, although the latter was not the medium of business in these Sabha. In other words, starting from the middle of the 19th century, Rata Sabhā in Nuwarakalaviya, being fully aware of the laws that were slowly being infused into their new province and in the neighboring provinces, and various individuals creating volumes on precedents and lore based on anecdotal history since about a century earlier, felt comfortable and empowered still to continue with Kandyan laws and customs as basis for their tribunals. My view is that in its heyday, the Kandyan kingdom did not make efforts to clarify its fringe relationship with Nuwarakalaviya and Tamankaduwa. But both provinces sure had the kingdom in their hearts, for even the hilly kingdom was in its last gasp of existence, two millennia ago, its primogenitors were nurtured in these two districts before they would become forested and forgotten until the late in the 19th century.

TWENTIETH CENTURY CONTRIBUTORS. As much as the raft of 18th and 19th century yeasty volumes of Kandyan laws and customs were a major contribution to frame them on record as the standard legal and social norms in the country at the time, a century later, the inimitable and enthusiastic role played by C. L. Wickremasinghe, the Government Agent of Anuradhapura (1931-1934) is remarkable for its vision and originality. For the first time in the province, or in the country for that matter, he assembled a coterie of 32 *mulādänivaru/ kāriyakarawannō* who were ordinary citizens but wise elders conversant with folklore and history of Nuwarakalaviya.

---

[98] Coperehewa, S. 2011, p. 35.
[99] Sivasundaram, 2007, p. 926-965.

The Government Agent's announcement calling for essays for a competition on traditions and customs in areas they lived turned out to be a novel and an extraordinary idea to enlighten the life and ancient traditions and customs practiced in the region. Until then, no literary work, either fictional or analytical, had been produced with the direct participation of local *mulādānivaru/kāriyakarawannō*, or any elders and intellectuals who could provide a glimpse of authoritative details of the life and ways of the region. It is also difficult to find a similar collective exercise attempted anywhere else in the country up to that time.

These essays came to be known as Wickremasinghe Manuscripts. The Government Agent's son, Lakshman Wickremasinghe, late Bishop of Kurunegala, inherited them, and in 1979, at his urging, the Royal Asiatic Society, Colombo Branch invited D. E. Hettiarachchi, Professor of Sinhala at the University of Peradeniya to edit them and publish as *Sinhala Sirith Sangrahaya* (SSS, 1979, 2019), the incomparable thesis written to date about the ways in Nuwarakalaviya.

The depth and details of topics covered in SSS are of remarkable likeness with the same class of writings as Ievers' *Manual* (1899) or works of the likes of D'Oyly or Sawers, nearly a century earlier. The *mulādenivaru* jotted down their exceptional essays, no doubt on coarse foolscap or exercise paper, and with assiduous attention to details of facts, history, culture, and their traditions, casting a patented aura of their own people. This feat elevates this motley collection of individuals with backgrounds representing the larger province, humble in their intellectual endowment, with little or no exposure to hallowed halls of learning, but only the experience and access to oral history. With enthusiasm of highest order, they stand today alone in their special place, as stellar writers who contributed immensely to build the law literature north of Kandyan Kingdom.[100]

Finally, to top it all, in the first decade of the 20th century, after a millennia long state of evolving and rendering service through well-entrenched traditions and customs, Rata Sabhāwa came upon its glorified moment. Its rules and procedures were deposited as a written treatise with unmatched authenticity and telling authority by a native son, a muralist of traditions – an unassuming aristocrat with a life full of humility, yet a scholar and poet of Nuwarakalaviya. It was Kapuruhami Madukanda Ratemahattayā, later Maha Dissāva of Vavuniya Sinhala Pattuwa in the North Province. This effort cemented him as the premier native scholar in the region in the first half of the 20th century. Up to that time, no one had taken up writing even a summary description of Rata Sabhāwa tradition. Thus, Madukanda Ratemahattayā's seminal and refreshingly evocative work no doubt deserves to be called the *magnum opus* of the Rata Sabhāwa tradition of Nuwarakalaviya. It is doubtful the Government Agent Wickramasinghe was aware of its existence while working on the SSS because its handwritten manuscript was in the author's possession, 35 miles north of Anuradhapura.

Writings about Rata Sabhāwa blossomed into another stratosphere after the publication of the Kapuruhami thesis in the *JRAS* in 1948, five years after his death, although written in Sinhala decades earlier. Until then, any written description of the Rata Sabhāwa hardly exceeded a few lines. While the Madukanda Ratemahattayā's

---

[100] See Appendix C for the list of the contributing *mulādenivaru* to the *Sinhala Sirith Sangrahaya*.

work stands shoulder to shoulder with other great writings about Nuwarakalaviya, the efforts of the duo of H. W. Codrington (1879-1942) of Ceylon Civil Service and historian Paul E. Pieris (1874-1959) coordinating its English translation and publication deserve our appreciation. Moreover, both Codrington and Pieris have contributed tremendously with their own scholarship on the culture and history of Sri Lanka in general.

Since its publication, anthropologists and sociologists found Kapuruhami's disquisition as the premier resource to study at granular level a well embedded but little-known judicial system in Sri Lanka. It encapsulated the workings of the Rata Sabhāwa in detailed fashion no other Chief anywhere had been able to do up to that time. I will discuss in later chapters Kapuruhami Madukanda Ratemahattayā's piercing and panoramic curiosity and contribution to the culture he represented.

The 32 elders and Kapuruhami Madukanda Ratemahattayā produced their documents independent of each other and close to 30 years apart. None of the 32 elders were from Sinhala Pattuwa of Northern Province where Ratemahattayā lived and held court. In their writings, none of the elders have made any reference to Ratemahattayā or among each other. It affirms the authenticity and originality of their submissions. All of them had held positions as officials or *kāriyakarawannō* or indigenous medical professionals (*veda mahatvaru*), professionals of diverse fields or simply autodidacts competent in social norms, history, and their permutations.

Brilliance of the collective work of the 32 *mulādänivaru/kāriyakarawannō* is well summed up by D. E. Hettiarachchi when he called the Wickramasinghe Manuscripts a social science mine.[101] It is not an exaggeration then to call Kapuruhami Madukanda Ratemahattayā's thesis, written a generation before the *Manuscripts*, an incandescent moment in literature about the culture of Nuwarakalaviya! His name will be associated with the Rata Sabhāwa of Nuwarakalaviya for all of history.

Then, a couple of decades after Kapuruhami's initials work, in 1938, with the abolition of native hereditary titles altogether, the role which the Chiefs played on social order for centuries ended. Since then, it would take nearly a half century before any kind of literature investment appear in the province. In the latter half of the 20th century, prominent scholars like C.M. Madduma Bandara, C.R. Panabokke, U. B. Karunananda, M. U. A. Tennakoon, Ranbanda Seneviratne, Piyadasa Ranpathwila, Shanthi Dissanayake, Ratna B. Ekanayake[102] and a host of other writers began to enrich the literary environment in their own way to present Nuwarakalaviya at its core.

---

[101] Hettiarachchi, D. E., ed. 1978, p. 2.

[102] For more information about Nuwarakalaviya literary figures, see *Wev Bendi Danawwe Nihanda Pera Gammankaruwo* by Ratna B. Ekanayake (2011).

8. CHIEFS, GRANT OF TITLES AND APPOINTMENT OF *MULĀDĀNIVARU*

$\mathcal{K}$andyan Chiefs were also called *radalakam peruwa* (Chiefs' Guild). During pre-modern times, titles whether regnal, hereditary, or non-hereditary, were an essential part of the feudatory customs and traditions in effect in the country to maintain social order and execute King's wishes.[1] A brief discussion about the hereditary honorifics and non-hereditary titles awarded during pre-modern times in Kandyan country is essential to fully understand the context of Rata Sabhāwa.[2] In 17th century, Robert Knox (1681, 1995) noted "…This people are very ambitious of their titles, having but very little else that they can boast in; and of names and titles of respect they have great plenty in their language… [*sic*]" (p. 95). There was no possibility for the Rata Sabhāwa of Nuwarakalaviya or *Gam Sabe* in Kandyan highlands to sustain their effective presence as a potent and essential institution without equally relevant group of nobility.

P. Arunachalam opines that the area between south of Jaffna and north of Anuradhapura was under Chiefs called *Vanniyars* whose original settlement was in Kottiyar in Trincomalee District. They spread out and formed small principalities, each ruled by a prince or a princess. As their influence extended to Anuradhapura district, their descendants came to be known as *Vannihuru*.[3] Considering the remoteness of the areas they lived and ruled, and claim to some singular historical events, kinship relationships bloomed between Anuradhapura and Mullativu families often as time passed.[4] Therefore, it is not improbable these Chiefs were referred to in the vernacular as *Vannihuru* and *Vanniyars* interchangeably by ordinary people in the North and Northwest Sri Lanka. It is also important to note that written accounts about these Chiefs are lean and diverse, and therefore, any inference to an exact definition about them is difficult.

Across the rest of the country, King endowed three types of regnal titles on individuals. As the name suggests, examples of regnal titles are – *Yuva Raja* of a *rata*, *kumāravaru* (princes) and *ādipāda* (*maha-pā, aepā*).[5] One had to be linked to a royal

---

NOTES

[1] For titles existed in Sri Lanka during the turn of the 19th century, see John D'Oyly (1835), *Sketch of the Constitution of the Kandyan Kingdom*. (191-252); Also see *Sinhala Ānduwa* the comprehensive disquisition by Medauyangoda Vimalakeerthi (1955) for titles existed in Sri Lanka in ancient times.

[2] Although we are quite happy and content to have leaders, and Chiefs and Kings and Queens in the past, not all societies subscribed to that idea. For example, *Ju/Wasi* people of Kalahari Desert live happily in the hardest of environments in Africa without a Chief or leader or headman, let alone a King (Thomas, 2006, p. 68).

[3] Arunachalam, P. 1906, *Sketches of Ceylon History* 2nd Ed, p. 46.

[4] In 1839, Tamarawewa Vanniya, later Ratemahattayā of Eastern Nuwarakalaviya visited Vattappalai Kovil near Mullativu (120 km) on the Northeast coast with 100 villages. Lewis, J.P. 1895, p. 265.

[5] Sans. *ādhi-pā* – lord, ruler.

blood line to have these titles.[6] But the tradition ended with the capture of the King of Kandy in 1815. And the granting of all other titles ended with the end of the colonial rule few decades into the twentieth century.

CHIEFDOMS ENDOWED. Chiefs got their names in diverse ways. The King complements a subject with a title and a new name when he endows the person who enters the fraternity of nobility. Departing from this practice, King often bestowed sacerdotal titles to Chief Monks.[7] A well-known example is the granting of *Sangharaja* (King of the Sangha) title to Valivita Saranankara, a monk well-known for his contribution to Buddhism in late 18th century. This title is obsolete in Sri Lanka now.

King can also add a new name to someone already holding a title after the latter does heroic or congratulatory acts usually beneficial to the King. Long names are regarded by many as evidence of lengthy royal patronage and obsequiousness. In ancient Sri Lanka, when a person takes a leading role in building a village (*gam bándeema*), an irrigation reservoir (large or small), or a religious or any other major structure, the tradition was that the King, a regional prince, or the community members themselves appointed him as its leader or caretaker. He then received a nobility title with visibility like *Dissava* or *Ratemahattayā* (master of the *rata* – region). Commoners like *mulādānivaru* (lesser officials, e.g., *gamarāla*, *vidāne*) received lesser positions with authority limited to their communities. Subsequently, the name of the *Dissavani* or the village becomes the prefix or the suffix of the official's old name.

Folklore in Nuwarakalaviya reads that Kala Wewa irrigation reservoir, south of Anuradhapura, has its namesake Kala Sitano living in the wild. When brought before King Dhathusena (455-473 AD), the man told the King about a large, naturally formed body of water in the forest. The King developed it as a reservoir and appointed the man as its caretaker and titled him as Kala Sitano. Some use the word *Sitano* as another type of rich personage of social prestige, but its use in the mainstream vernacular is almost non-existent now. It appears primarily in Buddhist religious literature that pertains to ancient times. Hurulu Wewa – known in ancient times as Challura Wapi, and Nuwaraweva, and Bulankulama Wewa are other tanks with namesake Chiefs. Padaviya Wewa in the northern border of Nuwarakalaviya had its namesake Chief Padavi Mudiyanse Vanni Unnehe. According to patronymic traditions of the Sri Lankan Chieftains, name of the village or area which they or their ancestors have received as a royal grant became their chosen name. They did not use "Senior" or "Junior," or Roman ordinals like "the II" or "the III" as a suffix to the name.

Following were the Chiefdom titles in Sri Lanka, in order of seniority: *Maha Adikārama* (1st, 2nd or 3rd) also called *Maha Nilame* – the Prime Minister, *Adikarama*, *Dissava*, *Muhandiram* and *Ratemahattayā*. Provincial Kings, e.g., Godapola Wijayapala of Matale (Fig. 8) awarded their own titles as Chiefs. In Maritime Provinces during

---

[6] Since 1739, after the death of Sri Wira Parakrama Narendra Singhe of Kandy, who is believed to be the last King with Sinhala blood line, the *Adikāramvaru* and the Buddhist clergy decided to invite a family member from a South or Central Indian royal family and crown him as the King. Predominance of patriarchy kingship traditions in Sri Lanka was only broken few times in its history. Anula, Lilawathie and Kalyanawathie are among the few queens regnant in Sri Lanka.

[7] Knox, (1681, 1995), p. 74.

the colonial times, the equivalents were Maha Mudliyar of the Governor's Gate, Muhandiram and Mudliyar. Except in Nuwarakalaviya, where there are no such titles, in Kandyan highlands and Maritime Provinces, these titles were conferred by the King or the Governor. In Nuwarakalaviya, the Maha Vanniya and *Ratemahatvaru* titles were simply passed down the family lines.

In *Sinhala Sirith Sangrahaya*, Ukkurāla Baddarāla of Welimuwapothana tells of folklore which illustrates the naming practices used for early Sri Lankan nobility. Vanni Bandara of Nuwarakalaviya got his long cognomen written on a Sri Sannasa from King Buwanekabahu V (1344-1359). Accordingly, following is the full name of Vanni Bandara of Nuwarakalaviya scribed on a *pata tahaduwa* (frontlet): *Sisila Gunakamala Sakalajanakaruna Manthriswara Warnawantha Saparipurna Rajarathna Rajapaksa Rajatilaka Rajakaruna Rajasundara Mitrasundeera Attanayake Thrisinhala Yasakeerthi Sri Wickrama Senanayake Hendath Herath Senevirathna Rathran Vanni Bandara.*[8] The full assortment of virtues and eminences proclaimed in this long name can be translated as follows, not necessarily in the listed order:

> "Gilded and acclaimed Chief of the Vanni (sylvan) Country with pleasant qualities of a lotus, kinder to all people, King's noble servant, the colorful, perfective, the gem of the King, the friend of the King, the receiver of the King's kindness, the receiver of compassion of the King, the giver of beauty to the King, the friend of the people, the leader with wealth, of the three Sinhala countries, the carrier of great qualities, the great leader, the leader of the troops, indefatigable worker, the aide with guns and, the golden General Vanni Bandara."

Each of these names is a phrase or word which expressed an extraordinary feature, an achievement, or uniqueness of some sort - a high premium expected of or ascribed to the Chief differentiating him from a commoner. For obvious reasons these types of long names have dropped from nomenclature traditions in Sri Lanka now, and if found, will sure evoke scorn.

In regular vernacular, however, a Chieftain's name was just his village name, irrespective of his achievements and other attributes. Thus, Vanni Bandara in this embellished appellation was called in any one of the following names: Nuwarawawe Vanniya, Nuwarawawe Unnehe, Nuwarawawe Mudiyanse, *Vanni Unnehe* or just Nuwarawawe Ratemahattayā.[9] Title of *Dissava* of Nuwarakalaviya appointed by Kandy King or Colonial government was abolished in 1834, and *Ratemahatvaru* listed

---

[8] Hettiarachchi, D. E., ed. 1979, 2019, p. 37.

[9] An unmarried son of an aristocrat was called *mahatmaya*. After marriage, he got an appellative suffix as *mudiyanse*, or *rāla*, or in Sabaragamuwa Province, *uppō* until he inherited father's Chieftainship. But if the son accedes to the title of the aristocrat after his death, he will acquire the full length of the name, though he had had no role in supposedly unique deeds of his ancestors. *Mahatmayō* was how a Chieftain's unmarried daughter was addressed. Prior to mid-19th century in the Kandyan country, once she got married to a male from another family of similar rank, she was called a *walawwe ammandee* or *walawwe paminitenannanse*. These women began to be called with the neoteric word with the prefix *kumari* (for Kumarihamy) only after the line of Sinhala monarchy ended in 1815. Until then only those with royal blood were called *kumari* (princess). She could also take the husband's village name as the appellation to hers. Thus, for instance, Ehelepola

above continued to hold office. Often, these officers were also called *Raterāla* or *Rālahami.*[10]

To keep its privileges safe, the gaggle of Chieftains in Kandyan kingdom glided in formation showing flattery and genuflection to the King regardless of his whims and brute cruelties he subjected citizenry to. Those who showed slightest dissent found themselves facing the King's ultimate ire – death by beheading. Pilimatalawa (Senior), Leuke, and Ratwatte are few Chieftains who found it too late for adjustments and paid the heavy price by losing their lives under the King's orders.

As discussed earlier, the King's only appointee in Nuwarakalaviya was the *Dissava*, one chosen from the fraternity of his *Curia Regis*, senior Chiefs in his Court. King did not have any direct role in appointing other officials in Nuwarakalaviya. This province had a history, tradition, and power within to maintain its line of Chiefdoms without involvement of any other potency. Occasionally the King gave letters of recognition called *Sannas Pathra* to Nuwarakalaviya Chiefs when they visited Kandy though such trips were far in between. Such a *Sannas Pathra* naturally became a treasured possession in the family line. After the British took full control of the country, the Government Agent of Anuradhapura appointed *Ratemahatvaru* and *kāriyakarawannō*. Thereafter, instead of "Sri" *Sannas*a (Royal Grant), the Governor presented an ornate certificate to the grantee (Fig. 54). With this, they retained the freedom to treat themselves as 'nobility.' Their descendants proudly displayed it as a family treasure.

Historically, independent of the King, Maha Vanniyā of Nuwarakalaviya held the prerogative and the responsibility of appointing *Ratemahatvaru*, also called *Mudiyansevaru. Mudiyanse* title in Nuwarakalaviya seems to have exercised an implied autonomy from the King's affairs although King did not hesitate to punish them if they vexed him for any reason as seen from the instance of imprisonment of Maha Vanniyā by King Rajadhi Raja Singhe (1782-1798). Over time, calling the Chiefs as *Mudiyanse* gradually fell out of favor in Nuwarakalaviya as these Chiefs themselves preferred to be treated with equal hierarchical appellations up to par with their Kandyan counterparts.

With the experience of 1818 and 1848 revolts, colonial administration with myriad of instances of going back on pledges, still chose not to involve with native traditions directly. For example, *Ratemahattayā* appointed lesser officials for native institutions. This allowed these institutions coated with shades of their own rules and directives to be overseen independently by nobility appointed by the Government Agent.

In 1851, Nikawewa Ratemahattayā of Ulagalla told A. O. Brodie, Assistant Government Agent of Anuradhapura, that his family folklore draws its ancestry from a ducal primogenitor who came to the island from Indian mainland with *Ayyanār Deyyo* (Ayyanāyaka), deity for sylvan affairs of Nuwarakalaviya even before

Dissava's wife who was of the Keppetipola clan before marriage, was called Ehelepola Kumarihamy. She performed no titular duties or responsibilities or received grants from the King. Since naming conventions followed patrilineal traditions, any agnatic appellations from her ancestral family were dropped after marriage, therefore were not transferable to her children.

[10] Pieris, R., 1956, p. 24; Jennings, 1952, p. 193.

the arrival of the Sacred Bodhi Tree in c 288 BC.[11] This seems to suggest the Nikawewa family in Nuwarakalaviya places themselves in the province sometime before any other oldest aristocratic families in the area. This claim stands in its own without any corroborative physical or written evidence.

Millenia later, as the region remained in isolation, different forms of independent regnal or semi-regnal rulers were in control of the province. From the beginning, Nuwarakalaviya, though its primogeniture status had abandoned it long ago, was not as significant to the Kings in the same way as the provinces around Kandy. They had other issues to be involved in, e.g., the Kotte Kings and later the colonial rulers. For a forested and distant land as Nuwarakalaviya, Kings had little interest to be imbued with its past allure.

Less inviting also was the insalubrious ground conditions in Nuwarakalaviya. According to Knox (1681, 1995), as far back as 17th century, *Chingulays* (Sinhalayo) in the mountains having used to pure spring water were scared to travel to Hurulle (in Nuwarakalaviya) for fear of diseases – violent fevers, probably malaria and aches (yaws) (p. 154). It is no wonder King did not have desire to be upbeat about the province. If given the opportunity to be away in a distant and insulated province, he feared the potential attempts to depose him by treacherous aristocrats in his Court. Thus, strategically he prevented them from being absent from the Court for long durations in areas further away.

Under the King's immediate control in the Kandyan region, *Ratemahattayā* was the last decision maker on issues concerning lands.[12] But it is safe to suggest that though the King regarded Nuwarakalaviya as part of his dominion, he had less political and administrative control over it, and he was satisfied with only the implicit recognition of his authority, even to the point of tolerating Maha Vanniyā administering the province as an independent principality. For an ordinary villager, the Kingship was a faraway reality: literally a 3 or 4–day trip to Kandy. Thus, in his way of thinking, the King existed in a distant province in tradition and name only. But Vannivaru participating in any hearing in Nuwarakalaviya effectively elicited a regal aura to the event. This provided an opportunity for them and other Chiefs to maintain institutions like Rata Sabhā independently with little meddling from the King.

Titular establishment in Nuwarakalaviya functioned like a local tradition, but the Chieftain families across country were usually peers and welcomed and fully embraced this brotherhood as seen from the long lines of kinship connections established between Nuwarakalaviya and Kandyan families since second half of the 19th century. This also helped to expand their matrimonial candidate pool as noted before.[13] As colonial powers tried to chip away at the independence of these distant semi-autonomous large principalities, *Vannihuru* began to build closer alignment with the Kandyan kingdom and a token relationship with the Maritime Provinces as a show of countering force.

---

[11] Ievers, 1899, p. 92; Arunachalam, 1906, p. 46.

[12] Seneviratne, H. L., 1978, *Rituals of the Kandyan State,* p. 7.

[13] For a moment of unusual circumstances that can lead to such matrimonial connections, see Appendix B, the fairytale-like story which took place over a century ago in Ulagalla and shared with me by Sanath Panabokke, a descendent of Nikawewa clan.

CHIEFDOMS EARNED. The second type elevation is honorifics earned by doing a favor to the King, wining his good grace by a heroic act usually beneficial to him, presenting an   exceptional gift, e.g., an elephant or its tusks – gift most likely to earn a guaranteed good return, precious stones, appeasing him with poetic encomia, special skills that could awe the King, or simply a significant financial contribution. For instance, in December 1811, a Navinne Mohottāla in Hath Kōrale paid 3500 ridi as *dākum* to the King for the title of *Rate Lēkam*, a title equivalent to *Ratemahattayā*.[14] An instance of endowing lower level of titles was when in 1803, Mullegama Dissava of Wellassa received a slave as a fee for appointing a man as a *Rate Rāla*.[15]

On their part, colonial authorities too believed that continuing this tradition was expedient to their control of the island. A businessperson named Jeronis Soysa with roots in the littoral received a Gate Mudliyar title from the British Governor in 1853 after completing charity work in the Central Province. Soysa constructed a road and renovated a small tank, Malulla, which cultivated 36 acres of paddy lands a few miles from Hanguranketa. He also had a coffee plantation in the general area. The labor cost for the project was only £200.[16] He got interested in this tank as it was believed to have been built by King Raja Singhe II in mid-17ᵗʰ century while living in Digligy Nuere (Hanguranketa) city after escaping a rebellion launched by his Chiefs in Kandy. Robert Knox wrote, the pond was "a musket-shot from his palace."

In the turn of the 20th century Kapuruhami Madukanda Ratemahattayā (1948) gave an authentic description of appointing feudal officers. He stated that appointing unqualified officials was prevalent then too, and lamented and cogently argued such practices would undermine the Rata Sabhāwa tradition (pp. 42-68).

MAHA VANNIYĀ – NO ORDINARY CHIEF. Not enough studies have been done, nor enough anecdotes or folkloric clues have been unearthed about Maha Vanniyā, his subordinate *Vanniyas* and *Ratemahatvaru* who ruled Nuwarakalaviya. No books or praise poems are known to have been written about them. Although they led a stately life in their comparatively large homes in this isolated and less travelled province, they were not well-known to the rest of the country like their counterparts in Kandy or Maritime Provinces. To the Kandyan country and Maritime Provinces, they were heads in a wild and little-known piece of the country.

A closer look brings into light interesting evidence of the standing of Maha Vanniyā in relation to hundreds of other Chiefs who held Court in other parts of the country. Based on their special relationship to religious and cultural establishment in Nuwarakalaviya, particularly the unique role of protecting one of the two holiest religious icons in Sri Lanka, the Sacred Bodhi Tree, the degree of independence the Maha Vanniya enjoyed with day-to-day decision making, maintaining cordial relationships simultaneously with the colonial powers in the Maritime provinces and Kingdom in Kandy, and King's loose policies and interest towards the region, it is not hyperbolic to suggest that this assembly of Chiefs in

---

[14] D'Oyly, 1917, p. 70.

[15] Lawrie, 1898, p. 610.

[16] Jayawardena, 2003, p. 177.

Nuwarakalaviya existed as something of a potent form of a sovereign aristocratic conglomeration.

Fig. 33. Mahinda Bulankulame, Relative of
Last Maha Vanniyā with Queen Elizabeth
c 1981. Photo: RoarMedia/Sinhala Century.

A letter by Governor Horton to Colonial Secretary in 1833, quoted by Sivasundaram (2013) states that Nuwarakalaviya region "has been hitherto almost beyond the control of the authorities in the interior (p. 156)." Although Sivasundaram thinks it as an admission by the British of their failure of engagement with the province, I believe it also an indirect way to recognize the strength of the region controlled by the Nuwarakalaviya nobility. Horton's officers have been able to ascertain the province "to contain a much larger population than was suspected to exist, and which in general found to be better circumstances than those of the neighboring Maritime Provinces." The Governor also found the inhabitants involved in a "very considerable commercial intercourse," some exports finding markets in India.[17] This is a testament to the job Maha Vanniyā, and his assembly of Chiefs were doing in the province with no participation of the Kandyan reign. The Chief held power with splendor and purpose which the colonial officers too would not miss to note in their missives home. But the Chiefs in Nuwarakalaviya also had their failings as found in some reports of their occasional harsh treatment of villagers stated in earlier pages.

Chiefs in Kandy and Maritime Provinces were Tenant-in-Chiefs only to the King or the colonial Governor respectively. But because Maha Vanniyā's historic mandate being the Chief of an area larger than any of the provinces under King or colonial Governor's control, and the richness and reverence attributed to the history

---

[17] Qtd. in Sivasundaram, 2013, p. 156.

of Anuradhapura no doubt placed him as a Dual Tenant-in-Chief – implicitly to the King and explicitly to the Sacred Bodhi Tree.

Before the Kandyan convention of 1815, Maha Vanniyā did not have to report to anyone, but maintained an important rapport with the Chiefs in Nuwarakalaviya and a reverential relationship with *Atamasthānādhipathi* while playing a leading role with the lay people in the Committee which selected this priestly leader. The responsibility of this task was set by tradition and not by any decree from a King or another Head of some recognition. Numerous written accounts suggest that in ancient times, King participated in this task as the principal layman. After the British declared sovereignty over the island, they introduced the Temple Lands Registration in 1856. It was the precursor to the various forms of legislation targeting the temple temporalities.

Culminating this policy was the Buddhist Temporalities Ordinance of 1889. With legislative attempts like this, the colonial government was sending signals for tacit oversight of the religious institutions, partly due to ideas floating around as to how to use the lands belonging to the temples. Even with the ordinance of 1889 and government secular involvement with the religious affairs, Maha Vanniyā enjoyed a level of significance and independence no other Chief in Kandy could ever place claim to – the trusteeship or the lay custodianship of the Sri Maha Bodhi, and experience the benefits and prestige that came with it. It may not be a stretch to suggest, and Chiefs in highlands would not have agreed, but this exclusivity of Maha Vanniyā and keeping the whole of Vanni area together placed him on an elite standing beyond the *Dissavaru* and Chiefs in Kandy.[18]

Strands of cultural and religious differences expressly outnumbered the similarities in Kandyan and Nuwarakalaviya provinces. They gave each other strong affirmation, though. One difference is the styles of expression of vernacular in the Nuwarakalaviya. As seen in the titulary nomenclature, Chiefs in Nuwarakalaviya were called Maha Vanniyā, *Vanni Unnehe, Mudiyanse, Vanniyā, Kālä Kōrāla* or *Vel Vidāne. Unnehe* is a word of art and an honorific only in Nuwarakalaviya to denote that someone was special and superior. No Kandyan Chief is known to have used the suffix *Unnehe* to their names.

According to Ievers (1899), British officials themselves hinted often with indirect comments that *Maha Vanni Unnehe* was partially independent, and the title as hereditary (p. 60). This says a lot about his lofty standing among the Kandyan Chiefs who never enjoyed any semblance of independence from the King or the colonial administrations. Their titles were not hereditary but granted at the pleasure of the King. Even the present day Diyawadana Nilame who heads the affairs of the laity in the Temple of Tooth Relic, and a position with term-limits, is elected from a pool of individuals with diverse backgrounds.

---

[18] Affairs of lay caretakers of religious institutions have changed extraordinarily a century later. Most notable is the present state of Diyawadana Nilame, the civilian caretaker of the Temple of the Tooth Relic in Kandy. After independence in 1948, with changes taking place due to influence of religious, cultural, and political winds, this title gradually ascended to a level of prestige, exposure, and influence which many consider on par with a cabinet ministerial level, but often capitulating to the whims of the governing hierarchy.

It is notable that, though the ancient titulary titles have disappeared in Sri Lanka altogether, their descendants have no role in affairs or activities their ancestors were involved with. Only exception is the descendants of Maha Vanniyā, presently the head of the Nuwarawawe Bulankulame family, and descendants of few other Chiefs in Nuwarakalaviya. Tradition allows and Acts of Law requires (particularly, the Buddhist Temporalities Ordinance of 1992 Part II, 9 [2a]) them to be a member of the 3-person committee of men that selects the *Atamasthānādhipathi*. And contrary to the Diyawadana Nilame of the Temple of Tooth, the Nuwarawawe Bulankulame family and descendants of other Chieftain families in Nuwarakalaviya have no term limits in the selection process or holding that office.

By the BTA stipulations, no woman, whether employed in the government or with any other profession is allowed to be a Trustee or vote in the selection of the Diyawadana Nilame. Thus, ironically, two premier Buddhist institutions in Sri Lanka are participants in a form of misogyny under the cover of government blessing negating women the same opportunity as men.

In 1981, on the occasion of Queen Elizabeth's visit to the Sri Maha Bodhi Tree, the ground zero of religious icons in Sri Lanka, Mahinda Bulankulame, a direct descendent of Maha Vanniyā and Head of the Nuwarawawe Bulankulame family at the time received the Queen and accompanied her to the Bodhi Tree representing the country in general and Nuwarakalaviya in particular, illustrating the premier position *Vannihuru* of the region held which no nobility elsewhere can claim (Fig. 33).

Another fact that distinguished the Maha Vanniyā from Chiefs in other parts of the country is his spatial role in control over economic resources in the province, including its fauna and flora. Elephants in the wild and their tusks were the property of the King. Ievers (1899) noted killing of elephants within the Kandyan kingdom were ranked with the offence of robbing of royal treasure or striking a priest. But its relevance decreased inversely from its distance from Kandy. This made it easy for Maha Vanniyā and his Chiefs in Nuwarakalaviya (and northern parts of Vanni, Tamankaduwa and Bintenna), to consider elephants as fair game. Ievers further noted that the Chiefs exercised power over the capture of elephants and regarded the tusks as their perquisites across far afield (p. 262). They even used foreign trappers (Afghani *Panikkiyo*) to catch elephants to be given to Dutch as annual payments, and kept the tusks when occasion allowed.[19] This was the practice in Northern Sri Lanka as the *Vanniyas'* cohorts in Vavuniya and beyond had Elephant Farms where captured elephants were sold to buyers, including Rajas in the Subcontinent.[20] Chiefs in Kandyan highlands did not dare to try this because elephant-related activities were the absolute prerogative of the King. He would consider a Chief in Kandyan highlands engaging a foreigner with any work or trade as spying and straying beyond his authority.

---

[19] Panamure Kraal conducted by Maduwanwela Dissava is renown in the land. It was conducted close to a century after the British took full control of the country. Thus, the British had the larger say in such activities. While it is not known whether an elephant kraal was operating in Nuwarakalaviya after the British took over, Maha Vanniyā and Nuwarakalaviya nobility had no such constraints when the colonists were controlling only the Maritime Provinces.

[20] Lewis, 1895, p. 110; Ferguson, A.M., 1868, p. 4.

In the 19th century, the British also seem to have recognized the importance of Maha Vanniyā overseeing a large, forested region holding, in their view, an important stretch of the colony with high economic potential. Some colonial officials have seen and heard of the agricultural potential of the large reservoirs in the region, some in working order, some yearning to be restored. It is well-known that decades after the fall of Kandy, as British were still scrambling to formulate its irrigation policies and restoration of irrigation infrastructure[21] in Nuwarakalaviya, Maha Vanniyā and Chiefs had a larger control of water from major reservoirs in and around the city of Anuradhapura and the countryside. This is an experience the Chiefs in Kandy could not get closer. Therefore, a closer analysis of all things considered about Maha Vanniyā title in ancient times reveals that it had a larger and free hand to operate than one holding the *Maha Adikārama* title in the Kandyan highlands.

Unlike some Kings before him, the last King of Kandy never led a battery of soldiers out of the city for war. He and his Chiefs in Kandy did not feed the soldiers when they were on guard duty. The reason supposedly was that soldiers were performing a service owed to the lords mandated by the feudal customs and traditions. Knox (1681, 1995) wrote that Maha Vanniyā fed his soldiers (p. 175) when they were deployed on duty, a remarkable difference of functionary and procedural responsibilities that set him apart from the King or his Chiefs. King would not move troops through Nuwarakalaviya without Maha Vanniya's knowledge, Knox noted!

Regardless of the independence enjoyed by Maha Vanniyā and other Chiefs in Nuwarakalaviya, Kandy Kings' belligerent actions against them have been reported in some accounts. Particularly the alleged execution of the Maha Vanniyā in 18th century by the King is one such moment. As reported by P.A. Leupe (1862), in the first decade of 18th century, an embassy of Chiefs from Kandy brought a potential bride-princess from India for King Sri Wira Parakrama Narendra Singhe (1707-1739) with the Dutch help (p. 115). After his *ganithaya* (astrologer) read the horoscope of the princess, he found her planets were on inauspicious axes.[22] After this revelation, as was the custom, an embassy from Kandy escorted her back to India through Nuwarakalaviya.

Folklore says Maha Vanniyā married this bride-princess of the "Sun Race" after intercepting the King's emissaries taking her to Madurai. This news infuriated the King. He went to the house of Maha Vanniyā disguised as a singing Sanyasi, caught, and executed him. In truth, a Kandyan King disguising as anyone, let alone a Sanyasi, and leaving the Court to exact retribution may be a story of fairytale variety, too

---

[21] Ievers, 1899, p. 153. During 1874-1886, colonial government renovated the Maha Medawachchiya tank on the North Road to supply water needs of Indian migrant workers who were passing through to Hill Country plantations.

[22] King who would not allow anyone to see his bare body save for the ailing hand (as Dutch Dr. Danielsz's reported earlier) was unlikely to send his horoscope information to an unknown astrologer in India for bride selection process. Only his in-palace astrologer (*ganithaya*) could read and interpret it. Leaders now routinely go to India in person to seek astrologers' service to remain in power.

good to be a fact. But on one hand, some folklore cannot be discounted simply as fiction.

Late in the Kandyan period, Kings' desire to marry princesses from South India was a well-known fact. D'Oyly (1917) wrote that sometime around 1811, King Sri Wickrama Raja Singhe brought two teenage sisters from the Malabar coast through Batticaloa as potential brides. He married them in January 1813 (p. 170). This was the time when polygyny (and polyandry) was common in Kandyan country. The practice lasted until the late 19th century.

However, after the King's 1813 marriage, there is no record whether either one of the two brides was sent back to India, nor there is any story of a Nuwarawawe Chief being executed by the King right before the fall of Kandy. Thus, which of the Kings who had involved in matrimonial interests in 18th century with South Indian princesses is not clear. If the King's reported retributive action against an independent Chief of an isolated district is true, it is no less than an instance of hyperbole. Undoubtedly, the King must have felt disparaged by someone interfering with royal property – the princess *Vanniya* belittled. His ego must have gotten hurt because someone with lesser lineage denigrated something imperial – the princess suitable to be his queen.

After the hill capital fell to British, in the back country of Nuwarakalaviya, contemporary written accounts show instances of Maha Vanniyā showing manifest resistance to the new rulers.[23] But the approach taken by the Chiefs based in the Kandyan highlands towards the new masters was tellingly different. As D'Oyly started residence in the Palace while keeping the adjoining Audience Hall as his base of operations, the Kandyan Chiefs scrambled to line up requesting his audience to keep the good grace of the British. They then requested D'Oyly to sort out host of issues, e.g., their emoluments, ancestral privileges, functional responsibilities, and getting briefed and acquainted with the protocols under the new administration.[24]

Meanwhile, at Vilachchiya land pass point, *kadawat* a, few kilometers north-west of Anuradhapura – Maha Vanniyā 's hometown, a *Kanakapulle* (a *canicopoly*), was levying duties on all merchandize that passed through it with the authority of the Chief as he has been doing since King's time. The collector of Mannar T.R. Backhouse wrote in his diary on October 8, 1818, which Ievers (1899) quotes: "this tax, it appears, has been imposed by the Vannia from time immemorial, both before and since the rebellion [*sic*] (p. 46)." He only paid an annual tribute to the King, "enjoyed a surprising degree of independence" and had policing and judicial powers even three years after the British subdued Kandy. "The inhabitants (of Nuwarakalaviya) established an identity which was separate from that created for them in Kandy."[25] Bryce Ryan noted in 1953:

> *Vanniyās* are more strictly a parallel group with the Kandyan
> highland Radala, although such an analogy is distinctly odious to
> the former. Nominally they are a feudal aristocracy tracing their

---

[23] Mannar Collector's letter, reproduced in Ievers, 1899, p.44.

[24] D'Oyly, 1917, pp. 225-233; See Fig. 46 for Captain William Willerman's sketch of the Kandyan Chiefs (c 1818) in conversation with John D'Oyly.

[25] Sivasundaram, 2013, p. 142.

descent from the royal overlords of the region (Nuwarakalaviya) during the period in which the area was a no man's land between Sinhalese and Tamil invaders. (p. 243)

The British working for years with their network of native spies were aware that the dynamics of Maha Vanniyā's relationship with whoever the King in Kandy was different than that of any other Chief elsewhere. Furthermore, D'Oyly did not have native spies in Nuwarakalaviya. He did not have to, for in his thinking too, the province was a different and a separate entity, loosely attached to the Kandyan kingdom, and had not carried any burden of importance both politically and militarily. For this very reason, before and immediately after taking of Kandy, the British were still courting the Chiefs in Vanni with a bi-lateral form of diplomatic protocol.

Ievers (1899) wrote that on or about March 12, 1815, soon after the Kandyan Convention, Suriyakula Kumarasinghe Vanniya of Nuwarakalaviya was in Mannar Kachcheri on a courtesy call, "seeking marks of respect and honor from the British government" (p. 44) and to discuss any potential harassment from the vestigial elements loyal to the King that may spill over to the Nuwarakalaviya countryside. This leads us to believe that *Maha Vanniya* had no immediate or significant interest in what was happening in the Kandyan highlands. To their credit, the new rulers accorded magisterial recognition to Maha Vanniyā when they received him cordially at Mannar. The reception he received there from the Assistant Government Agent was with diplomatic fervor and friendly as seen from the conveniences the British placed at his disposal for the trip back to Anuradhapura. He was given a "country palanquin, accompanied by some of the Kachcheri servants, including Arachi of the sitting Magistrate and two Kachcheri lascoreens [*sic*]."[26] Three months later, despite the British slowly cobbling together their expansion to the reaches of all corners of the country, Maha Vanniyā was still showing his control and authority over Nuwarakalaviya, as shown in the incident of refusing a D'Oyly's passport-holder to cross the land pass point at Vilachchiya.

One other little-known fact needs mentioning. It involves an oft quoted claim by Chiefs in Nuwarakalaviya and in the northern, northeastern, and northwestern coastal regions. They have claimed that their ancestors were on the island many centuries before those of the Kandyan highlands or Maritime Provinces. For example, Suriyakula Kumarasinghe Maha Vanniyā claims ancestry to the entourage of the Bodhi Tree in 3rd century BC. In the Bodhi Tree entourage, there were eight princes of *Setthi* caste who were part of this group.[27] King Devanampiyatissa granted them the title of Bo-dhāharanakula (Caste keeping the Bodhi Tree).[28] Citing H.Ellawala, Shirley Pulle Tissera suggested that the word Chetty in Sri Lanka is identified with the word Sethi in pali, Hetti or Situ in Sinhala. As described earlier, a similarly intriguing pedigree is claimed by Nikawewa of Ulagalla and Hurulle of

---

[26] Letter on record at Mannar Kachcheri, provided by M.S. Crawford, Esq., Asst. Govt. Agent, reproduced in Ievers, 1899, p. 44).

[27] See page 64 n43 for the names of these princes. They were also called Bodhiwansadeva princes, or Bodhi Bearers' Guild.

[28] Turnour, 1836, p. 132.

Morakewa.[29] Accordingly, their ancestors have come to Sri Lanka with *Ayyanar Deyyo* even before the bringing of the Sacred Bodhi Tree to Sri Lanka. But there is no evidence, historical or folkloric, to suggest that a Chief in Kandyan highlands descended from a deistical or a regnal lineage equaling these claims.

WALAWWE MOHOTTĀLA, AND MUDLIYAR OF THE GOVERNOR'S GATE. Walawwe Mohottala's duties include *Maha Vanniya*'s public relations officer, senior aide, secretary, or head of the work crew of an important person today. From the perspective of duties performed, I venture to suggest that *Walawwe Mohottāla* as a juxtaposed version of the Mudliyar of the Governor's Gate in the Maritime Provinces during colonial times, though not had the same cultural weight and traction as the latter.

While the British Governor was the ruler of Maritime Provinces, Maha Vanniyā ruling an area as large or perhaps larger than the Maritime region was as every bit as same eminence as the Governor. He was also of the same level as King's *Dissava.* According to Ievers (1899), in 1833, in a list of names of *mulādenivaru* and Vanni Mudiyansevaru (s. *Mudiyanse*) sent to Government Agent in Kandy by Assistant Government Agent in Kurunegala (p. 82), *Walawwe Mohottāla* (named Pahalawalawwe Appuhami – Appuhami of Lower Walawwa) with the title of *Atapattu Mohottāla* of all seven *pattus* was listed right below Maha Vanniyā but above all Vanni Mudiyansevaru, i.e., *Ratemahatvaru.* The fact he resided in a Walawwa (residence of a Chief) suggests that he was not an ordinary *mulādäniya* or *Mudiyanse* but a title holder equal to or above a Vanni Mudiyanse. He was involved in coordinating official functions in walawwa and revenue collection for the Maha Vanniyā's administration and outreach to Vanni Mudiyansevaru, *mulādenivaru* and constituents in other *pattus*. In modern terms and vernacular, *Walawwe Mohottāla* would have been the private secretary of the Dissava in Kandyan country. He was one of the four Mohottalas[30] in Kandyan country and Nuwarakalaviya.

Walawwe Mohottāla administered the *nindagam* and other private property of the Maha Vanniyā and his household staff. He could write *sittu*, detain people until they pay the fine, and had pretty much all powers enjoyed by the Dissava.[31] In a similar way, duties performed by the Mudliyar of the Governor's Gate to the British Governor in Maritime Provinces also were functionally similar in that they both supervised the attending house staff of the two houses and subaltern Mudliyars across the district.

When Governor Horton (1831–1837) wrote to the Colonial Office identifying his 42-member native House Staff as "attendants" and one of them as their leader was given the title of *Mudliyar of Governor's Gate and Guards* [emphasis added], he noted that conferring this title was "the highest and most valued distinction in his power."[32] Over time, as the colonial influence extended to all corners of the country, recipient of the British title Governor's Gate and Guards (and other colonial titles for that matter) seemed to have received a glittery exposure which increased holder's

---

[29] Ievers, 1899, op. cit. p. 92.

[30] 1. *Dissave,* 2. *Atapattu,* 3. *Kodituwakku* and 4. *Walawwe.*

[31] Vimalananda, T. 1963, pp. 388-389.

[32] Governor Horton's letter to Colonial Office dated November 21, 1831, cited in Sivasundaram, 2013, p. 288.

political and social stock. In the same time span, *Walawwe Mohottāla* faded into insignificance after the Heads of the Nuwarakalaviya province ceased to be relevant under British rule.

KŌRĀLA. This third type of lesser Chief is the head of a smaller district, *Korale*, which consisted usually of three or more *tulān*, each headed by a *mulādāniya* or *Arachirāla*.[33] During the feudal times, Korāla was appointed by the *Ratemahattayā* or Maha Vanniyā. During the colonial times, it was the role of the Government Agent.[34] In Nuwarakalaviya, in the context of line of authority, *Korāla* title was one that stood between *Ratemahattayā* and *kāriyakarawannā*. Often with the unbroken manner it passed along a family line, some thought it as a hereditary title. But there is not enough evidence to determine whether this is true even during Kandyan Kings' times. But *Korāla's* son stood in the inner circle with better chances for consideration for a mid-level position under the feudal traditions. Copious written accounts show that sons of many *Korāla*s or those who already hold minor titles like *atukōrāla, muhandiram, vidāne, or Lékam Mahattayā* drew attention for a vacant *Korāla* position.

Korāla's responsibilities during British times included protection of forest resources, assist in *Gam Sabhāwa* functions, issue licenses for chena cultivation. He also functioned as the representative of the government in affairs of his *tulāna* jurisdictions. He dealt with the issues of a villager with matters of forest (*kálā*) like chena and timber needs. Primarily for this reason, this official was also known in Nuwarakalaviya as *Kálā Kōrāla*. Together with *Ratemahattayā* and other officials, *Korāla* had to attend monthly meetings called *palāth dinaya* (Provincial Day) at the kachcheri.

Indirectly, the Rata Sabhāwa made it possible for the *Ratemahattayā* to consolidate his power across his *Rata* or *Pattuwa* – the collection of few *Korale* districts under him. The *Ratemahattayā* or Maha Vanniyā knew that the *Korāla*, another person obliged to answer to the Colonial government Agent, wielded considerable authority and influence in his district. As *Korāla* also sometimes presided over Rata Sabhāwa, if *Ratemahattayā* wanted to assert his authority and shape the traditional functions in such institutions in accordance with his wishes, having a *Korāla* who can work with him without any friction was an advantage to him.

As I have noted earlier, in the 19th century, the officials of lower-rung titles in the province (*gam mulādāniya, wew lékama*, etc.) conducting the Rata Sabhāwa business were also happened to be officials appointed by the *Ratemahattayā* under the authority vested in him by the traditions. Leach (1968) writes that *Ratemahattayā* uses this political capital – the invested allegiance of these minor officials to regulate the official appointments associated with village councils (tribunals) by the colonial government (p. 76). He can also extend this influence on the selection process of *Korāla* overseeing the villages in the Rata Sabhāwa area.

Ratemahattayā's advantage in this context became substantial and expansive when a Rata Sabhāwa jurisdiction crossed into the multiple Kōrale districts (Fig. 34). I have a good example I am personally aware of this. In 1849, colonial government

---

[33] See Fig. 3 & 4. for the Division of districts and placement of each official in the titular structure in Nuwarakalaviya.

[34] Multiple sources in Karunananda, 1990, p. 20-21.

subdivided the Kändä Kōrale after deciding it was too big to administer. The new district carved out became Kanadarā Kōrale (Ievers, 1899, p. 72).

My birth village of Maradankalla (formerly known as Maradankadawala) is in Kanadarā Kōrale. Kändäwa and Kallanchiya villages where my extended family lived are in Kändä Kōrale, and Uttimaduwa in Ulagalla Kōrale is where my mother was born. But all four villages were part of the Gam Daha Ata Varige with its own Rata Sabhāwa in which, as noted before, my great-grandfather was the Mohottāla.

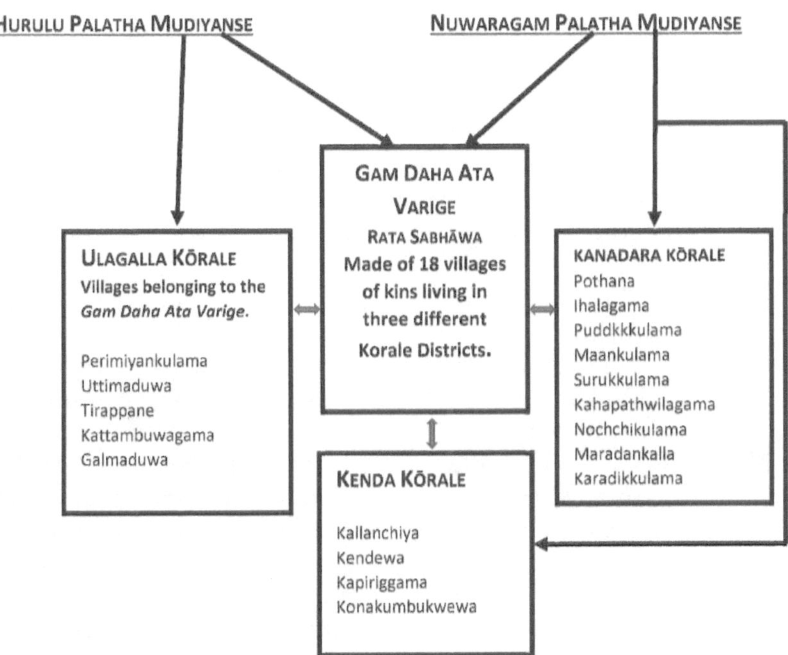

Fig. 34. Villages in a Variga Sabhāwa Under the Administrative Control of Three Korale Districts and Two Ratemahatvaru (Mudiyansevaru). Sourced from the folklore in the region.

The structure of this Rata Sabhāwa proves Leach's observation. It came under two *Ratemahattayā*s. Some member villages were in Kōrale districts Kanadara and Kändäwa under the *Ratemahattayā* of Nuwaragam Palatha while some in Ulagalla Kōrale under the *Ratemahattayā* of Hurulu Palatha. With the traditional powers vested with them on the Rata Sabhāwa or Variga Sabhāwa of the Gam Daha Ata Varige, these Chiefs could indirectly influence the outcome of the selection process of the three *Kōrālas* (Fig. 34). In 1888, Rajakaruna Dissanayake Mudiyanse Wijekone Banda Wijekone of Kändäwa was its Ratemahattayā (Fig. 35).

This unusual placement of villages in three different *Kōrale* distrticts in the province but belonging one Rata Sabhāwa augmented the *Ratemahattayā*'s ability to approach (if he so desired) its officials each time a *Kōrāla* vacancy opened in a district where its *mulādenivaru* may often be consulted by the Government Agent if needed. This fact affected in an unintended and unbeknown way the colonial government's workings in appointing *Kōrāla*s. The *Ratemahattaya*'s advantage extended not just in financial, but social and political terms as well.

MINOR TITLES. The fourth layer of officials are the commoners who received titles (*mulādāni or vidāne*) under the feudatory customs (Fig. 36-39). These were *Mohottāla, Baddarāla, Lēkama* and *Undiyarāla, Vel Vidane, Arachchirala* and *Gamarala*.[35] Rata Sabhā officials and *mulādānivaru* titles were usually temporary and lasting for short durations. Unlike the *Ratemahattaya* or *Kōrāla*, as shown by the name of the title itself, the *mulādānivaru* had specific duties and smaller jurisdictions – overseeing few villages or few variga assigned to them. The scope of their authority was comparatively smaller. The chain of officials and Chiefs in Nuwarakalaviya are shown in Fig. 40.

Usually, *mulādāni* office provides three benefits to its holder.

(I) **Prestige and exposure**. It brings prestige among the villagers, accoutrements like the cane, round hat, and the like presented by *Ratemahattaya* or Maha Vanniyā.

(II) **Economic Advantage**. Receives a share of fines imposed at a Rata Sabhāwa.

(III) **Ease of job succession**. Although in theory and tradition these were non-transitionary titles, in Sri Lanka, in general, a father's capital of holding the office of *mulādāni* already usually places the son a step closer to being considered for the same title over someone who did not fit into that criterion or privilege.

(IV) **Audience with the Chief.** Per Kapuruhami Madukanda Ratemahattayā, anyone who wants to be a *mulādāniya* goes to walawwa for an audience with the Chief and offers a hand of 40 betel leaves (*bulathurulla*) to him and make a request to be honored with the title.

Henry Marshall, 1846, 1954, *Ceylon*: p. 30, called *bulathurulla* a form of bribing the Chiefs. This description behooves comment to address misinterpretation it can provoke. He is right that bribe in any form is a crime. But *bulathurulla* is a solemn custom in Sri Lanka stretching out to Medieval Ages. It was a practice accepted as good diplomacy and show of friendship, valued etiquette when meeting a Chief in Sri Lanka. Marshall would not see it that way since he never had to do it with a Chief because British Civil Servants regarded themselves as an extraordinary fraternity and were not bound to do it. In Dickensian England, a beadle paid five pounds to anyone accepting an orphan fully knowing that he would sweat in a workhouse! Contrary to what Marshall saw, D'Oyly (1835) correctly wrote the practice as "being established universally by custom, it is a token of respect and not a bribe (p. 233)." Its formality is evident in the *Gam Sabe*, when a fee is given as a present to the Chief, usually placed on a hand of betel leaves at the beginning of a hearing, it must be returned on demand if the suit is lost (D'Oyly, 1929, p.28). This rings similarities to when a commission is paid as a way of doing business, and it is not considered a bribe! As Ievers (1899) showed, for those who were waiting at *kadawat*, it was common to exchange gifts to cross it (p. 113). Similarly, dignitaries of both native

---

[35] *Undiyarāla* was responsible for collecting taxes due to King or Maha Vanniyā. *Undiya* – Bundle. In Nuwarakalaviya *undigahanawa* means miserly hoarding of wealth.

Fig. 35. Rajakaruna Dissanayake Mudiyanse Wijayakone Banda Wijayakone, Kändäwa Ratemahattayā, formerly *Kálä Kōrala*) (? – 1888). Photo: Hasala Senevirathna.

Fig. 36. Minor Official. From *Ceylon in 1893*, by John Fergusson (1893.

and colonial governments exchanged gifts (Bertolacci, 1817, p. 53) as a form of proper diplomatic protocol.

Fig. 37. Senevirathna Kapuruhami Dingiri Banda, *Vel Vidāne*, Manakkulama. c.1950.Writer's grandfather. Author's Family Archives.

Customarily, at the time of presenting a *bulathurulla* the petiole-side of the leaves is directed towards the recipient.[36] This has been a practice as far back as the Dutch time.[37] This was called *penum* or *dākum* (appearing before the King or a Chief with tributary payments).[38] As a mark of acknowledgement of the privilege of the audience granted and as a tribute to the Chief, a rupee is also placed on the *bulathurulla*. And if the giver gets his wish granted, he will return later with another hand of betel leaves called *pudapēruwa* (*puda* – offer; *pēruwa* – title). The *pudapēruwa* that would be offered to the Chief later by the grantee had a set value. For a recipient

---

[36] See Lawrie Vol. I, pp. 5 and 98. D'Oyly (1917) wrote on October 6th, 1810, that when Dissava of Sabaragamuwa went on circuit and stayed at Ruwanwella rest house, people came to see him and offered *bulathurulu* with a rupee on it as *dākum* for the privilege of the audience (p. 22). Often a dry leaf of tobacco is also placed on the betel leaves.

[37] Pieris, P.E. 1918, p. 153; Knox, 1681, 1995, p. 51; *Kurahanmalaya,* (author unknown, n.d.) p. 56 qtd. in Norman Siripala (p. 33).

[38] On Dec. 28th, 1811, an informant told D'Oyly about a man in Gomagomuwa (close to Kuliyapitiya) bringing a large white horse from Chilaw as *penum* to 2nd Adikārama Ehelepola, soliciting an office from him.

of a *mulādāni vasama*,[39] the tribute fees are as follows: *Mohotti vidāne*: Rs. 30-40; *Badde Paiyandaya (Baddērāla)*: Rs. 20-30; and *Lékam Paiyandaya*: Rs. 10-20. With the consent of the Chief, this amount can change. Often a fee given in the past as the *pudaperuwa* was a cow and her calf (*wehi passe*) or a young bull.[40] There was no land grants given to *vidānes*.

Fig. 38. Wannihamy Senevirathna
Arachchirālla of No. 23, Kandu Tulana.
Photo: K.B. Senevirathna.

An official who was granted a title must be from the same caste as of the village(s) where he was assigned to serve in the Rata Sabhāwa or in other roles. Upon conclusion of the formalities of investiture, the *Ratemahattayā* or *Vanniyā* presented the grantee with the insignia of the office. To confirm in the title, the Chief must then tie a cloth strip or metal plate or the frontlet (*pata tahaduwa*) on the forehead of the grantee and give him a silver-colored cane. In the past, such elaborate functions had been used to bestow princely titles as well. The number of insignia increased or decreased in proportion to eminence and importance of the rank or the title.

The following is a general description of the insignia received by each level of recipients:

Mohottāla — *damwel bendi sembuwa* (brass or copper pewter pot with a chain), *Mohotti bámma* (a turban-like head cover), *Sammukkalama* (cotton sheet to wear

---

[39] In general, *vasama* is another word for the title of a minor official. Head of the village (gama) holds the title of *gam vasama*. But in the vernacular of the region, *vasama* also has other meanings. The area of the office holder conducts his duties is his *vasama*, or in a village, the plots of lands reserved for *gamarāla* are also called *vasam* lands.

[40] See Tillakaratne, 2015 p. 122 for description of this practice in other situations in 1950s in a village in Elimeda Tulāna in Kanadarā Kōrale in 1950s.

around waist)[41], *Navariyan Maha Uramalaya* (a towel of three meters)[42], and the cane called *naga pirambuwa* (*naga* – snake, *pirambu* – cane). Next, the Chief announced boundaries or names of the villages that came under the title holder's oversight and wrote a *sittu* (act of appointment) describing other requisites, specificities, and duration of the title. Thereafter, he addressed the *mulādāni* for the first time with the appropriate title appellation. Thus, Maradankadawala Senevirathna Banda *Vel Vidāne* (see name in *Sinhala Sirith Sangrahaya*) began to be called Senevirathna Banda Appuhami Mohottāla. He then became a *Varigeta patabándek (*a title holder of the *Varige*). He had no restrictions from using his insignia for occasions beyond Rata Sabhā functions. So, a *patabándā* may come to a marriage ceremony or religious occasion at the temple attired in his regalia for ostentation or to honor the exceptional nature of the occasion.

Baddarāla – *tuppottiya*, the cylindrical *karapus* toppiya and *vévála* (cane).
Lékama – *vévála.*

Fig. 39. Senevirathna Appuhamy Kalubanda
Senevirathna   *Gamarāla* of Maradankalla.
Photo: Niranjala Tillakaratne.

After the person was declared as a *patabándā,* he goes home with the new title. Villagers then hold a reception for him. Residents of adjoining villages too take part in this celebration. The reception includes showering him with a feast and gifts and fun activities that shall be described in a later chapter. The common gift is the

[41] Also called *Samakkattu:* any item bestowed by the King on his subjects (D'Oyly, 1917, p. 243; Casie Chitty, 1834, p. 283).
[42] A length of about 45cm or distance from one's elbow to the tip of the middle finger. Also called a cubit.

traditional *bulathurulla*. A few days later, *patabándā* invites villagers to his house where he hosts them to an elaborate feast in a *Maduwa* or *pandalama* (a temporary shed on stilts) covered with a *viyan* (ceiling awning) of white linen.

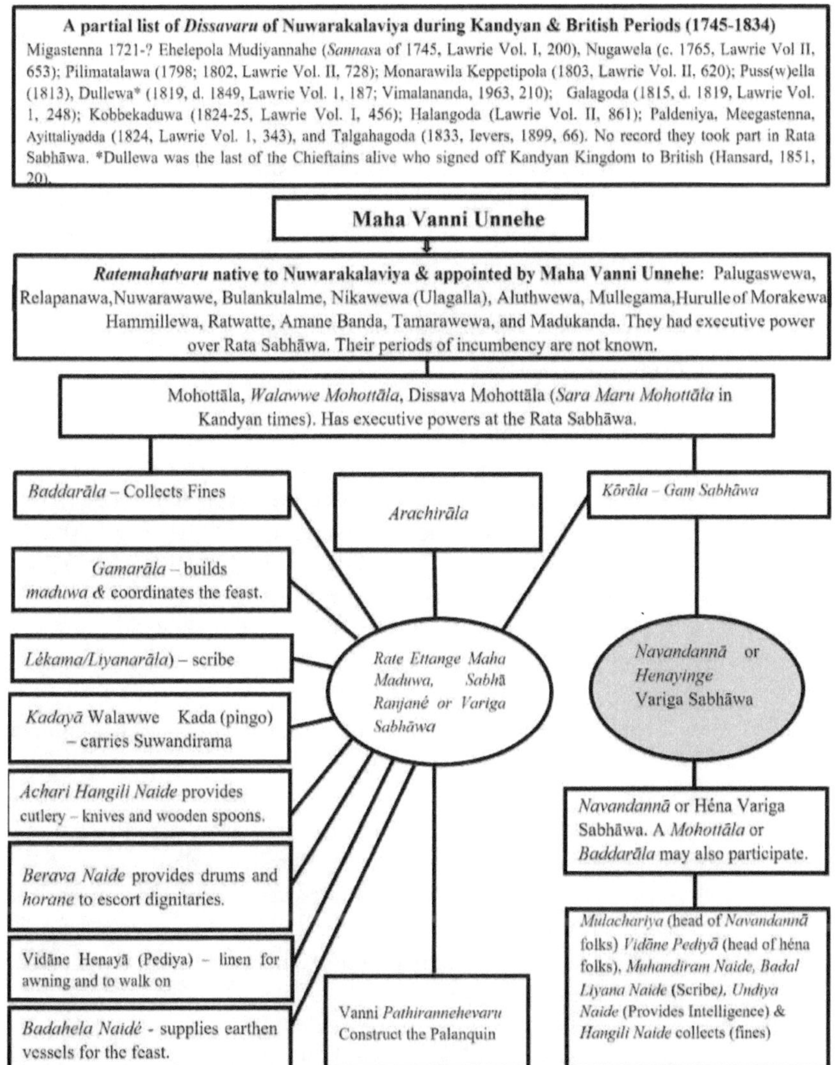

Fig. 40. Chain of Officials in Rata Sabhāwa in Nuwarakalaviya c 1910.

To share the community spirit and highlight the new *patabándā's* substance, relatives, and well-wishers make felicitating remarks after the feast. In 1996, Kandathe, a villager in his 80s recalled one such meeting and the feast at Kukulawa, a village referenced in earlier pages. He told anthropologist James Brow (1996) that after a new member of the Variga Court was first introduced at a feast in his village, an elder stood up and declared, "you people take care! Don't violate the laws of the

Varige. This man is a new cobra. His teeth are not broken. So, don't you women run away with outsiders. He can tear your limbs, and he can punish you as he likes. So, beware of him, and don't break the laws of the variga [*sic*] (p. 117)." If the above introduction was given verbatim or as a metaphor or not, what is clear is the degree of importance attributed to the authority wielded by a Variga Court member.

Few days after the feast, the *mulādäniya* goes back to Chief's walawwa to present *dákum pudaperu* (tributary presentations). Some of the relatives, well- wishers and a *kadayā* (pingo carrier) carrying sweets and other victuals accompany *patabándā* on this trip. He carries the *bulathurulla* with the appropriate fee as promised. Only now the title is confirmed. This must have been an arduous task. For example, for this phase of the investiture, my great-grandfather Senevirathna Banda Mohottala of Maradankalla must have walked or rode a bullock cart 20 kilometers to Anuradhapura where Ratemahattayā of Nuwaragam Palatha lived. There was no motorized public transport between this village and Anuradhapura until the 1970s. Having to make this trip twice for the process is proof of how important receiving a title must have been to a *patabándā*.

CHIEFS' DRESS & INSIGNIA. After the Chief gets titled, he will also get his insignia of office and gifts from the grantor.

1. *Atamulu toppiya*. Those individuals who were ennobled as a implicit birth-right or at the pleasure of the King received eight-cornered puffed berets) for *Adikāramvaru* and Maha Vanniyā. D'Oyly wrote that among the missives he received from Ehelepola Udagampahe Adikārama, there were requests for green velvet fabric, among other things, to make caps. The messenger told D'Oyly that anything made of green velvet was special and selective; except *Adikarama* or *Dissava*, no other Chief or person could wear green colored caps.[43]

2. *Hatara mulu toppiya* (four-cornered puffed berets) for *Dissavaru* and *Ratemahatvaru*. These hats were also called *jagalat toppi* (*jagalat* – important).

3. Sword, or a lance or a gun commensurate with the rank or title which D'Oyly called according to the *pavula* (family or clan).[44]

4. *Dissava* received an elephant or a horse.[45] There was no shortage of elephants around Kandy, either in the wild, particularly in the surrounding forests or tamed and tethered in King's *kuruwe* stalls (elephants' section).

5. Great Flag of the *Dissavani* (*Maha Kodiya*).

6. Stylus, ornamented and made of high value metals. Usually carried wedged in grantee's waistband. It is an essential item the Chief must have to write on palm leaf strips.

7. Lands or whole villages as *nindagam* (also called *accomodessan* during Dutch time) – villages a grantee lived in and worked for the grantor.

---

[43] D'Oyly, 1917, p. 52.

[44] D'Oyly, 1917, p. 21.

[45] Minutes of Government Agent at Ruwanwella in 1815 CGA, B-262b, qtd. in Ralph Pieris p. 23.

The bloated mid-area of the Chief's dress ensemble looked peculiar. The following is how Reginald Farrer (1908), penetratingly described a Kandyan Chief dressed in his utterly dazzling and refulgent regalia (Fig. 41):

> At last, the chieftain emerges! No wonder that his preparations took time, for he is the most gorgeous spectacle. A magnificent old man, stalwart, tall, erect, portly, with a face at once beautiful and royal; serene, aquiline, with streaming beard of gray – the very face of the Oedipus the King. And he is clothed in pantalettes of white muslin, rucked round his ankles like a ham-frill. About his middle is wound some six miles of similar muslin, starred, and spangled with gold, until his figure has the shape of a bobbin or peg top. His shirt is snowy fine, and over it he wears an Eton jacket, very short, with puffed gigot sleeves. Its material is of some marvelous brocade, stiff and opulent, in which the ground color, of hot rich salmon, glimmers and glows through a film of pure gold, shifting, changing, darkening, disappearing in altered planes and folds of the fabric as he moves. His cap or crown is a big, flattened biretta, hard, four-sided, of crimson satin, hidden from sight with jewels and embroideries of gold. In state this commanding figure comes advancing down the cloister, makes his welcome to the visitor … Here, with some ado, the crowd is beaten aside to make place, and we wait […]. (p. 71)

Since writers took pains to describe a Chief attired in his ceremonial livery, the corresponding elegance of a Kandyan lady in full dress (Fig. 7) also behooves space here. From the 18th and 19th centuries, with the influence of diverse colonial dress styles in the Maritime Provinces and silk and cotton cloth and fine jewelry worn by Nayakkar women in the Kandyan Court, a dazzling and fashionable portrait of Kandyan woman began to take shape.

A sari was her chosen dress. She meticulously folded the first quarter of its 7-meters lengthwise a few times and threw it diagonally across the bosom, over the shoulder like a shawl and let it drop faithfully down on the back, its end reaching just above the ankle. This shawl is called *osariya* or *ohoriya* and is tucked in place just below the naval with a cord. Next, she gathers the next part into pleats and the pleated frill is then pulled out through the cord to hold them in place. She wraps the rest of the saree around her waist so that the decorative panel of the saree covers her front below the waistline. She wears a long- or short-sleeved jacket, embroidered and puffy at shoulders – a mix of a short version of *kabakuruththuwa* worn by women in old Maritime Provinces. A few strands of tiny trinkets sewn to it embraces the upper body.

She illuminates herself with seven gold necklaces – *hath male* – with varying lengths, longest falling in front below the waistline stunningly in harmony with other six like rolling waves on a calm ocean. Shiny strings studded with several pearl-like ornaments are pinned and set in place on her neatly combed steel-black hair by peacock-shaped brooches glistening with droplets of stone. The half-moon-shaped frontlet with shiny globules jiggles touching the eyebrows with artful crafting emulating a gaggle of golden geese in flight. Equally lovely armlets, bracelets, bangles, and a glistening waistband holding the sari to the bare naval area redoubled her charming air. Long earrings made of silver or gold dangle from the earlobes and dance to the slightest movement of her head. As she walks, the bottom edge of the sari folds swing with pretty anklets fit for a dancing queen. This assemblage of regalia on her made the sight an impeccably beholding experience and an eloquent language of beauty.

Fig. 41. Kandyan Chiefs Waiting for Prince of Wales in Kandy, 1876. Faded lines below the bottom are the names T.B. Panabokke, President of Tribunal Dumabara (left), Girihagama (middle) and Paranagama (right). Sketch by unknown artist of the colonial government, Ceylon. The Miriam and Ira D. Wallach Division of Art, Prints and Photographs: Picture Collection, The New York Public Library.

9. RATA SABHĀWA, WOMAN, CASTE, AND FAMILY

*J*t has been suggested by anthropologists that caste purity ran through women.[1] Everyone hoped to have a conflict-free marriage and protect caste purity which was a beacon for social stability and kinship fundamentals. It alleviated threats and inconveniences born out of any aberrant deeds and unacceptable practices. Rata Sabhāwa also seems to have looked to other legal traditions for precedents and familiarity to regulate male-female relationships and associated customs. For example, we find in *Niti Nighanduwa,* edited by LeMasurier and Panabokke in 1880 that:

> If a woman without regard to her caste and rank, goes off to a man of lower caste than her own, she will lose her right of inheritance whether her parents disinherits or not; and even if she thus disgraces her caste after her parents' death, her paternal and maternal inheritance through her parents and her any other relatives will be forfeited absolutely. (p. 54)

In *Niti Nighanduwa* and *Armour's Grammar,* especially notable leitmotifs were the rules in use in Kandy as to how a marriage should take place. On the other hand, in Nuwarakalaviya, Kapuruhami Madukanda Ratemahattayā c 1910 and the *kāriyakarawannō* in *Sinhala Sirith Sangrahaya* in 1932, emphasized how a marriage should not take place. Section 14 (1-9) (Fig. 42) of *Rata Sabhāwa* shows such select instances of marriage-related issues. Nuwarakalaviya traditions, while existed strong on their own merits and terms, seemed to have picked only those they considered relevant and important to their regional purposes, which was important, if not central, to the purposes of villagers' institutions – variga, caste and the womanhood. Yet, women as an institution show how relevant, influential, and involved they were to social fabric of the people. In this light, it should not be forgotten in us that even for descriptive purposes we have no right to disregard the prism of past ages in favor of the prism of our own age in viewing multidimensional caste concepts and traditions a woman was subject in the past.

Rata Sabhāwa customs are silent on whether polyandry or polygamy was considered a violation under its rules. In the context of women, Rata Sabhāwa paid more attention to norms society expected rather demanded from women, particularly in marriage-related customs, for it was considered the cobblestone that built the *pavula,* a micro-caste as described earlier. In other words, Rata Sabhāwa placed a high bar on the modesty of women, ethos of marriage and rights a man claimed over his wife. At the same time, Rata Sabhāwa was a misogynic system without doubt. Women participated in the Sabhāwa activities either as accused, complainant or cooks in the kitchen for participants who may be just spectators. Women had no role in decision making in a case before the Sabhāwa. See page 191 for another instance of misogyny in Sri Lanka.

NOTES
[1] Robinson, Marguerite, 1968, pp. 402-423.

Marriage situations not in accord with Kandyan Laws existed c 1860 in *Armour's Grammar*.	Marriage situations not in accord with Nuwarakalaviya customs existed c 1910 in *Rata Sabhāwa* & c 1932 in *SSS*.
SOURCE: Joseph Martinus Perera (1861). *Armour's Grammar of Kandyan Law*.	SOURCE: 1. K. A. Kapuruhami, Rata Sabhāwa, *JRAS (Ceylon)*, 28 (106) (1948), pp. 42-68. 2. *Sinhala Sirith Sangrahaya* essays of *mulādänivaru*, D. E. Hettiarachchi, ed. (1979, 2019).
Non-conservative Marriage (Chapter II.	Non-conservative Marriage (Kapuruhami, Sec. 14).
Sec. 3 p. 5 – Appendix C, p. 129 arriage not done according to traditional *Pas- Mangul* (Five-step marriage ceremony. See page 216).	There is no comment in *Rata Sabhāwa* on *pas mangul*. But *SSS* makes references to it as a tradition in some villages (p. 99-109). See also Tillakaratne, *Millstone*, 2015, p. 3).
Sec. 4 p. 6 – Marriage between couples of different castes. Sec. 8 p. 8 – Higher caste woman marrying man of lower caste. NOTE: Variga customs as in Nuwarakalaviya were not practiced in Kandyan region.	Sec. 14(1) – Higher caste woman marrying or having relationship or eloping with lower caste or low-country (litoral) man (*pāthayò*). Sec. 14(2) – Higher caste woman, or man living with a lower caste. Sec. 14(3) – Higher caste woman openly having an improper relationship with a man of lower caste. Sec. 14(4) – Higher caste woman suspected of having an improper relationship with a lower caste man. Sec. 14(5) – Woman becoming pregnant with child having no legal or known husband. Sec. 14(6) – Marriage out of the *Varige*.
Sec. 8 p. 8 – Prohibited marriage between non-ávessa woman and man (not cross-cousins). Sec. 8 p. 8 – Marriage between children of two brothers or children of two sisters.	Sec. 14(7), (8), (9) – Contracting or proposing for Marriage, or having illegal connection between a couple of Prohibited Degrees of Relationship.
Sec. 9 p. 9 – Incest.	Sec. 14(7), (8), (9).

Fig. 42. Marriage situations not in accord with Kandyan Laws per *Armour's Grammar* (c 1860), *Rata Sabhāwa* (c 1910) & *SSS* (c 1932) in Nuwarakalaviya.

This is not surprising as we see that an exegesis of the 25 violations or breaches listed in Kapuruhami Madukanda Ratemahattayā's thesis on Rata Sabhāwa shows that the first nine are associated with marriage-related improprieties weighing heavily upon a woman's improper sexual conduct or romantic relationship with a man. If the alleged relationship was with a man outside of the caste or *Varige*, then special provisions were in place to deal with it.

Nuwarakalaviya *mulādānivaru* contributing to the *SSS* (1932) also noted the importance of marriage customs. That all of them started their essays with the subject of marriage and caste issues, and the first half-dozen violations under the purview of Kapuruhami Madukanda Ratemahattayā's *Rata Sabhāwa* also relate to marriage and caste subtexts underscore the importance Nuwarakalaviya people had placed on the institutions of marriage and caste.

Often a man in Kandyan times, regardless of his title or caste, shared a wife with his brother (polyandry – *bahu purusha vivahaya*). There was also a custom where a man may marry and live with two or more women (polygamy – *bahu bharya vivahaya*). This custom was universally called *eka gei kāma* ('eating and living in the same house'). In such arrangements, the two men sharing a woman were called associated husbands (*sahabhaga purushaya*) and two women sharing a husband were called associated wives (*sahabhaga bharya*). The rigors of life in the past behooved and tolerated both these customs that are ostracized, abhorred and illegal now. This practice also helped to keep family holdings (land and movable property) within the kinship group and mitigate complexities, urgencies and potential hardships to the surviving family arising after sudden death of the husband or wife.[2]

In Nuwarakalaviya, caste customs were practiced with painstaking effort and *kula sirith* (habits or practices) were 'jealously guarded.'[3] Arthur A. Perera elucidated caste in the following manner:

> A caste consists of a group of clans, and each clan claims descent
> from a common ancestor and calls itself either after his name, or
> the office he held, or if a settler, the village from which he came.
> The clan's name was dropped when a person became a Chief and
> a surname which became hereditary assumed. The clan's name was,
> however, not forgotten as the ancestral status of the family was
> ascertained from it. (p. 32)

But caste tenets of marriage were in a separate sphere of its own in the past. As far back as 1600s, Robert Knox (1681, 1995) observed that a person's dalliance with a lower caste man or woman were subjected to even expulsion from the family or the village or the *Varige* (p. 66). In Kandyan times, D'Oyly (1835) wrote, marriage between a low caste man and higher caste woman was a "barbarous custom." Consequently, "... female was consigned as a Slave of the Crown to the Royal Village of Gampola, and the Family was ordered to deliver some Provision to the Royal Store and by this act became purified [*sic*] (pp. 191-252)."

---

[2] Before the medical advancements of the 20th century, a person could die from contracting common cold or consumption (tuberculosis) that were rampant in communities.

[3] R. Pieris, 1956, *Sinhalese Social Organization...* p. 252.

Review of state of property rights of women centuries ago provides evidence of ill treatment with social and cultural restrictions they were subject to.[4] Bertolacci (1817) found that in the 18th century, a married woman was only the 5th in line to inherit husband's property (p. 473). And at the time of fall of Kandy, not the wife, but inheritors of *paraveni* rights of her husband had the right to any *Sannas*, weapons, gold chains, *pata tahadu* he received as gifts or awards from the King.[5] One of the most abhorrent customs was the naming of the child born out of a relationship (not kinship) between a higher caste man and his low cate mistress. Man disowns the offspring as if he had no role in it and shirks the obligation to name the child after his colorful name. Child bears the mother's caste name. Obviously, this practice denies the child and the mother any traditional rights endowed under the patronymic naming ways![6]

Violations and indiscretions involving a woman were called *māgam sōli* (*māgam* – women, *sōli* – improprieties, faults). If she was harassed – sexual or any other manner, or got pregnant out of wedlock, such acts were called *mahā sāvadya kula veradi* (breaches and disgraceful acts of major kind). Other minor violations involving women were called *alpa sāvadya kula veradi* (breaches and disgraceful acts of minor kind).[7]

Rata Sabhāwa, with its generations of experience, must have found the need for special provisions to curb potential improprieties by women, or threats against them. Someone today might rightly say this institution was biased against women. But in fairness to the times and culture they lived in, this is what they thought best way to protect the family honor and survival. While men rarely faced consequences for committing all sorts of indecorums, only women had to answer when faced with similar accusations. Such bias can only be defined as a malicious and inequitable legacy practiced in Sri Lankan history. Sadly, this is true universally even now. In the 1970s TV sitcom *Threes Company,*[8] John Ritter famously declared, "Men don't have to worry about their reputation!"

If the woman was at fault, Rata Sabhāwa placed restrictions or interdictions – *tahanam* on her and her close relatives. Afterwards, no one can visit her house. She also will not get fire (fire sticks) from another house to light her kitchen hearth; not allowed to bath at the *nānamankada* – common bathing ford in the village tank or collect drinking water from the *diyamankada* – a dedicated spot away from the bathing ford to collect drinking water. Nonetheless, Rata Sabhāwa, though had not done any statistical study, undoubtedly noted the preponderance of aggravating acts against women and incorporated them in the category of objectionable acts under its purview. Threats to women as small as an insult received stern and judicious response from the Rata Sabhāwa.

---

[4] Even in the middle of Kalahari Desert, female members of bushmen bands had to obey inequitable social restrictions. Men among the Ju/wasi people can move between neighboring campfires at night just to chat, but for a woman, she just had to stop at a distance and shout out (Thomas, 2006. p. 188).

[5] Perera, J.M., 1861, p. 21.

[6] A. C. Lawrie (1896 and 1898) refers to multiple instances of this practice in 19th century Sri Lanka.

[7] Hettiarachchi., D. E., ed. 1979 p. 21.

[8] Based on the BBC sitcom *Man About the House.*

Writing essays for the *SSS* in 1932, *mulādenivaru* noted that King Buvanekabahu V (1388-1408) advised the *Vanniyars* of Nuwarakalaviya and Vanni area about their responsibilities and duties (p.7). These guidelines emphasized that in the higher castes like Goigama or Vanniyar, if a woman married with a lower caste man or started a relationship with him, she was said to have fallen into disgrace – known as *kula pali vāteema*. That called for the accused woman to be expelled from her caste with a *tahanama*. Following this tradition, the Rata Sabhāwa punished her fittingly after a hearing. The Sabhāwa afterwards removes her disgrace by cleansing it (*kula pali arinawa*). The decision is next confirmed by a declaration to all village(s) concerned.

Nikawewa Ratemahattayā who asserted superior status over Vellala caste would only pause to condemn the caste-based marriage issues involving women. In 1851 when asked by A. O. Brodie, Assistant Government Agent in Anuradhapura, what he would do if a woman of his caste married a Vellala caste man, he replied: "In the Kandyan Times we should have killed her at once, but now – hump! – well : I don't know what else we could do with her now either [*sic*]."[9] In the past, Ratna Irugal Vanni Bandara who lived in Kelaniya was found having an illicit relationship with a Tamil woman who came to his house to coat a room floor with cow dung in order to keep the dead body of a member of the household. Oddly enough, a Rata Sabhāwa held at Yapahuwa convicted not the man but the woman to death by drowning in the Sarasna tank.[10] This suggests that at some point in time around Middle Ages, a variant of Rata Sabhāwa had authority to levy capital punishment, particularly on breaches involving caste, ethnic identity and gender. Some believe the Vanni Bandara in this case had been granted the area including Kelaniya near Kolompura also called Labuveriya.[11] D'Oyly wrote in his *Diary* on February 21, 1813, that grandson of Kulasekara Brahmana who built Kelaniya Dagoba "mixed with Patti women (herdswomen of a lesser caste) & lost his caste" (p. 171). British administration in Sri Lanka continued to sentence women to death by drowning until 1826 when Governor Edward Barnes outlawed the practice by a proclamation dated March 23.

Seldom there had been reports of dishonor of this kind perpetrated by males of the upper castes as well. It is not clear whether that situation also was treated as a *kula pali vāteema*. According to an anecdote in the Ulagalla Kōrale, there was once the son of a Chief who fell in love with a woman in a lower caste village near Uttimaduwa. The elders then expelled the man from the village. He moved out with his new wife to a small village, one of his father's *muttetugam* in a far corner of the *Kōrale*.[12] It is not known whether any caste stigma followed this expulsion. Had there been any, it went unknown under the depth of history as time seems to have healed the alleged impropriety (*kula pali*). Now there are families in the area that have assertively adopted the same last name and a new subcaste or *Varige*!

---

9 Ievers ,1899, p. 92; Arunachalam, 1906, p. 46. D'Oyly, 1917, p. 242 had included this fact in his *Sketch* but only refers to it as "ancient usage" as in practice for some time prior to the fall of Kandy (p. 242).

10 Hettiarachchi, D. E., ed. 1979, p. 7.

11 Hettiarachchi, D. E., ed. 1979, pp. 34, 168.

12 K.B. Ranbanda of Uttimaduwa (Personal communication, June 20, 2014).

However, Ryan (1953) noted that by 1950s caste system began an irrevocable evolutionary process. He found, though exceptional, instances of hypergamic and hypogamic marriages between *Radala* and *Vahal* (slaves) emerging. Wealthy families of lower caste status could usually find grooms among impoverished aristocratic families. Subcastes began a gradual process of merging (p. 157). Until that time, there was a perceptible pattern associated with a person's name associated with a certain profession, group, religious affiliation, ethnicity, caste, region, or the village he or she belonged to. By and large, name is a fair indicator of a person's caste standing up until the latter half of the 20th century.

But by the 1980s, newspaper obituaries often showed shifting kinship topography and its assortment of diverse caste affiliations (generally implied by way of names listed) of the kindred of the deceased person. In the Sunday paper, the text of matrimonial announcements is toned-down and phrases like "no caste preferred" or "caste immaterial" are becoming common. In the 21st century, naming conventions have evolved so much so, they do not represent the named person's social, caste, religious, ancestral, or professional affiliation, attributes that were easy markers in the past. Now credit cards buy baby's name online from the so-called linguists. A good book of alphabetically arranged names will do the job. This trend is a business venture which needs zero capital!

According to Nuwarakalaviya traditions, the intent and purpose of the Rata Sabhāwa was to safeguard and preserve the purity of the *Varige,* lodestone of the social order which is composed of nine honors (*nava nambu*).[13] In the context of marriage, Variga concept was not seemed to be widespread outside Nuwarakalaviya. With such strict social tenets being relevant often giving wide berth for interpretation of customs, it is not improbable that not just marriage to a lower caste, any mesalliance could have resulted in the parties summoned before a Rata Sabhāwa. Rata Sabhāwa customs allowed endogamy between members of one *Varige* only.

Typically, this happens when the caste purity of the variga members is not in question. In some instances, however, person A of caste A may not know the caste affiliation of person B who is unable to guarantee his or her *Varige* or caste affiliation. When this happens, in most cases, he or she is branded as a *pita varigakkārayā* (exo-variga member). Then, if possible, at all, the relatives do not consent to the marriage of A & B taking place.

One of the underlying purposes of this stricture – ban to marry outside the *variga,* and between those who are not cross-cousins (*ávessa massinā* or *ávessa nänā*) – is to prevent fragmentation of holdings of a kinship group. Any marriage outside of this conformity threatened the splintering of land into smaller lots, weakening the economic well-being and stability of the family, the important building block of a *Varige. Ávessa* marriage as outlined then contributed to marital share consolidation. Obeyesekere (1967) noted that it also made possible for women to become outright landowners or at least enabled them to inherit shares (p. 254).

---

[13] One version of *nava nambu* are: Religion, Country, Government, Education/Learning, Variga/Clan, Relatives, Friends, Parents and Teacher. Another goes as: King, Country, Ethnicity (*jatiya*), Teachers, Parents, Woman (wife?), Children and Slaves (*Vahallu*) (Hettiarachchi, ed. 2019 p. 164).

VARIGA COURTS IN KUKULAWA. In 1983, James Brow was able to interview mostly 2nd and 3rd generation descendants of Albert Fernando, a Catholic of karāva caste from the Western Province who worked as an overseer in the Survey Department in Anuradhapura in early decades of the 20th century. After retiring in 1924, Fernando settled down with his wife Millie in Kukulawa, a small village near Maha Kanadarāwa wilderness off Anuradhapura-Trincomalee Road (A12). The information Brow was able to cobble together, particularly about marriage practices and customs involving cross-caste families showed what the present-day Kukulawa villagers had heard and experienced in their teenage years when the Rata Sabhā and Variga Sabhā customs had begun to fade into sunset.

Kandathe, a Kukulawa resident told Brow (1996) that he remembers hearing difficulties of karāva caste woman named Podi Nona had to experience after marrying Bandathe (? - 1976), a Goigama caste man. She was a relative of Millie and Fernando, whose clan expanded over the years and still live in Kukulawa and nearby Samādhigama. They are nonchalant about past Variga ways. The villagers shunned this marriage, forced the couple to leave the village to Sippukulama, a few kilometers away. This was equivalent to expulsion from the *Varige*. After their child Tikiribanda was born, the couple went before the Variga Sabhāwa and got consent to join the *Varige* after paying 550 ridi. In 1983, after locating Tikiribanda, James Brow was able to speak to other relatives of Bandathe as well. In another instance, a couple was represented by the groom's father and after paying a fine of 550 ridi and feeding the villagers for three days, the marriage was approved, and the couple was accepted as *ape-minissu* (our people, our *Varige*) which allowed them to move back to Kukulawa (p. 115). As will be described in another instance, a man from *pātha rata* who intended to marry a woman in Pul Eliya near Anuradhapura nearly got expelled from the village when he refused to be subjected to Pul Eliya communal norms and pay Rs. 200, the fine imposed by the Rata Sabhāwa for the privilege to join the *Varige*. Generally, categorizing residents of Maritime Provinces as a separate caste runs back as far back as early 19th century as found in D'Oyly's (1917) writings (p. 240).

After the *Ratemahattayā* system ended, variga concepts in general with occasional exceptions, have become outdated. For example, Ukkubanda of Kukulawa said that anyone who married to his variga (regardless of other variga affiliations) was treated as belonging to his *Varige*. "After all, we are all human beings!" But Brow found this was not universal. Some folks in their golden age still refused to participate in ceremonies with the Fernando clan. In their thinking, Fernando's was still a *pita varigakkarayā*. Kandathe told that on some occasions, in the heat of an argument, an angry villager would throw an insulting counter punch like "you bitch, you're married to a karāva man!"[14] Notwithstanding how much had changed in the social fabric in a village, such instances show how deeply and influentially entrenched the old ways in the psyche of some descendants who has nothing to do with it now even after pertinent customs had been defunct for decades.

Brow also observed that in 1920s the Kukulawa villagers held the Fernando

---

[14] Brow, 1996, p. 120.

family at a certain social distance because of its origins with direct connections to karāva caste. Brow thought it has more to do with being envious of Fernando's family success with a lone long-running grocery store in the village and exposure to outside ways and urban manners than variga exclusiveness. Another reason is the Fernando clan members' disregard and disrespect for Kukulawa traditions of propriety, which naturally drew discontent from the villagers.

In 1973, four decades after Rata Sabhāwa became extinct, A. P. A. Gunasekara, a novice Civil Servant Administrative Officer (DRO) stumbled upon a reincarnation of a Variga Sabhā moment during a *Palāth Dinaya*, the Provincial Day, also called Division Day conducted by Kachcheri officials. The DRO awaits the villagers if not in the village, in the nearby Rest House in Horowpothana, about 50 kilometers east of Anuradhapura. On this monthly pre-scheduled day, the DRO makes this formal visit to hear villagers' concerns and disputes and resolve them right there, if possible. If the issue cannot be resolved on this day, an alternate official from Kachcheri will follow up later and resolve it.

On this day, a 70-year-old man came to meet the young official seeking a resolution for complications thrust upon him to deal with his son who married an out-of-*Varige* woman. The man told the DRO that he will expel his son from the *Varige* because the disgrace he had to face following this unconventional marriage in early '70s. Complicating this request further, the man wanted the DRO to give him assistance with documentation to get the plot of land he deeded to his daughter who had allowed her offending brother to build a house in it. It is notable how ingrained was the rational dissonance of caste and *Varige* themes in old-timers, a generation after the Variga Sabhā practice ended. For the father, his son's incompatible act made him worthy of expulsion from the *Varige* – an erstwhile concept but embers still burning below the surface of his thoughts. He wanted his daughter punished as well by annulling the deed to the land. After rookie Administrative Officer who in his own words tellingly admitted not knowing "North or South of Anuradhapura," sat and listened, he had no choice but to enrich himself with the Variga Sabhā traditions of the past when the old man was in his 30s.[15]

The man brought his experience with Variga Sabhāwa and influence of its traditions to the young officer's attention. On that day, this man must have been one of the few adults of the genre who was still living and had witnessed a Variga Sabhāwa in action. He had seen the effectiveness of the system with his own metrics. To him the DRO who could resolve the issue was the highest voice of the new genre of officialdom, akin to the avuncular *mohottāla* of his younger days. The villager's argument cut across practicality desired by all villagers of his generation. As unrealistic as it may seem to us now, he was living in the past and untethered from reality. The villager was familiar with the Variga Sabhāwa and its simplified dispensation of order which he now sees as lacking in the Administrators mantra on this highly publicized Division Day. He feared his concerns would be tabled for a future meeting, then perhaps get buried in the bureaucratic maze. He probably had seen the lethargy of the government service before Division Day.

---

[15] Gunasekara, 2004, p. 131.

What he was asking was the convenience of resolving issues without the weight of the bureaucracy the young DRO was bringing to these meetings. To this villager, the dissolved inertial potency of the collective community memory of an erstwhile custom which he had known as the norm four decades ago must have felt so tempting and trusting, he began to insist on it to the surprise, and to a point, frustration of the DRO. His efforts to come to terms with the prospect of having to adapt to a new way of conflict resolution was like, as Chinua Achebe said, trying to become left-handed (to write anew). The DRO's tutoring was from codes of law and volumes of procedure unfamiliar to the villager who instead wished only the old ways. With this man's estimation, it would take no more than a day to reach an acceptable solution. With this hope, he clung to the dreams of yesteryear when, before long, that time called 'long ago' shall have been merged in with the changing realities of modernity which the DRO embodied.

INCEST. In *Sinhala Sirith Sangrahaya,* Hettiarachchi (1979, 2019) found reference to instances of incest and how Rata Sabhāwa resolved such situations. An unconventional union like incest was called *nekam bändeema* (prohibited degree of relationships). In the past, such situations called for death of the man by impaling, but the Rata Sabhāwa, having no powers to impose capital punishment, opted for the maximum fine allowed within its authority – 550 ridi or expelled the parties from *Varige* without pardoning or any reconciliation as a form of reckoning with the issue (p. 169). Rata Sabhāwa will also impose maximum punishment on those who plans or proposes such a preposterous idea too.[16]

Sometimes instances of inadvertent incest situations came before Rata Sabhāwa. This happens when a couple enters a marriage while kinship boundaries are unclear or vague or distant kinship with unclear relationship come to light after they married and had children. Long after they had children, if it becomes known that the couple may not be cross-cousins, or their variga identities have dubious origins, then obviously the resulting murky situation had to be resolved. Now to avoid potential dishonor, and danger of ostracism, particularly aimed at the children, the couple itself or the relatives or the villagers who have other vested interests bring the quandary to the attention of the Rata Sabhāwa asking it to review and decide upon it to clear any lingering misconceptions about acceptability. After weighing the mitigating facts and evidence, the Rata Sabhāwa on its part imposes a fine and declares the whole family as legitimate members of the *Varige*. Furthermore, if the need arises that such a marriage has become an absolute and exigent imperative, then too, the parties could pay a fine before marrying to avoid any legal hassle later. H. M. K. Mohottāla Kōrale Lékama of Horowpothana noted that in ancient times, marriage between siblings in a royal family was considered an acceptable custom.[17] Since the marriage took place in the royal household, it is highly improbable anyone would ever subject it for any judicial clarification. Nor anyone would dare to bring it up. It may well have been a tolerated custom in the past.

On the other hand, when the marriage was certified or registered in the books, this colonial conception was accepted as a binding union between a man and a

---

[16] Kapuruhami, 1948, p. 42-68.

[17] Hettiarachchi, D. E., ed. 1979, 2019, p. 102.

woman while all other types of unions under the long-standing traditions were not given recognition. But Nuwarakalaviya had a rational process to make the union acceptable for all intents and purposes after completing ingrained process called *pas mangul*, community celebration that involved a five-step marriage protocol.[18] In terms of perpetuity and community validation, decision of a Variga Sabhā session parallels a marriage ceremony in the village. The community memory of the decisions taken at both events makes them "legal" and binding.

In the village, there was no recording of the marriage in a public document, i.e., register. Discussion of prospective property rights, dowries, and so on took place in the presence of the villagers at a feast by a gathering of people who came to witness and celebrate the union. This too makes the occasion embodied in the community memory as a fact in perpetuity, witnessed and accepted by all. Henceforth, people's willingness to accept the conclusions of the 'convention' that two people have joined hands to live a life together becomes the 'record.' Similar understanding of the community is the premise for calling a Variga Sabhāwa a *Sammutiya* – a convention – of variga members agreeing on an important matter with community blessing. Underlying meaning of a *Variga Sammutiya* that consist of *tahanam arina vākkiya* (proscription lifting incantation) and *tahanam vattiya* (proscription tray) demonstrates the reinforcement of such a public agreement and pronouncement. The union was accepted as valid albeit without documenting it in a book. The marriage then earns the 'officiated' label if it were witnessed and celebrated by the villagers culminating with a grand feast.

Furthermore, non-action or non-response by a Rata Sabhāwa on such a union was tantamount to a tacit 'certification" and validation of a couple as married under the social norms.[19] A 'correction' to questionable marriage(s) under instances outlined before also cleared of any doubts, and 'authenticated' with or without a fine after it went through the Rata Sabhāwa review process.

Variga Court often showed favoritism during hearings related to marriages where caste authenticity was clouded. Then the court ordered the paramour to pay a fine to purge the offence. Leach (1961, 1968) believes such payment was something tantamount to a fee for admission to the *Varige* (p.72). Paying an admission fee was not a custom: it was always a fine paid as a reminder to the wrongdoer for shirking communal responsibilities.

INFANTICIDE. Three instances of infanticide existed in Kandyan kingdom as D'Oyly (1835) reported:

    a.   When parents already have many children and believe they cannot support another because of their indigence.

    b.   When the child is believed to have been born under the spell of an evil star, which is likely to threaten the family and the child to suffer misfortune.

---

[18] *Pas Mangul* are: 1. Proposal brought by groom's kinfolks to bride's; 2. If willing to proceed, bride's parents give the horoscope to groom's; 3. If horoscopes match, groom and his kins visit the bride's folks to discuss logistics of the marriage ceremony; 4. Marriage ceremony and escorting the bride home; and 5. *Kat Bendi Mangula*, the occasion when a week or two after the feast, bride's parents and kins go with a *kada* (pingo) full of sweets to see the daughter in her new home.

[19] Tillakaratne 2015, pp. 3-5; Hettiarachchi, D. E., ed. 1979, 2019, p. 74.

c. If the child were born because of an illicit relationship and mother is ashamed of it.

I believe the misnomer "death sentence" by Rata Sabhāwa in the folklore may have its origin based on instances of infanticide, primarily of girls, reported in Nuwarakalaviya and Kandyan country[20] (p. 243).

There were instances when the mother herself was forced to infanticide by her master or circumstance.[21] In early 1800s, a slave woman who worked at a walawwa in Wattegama gave birth to a child. Lawrie (1898) found folklore that the Chief who she worked for then asked her to kill the baby as he worried the new baby would be an added burden to the slave mother who had to care for Chief's children as well. Over time, with Chief's continuous urging, this woman buried altogether eight of her children (p. 923). The scale of this heinous act is so extreme, one may be inclined to think it as a spurious tale or imagination shared with Justice A. C. Lawrie by one of his overzealous and fudged informants in the course of his research or witnesses in one of the cases he found in the record room in his Court. Two centuries ago, with the way women, whether slave or not, were treated, it is difficult to doubt if a Chief would not resort to such a series of devilish acts to protect his own interests at the expense of a mother. A well-known example is Chief Ehelepola who let his wife and children be murdered to protect his skin. Pandulagama-Kattambuwagama Wijepala Kumarasinghe told me of a story circulating in Kanadarā Kōrale where in 19th century, an infant born out of wedlock was killed by feeding her with a plant extract called *kabara* oil. But it should be noted that the story does not involve Rata Sabhāwa as having played any role in it.

Kapuruhami Madukanda Ratemahattayā does not make any references to infanticide. With instances of teenagers making fun of Rata Sabhāwa traditions[22] I wonder whether a generation after its demise, with stories like the above, did wild speculations began to build surrounding this institution?

MARRIAGE, *ARMOUR'S GRAMMAR*, *NITI NIGHANDUWA* AND RATA SABHĀWA. In the 19th century, the three landmark documents, *Armour's Grammar of Kandyan Law* (1861), *Niti Nighanduwa: A Vocabulary of Law* (1880), and *A Sketch of the Constitution* (1917), have taken great pains to outline laws and prohibitions in place on marriage customs in Kandyan provinces.[23] An exegesis of these works reveals criminal and civil procedures existed in 19th century, including those related to marriage customs and traditions. Similarly, to a considerable extent, these traditions had remarkable influence on marriage traditions Rata Sabhāwa of Nuwarakalaviya had to deal with (Fig. 42).

---

[20] Knox, 1681, 1995, p. 94; D'Oyly, 1917, p. 80.

[21] Infanticide was found among peoples who live in very rigorous living conditions. The *Ju/wasi* Bushmen, also called First People – being the first in the Kalahari Desert in Africa – practiced the custom without any discrimination of the sex of the child. The hunter-gatherer living is so challenging, they had to do this for "spacing of children" to make sure a mother can only nurse one child at a time to save herself and the child (Thomas, 2006, p. 196). On the other end of the world, the Netsilingmuit, a group of Inuit people in the Canadian High Arctic killed newborn "because the struggle for existence is so hard," (Danish anthropologist Knud Rasmussen, 1922, qtd. in Paul Watson, 2017, *Ice Ghosts*, p. 185).

[22] Leach, 1961, p. 78.

[23] D'Oyly, 1817

In large measure, marriage limitations, vicissitudes, and exclusions exist similarly in both systems – Kandyan proper and Nuwarakalaviya, an indication that they both sprang from analogous traditions but ending up in their own trajectories showing minor differences such as variga concept which was only practiced in the latter. *Niti Nighanduwa* and *Armour's Grammar* summed up the manner of maintaining civil administration with attention to criminal behavior of people. Rata Sabhā customs maintained a sociable process on its own where emphasis was not so much on deeper shortcomings of people, but of minor conflicts, marriage, caste and variga purity issues and etiquette at public gatherings. They were considered collectively as disgraceful or inappropriate conduct calculated from a social point of view. Rata Sabhāwa believed that if no strictures regarding essential components like family (building unit of the society), criminal or civil conflicts (social order), customs (social behavior) were imposed, resulting chaos would result in weakened foundation of variga and caste principals and traditions, eventualities without doubt would have certainly led to deterioration of life in all fronts. Thus, with institutions like marriage in steady footing with a regulated approach under the concepts like Rata Sabhāwa, Chiefs and populace in Nuwarakalaviya were confident of a robust way of life and solidarity among communities.

As explained in *Niti Nighanduwa* and *Armour's Grammar*, between the two premier Kandyan institutions to wit: the *pavula* (family or band), and *uruma* (inheritance and property rights),[24] there are about 430 instances that had the potential for needing assistance of the law (traditions) of the land.[25] Importance of this was proved with what followed after the fall of Kandy in 1815 when the mad rush of people seeking clarification and validation of their traditions and social customs in the context of English law began to collect speed as an urgent matter as never seen before.[26]

Although writing about family laws was not the forte of Nuwarakalaviya Chiefs, most of their families had kinships established with other families of equal standing spread across the Kandyan provinces. The result of this convenience was their ability to expand and update the knowledge base of unwritten customs and traditions encompassing multiple regions. Hurulle of Morakewa family near Horowpothana was related to both Nikawewa and Galagoda Dissava in Kandy who signed the 1815 Kandyan Treaty representing Nuwarakalaviya. He continued to live in his ancestral village in the Kandy area. Nuwarawawe and Bulankulame families had relatives in Matale, Kandy and later in Hath Kōrale. Nikawewa *Ratemahattayā* of Ulagalla was related to Panabokke family in Kandy. T.B. Panabokke, President of Dumbara Village Tribunal was an accomplished scholar as seen from his co-authorship of *Niti Nighanduwa: A Vocabulary* in 1880. Reason for cross country marriages was the

---

[24] In 19th century Kandyan Law theses, four main types of rights of succession (*uruma*) of an individual are given. They are namely, Paternal (*Piya*), Birth Child (*Jataka*), Maternal (*Mau*), and Parturiated Child (*Daru*).

[25] Perera, J. M., 1861, pp. 6-120.

[26] Fondness of Sinhalese for litigation is proverbial; their cases in Court abound, even to disputing about the fractional part of a coconut tree (John Ferguson, 1893, p. 33). A generation after the fall of Kandy, by 1862, Sri Lankans have litigated 101,319 cases in the colonial courts as reported by Ferguson, A.M. (1868) in *Ceylon Directory* (p. 133).

tradition of exclusive caste endogamy practiced by these families that identified themselves as Radala caste. In short, any Chief, whether he claimed ancestry to Kandyan villages, or Vanniya families in Nuwarakalaviya, or bourgeoning capitalist class of the 19th century Maritime Provinces had open lines of communication regarding marriage opportunities. The dearth of qualified partners for marriage from the same caste made them scramble all over the country looking for families that had brides or grooms in waiting. This helped widen the knowledge base on customs across the Kandyan and even Maritime Provinces and far out in the Nuwarakalaviya.

The *Niti Nighanduwa* and *Armour's Grammar* had been in circulation in some form for several decades by the time Kapuruhami Madukanda Ratemahattayā began to write *Rata Sabhāwa* thesis. How big an influence it had on him is not known. But knowing his superior scholarly attributes[27] and penchant for ethnographic interests, it is not out of the realm of possibility that he could have been aware of the new scholarly works about Kandyan laws published in Colombo. In summation, both primers, *Niti Nighanduwa* and *Rata Sabhāwa*, can be best described as a fusion of legal elements and customs existed in the Kandyan kingdom and Nuwarakalaviya.

Even as stood as neighbors, these two regions stood apart with expansive stretches of forest and geographic characteristics that naturally made some customs and traditions remain a bit disparate. Examples are the Variga Sabhāwa and *Variga Sammutiya* which the Kandyan highlands did not have. Instead, it had *Gam Sabe*. And there is no record an *ambalama* was used in Nuwarakalaviya for Rata Sabhā sessions because there was hardly any *ambalama* in the province. Due to logistical drawbacks, it is unlikely a *Gam Sabe* session held in an *ambalama* could have a feast with the same level of gaiety as a feast in a *Maduwa* after a Rata Sabhāwa session.

Thus, on some occasions, adherence to different approaches for social order and life in Nuwarakalaviya were predictably unavoidable. Reasons like these also influenced how Chiefs often conducted their business. D'Oyly (1835) noted that dating back to ancient times Nuwarakalaviya and Vanni Chiefs had used near autonomous power they inherited to grant *sittu* decisions, equivalent to judicial decisions. While it was illegal for a *Mohottāla* in Kanda Uda Rata to issue a *sittuwa*, *Mohottāla* in Nuwarakalaviya had no prohibition to do so (p. 230). So, it is conceivable that they had a larger role in how traditions and customs were managed in this nearly secluded region. Kapuruhami Madukanda Ratemahattayā too wrote that each Rata Sabhāwa operated with rules specific to its area or part of it, an indication of the level of independence, flexibility, and a certain degree of autonomy each Sabhāwa enjoyed. This was, among other things, due to an indirect result of the absence of a central document governing the institution. But both systems – the Kandyan and Nuwarakalaviya, functioned with comparable epistemological principles, the core of which was to maintain communal solidarity, social order, and upkeep of the traditions dear and essential to the people. In this series of necessities, women carried a heavy burden.

---

[27] Tillakaratne, *Daily Mirror*, Sri Lanka, February 15, 2017.

10. DEVELOPMENT MATTERS, FISCAL AND BENEFITS TO OFFICIALS

The Chiefs and *mulādenivaru* savored feudal and financial advantages they received from Rata Sabhāwa traditions. The King had no role or interest in these traditions, pecuniary or feudal. Therefore, Chiefs received no compensation from the King for this work. After the King was deposed, the colonial government too continued to follow suit and the repertoire of Rata Sabhāwa narrative did not get any space in the national arena. And according to Ievers (1899), the British did not consider feudatory services as "revenue" in their "sense of the word" (p. 112).

By 1833, however, the colonial administration began compensating the *Kōrāla*s, *Ratemahatvaru, Vanniyas* and *Dissavaru.* Salary of *Ratemahattayā* was £20 a year, and Nuwarawawe Mudiyanse *Maha Vanni Unnehe*'s salary was £45 a year (Ievers, p. 66). Ievers did not list salaries of other Chiefs or *mulādenivaru.* The government did not recognize the Rata Sabhāwa officials as worthy of including in their pay structure. But the Rata Sabhāwa tradition allowed pecuniary benefits upon such officials by its own age-old ways. A. O. Brodie (1894) noted that *Ratemahattayā*'s salary was set at £2 s10 a month. He also collected 5% of the division's revenue, a form of commission (pp. 136-161). Since Rata Sabhāwa was an unsanctioned scheme, this salary does not seem like associated with anything to do with it but meant for any other affairs related to the government. Included in the list announcing the names of Chiefs and officials also was the last *Dissava* of Nuwarakalaviya Talgahagoda Jayatilaka Rajakone Mudiyanse.[1] He lived in Kandy. But it is unlikely Talgahagoda was not compensated comparably since the British understood it was in government's best interest to keep the Chiefs happy whatever region they were in following the discontent that was pervasive amongst them during the short history of the government. As the British rule continued, the Governor seemed to have a practice until 1938 to elevate select senior *Ratemahatvaru* to *Dissava* titles.

DÁKUM, PENUM,* AND *KÁNDAWEEMA. To be seen, seeing, or the sight and the view, generalized as *Dákum, Penum* and *Kándaweema,* have a wide range of formulative and expressive connotations. They are also the principal modality of show of benevolence or malevolence, whether before the serenity of a religious icon, King in the Court, or a crude clay figure of a *yakka*/deity leaning against the trellis at a *yaktovil maduwa* in the village.[2] These customs usually brought a variety of presentations – floral, something of pecuniary value as small as a coin, even a whole village often or living objects. In the most mundane instances, in a traditional ritual hall, this practice evokes healing and peace of mind. In formal situations, it is the higher honor one can bestow upon another. The circumstances under which *Dákum, Penum* and *Kándaweema* occur in celestial or ethereal situations are diverse. Although

---

NOTES

[1] Name spelled as *Tallayakagodekarone Jayetilleke Rajegoen Mudiyanse* (Ievers, 1899, p 80).

[2] For an insightful discussion of glances, both malign or benevolent in rural Sri Lankan life, particularly village rituals, see David Scot, 1994, *Formations of Ritual: Colonial and Anthropological Discourses on the Sinhala Yaktovil.*

they mean the same in general, i.e., standing in front of a higher or powerful host –
the King, deity or a *yakka*, an exegesis of the context of the implied meanings points
to their well-defined and disparate purposes.

1. **Dákum** is the unsolicited and non-obligatory appearance before the King
(*dákeema*, to see) or Chief to offer courtesies and gifts. An example of this is the
ambassadors coming to see the King. They naturally bring presents of their choosing
– a sword, a colorful and unusual object not found in Sri Lanka, precious stones,
jewelry, animals, or anything that is known or potentially pleases the King. Invited
subjects too came to see the King on special occasions – New Year, wedding at the
palace.[3] They bring special gifts like a gemstone, if the visitor is a Chief – a pair of
tusks, a sword ornamented with carvings, and precious stones.

2. **Penum** is the annual appearance wherein subjects were obligated *to be seen*
(*Peneema*) by the King based on mandatory or obligatory *rājakāriya* duties under the
feudal or royal protocols. They bring tax money (*uliyam badu*) or crops from
gabadagam or nindagam. If the person is destitute, he may bring only a hand of
betel leaves.

3. **Kándaweema** (summons or subpoena to appear) was the other form of
appearance before the King. This signifies the requirement for certain people to
appear before the King or Chief by order or pursuant to any reason other than feudal
or royal obligations. It is a summons which the subject individual must abide by.
Examples are summons – *tudapath*, royal edicts to an offender to appear and answer
an accusation against him, or to be punished if convicted already. King's call to
members of royal household for various chores can also be a form of *kándaweema*.
In scenarios 1 & 2, if the person appearing before the King is unable to afford a gift,
he can bring a *bulathurulla*. I have not been able to find whether a person summoned
to answer a charge, or an informal accusation gives a gift or hand of betel leaves to
the summoning authority.

Chiefs also enjoyed monetary, or material receipts from their subjects and
tenants in the districts under the same custom called *dákum*. This is often done by
sending a *sittu*, or an object symbolizing an order to appear or a notice to abstain.
Often in Nuwarakalaviya, this is done with an object, a broom called *bol atta* – an
anabōla (Fig. 22). *Lékam miti* describing transactions of payments of taxes or other
tributes made by Chiefs in Nuwarakalaviya to the *Maha Aramudala* in Kandy, or
contributions they received from residents in the province as fines are hard to find.
I have not been able to find *lékam miti* for tributes the Nuwarakalaviya Chiefs made
to the *Dissava* representing the King. This makes it difficult to ascertain the extent
of this economy.

However, only a note about the receipts of *dákum* and *bulathurulu* received by
Dissava of Sabaragamuwa in early days of British occupation in Sri Lanka reveals a
snippet of the finances of a Chief. Towards the end of Kandyan kingdom, this
Dissava received 13392 Ridi as *dákum* and *bulathurulu* from the *mulādänivaru* in his
province. The receipts ranged from 1 Ridi from a *vidāne* for an axe to 500 Ridi from
a *Dissave Mohottāla* (a title like Walawwe Mohottala), fee he paid for his appointment

---

[3] Also called Panduru-mila or Gam-panduru.

to the title. Out of the total annual contributions the *Dissava* received, he credited 3643½ Ridi to the *maha aramudala*.[4]

A Chief paid the King direct and guaranteed revenue as *dákum* or *penum* for the honor of being the *Dissava* of Nuwarakalaviya province or if called to or when he came to see the King. As the *Dissava's* residence was in Kandy, he did not incur any housing expenses in Nuwarakalaviya.[5] Although the province extended half a country to the North to the edge of the purported boundary of the Kingdom, this *Dissava* only had to step out of the walawwa and walk up the street for an audience with the King! *Dissava* left Kandy only when State business required, which ostensibly was not much as the nether province of Nuwarakalaviya was only trekked through interminable sylvan country.[6] On other times, he rarely ventured out to the densely wooded province because the trip to Anuradhapura, largest city in the *Dissavani*, took at least a week back and forth. On rare occasions, when he went to Nuwarakalaviya, the expenses would have involved support for his entourage consisting of palanquin bearers, *tawalam* operators, scribes, cooks, and a host of attendants. *Dissava* would not compensate the attendants helping him in these trips directly as most of them occupied and lived off his *nindagam* and were required to perform services free of charge as mandated by *rājakāriya* obligations.

Due to diverse cultural and traditional reasons, the influence of a Chief based in Kandy upon a villager in Nuwarakalaviya was not as acute as that upon a villager in Kandy who was under some form of feudal obligations to the Chief. Kandyan villagers also had obligations like taxes and other dues under *rājakāriya* tradition to the *Maha Aramadula*, temples, and Chiefs in the area. These dues may consist of taxes (*uliam* and *marala*, etc.) and *dákum*.

Irrespective of the inherent power and benefits enjoyed being somewhat of independent rulers, the Chieftains in Nuwarakalaviya were occasionally tardy in paying the taxes to the royal treasury. Maha Vanniyā must have known that the King did not accept tardiness for an excuse to offer *dákum* or *penum*. But if confronted by the King, Chiefs offered excuses like drought, wild elephants – King's own property – causing crop destruction, and diseases to people impeding earning opportunities as reasons for delay and ask for his sympathy (*anukampāwa*). King was aware of the dreadful conditions in the region. He certainly considers granting his sympathies following such entreaties. In any case, the distance between Kandy and Nuwarakalaviya also made *dákum* to the King unenforceable.

But diplomatic protocols continued. So, paying *dákum* (*dákum mangalle* – gift ceremony) on special occasions when the Nuwarakalaviya Chiefs visited the Court continued but not to the same level as from a Chief in Kandyan highlands.[7] One may argue, as shown before, that these conditions influenced the low value of *dákum*

---

[4] Government Agent H. Wright qtd. in Ralph Pieris, 1956 p. 132.

[5] Ralph Pieris, 1956, p. 249.

[6] De Silva, R. K. and Buemer, W.G.M.,1988. *Illustrations and Views of Dutch Ceylon 1602 -1796*. p. 108.

[7] *Vannihuru* or *Vanniyars* offered *dákum* (*penum, penumkat*) to the Nuwarakalaviya Dissava (based in Kandy) when he came down to the province, but not to the *Maha Aramudala* (D'Oyly, 1929, 51). This could have been no more than a gesture plainly to show collegiality and common courtesy on behalf of Nuwarakalaviya people to the King's ambassador.

and *penum* offered by Maha Vanniyā to the King than Dissavaru in and around Kandy.

Furthermore, as stated earlier, mainly due to its isolation, the Nuwarakalaviya village enjoyed a high level of economic and political independence insulating it from the dues to royal establishment or participating in public work assignments under royal supervision like construction of the Kandy lake.[8] In the two provinces of Nuwarakalaviya and Tamankaduwa, however, majority of small villages were obfuscated in the jungle, and few knew whether they even existed or if they had any *rājakāriya* duties at all. On the other hand, even with their independent feudal authority, the Maha Vanniyā or other Chiefs in Nuwarakalaviya did not pay villagers for public work projects or not known to direct such work programs in their districts at all. Had there been any, it was only a handful of Chiefs in recent history. Ievers (1899) writes that the stone parapet wall around the Sri Maha Bodhi Tree was built by Maha Vanniyā (p. 50). But he fails to provide more information to verify it.

Nevertheless, citing *Sangharāja Sādhu C(h)āriya(wa)* (c late 18th century) Ven. Kotagama Wachissara (1961) says this wall was built in 18th century by Ilupangamuwe Terunnanse during the time of Valivita Saranankara Sangharaja (pp. 277, 426). Authorship of *Sangharāja Sādhu Cāriya(wa)* is credited to Ayittaliyadda Muhandiram Nilame of Kohonsiya Pattuwa in Matale.[9] In Lawrie (1896) we find that he was sent to Siam in 1750 AD by the Sangharaja with a deputation to bring *upasampada* (Buddhist higher ordination) for which he was given a *Sannas*a by the King Kirthi Sri Rajasinghe (1747-1782). Ayittaliyadda was the son of Owille Dissanayake Nilame and his grandson was the Ayittaliyadda, Nuwarakalaviya Dissava in 1834.[10]

It is possible, therefore, Maha Vanniyā who was related or acquainted with Owille family since decades earlier and with his close association with Anunāyake of Atamasthāna could have welcomed Ilupángamuwe Terunnanse to provide assistance for restoration projects of the Bodhi Tree complex. As a guest, Terunnanse obviously could not have undertaken such a massive project without the participation of influential devotees in the area who could provide the labor force for it. Vanniya too must have borne some cost of the project. Kotagama Wachissara

---

[8] About 2000 or 3000 men were in Kandy as of February 1812, brought down from Dissavanis to work on the dam of the lake (D'Oyly, 1917, p. 89). It is not known whether citizens of Nuwarakalaviya provided any labor for this project. A Tikiri Gammahe (smith) of Gannoruwa near Kandy said in 1819 that he was imprisoned after the King found his work on the dam was not satisfactory. Released after 18 days in prison, he escaped to Vanni (Lawrie, 1896, Vol. 1, p. 278). It is likely that Nuwarakalaviya did not have a labor pool earmarked for this project, thus there was no need for King's agents to look for absconders as evinced from Gammahe choosing Vanni a safe place to hide. Forest in Vanni areas was also the favored destination for other kind of escapees from the North. In 1803, Wany Wenjin, a Nalavar slave from Jaffna escaped from his master and joined Pandara Vanniya who waged war against the British in Mullativu (Wickramasinghe, Nira, 2020, p. 121.

[9] Gamlath, Sucharita & E.A. Wickramasinghe (1996). eds. *Ayittaliyadda Muhandiramge Sangharaja Sadhu Chariyawa*, Colombo: S. Godage Brothers.

[10] Lawrie, 1896, Vol. 1 p. 343.

(1961) says Ilupángamuwe Terunnanse was first a *ganinnase*,[11] and later received the full monkhood under the Sangharaja as his second disciple. He was one of three companions of the Sangharaja. It appears he was a well-travelled monk: He accompanied the Sangharaja once to Hath Kōrale when the latter went there for a sermon at Kanukatiyegedara (Kanugahagedara?) (p. 278). Ilupángamuwe was also familiar with building or restoring religious places. He visited and worked to help repair Tissawa Vihara (near Katupotha, 12 kilometers from Kanugahagedara, in Hath Korale) part of which was built by the Sangharaja. Ilupángamuwe came to Anuradhapura, with the urging of his teacher, and died while working on improvement to Atamasthāna, including the aforesaid wall (Wachissara, p. 426).

However, there is very little of any other major works known to have been completed by Maha Vanniyā and other Nuwarakalaviya Chiefs. Even if any major structure was built by a Chief but did not have it named after him, it could be that the structure had already been designated with someone else's name in the past before most *Vanniyas* established their roots in the dark period that came after Anuradhapura period. If they wanted to build such a structure, insufficiency of labor and other financial resources could also have prevented them from launching it.

Thus, Hurulu Wewa remained fallow, although Hurulle and Ulagalla families were said to be the main benefactors from it until the colonial government began to survey it in 1876. Nuwaraweva reservoir remained partially functional until the Colonial Engineers renovated it in 1887 to complement their agriculture development program. Yet, Chiefs obviously had their small irrigation tanks in excellent shape to support their own *nindagam* and fields. The surplus weir (*pitavāna*) of the small Morakewa tank by Anuradhapura -Trincomalee Road (A12) is built with square granite blocks, each with the size of a gunny bag of rice. They show a high degree of stone workmanship and engineering existed even in hard-to-reach areas in Nuwarakalaviya. Such stonework could not have materialized without the participation and support of the villagers. Morakewa is a typical rural tank and supplied water to the *nindagam* fields of the Hurulle of Morakewa family.

LACK OF INCOME FROM ROYAL VILLAGES IN NUWARAKALAVIYA. Ievers (1899) had heard of a *gabadagama* in Unduruwa, situated between Kalaweva and Kekirawa. He was also aware of a few *keth* (King's rice fields) located below the Minneriya Wewa in Tamankaduwa. As the story goes, this field ended up being bought by someone (p. 112). There is no other report of *nindagam* in Nuwarakalaviya owned by the *Dissava* sent from Kandy. The King even did not have a travelling palace, *gaman maligawa*, in this province. Therefore, it appears his 'pecuniary legacy' in the province is not substantial. When the *Dissava* visited Nuwarakalaviya, only way he could stay few days was as a guest of someone with similar rank like Maha Vanniyā or a Chief. For fear of threat to his reign, King kept a tight control as talons of a falcon over his Chiefs. With his strategy for moving *Dissavaru* between *Dissavani*s in short intervals for tactical reasons – the deep-seated suspicion of their

---

[11] Secularized 'monks' who are un-ordained and non-reclusive but attending all religious activities as an ordained member of the Sangha community. *Ganinnase* either lived in a temple or while living outside supported a wife and children, engaged in agricultural activities like any lay person. This practice ceased to exist sometime in the middle of 1900s.

potential for plots against him – any grant of villages located in this distant *Dissavani* as immovable property to them was also meaningless as the management of such villages obviously became extremely impractical due to *Dissava* not living in the province.

The sale of the *keth* stated above below the Minneriya tank makes me to ponder whether this was something like the game of Chinese Whisper where something uttered is whispered down the line (of people and decades) and comes out at the other end of it with an entirely different meaning. Someone could have coined a reference to royalty about an ordinary plot of land which gained its own meaning as time passed. But nothing similar has happened.

Not just the crops from *muttetugam* and royal villages, the Chiefs and the King profited regularly by selling areca-nut, cinnamon, and host of other kinds of spice to Maritime Provinces or traders in South India. Regardless of the paucity of diversity of commercial products, their control of acreage, including claim to sea-like reservoirs for irrigation, and independence placed the Nuwarakalaviya Chiefs at a considerable economic advantage in comparison to a Kandyan Chiefs. For example, Hurulle of Morakewa and Nikawewa of Ulagalla families owned fields under Hurulu Wewa which was in working order until 1803-4.[12] Nuwaraweva, the large reservoir in the area in the outskirts of the old city of Anuradhapura, and large tracks of fields under it were said to have been in the control by Nuwarawawe family[13] until the British took over the management as part of their comprehensive irrigation restoration and restructuring efforts.[14]

While Chiefs in Kandy were obligated to 'share' harvest with the King in the form of annual *dákum* and payments, no such mandate seemed to have played a role in any significant way on the harvest from fields under the tanks owned by Vanni Chiefs. For example, Vimalananda (1963) wrote that compared to 12000 ridi a Kandyan *Dissava* paid as annual *dákum* to the King, Maha Vanniyā paid only 1000 ridi (p. 318). Unlike in Kandy, geographical and health impediments (footpaths as roadways, medieval transport methods and diseases like malaria and yaws) played a gloomy role on marketing potential of the agricultural products of the Vanni Chiefs. Any shortfall from this disadvantage did not seem to impinge on their total gains as they continued to enjoy their own form of *dákum* and *penum* when they appointed *kāriyakarawannō* in their districts. Fines imposed under the robust Rata Sabhāwa tradition also remained a sure source of income to them.

His indifference to pecuniary matters notwithstanding, the King never bothered to supply labor for any infrastructure and religious or cultural enhancements in Nuwarakalaviya. One of the major construction projects of the last King was Kandy Lake. He built it by damming and inundating the large paddy field called Tingolle Kumbura. This project did not cost him much. Upon the King's

---

orders, thousands of villagers were brought by *Dissavaru* from their districts and fed the workers.

King left Kandy city boundary only if there was a threat to his security or to show his authority to regional overlords and the colonial rulers in Maritime Provinces. He only went to his palaces in Kundasale, Hanguranketa (Digligy Nuwara) or Nillambe near Galaha or to the west coast near Kalpitiya.[15] Historians believe the trip to the west coast was to show-off his authority over dominion loosely held by Dutch or the British. A *talpotha* written in 1753 reproduced in Lawrie (1898) records that a Kawrala twice accompanied the King to Kataragama by (p. 809).

Except for such trips, due to the interminable jungles with footpaths barely enough to walk single file and crossed open waters in rivers to reach the 'nether province' of Nuwarakalaviya, the King was less willing to waste resources to assert full authority over it. But in his mind, having a claim to this important and historic 'Country of Kings' was as better placed as having an actual and proactive controlling role on it.

ECONOMIC ACTIVITY AT KADAWAT (GRAVETS). While King of Kandy had his land pass points spread across the kingdom staffed by batteries of his agents as outlined earlier, Nuwarakalaviya had its own system of *kadawat*. Maha Vanniyā had four land pass points on the boundaries with Maritime Provinces. These were more than tolling stations. Closest land pass point to him was at Vilachchiya on the road to coast at Arippu, about 40 kilometers northwest from his home in Anuradhapura. Land pass points checked travel documents of people who pass through them in either direction and provided a modicum of security by acting as a gate or a 'fort' manned by a motley battery of guards and collected tax and other dues from individuals carrying commercial products through it. Maha Vanniyā also received gifts and presents at these *kadawat*.[16] Ievers (1899) doubted whether any revenue collected at *kadawat* in Nuwarakalaviya ever reached the King (p. 112)! Procedures and etiquette at the time of crossing these *kadawat* were described as oppressive which led the British to determine such stations as restrictions for trade. Finally, they abolished the posts on boundaries in 1816 showing their burgeoning reach to outer areas in the colony.

It is interesting to note that the British did not consider most feudatory services performed by villagers as an income for the Chiefs. British also did not have an idea about the wealth in Nuwarakalaviya villages. Also, as these villages were spread across the width of the province, communication between them must have been difficult and economic activity in any form must have been difficult to gauge. This was not helpful to get any measure of total output of the fields in the villages too.

ELEPHANTS AS INCOME. Although their control of the thinly populated stretches of the coastal belt was no more than few miles inland in some places, Dutch and Portuguese still demanded elephants and tusks be part of the annual *dākum*, dues

---

[15] As seen from two different names marked as *kadawat – Saut Pan* and *Saut Pannen –* in Knox's map of Ceylon a short distance inland from Kalpitiya but near each other makes one to think that one of them could have been under the control of the Kandy King, inland on the border of his domain (See page 37).

[16] Ievers, 1899, p. 113.

paid to them by *Vanniyas* in the region. These *Vanniyas* were often called *Kumara Vanniya*s, a hint to their secondary level of authority extending deep into the countryside beyond the border of the occupied littoral. These 'trade' transactions may have been one of the brands of diplomacy that existed then, or simply a form of ransom or coercion by the colonials who looked ways to pressure native Chiefs and King's authority along fringes of his Kingdom to gain economic advantage.

It is difficult to ascertain whether the King pressured *Vanniya*s to pay *dákum* with valuable property like elephants. On the other hand, according to what D'Oyly (1917) wrote, there was not much of a need for it. Wild elephants roamed in plenty on the outskirts of Kandy (p. 31). Chiefs conducted elephant drives as part of their duty and to appease the King. These drives were held regularly in the heart of Kandy. All four entry roads to Kandy fell through narrow mountain passes. As wild elephants wandered on to lower elevations of these passes that converged on the city, it was easy for King's *kuruwe* people to approach them with decoy elephants and nudge their wild cousins into the esplanade in front of the Pattirippuwa, the ornamental balcony with Octagon-shaped conical roof annexed to the Temple of Tooth Relic. It was the King's gladiatorial spectacle where one unwilling, scared, and confused participant was chased around in the arena - the historic esplanade in Kandy. The King watched this 'show' with his queens while citizens stood all around the esplanade providing reinforcement emulating a stockade. Once the bewildered legion of elephants got trapped in the esplanade, mahouts moved in with their tamed elephants. The skilled catchers (*panikkiyo*) sat on large wooden pillars mounted in the esplanade guided slipping nooses. They also leg-noosed elephants with ropes made of deerskin (*wara-manda*) by furtively sidling closer with the cover of guide-elephants. D'Oyly wrote in his diary on Oct. 23, 1810, that there were four wild and 38 tamed elephants tied to trees on the esplanade along the border of the Wewa which was nearing completion (1917, p. 31). It is not known that the King built a kraal on the esplanade in Kandy or its outskirts. D'Oyly (1835) labelled elephant roundups as public work projects (p. 199). There is no doubt the Chiefs who were not involved directly in these drives but living in the city too came down to assist in the operation. They had no choice but to participate to earn the King's good grace! But there was no compensation to them for this task.

Chiefs in Sabaragamuwa, Hath Kōrale, Uva, and all the way down to the Kelani River near Ruwanwella operated elephant kraals. In other areas too Chiefs must have captured elephants for *dákum*. A copper Sannasa executed in 1545 state Raja Vanniya [*sic*] presented 30 pairs of elephant tusks to a regional overload (a yuva raja?) named Tani Walla Bāhoo of Madampe. The overlord then bequeathed to *Vanniya* the western coastal belt between Kudiramalai and Paramakanda, the area between the present-day mid-point of Wilpattu National Park and Anamaduwa.[17] Dutch also demanded a considerable harvest of tusks and elephants from Raja Vanniya. But according to Thomas Nagel, though the annual tribute was 30 elephants, it appears in the books as never given.[18] Gifting elephant tusks annually to Portuguese, Dutch,

---

[17] Pridham (1849), p. 467.

[18] Lieutenant Thomas Nagel, 1948, Account of the Vanni 1793. *The Journal of the Ceylon Branch of the Royal Asiatic Society of Great Britain & Ireland*, Vol. 38, No. 106, pp. 69-74

or Sinhala Kings to ensure cordial relationship and ingratiate themselves with their favor was an economic and political advantage to the Chiefs.

Flat topography, thorny forest, and low population density in the interior still made elephant roundup in Nuwarakalaviya difficult. While crossing Nuwarakalaviya between Anuradhapura and Arippu, Knox (1681, 1995) encountered many herds of elephants, and he described the typical forest he passed through as "…bushes and thorns, and in others a great many. So that our shoulders and arms were all of a gore, being grievously torn and scratched [*sic*] (p. 165)." However, in comparison to Kandyan highlands, elephants roaming here did not have natural barriers like rivers, deep gorges, or tall mountains to impede their movement. But even with guide-elephants and hundreds of trackers and handlers, a herd of wild elephants still could disappear in minutes in the limitless bush in Nuwarakalaviya. Operating under these dreadful conditions, catching elephants in Nuwarakalaviya was not an easy undertaking.

Although, according to D'Oyly (1917), an instance of capturing elephants in Kala Wewa by Matale Dissava Ratwatte who also had relatives in the area in 1810 is known, history about elephant kraals in general within borders of Nuwarakalaviya operated by its Chiefs is largely silent (p. 38).[19] In Maritime Provinces (like the kraal at a place called Topoe near Negombo in 1801), herds being large, and wet country devoid of thorny bush allowing easy chase made operation relatively easy. Also, building a kraal and driving herds of elephant to it required hundreds of men and resources making it a costly operation to say the least. Cordiner (1807) wrote that in the in early 19th century, at the Kotawy kraal near Tangalle, 3000 men participated for two months to capture 42 elephants. Elephants dying during these roundups was common. In Kotawy kraal alone, at least half dozen elephants strangled to death while tethered to guide animals or trees (p. 237).

Therefore, there is no doubt that Nuwarakalaviya and Tamankaduwa Chiefs preferred to employ Afghani *panikkiyans*, who used different methods for this operation. They did not have the luxury of kraals. They used their hunter-gatherer-type knowledge to do the job instead. Topography in Nuwarakalaviya did not deter them operating with or without guide elephants. So, their modus operandi was not to build kraals, but for few to use startling archaic methods based with or without guide elephants to sneak or crawl into the fringe of a herd in a *patana*, a dried-out marsh or an irrigation tank, and leg-noose an unsuspecting animal. It was cheaper and did not involve a large workforce because a herd then was made of hundreds of elephants making *panikkiyo*'s task that much easier.

In the 1830s, because of their incessant role of interfering with the government's agriculture revival efforts, the elephants became a major problem for crop output. As seen from historical records, elephants in Northern Sri Lanka were as numerous as herds of cattle. Although the colonial administration did not have any role in the Rata Sabhāwa customs and share of its economy, the trying state of rice cultivation in these villages and the need for the resuscitation of the irrigation

---

[19] In 1960, as a 12-year-old, I participated in a kraal operation – not the elephant kind, but a buffalo – close to an abandoned tank called Vallemorana bordering the Mihintale hill. For details, see Lokubanda Tillakaratne, *Echoes of the Millstone* (2015), p. 122. Basics of both were the same.

infrastructure - irrigation tanks and canals – were both a political and economic concern for them.

As the administration scrambled for solutions within its budgetary limitations, in a quirky and sad way, elephants became a huge discovery as an impediment to the economic uplift of the country. They got a bad reputation as pests. But in being pests they also became revenue sources to some. For example, when an elephant was killed, as proof the tail was sent to Jaffna kachcheri, and the reward paid was 10s. Ievers (1899) noted that in 1846 alone, 40 tails were sent to Jaffna (p. 56). Hunting elephants as a sport was also allowed to British game hunters. During 1831-1847, 3561 elephants were killed in Mannar and North Central (Northern?) Province alone.[20] Ferguson, J (1893) reported that in the span of 30 years in the mid-19th century, Indic Courts imported 2100 elephants from Sri Lanka, 261 just in 1865 alone. In return, Sri Lanka imported 16500 horses (p. 91). During 1857-1862, 1600 elephants caught in kraals were exported to India from Northern province.[21] Haughty Indian princes used elephants to show their wealth and to support their war efforts. It is difficult to find evidence that the Maha Vanniyā was involved in either cutting tails of elephants or exporting live animals to India which had been happening during their tenures.

As they did with Dutch and Portuguese, it is possible that *Vannihuru* of Nuwarakalaviya have gleefully appeared before the King few times and presented elephants or tusks to ingratiate themselves with his favor. In those days, elephants were plentiful, and finding a couple of dead tuskers a year was not unusual. With thousands of elephants roaming in Nuwarakalaviya, villagers occasionally found dead elephants, including tuskers in jungles around their villages, as this writer once saw in his pre-teens. Because of their indifference to aesthetics or commercial value of tusks, and fear of stringent edicts of the King about everything elephants, the villagers did not want to attempt anything to do with it. Like the King, a Chief himself could be in the privileged position to receive gifts from the lower rung ranks in his chain of command in the province. It is not out of the realm of possibility to think of a *mulādäniya* in the village stepping up to take over the retrieval of the tusks from a dead elephant and taking them to the walawwa to appease the Chief. When such an opportunity presented, it was a more notable *däkum* or *penum* than taking a traditional *bulathurulla* to the King, or the Chief.[22]

---

[20] National Archives, AGA's diary of May 1847 qtd. in Leach, 1968, p. 34.

[21] Ferguson, A.M., 1868, p.4.

https://www.google.com/books/edition/The_Ceylon_Directory/ePEdchQYbl8C?hl=en&gbpv=1&bsq=elephants

[22] As a preteen, this writer once got an extraordinary real time opportunity to reconstruct how this could have happened in Kings' times. In 1956, I saw a bony tusker stuck in the mud under the frying sun in the tank bed of Siyambalawa, an *olagama* of Uttimaduwa, my mother's birth village in Ulagalla Korale, 20 kilometers east of Anuradhapura. Few days later, the animal gave up and died. The *gam mulādäniya*, already in the scene with a saw, soon cut off the tusks and hauled them away. He told everyone he was taking them to an important person in Anuradhapura. Villagers had no qualms about this because dealing with important people in the city was part of the headman's job. Few months later, his son started working in an administrative board created to oversea the preservation activities of the old and the adjoining new city! It is conceivable that with access to

The King's kinder attributes were rare. This too did not help the regularity of pecuniary emoluments coming into the *Maha Aramudala* from his Chiefs. Furthermore, King's history of charitable disposition on certain occasions, often borne out as a political stratagem to appease the Chiefs or just wanting to express benevolence to his subjects even with the loss of income to the *Maha Aramudala* was not good economics. Lawrie (1896) found that King Sri Wijaya Raja Singhe (1739-1747) appointed Ehelepola Mudiyannehe as Dissava of Nuwarakalaviya (told in a family *Sannasa* in 1745). Among the gifts and privileges granted to him on this occasion on a "Sri" Sannasa was the freedom from all *pali* (character assassinations; name callings), *marāla* (heriot – death duty), and *madi hungam* (tax on *tawalam* paid at *kadawat*) "for ever and ever" for him and his descendants (p. 201). The treasury must have lost considerable income from the decisions of the King.

Since the rank of villages in the Nuwarakalaviya was spread thin across a large area in the 19th century and well into the 20th century, no accurate information about their economic activity was available. This economy usually included harvest from the fields and chena cultivation and share of the fines from Rata Sabhāwa retained by the Chiefs and lesser officials. Paid employment was not a concept in the lives of villagers until the arrival of the Europeans. Since there was very little currency in circulation, either in the form of coin or paper, life was imbued in cultural norms that had other tenurial customs where employment was provided as a form of two-way service. For the trouble of providing service to someone, recipient of such service allowed the provider to work his land freely and keep a portion of the harvest (*anda-muttetu*) or fully (*ninda-muttettu*). Religious entities (with *viharagam* – villages belonging to temples), others titled and important, and the service providers jointly benefitted from such arrangements. *Rājakāriya* – service tenure – was based on this principle. Between equals, *attama* or *kayya* (community member participation in helping each other en masse in one member's field at a time) came close to this concept, although the practice was not a feudal requirement and something that cannot be forced upon someone. In this practice, someone worked for the other to offset equally what each other owed in service. Then, there was slavery. Those in vassalage worked for a master and got nothing in return except food and subpar lodging. Also, owners sold slaves as property, as loan payment, or as dowry to the children marrying away.

Dákum or *penum* were offers to the feudal lords or officials hoping in return to receive their good grace and advantages based on the visit. But fines exacted from convicted persons at the Sabhāwa proceedings obviously ought to have been termed as involuntary and payments that were mandated. With the King's crystallized disconnect with Nuwarakalaviya, it is unlikely if he knew of the nuances of extracting these fines by the Rata Sabhāwa. If he knew of it, then he accepted it as *Vanniya*'s prerogative during his regular administrative functions.

Besides enjoying the freedom to collect fines from those who were convicted in Rata Sabhāwa, the Chiefs set conditions and percentages on how to share them among themselves, *mulādānivaru/kāriyakarawannō* and villagers. Their subjects – the

---

dead tuskers made possible by their large numbers, a Chief centuries ago would have done the same.

villagers – assented to this practice with the long-ingrained belief that the Chiefs had the authority to determine such fees, and secondly, they also agreed that it was a fair compensation for them for the trouble of conducting a Sabhāwa session. Fines were levied and apportioned in the following manner:

(a) First 25% to the Maha Vanniyā, *Ratemahattayā*, or *Kōrāla*, whether he was in attendance or not. Vimalananda (1963) believed they regarded this money as an entitlement which came with their hereditary privileges (p.335).

(b) 25% to the *Mohottāla*.

(c) 25% to variga members and the *Vidāne Henayā*.

(d) 25% to the *Baddarāla, Lékama (Liyanarāla)* and *Undiyarāla*.[23]

As seen above, no share of the fine went to Maha Aramudala in the Kandyan times, or later, the treasury of the colonial government. Although not a legally sanctioned process in   their books, the colonial government did not object to the Rata Sabhāwa practice. As there was no law overseeing the collection of its fines, the whole process looked more like a quasi-tax collection matter, a tradition agreed upon by the communities, and an economy that remained localized.

Except for the traditional *dākum, Ratemahathvaru* paid to Maha Vanniyā *hungam (sungam) badu* or *suvandiram (huwandiram) badu*[24] or any fees for the Rata Sabhāwa fines they pocketed. These fines were in addition to the income they already enjoyed from several other sources e.g., the *nindagam* and *paraveni* lands – both *goda* (gardens) and *mada* (paddy fields & *wev-tavalu*), *walawwe kada, dākum* and *penum* presented on a *bulathurulla* also called *gam-panduru* or *panduru-mila*. It can, therefore, be assumed that upholding a robust Rata Sabhāwa tradition with or without the sanction of the King, or later the colonial administration, was a profitable economic notion for *Ratemahatvaru*.

While the Rata Sabhāwa continued in the 19th century, the colonial administration introduced a new edition of the *Gam Sabhāwa* with Ordinance 2 of 1835. The difference between this *Gam Sabhāwa* and Rata Sabhāwa was that the former was a system created with laws promulgated by an Act of the Governor. It had the blessings of the government and full weight of the English law. Its officials – magistrate and *Kōrāla* – were employees of the colonial government on a fixed salary which was set on the guidelines and control of the fiscal structure proposed by the Governor and approved by his supervisors who lived in British Metropolitan. This *Gam Sabhā* contrasted with the Rata Sabhā fiscal structure. Rata Sabhāwa was simply a device of feudal customs whereby the Chiefs and officials – the lords and law of the occasion – collected fines at the conclusion of proceedings. On the contrary, *Gam Sabhāwa* officials did not have the authority to pocket the fines. Any fine became the crown property the moment it was paid.

With no major economic advantages, but quite easily the potential to reach higher titles like *Kōrāla* or *Walawwe Mohottāla* opportunities, being part of the Rata Sabhāwa was an advantage and good investment its officials could look up to. A

---

[23] Hettiarachchi, D. E., ed. 1979b, p. 6; Kapuruhami, 1948 (42-68).

[24] Chiefs including Maha Vanniyā expected payments from villagers as a hereditary right. Such payments were also called *walawwe kada* or earnest money.

kāriyakarawannā is lower in rank than a *Kōrāla*. But a sitting *kāriyakarawannā*'s potential to become a *Kōrāla* was better than that of an ordinary villager who was not an 'official' in the system.

Therefore, being a *kāriyakarawannā* was also an excellent position to make inroads to new kinship spheres. Review of genealogical charts shows how this has become a reality in many instances. In the case of *Kōrāla*, some even have gone up the ladder to become a *Dissava*. Even without kinship opportunities, simply earning prestige in the community by gaining a new appellation as *Kōrāla* and higher visibility that came with it were valued cultural desiderata in Sri Lanka. Naturally, besides the financial gains, the descendants could not be happier and prouder of their ancestry when they have the luminous and showy insignia, and in later years, the grainy photos of the titular past of the family displayed in the corridors of the house.

Ratemahatvaru or *kāriyakarawannō* did not receive any funds from the King or the Colonial government to cover the expenses of convening and conducting a Rata Sabhāwa. But from Maha Vanniyā to *Vidāne Henayā* — their incentives were the economic gains and prestige that came with their involvement in this tradition.

But for the respondent who had to stand before them, and the *gamarāla* (Fig. 39) who had to take on much of the logistical support for the occasion, it was a different narrative in economic terms. Cost and logistical matters of construction of the *Maduwa* to hold the proceedings was the sole responsibility of the *gamarāla* and the respondent. Ratemahattayā did not reimburse expenses to the officials for holding the Sabhāwa. The villagers usually assisted in it with labor which the custom demanded as required being a community member. Responsibility for the *gamarāla* and accused continued even after the Sabhāwa proper. They prepared and set up the feast for all participants and spectators who came to witness the event.

Moreover, *gamarāla* did not get a share of the fines, nor could he ask the colonial government or the King in the past to give immunity from any mandatory work like *rājakāriya* not related to the village. Ideally, like other officials, *gamarāla* should have been included in the chain of economy of fines. Instead, the quirky feudal ways would prefer bundling mostly unreliable returns of the crops from the *gamwasama* in the fields as his reward for the expenses. He was obligated to do these duties in lieu of the non-monetary compensation that came with the *gamwasama* (usually the *vanat liyadi* in the field – the lots closest to the tank bund or at the farthest end of the field). Although he got the opportunity to carve out a largest plot in a community chena free of any community work obligations, he did not get a centimeter added to his chena lot for the responsibility of involvement in the Rata Sabhāwa affairs. His general restitution was being free of certain *rājakāriya*-type assignments others were subject, or other community work which *pangukārayō* in the village were subject. Obviously, the accused in Rata Sabhāwa was out of luck altogether as he did not have similar immunities. In a way, while the *gamarāla*'s burden was somewhat remedied as outlined above, the accused too can look for some hope. Officials might consider his expenses for the feast as an extra burden associated with the punishment and use it as a palliative factor warranting reduction of the time to be served or fine to be paid.

11. RATA SABHĀWA IN SESSION

*A*ny villager who has a grievance that requires resolution brings it to the attention of an official of the Rata Sabhāwa. This official can be the *Mohottāla, Gamarāla or Baddarāla.* If the latter two live in the same village, which is usually the case, the villager can first place his concern before them who will then take it to the attention of the *Mohottāla,* if not in the village, probably a walk to the next through few kilometers on multiple footpaths. If the villager is living in the same community as the *Ratemahattayā,* he can go directly to the walawwa.

In Kanda Uda Rata, where the equivalent of Rata Sabhāwa was *Gam Sabe,* if a villager believed that he did not get a fair hearing for the alleged injustice perpetrated on him, he could appeal to the *Dissava* and finally to the King. A villager in Nuwarakalaviya is hardly resolute enough to try this because of the considerable logistical inconveniences like travel, lodging and meeting the officialdom that takes over the process in Kandy. The ease and confidence of taking his concerns to the officials in the familiar setting of Rata Sabhāwa in his village or within a few villages away outweighed the arduous trip to Kandy and faced the uncertain and often scary response of the King.

If the King was in the palace, the villager could go in front of the gate and present wrongs done to him and other concerns by shouting out loud in that direction. Or he can sound the *Yukthiya Istakireeme Ghantāwa* (Bell of Justice) which was set up on a belltower in the *weli maluwa* (sand court) of the Natha Dewale compound across the street from the palace (Fig. 43).[1] When the King was away in the countryside on his occasional outings, a villager could walk up and genuflect before him and state any grievances.

As reported by Bertolacci (1817), a learned Buddhist monk in Kandy answering questions put to him by the Dutch Governor Falck on August 12, 1769 about Kandyan customs told that if a villager did not agree with a Chief's decision on a similar case, he may even go to the palace compound with his children. The villager prostrates in the direction of the King, gets up and strikes the children to make them cry. When the children begin to cry, the father shouts out his complaint to the King (p. 466). The appellant also could bring his case before the King through a third party, usually an official of the palace. Or he may also seek refuge in the Temple of the Tooth Relic or the treasury, *maha aramudda*la, both located in the palace complex, and makes the appeal to the King through the house staff. If the King agrees to hear or take any remedial action on the request, the appellant villager has to pay a fee to the King. Once, when the decision in a case favored the accused Chief named Attaragama Nilame, a family member of the plaintiff named Kande Appurāla – a violin player, climbed up a coconut tree on the sand court of

---

NOTES

[1] This bell had a dual purpose. Calling out devotees of the Natha Devale on the premises for service and draw attention to the King by ringing it and shouting at the palace for him to hear the purported travesty.

the Natha Dewale and cried out to the King for redress. After hearing this, the King ordered to re-examine the case, but no hearing seems to have taken place.[2] Knox (1681, 1995) in 17th century observed that the King was not always pleased with this gesture of his subjects, often sentencing them to be chained for years (p. 54)! In the case of Rata Sabhāwa, there is no record of a decided case remanded back to *mulādenivaru* for reconsideration.

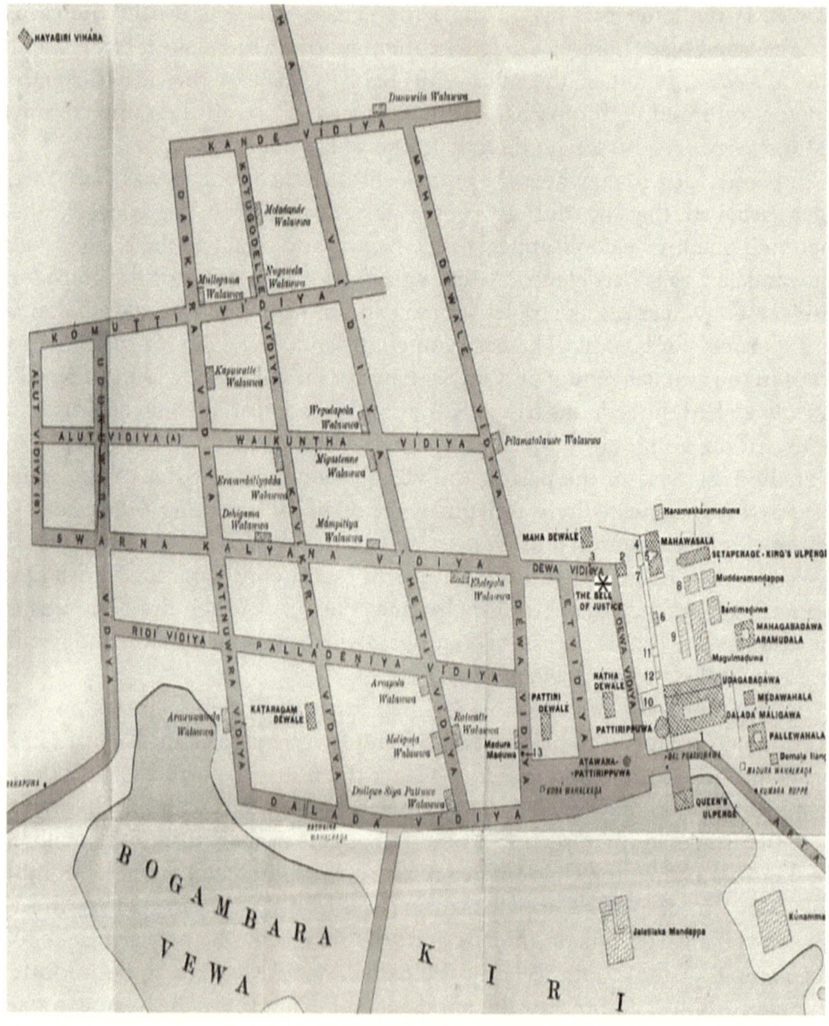

Fig. 43. Map of Kandy Town c 1815 (T.B. Keppetipola). Bell of Justice is at top corner of Natha Dewale square across from the *Maha Wāsala* (where Dewa Veediya turns to Swarna Kalyana Veediya, shown with an asterisk). Ceylon Survey Dept. 1918.

Except for sending a note to the Chief with a *dada mudippuwa*, it is not known whether a Variga Sabhāwa or Rata Sabhāwa held in a village kept records of the total proceedings or decisions in a *Lēkam miti*. After the case was decided upon, everyone understood that it is a matter that had been adjudicated to the satisfaction of all – a *res judicata*, and it may not be relitigated.

This principle is like other forms of *res judicata* existing in the village. A villager clearing a threshing-floor-sized area in the forest establishes his claim to multiple hectares of land around it to develop as a homestead or a chena. Everyone in the village – the court of public knowledge – understood the fellow villager's intent, regardless of whether others knew who he was or not. Everyone will honor the ownership claim of another villager who had cut a notch on a tree in the forest with an axe to mark it for timber.

A lower caste village must have permission from the Maha Vanniyā or *Ratemahattayā* to conduct a Sabhāwa. According to Hettiarachchi (1979, 2019) such Sabhāwa was *Navandannā Ayage Sabhāwa* (Session of the people of Navandanna caste). It was officiated by *Mulachariya, Muhandiram Naidé, Hangili Naidé, Badal Liyana Naidé and Undiya Naidé* (p. 40). A *Mohottāla* may participate in this Sabhāwa only if invited by the villagers or asked by the Chief. I have not been able to find if a Chief ever participated in a *Navandannā Ayage Sabhāwa*. Villages known as *Karae Poth dun gam* (villages declared as slave villages after receiving *Karae Poth* – deeds declaring a person as a slave) cannot convene a Rata Sabhāwa. Only if they are emancipated by receiving an *ittan karae* (deed of manumission), they may hold a Rata Sabhāwa like non-vassal people. As seen in coming pages, it is plausible that although slavery in Sri Lanka was outlawed in 1844, its residual customs in the context of Rata Sabhāwa could have continued in some form.

Kapuruhami Madukanda Ratemahattayā (1948) wrote that by 1910 only *Vidāne Henayā* continued with the Rata Sabhāwa functions while other *tovil kārayo* like *achariya, kadayā* (pingo carrier) and *berawa naidé* – providers of caste-based service tenures, had stopped participating as they had begun to think more and more outside the caste perimeter. Rata Sabhāwa had no way to enforce this (42-68). This *Ratemahattayā*'s writings illustrate the social shifts that had been gaining ground at that time, perhaps by collateral changes like minimized participation in *rājakāriya* custom occurring following a century of British colonial presence. Ryan (1953) points out that from the beginning of the 20th century, caste conventions and elements of feudal essence have begun to get weaker and fade away from the Sri Lankan life (p. 89). As Kapuruhami Ratemahattayā (1948) authored his thesis in the early 20th century, he bemoaned the possibility of Rata Sabhāwa losing its "luster and power" in the face of such changes (pp. 42-68).

COMMUNICATIONS. Villagers had to travel on roads to the village where a Rata Sabhāwa session was held or to meet a *mulādāniya*. They were narrow tracks that allowed a group to walk only in a single file. In pre-modern times, road infrastructure in Sri Lanka was abysmal. Even as late as the 1940s, Nuwarakalaviya villages connected to each other with footpaths, or at best a cart road cut through narrow clearings. M. U. A. Tennakoon wrote in the Forword on the beginning pages of this book (p. xii) that the travel time can be half a day or about 20 to 25 miles. The firsthand account of Marshall (1846) gives us an unobstructed picture of what these roads looked like in early decades of British occupation in Sri Lanka:

> The roads in the island and upper country were … chiefly narrow paths, by which men on foot might pass singly, climbing over the rocks, and penetrating through the thickets in the best way they could. Bullocks, the common beasts of burden, even with light load, were with great difficulty able to get over the precipitous parts of some of the passes. […] indeed, making roads was discouraged by (Kandyan) government. (p. 3)

The difficulty of transportation was embodied as a strategic design into the security structure by the King. It was a well-thought-out strategy to keep away domestic and foreign threats to the State. Knowing this tendency of the King, the Chiefs in Nuwarakalaviya, though they ought to have tried otherwise, followed his desire to the letter making travel between villages for Rata Sabhāwa functions difficult. It seems though, if the palanquin bearers could carry them anywhere on footpaths, the Chiefs would see them as highways!

Under these conditions, if a person wants to place a grievance in person before the Chief or a *mulādäniya* in the walawwa it is a long round trip. In an oral history video recording my father tells that in 1920s it took three days roundtrip of 25 kilometers on a bullock cart from Kahapathwilagama to Anuradhapura to participate in the brick-laying activities at the Ruwanweliseya, one of the largest stupas in the country. Albeit with this level of difficulty, if a villager chose to go to the walawwa to place a grievance, it was a testament to his sense of trust in the tradition and the strain of responsibility that bound the officials to discharge their duties reasonably and fairly. His own responsibility and role to safeguard the stability and honor of his family and the *Varige* stood to guide his decision to follow this difficult course.

Even if someone approached the walawwa with a request to hear an injustice, it was possible the Chief might not know of it right away as the *Walawwe Mohottāla* who assisted *Ratemahattayā* sorted out the preliminary formalities. After consulting the Chief, and when he gives approval, *Mohottāla* notifies the *mulādenivaru* in the village. *Walawwe Mohottāla* sends out a notice either verbally, possibly with an *ana bera* (messenger drums) or written on palm leaf *ola* to the *Mohottāla* of the *Varige* with instructions to convene the Rata Sabhāwa for a hearing. If the Chief wants to attend in person, *Walawwe Mohottāla* notifies that too.

Then the Rata Sabhāwa officials can coordinate the logistics of the Sabhāwa appropriate for a Chieftain's visit. The notice sent by the walawwa contains date and time of the hearing, place (village), names of the litigant and respondent, and whether the *Ratemahattayā* or Maha Vanniyā will participate. When a session to be attended by the Chief is thus proposed, Maha Vanniyā or the Chief sends encrypted messages using symbols or specially designed objects to warn of a fact or what to expect. To act, these encryptions must be decoded by the recipient. This symbol may be a chili fruit, or one or two knots made on a coir string or *kiri wel* (a creeper growing on the forest floor, used as a string to tie things or make baskets). A sealed message with a chili fruit denotes that the Chief is arriving immediately. One knot on the string denotes Chief will stay for one meal; two knots mean two meals with overnight stay.[3]

Upon receiving a complaint, the first act of the Maha Vanniyā, *Ratemahattayā* or *Mohottāla* was to impose a *tahanama* (proscription or ban) on the alleged miscreant. It is done by reading an invocation called *tahanam vākkiya* (banning incantation or sentence; pl. *tahanam vākki*) outlining the nature of the alleged impropriety, individuals who are subjected to such banning, specific and activities they are prohibited to participate. *Tahanam vākki* and other formulaic incantations that follow later in the proceedings framed the vignette that was the essence of the authority of the Rata Sabhāwa.

Kapuruhami Madukanda Ratemahattayā (1948) gave an example of a *tahanama*. It was a dispute between two people in the same village. This is not unusual. Both parties appearing before a *Gam Sabhāwa* or Rata Sabhāwa were usually known to each other. A man named Punchirāla accused a woman named Ranmenika from the same village as having involved in an immoral act. The *Ratemahattayā*, or the *Mohottāla* on his behalf, imposed the following proscription on Ranmenika (as translated from Sinhala):

> 1.   *"(Mr) Punchirāla of the village of .... has brought before us ostensibly incriminating and defaming information against* (Mrs) *Ranmenika of the same village as having participated in acts injurious to and incongruous of the honor and purity of the caste. Therefore, it is ordered hereby that Ranmenika and her blood relatives namely, ..., ..., and...... shall not participate in ilav mangul* (funereal or matrimonial celebrations) *and tovil* (service tenures under caste customs) *with anyone in this village or Varige. From this day forward, it is also prohibited for all persons to keep any company with the aforesaid Ranmenika and her blood relatives. Prohibited, if they are aware of the decree of the Great King of Sinhale, Great King of Colombo, Nuwarawawe Kumarasinghe Mudiyanse or the Dissa Mahatmaya who imposed such decree. Prohibited twice, thrice, prohibited, prohibited, and prohibited."*[4]

If Ranmenika's husband was separated and living away at the time of the alleged indiscretion, or he left the house immediately after, he would not be subjected to a *tahanama*. Family members of Ranmenika would also be subjected to the same *tahanama* as she is. On the other hand, if the *mulādäniya* or the Chief believed that there was no sufficient evidence to determine Ranmenika's guilt, or her accuser failed to submit exculpatory evidence, then the accusations were determined to be potentially frivolous, farcical, or unsubstantiated. He then turned

---

[3] Hettiarachchi, E.D., ed. 2019, p. 23.

[4] .... ගමේ රන් මැණිකාට ඒ ගමේ පුංචිරාල විසින් කුල දුස්සිය වචනයක් අඩ ගහා කියා තිබෙන නිසා රට සම්මුතියක් බැඳ සුද්දකර ගන්නාතුරු රන්මැණිකීටද ඒ ඇත්තීගේ ලේ නෑයෝ වන ......, ..., ටද ඉලවි මගුල් සහ තොවිල් තහනං. අද පටන් මේ ගමේ හෝ වරිගේ ඇත්තන් සමග කිසිකෙනෙක් සමාගම් පවත්වන්ට බැරි හැටියට තහනං. සිංහලේ මහ රජ්ජුරුවන්ගේ අණ දන්නවා නං තහනං. කොළඹ රජ්ජුරුවන්ගේ අණ දන්නවා නං තහනං. නුවරවැවේ කුමාරසිංහ මුදියන්සේගේ අණ දන්නවා නං තහනං.   මේ අනාඥාවදුන් දිසා මහත්මයාගේ අණ දන්නවා නං තහනං. දෙවෙනුවත්ව, තුන්වෙනුවත්ව තහනං - තහනං - තහනං. [*sic*], Kapuruhami, 1948, pp. 42-68.

back and placed a *tahanama* on Punchirāla as well. In that case the following was the proscription proclamation (as translated from Sinhala):

> 2. *"Moreover, Punchirāla has brought before us allegations incriminating Ranmenika as having participated in acts injurious to and incongruous of the honor and purity of the caste. Hence it is hereby ordered that until an examination done to ascertain veracity of the allegation, said Punchirāla too shall also have no ilav mangul* (funereal or matrimonial celebrations) *with anyone, and any tovil* (service tenures under caste customs) *from anyone who provides such tovil. From this day forward, it is also prohibited for any other person to continue any conventions with him."*[5]

After these preliminary steps completed, if the Chief determines that the alleged injustice is one that has merits and requires a hearing, he appoints a committee consisting of *Mohottāla, Baddarāla, Lékama, Undiyarāla* and advises them to proceed with a hearing. Naturally, *Mohottāla* summons the officials living closer to the accused's village to participate. He notifies the elders as well. An interesting side note to this is that no record exists of an instance where a woman was ever appointed as a judge or official in a Rata Sabhāwa or Variga Sabhāwa hearing.

Not all respondents who received the notice of the *mulādäniya* or *Ratemahattayā* to attend a Rata Sabhāwa session in the village or at the walawwa complied with it. If such an instance arose, *Ratemahattayā* gave an *anabōla* to the *mulādäniya* to be delivered to the respondent. In this case, it is an order asking to be present to respond to the allegations against him on the stipulated date and time. Modern equivalent of this procedure is a summon issued to someone by a court to appear. Anabōla, also called *Bōla-Atta*, is a bunch of *bōlpanā* twigs (*Blycosmis angustifolia*) tied together to be used primarily as a broom to sweep the threshing floor, *kamatha* (Fig. 22). When used as a symbol of authority, its bristles are covered with a piece of white linen. It was designed as a notice to all villagers and passersby. It is a proclamation or a notice of prohibition to stay away from certain activities about the location. An *anabōla* mounted upside down on the boundary between two plots of land or sections in a paddy field is a warning to all: stay away from the place until further notice! An *anabōla* standing in the middle of a receding tank is an order that no fishing is allowed. Removing this is a punishable breach under common customs, like withholding the share of his fish haul at the next permitted community fishing event in the tank.

Mohottāla hand-delivered the anabōla to the accused villager or left it standing by or propped up against his *idikadulla*, the gate of crossbars. Obviously, disregarding this order results in more punishments or increased fines from *Ratemahattayā*. Using French novelist Alexandre Dumas' analogy, a *mulādäniya* bringing an anabōla from *Ratemahattayā* is a "statue of law (of tradition), cold, deaf, and mute."

---

[5] තවද, පුංචිරාල විසින් රංමැණිකිට නොබිනා කුල දුස්සිය වචනයක් අඩගහ කියා තිබෙන නිසා රට සම්මුතියකින් ඒ ගැණ අහ විභාග කරණිතුරු, ඒ ඇත්තාටත් ඉලව් මඟුල් සහ තොවිල් තහනං. අද පටන් ඒ ඇත්තා සමග කිසිම කෙනෙක් සමාගම් පැවැත්වීම තහනං (Kapuruhami, 1948, pp. 42-68).

Gamarāla assisted by relatives of the respondent supervised the building of the temporary *pandalama* or the *Maduwa* to conduct the Sabhāwa. The village carpenter appointed it with chairs and benches. A pandal decorated with colorful bunting and artfully slivered coconut fronds, arched, and hung from the entryway, adding color and grandeur to the occasion. On the head table and on strategic spots on the floor were placed *punkalas* (pots filled with water) with bunches of inflorescences of a coconut flower arching down from their rims. This is a common feature at any ceremonial occasion. The exquisitely bedecked *pandalama* is now called *Sabhā Mandape* (Conference Chamber) (Fig. 1). Also placed in this chamber were brass pitchers of water (s. *sembuwa*) to freshen up, and spittoons (*padikkama*) and a kettle (*kendiya*, pl. *kendi*) with drinking water,[6] a short pedestal betel salver (*Ilatthattuwa*) for those who are seated on mats, and a tall pedestal salver (*seruwakkala)* for those distinguish guests who are seated on the chairs or the bed.

While Rata Sabhāwa's meeting place in Nuwarakalaviya was the *Maduwa* built in the front yard of the house of the respondent, in Kandy district, there are records that it was held in temple premises, e.g., Asgiriya Temple in Kandy stated earlier.[7] There is no record of using a temple premises to conduct a Rata Sabhāwa in Nuwarakalaviya or sacerdotal participation in it, perhaps for the reason that not all villages in the region had temples. Another reason is that unless it was a case involving a land dispute of the temple or someone shirking communal responsibilities like *rājakāriya* due for the benefit of the temple, the idea was not encouraged for its potential for disclosure of lascivious conduct of the litigants that may be the subject of the proceedings. Such a situation was obviously inappropriate and even sacrilegious to the sanctity of a sacred environment.

If the Sabhāwa were to conduct the session in the walawwa, it was usually held in the small courthouse in the same compound (Fig. 6) or courthouse in a specially designed room in a section of the walawwa.[8] An *ambalama* by the roadside (Fig. 44) or *bana maduwa* (sermon hall) of a village was also used to conduct Gam Sabhā sessions in Kandy region. But Nuwarakalaviya had neither. An *ambalama* was not needed usually in an area with lean travel volume between villages. Walking on trails in monotonous terrain of Nuwarakalaviya was not as strenuous as walking through the landscape of mountains, passes and streams in the Kandyan highlands. Therefore, the need of an *ambalama* to refuel a hard walk was felt less of a need in placid terrain in Nuwarakalaviya than on a laborious mountainous road. A *bana maduwa* was seasonal and a temporary structure, a rarity in Nuwarakalaviya because a village usually occupied by less than half dozen families could hardly support a

---

[6] "They never touch the lips to a drinking vessel always holding it a little above the upraised mouth and skillfully pouring," wrote Howland, W. W., 1877, in Caste as Affecting Christians in Ceylon, *The Missionary Herald,* Vol. 73. No. 8, pp. 233-237. Also see illustration in Robert Knox (1681, 1995) verso p. 87. However quaint and rudimentary this practice may have looked it is hard to discount the public health consciousness of villagers with unpretentious nuances like this in Sri Lanka in ancient times. An example already discussed in previous pages is the villagers collecting drinking water at a designated spot far away from public bathing ford in the tank.

[7] Goonesekere, 1958, p. 142; Lawrie,1896, Vol. I, p. 71.

[8] Karunaratne, M. W. E. *Historic Maduwanwela Walawwa...* Undated pamphlet; Tillakaratne, *Daily Mirror,* Sri Lanka, February. 15, 2017.

year-long temple or its *bana maduwa*. If the *Vanni Unnehe* or Maha Vanniyā were to participate, a passel of his attendants brought him to the village enthroned in a palanquin. He gets off the palanquin and walks grandiosely on linen sheets – *piyavili* – rolled out along his path. Often if there is not enough fabric to roll out as *piyavili*, the alternate option is to roll out reed mats. The Chief is decked out in his ineffable

Fig. 44. Yatiwawala Ambalama on Kandy-Kurunegala Road. See half walls-built with different heights to fit caste ranks. Photo: Chula Wanigasekara.

and finest regalia: pleated *tuppotti* wrapped around from his waist down, silk blouse with puffed-up shoulders and gold embroidery in trefoil-like designs, sword or dagger wedged on the waist belt, royal insignia – the cane arched on top with a silver-headed snake, *naga pirambuwa*, gold necklace, *peras mudda* (signet ring), *atamulu toppiya* or *hataramulu toppiya* (eight-cornered or four-cornered puffed beret (*toppihaluwa* in Nuwarakalaviya), generally made of green velvet or tweed fabric as the case may be based on the rank of the Chief who is bedecked in it. He walks barefoot. Attendants carry Chief's *bulath kadaya* (betel box). To illuminate the exquisite style of this box, it is fitting to see how a colonial writer saw one carried by a Muhandiram, a Chieftain of similar rank in Maritime Provinces. Robert Percival (1803) wrote this box as "made very handsome as if to denote the quality of the owner: they are usually of ivory, tortoise-shell silver, or calamander (ebony) inlaid [*sic*]."[9] It is no wonder, thus, a sight like this was a remarkable treat for the villagers.

If *Vanni Unnehe* came for a night hearing, his aides brought *pandam* and *vilakku* (torches). Mohottāla of the village or the *Varige*, other Rata Sabhāwa officials and villagers walked to the Kada-Ima (boundary of the village) and received *Vanni Unnehe* by offering hands of betel leaves and *watura sangraha* (offering water to drink). After concluding the reception formalities, villagers conducted him in procession to the Sabhā Mandape.[10]

---

[9] Robert Percival, 1803, p. 239.

[10] Not only when a *Radalakam Peruwa* (Chiefs' Guild) comes to the village, but when a group of guests from a neighboring village came to participate in an important event or brought a *pujāwa* (votive offering) to the annual religious sermon (*bana pinkama*), elders walked up to the village boundary to receive them (Tillakaratne, 2015, p. 187).

The Chief walks in this procession escorted by whip-crackers, drummers, dancers, and horn-blowers, all playing their own opus. The earnest crowd was made up of the villagers, *Vanni Pathirannehes* – *andoru karayo* (palanquin bearers or *uliyamkarayo*, *villidurai* (valliduri) who brought the umbrella (*sesatha*), and *pawan atu* by *vadana atu daranno* (holders of ceremonial talipot umbrellas). The servants and aides of Maha Vanniyā – standard bearers (*kodi daranno*), bearers of heraldic insignia (*muravuda daranno*), and food servers (*may wadanno*) also came. The retinue of the Chief got appropriate accommodation and conveniences. A *diyage* (shower stall) and a latrine, probably a pit with a lid to sit, were set up close by. Water for these visitors was brought from the tank and warmed up on a kitchen fireplace built closer to the *Maduwa*. *Vanni Unnehe* gives his *atamulu toppiya*, cane and *bulath kadaya* to his attendants who place them on the *perāsane* (short side-table). These items are symbols of the Chief's title and authority. In 18th or early 19th century, an unknown author wrote the following praise poem describing the March of the Dissava of Hatara Kōrale:

කොඩියකුත් රතු බැඳපු සවරන් සදන යුදයට පෙරමු ෙණ්
කොතවියත් සහ පච්චලංෙස් දවුන්ෙඩකුත්   සමගි ෙණ්
කොඩියකුත් තව පිහිටි ඉර හඳ මාන පස මේ   සමගි ෙණ්
මෙම සිරිත් ඇති සතර කෝරෙල දිසාෙවෝ යති පෙරමු ෙණ්
(මහ ලේකම් මිටිය)

"(Escorted by attendants), the *Dissava* of Four Korales, who as the established custom bears the five marks of honor, viz., the flag with figures of sun and moon, *pachcha lansa*, *davunde* (*davula* – drum), *kotaviya* (a spear with a pointed head on a wood shaft), and red flags (with *savarin* – strips of clothes attached to the four-corners of the flag) goes in front to the ever victorious war" (*Maha Lekam Mitiya*).[11]

In the event of Maha Vanniyā or Ratemahattayā is not coming, Mohottāla, now the presiding officer, places his cane and the *Mohotti bámma* on the side table as a display of his authority. He then freshens up with water offered in a brass or copper pot (*sembuwa*). It was covered with a piece of white linen. Afterwards, he settles in his chair covered with three layers of white linen. Villagers offer him hands of betel leaves with small amounts of money as much as they can afford. This was called *radala dekma* (Presentation to the Chiefs). Sometimes, *Ratemahattayā* makes a cameo appearance without any active participation but just to observe.

SEATING. A graphical representation of the seating plan in a Rata Sabhāwa meeting hall is shown in Fig. 45. This plan followed community seating traditions extant at the time. It ensured adherence to hierarchical protocols in line with the title or the caste of those who were present at the seating location. Architecture of some ambalam shows how physical space was designed to achieve this social norm even in remotest areas and simplest forms of seating. For instance, the design of

---

[11] *Maha Lékam Mitiya* n.d. Quoted in Bell, 1904, pp. 126.

the Yatiwawala ambalama on Kandy-Kurunegala Road near Katugastota (Fig. 44) conforms to four levels of rank or caste representation. Its roof rests on four columns. The 3-meter-long half-walls between the columns serve as benches. The atypical nature of these walls is that they are of four different heights, the tallest being about a meter high which was intended to be used by travelers of higher caste or holders of higher titles. The shortest wall called *kairuwa* was where the travelers of lowest caste sat. Mostly all had a fair inkling of his or her place in the caste or titular hierarchy. They knew the wall-bench appropriate to sit or at least to keep the right social distance (in seating).[12] The four levels of seating do not mean only four castes could sit here or was the number of castes existed at the time. In the heyday of caste traditions, there were over three dozen castes in Sri Lanka. But the symbolism displayed by the disparity of wall height is clear. In the past, in many homes without furniture, a half-wall was built either at the corner of the verandah or running around it for seating purposes as well.[13] In villages where an *ambalama* was not available, a *pila* in the house, a part of the floor raised along the wall intended to be a bench extending out towards the front yard mimicked the *ambalama*-style seating practice. According to D'Oyly (1835), When a parley or a hearing was taking place in *Maha Naduwa* (Great Court or *Mangul Maduwa)* in Kandy, Judges – the Chiefs – sat from right to left in order of rank and seniority (p. 223). When the King was present at a hearing, this place became the *Wāhal Habe*. If the case was not in the *Mangul Maduwa* (Hall of Celebrations or Audience) but in the palace, King usually sat in a room and watched through the window as his Chiefs conducted the proceedings in an adjoining hallway or a reception area.

At the Rata Sabhāwa in Nuwarakalaviya, it appears the number of mats spread one over the other, or sheets of white linen spread out in the same manner on the seating surface – chair, bed, a short wall, is harmonious to Yatiwawala *ambalama*. Multiple layers of sheets or mats laid out for seating signified correspondingly a higher rank.[14] Not all homes in the village had chairs, so it was not unusual to use wooden bed at the head of the *Maduwa* for the Chief to sit. On this bed were rolled out two reed mats – one over the other – and a white linen over them.

Customs like these have a universal presence as historians have found. For example, seating of Kings and other hierarchical persons in pre-Colombian South and Central America followed the same practice. In Quiché society of Maya

---

[12] Two hundred years ago, Yatiwawala village seems to have been a popular rest spot for travelers to Kandy from Hath Kōrale, i.e., Northwestern Province. D'Oyly has multiple entries in his diary about his spies stopping at the Yatiwawala temple close to this *ambalama* to spend the night for few hours before starting next morning the last leg of the trip. With letters and gifts to or from D'Oyly in their possession, for safety reasons, native spies preferred to rest in secure places. Since a temple usually has a *bana ge* (preaching hall) usually open round the clock, and if *ambalama* ran out of space, travelers could go to the temple to rest.

[13] Gnanaharsha Beligatamulla et al., A Critical Reading of Seating in Non-Secular Buddhist Contexts in Colonial Sri Lanka. *Making Built Environments Responsive.* ed. Rajapaksha, Upendra, 2015, pp. 491–505.

[14] Once in the early decades of 19th century Coomaraswamy Mudliyar came to a wedding in Colombo in full panoply of livery "conducted under canopy and over white cloth spread over on the ground." He then sat on the place of honor - two carpets decked with spotless white linen (Vithilingam 1971, p. 45-46 qtd. in Jayawardena, 2003, p. 211).

civilization, King sat on woven mats as his throne and advised his people. "The mat not only symbolized the ruler, but the power of his people. Its interlaced reeds represented the unity inseparably linked within a community with a common

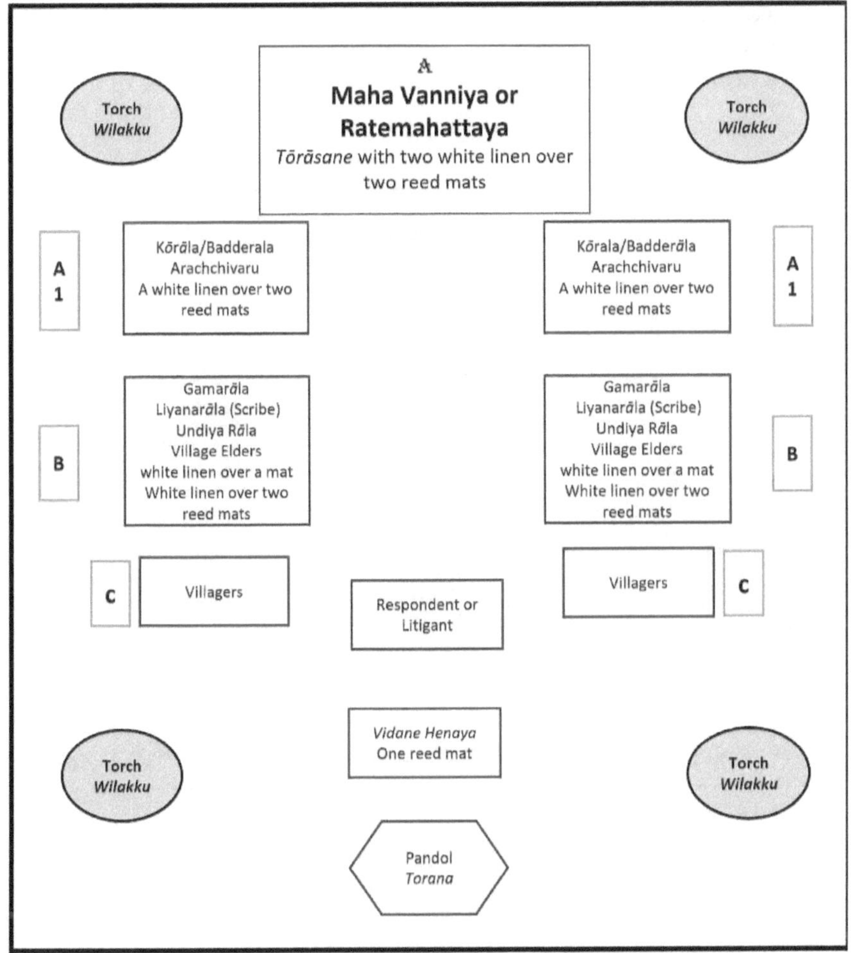

Fig. 45. Schematic Representation of a Rata Sabhawa Seating Plan. After Kapuruhami, 1948. Sketch by Niranjala Tillakaratne.

purpose." Correspondingly, in villages too, the community leader sat on the mat during a parley. Therefore, the mat was called "Counsel Mat"[15] and the King or the community leader of the village was known as "He of the Mat."[16] Knox (1681, 1995)) wrote that in ancient Sri Lanka, there was a direct association of power with the style of the seating (p. 86). As late as mid-17th century, only the King could sit

---

[15] Christenson, Allen J. 2003. *Popol Vu: The Sacred Book of the Maya.* p. 64.
[16] Christenson, Allen J. 2003. p. 231 n612.

on a stool with a back.[17] He sat cross-legged on the seat. During those times, even if she is the wife, no woman was allowed to sit on a stool before a man.

A sketch by Lieut. Col. William Willerson (1815) shows D'Oyly seated in conference with three Kandyan Chiefs – Ehelepola, Molligoda and Kapuwatte – on chairs covered with ruffled and loosely arranged plain sheets of fabric indicating they probably could have been white, the custom of the day (Fig. 46). Nowadays, in a laity's home, monks always sit on chairs covered with a layer of clean white linen.

Fig. 46. Kandyan Chiefs in Conference with John D'Oyly seated on chairs (1815) covered with linen. Reproduced from a Sketch by Lieut. Col. William Willerman, ADC to Governor Robert Brownrigg. Courtesy National Archives. Dotted lines and the italicized text above and under them by Niranjala Tillakaratne.

In an honored occasion, a white sheet of linen was also hung covering the ceiling as an awning. Saddhatissa Upasakatena reminds us that in such an instance, no decorative items like certain flowers, leaves, twigs, or other objects and *malolombu* (leis) were hung from the ceiling canopy as done for *Maduwa* constructed for religious sermons or ritualistic events. Rata Sabhāwa functions were cultural

---

[17] Knox, 1681, 1995, p 86.

events, and plain white awning covering the ceiling of the *Maduwa* shows the absence of ritualistic or religious undertones in it.[18]

To minimize interruption to agricultural and other day-time chores of villagers a Rata Sabhāwa was rarely postponed for another day. It usually commenced in the evening and ran deep into the night. This helped to reduce the cost burden and inconvenience experienced by those who hosted the event and those who participated as interested parties or spectators.

COURT IS SEATED. Now the Sabhāwa is ready to begin its proceedings. A villager toiling on a field a few hours ago is now a judge, seated solemnly and purposefully with his fellow judges in the *Maduwa* but with a magisterial aura to deliver rule of law. After the din around the *Maduwa* subsided, this villager, the *mulādāniya* – usually the *Mohottāla* – gets up and calls the court to order. His speech is authoritative and carries a grave tone. He recognizes the graceful presence of *Ratemahattayā* or Maha Vanniyā by extending utmost respect and felicitations. Thereafter he announces the reason for gathering and addresses the audience with a stately mien. He reminds the gathering that henceforth this Sabhāwa shall be called *Sabhā Ranjané*, a distinguished assembly. According to Kapuruhami (1948), the introductory proclamation to announce their authority to hold proceedings to follow immediately goes like this:

> "*We are assembled here today to conduct this* Sabhā Ranjané *in the presence of infinitely powerful hatara waram deyyo (*four supreme deities*) who govern and protect this cherished bhumi* (earth), *portentous deities who preside over all four cardinal directions, and the boundaries of this village. These mightiest and eminently judicious deities and any other lesser deities will bear witness to our efforts that we will recognize and hear the grievances to be placed before us for examination, true to the customs and facts made available to us. After such an examination, we will submit our decision to the said assembly of deities. We will also submit our just decision to the King's Council*" (42-68)

In this invocation, even if it implies the submission of the decision to "King's Council," there is no record that the King of Kandy or an European King had any purview or oversight or interest on Rata Sabhāwa of Nuwarakalaviya. On the other hand, it is doubtful Rata Sabhā decisions were in fact shared with the King because these Sabhā functioned traditionally under the authority of Maha Vanniyā. King's only interest in Nuwarakalaviya was the insignificant income he received as *dákum*, receipts from *kadawat*, and its geographic attributes as an effective buffer against other powers – domestic or external. Granted, "*Submit our present decision to King's Council*" in the opening pronouncement may be a metaphoric expression modelled in line with the "Fount of Justice" principle of a monarch, in this case Maha Vanniyā and his deputy Chiefs, who impose their supremacy and authority over the Sabhāwa traditions. As shown in previous pages, lauding the colonial power in equal terms with Sri Lanka's former Kings[19] had already started after the fall of

---

[18] In ritual houses, temporary or permanent, red, or blue is the usual color of the bunting and screen used to decorate the walls and stands.

[19] Sivasundaram, 2013, p. 6.

Kandy. But colonial rulers had no role in either formulating laws or appointing officials to Rata Sabhāwa as their customs were only originated and inherited with time-tested consent and practice by the community.

The *Mohottāla* next outlines the rules and procedures of the session to the participants. He is authoritative, lucid, eloquent and warns of the consequences of making perjurious statements. He reminds about decorum within and out in the immediate vicinity of the *Sabhā Ranjané.* The modalities include no one can exit or enter the court room without permission while the session is in progress. Anyone who does not heed to these provisions is subjected to fine or other penalties.

There is no custom to take an oath to promise and affirm what would be said at the hearing inside the meeting hall is nothing but the truth. But an oath contextualized after cultural norms could be administered only if there was a specific need, or respondent or plaintiff offered to resolve the issue under review 'out of court' by submitting to a voluntary oath. When parties agree to this method of resolution, prior to appearing before the Sabhāwa they go with a *mulādāniya* to a temple, *dēvāle* (house of a deity), or a Bodhi Tree, and take an oath. This oath can range from simply making a declaration before the deity or subjecting to physical pain like dipping the hand into a pot of hot oil or picking up a coin from the bag where a snake is confined. This then is a substitute for oral evidence.[20]

Dipping hand into hot oil was obviously so horrific, it was called 'trial by ordeal.' This was in practice until the late 19th century. J.P. Lewis (1895) writes that a man accused of stealing a gun near Vavuniya dipped his hand in hot oil at the suggestion of his mother, got badly burned and had to go to hospital (pp. 176-185)!

D'Oyly (1929) found in Kandyan highlands witnesses taking verbal oath after giving evidence at a hearing. The oath was given at a temple or *dēvāle* after the court was closed for the day. Witness was taken there by *Liyana Arachi* or *Peon Arachi* and *Hirage Kankanama.* Standing in front of the image of deity, the witness raises his hand declares: *"It is true that I did give evidence before the Court,"* instead of averring *"I declare that what I have stated in evidence before the Court is true* [*sic*]." He also evokes that if what he says were false, his raised hand ought to be crippled (p. 79).

The method of giving evidence in Rata Sabhāwa was *viva voce.* Writing word to word of the progression of the proceeding was not a legal or traditional requirement 200 years ago in Sri Lanka. There was no fast-writing method in rural Sri Lanka to keep up with a continuing flow of oral proceedings at a Sabhāwa.[21] It was a challenging task as well, given the outdated writing technology available in Kandyan times. Shorthand (stenography) too was not a scribing method widely available in the early 19th century. A written record, usually on strips of palm leaf, is needed only to provide proof of ownership, transfer or grant of property or titles. Understandably, writing on palm leaf strips is still a form of slow-paced engraving. Scarcity of paraphernalia needed, and time consumed in producing multiple strips

---

[20] See Ievers, 1899, p. 108; Vimalananda, 1963, p. 319, and Hettiarachchi, D. E., ed. 2019, p. 42 for types of oath practiced in Nuwarakalaviya and Kandyan highlands.
[21] Other writing surfaces in villages in earlier days were a smooth layer of sand, slate tablets framed with wood strips, bark of a tree or its trunk after the bark peeled off, or face of a flat rock.

of them were hardly an inviting process. Instead, the impediments that kept the proceedings of a Sabhā session in written form were mollified with building a lasting community memory. Over time, the essence of the event became permanent 'record' we now call 'oral history.'

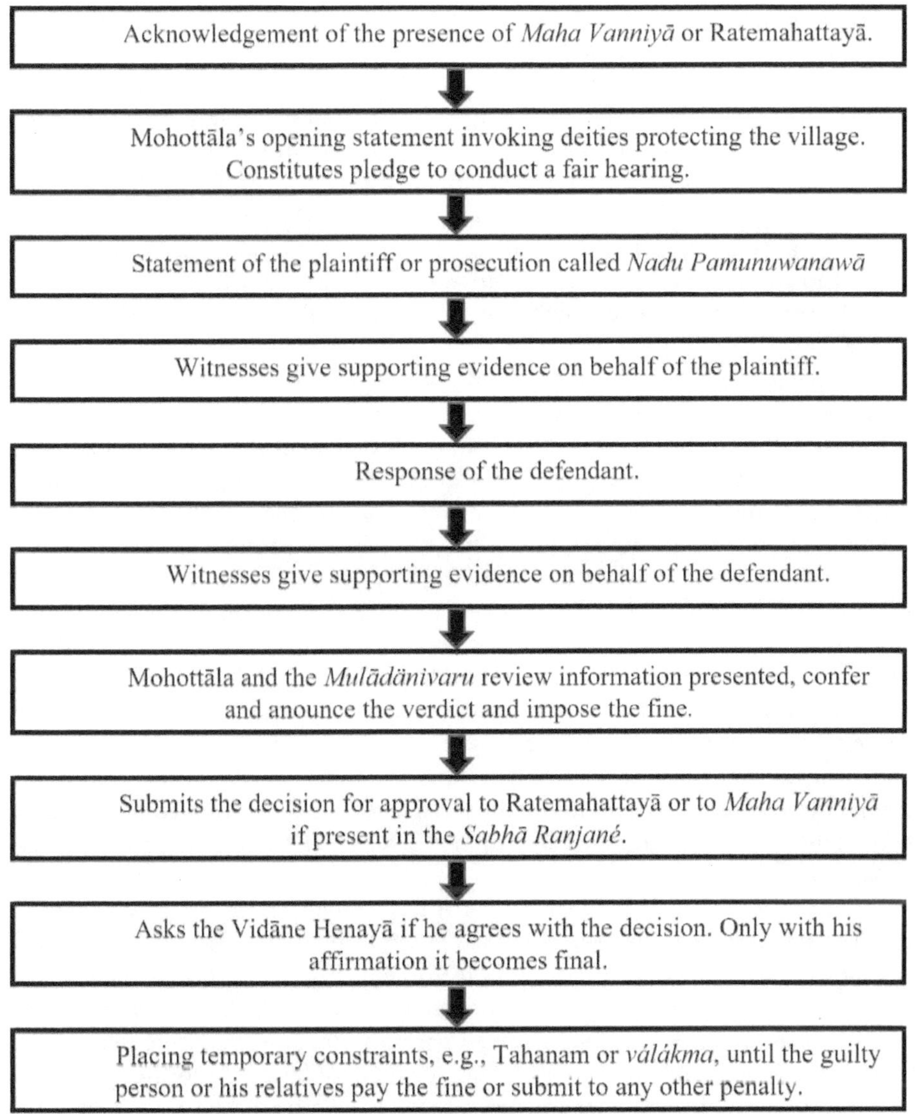

Fig. 47. Rata Sabhāwa Hearing Sequence. Sketch Niranjala Tillakaratne

Hearing starts when the Chair asks the litigant to step forward and present his or her grievances (Fig.47). The litigant standing in the middle of the Maduwa with both hands wrapped around the chest, acknowledges all dignitaries from Chair down to the last of the *mulādāni kattale* (Officials' Guild). He then begins to narrate his case. This is called *Nadu Pamunuwanawā* (presenting the case). Once they got the opportunity to talk, the litigants or respondents or witnesses continued to pour out their rigmarole and discursive accounts without a plan or following any semblance of logic. This is unavoidable given the lack of advanced knowledge on the practice of jurisprudence methods, both on the part of the *mulādānivaru* and participants of the Sabhāwa. Often witnesses who are shy or modest or have stage fear would talk quietly. Naturally, the officials then ask them to raise their voice. If the subject of discussion is a tabooed activity with immoral undertones, the witness might be less likely to narrate the story loud enough for all to hear. But Rata Sabhāwa, functioning on its own terms, rudimentarily but independently, strived to the best of its ability to prod out information from witnesses to resolve conflicting situations arising between any number of individuals in a community. Therefore, conventional jurisprudence was a relative concept for the villagers. Trust in the *mulādānivaru* was the essence of the 'law' that guided the villagers to this form of justice.

While *Mohottāla* is conducting the proceedings as the convener, *Vanni Unnehe* or *Ratemahattayā* might also come to participate or observe. The Chief takes his seat of honor. He sometimes injects a question or a comment.[22] After litigant submits his case, officials have the chance to ask questions. This happens in a hierarchical order. There may be a secondary line of questioning, but it does not amount to anything more than an attempt to clarify issues already presented. There were no lawyers, and it is doubtful whether there was any form of cross-examination since the rule of evidence as we know now was a concept unknown in Kandyan times. The Chiefs or *mulādānivaru* had no legal training whatsoever. Lawyering had not become a profession in Sri Lanka until mid-19th century.[23] The 'laws' (traditions and customs) that worked for villagers for centuries perforce made the need for lawyers an irrelevant matter. Rata Sabhāwa existed as an essential rural institution, and villagers were quite adept at functioning within its traditional framework, the primer they depended upon without the assistance of experts. Guided by unwritten codes and traditions, *mulādānivaru* examined issues that came before them as best as they could.

While the hearing is in progress, the officials often confer with each other. To do this, they may even step outside the *Sabhā Ranjané*. If necessary, they also ask questions from someone appearing before them. From the tone or line of the questioning one could get the impression that even before the hearing commenced, officials were imbued with preconceived partisan opinions about the issue under review. Shreds of similar conduct are still seen in legal traditions today.

By about midnight, Sabhāwa takes a break for dinner. When reassembles, the officials will continue to listen to the accounts of all interested parties. At the end of all oral and material submissions, *Mohottāla* and other officials will begin

---

[22] Hettiarachchi, D.E, ed. 2019, p. 41.

[23] Colombo Law College started only in 1874. Until then, the well-to-do families sent their children to Britain to train as lawyers. By 1890s there were 400 practicing lawyers in Sri Lanka (John Ferguson, 1893, p. 33).

deliberations. They will look at all mitigating and exculpating facts, and other pertinent information before agreeing on the judgement. Sometimes, efforts by the respondent to contrite for the infraction can also be accepted for consideration. His ignorance of the severity and nature of the breach, and inability to pay due to poverty are common reasons presented for consideration. Relatives of the respondent can now submit facts bearing on extenuating circumstances. The Chief or the Rata Sabhāwa officials can consider these to amend or commute the fine. If Maha Vanniyā or *Ratemahattayā* is in the session chamber, he will accept the decision of the *mulādānivaru*. The Chief has power to modify the sentence with or without an appeal from the guilty individuals. If he is not in attendance, the decision will be written on a *Sittu* and sent to the walawwa. There is no record in folklore that after this phase onward, a Rata Sabhāwa decision was relitigated.

In 1973, A. P. A. Gunasekara, during his conversation with the old man described earlier found that on some occasions a person convicted by a Variga Sabhāwa could submit an appeal to *mulādänivaru* through *henayā* who is sitting in the *Maduwa* in his official capacity. He may ask the *mulādenivaru* for a review and reduce the fine. For that to happen, *henayā* could make a verbal request to the *mulādänivaru* or the Chief sitting before him with the following address (tr.):

> "*I am the one who washed your dirty clothes. For all this time, I am also the one who washed dirty clothes of this convicted* etta *(person of higher caste).   I provided laundered linen for your* ilav *(funeral). I provided laundered linen for your* mangul *(celebrations). I covered the ceilings of this Maduwa with laundered linen. I laid out white linen for you to walk here. For all this time, I provided to this* etta, *now the respondent, all those services as well. In the future too, I will be the one who will perform all the said tasks. I believe the fine of 25 ridi you imposed is too burdensome to this* etta. *Therefore, I implore you with utmost respect and in earnest to be compassionate and endow him with relief after accepting a* bulath nambuwa *(hand of betel leaves) or a* bat nambuwa *(feast)*!" (p. 140)

Although the officials strive to be not prejudicial or unfair, a convicted person may still not accept their decision. With fairness and neighborliness in mind, the council may then make conciliatory efforts to resolve the differences. If the refusal to oblige with Sabhā decision continues, the officials will not budge. If appealed, the process may accommodate more witnesses who can submit exculpatory evidence.

Naturally, the Chief will then commute the sentence to be less severe. Injection of his own judgmental views was a way for Chief to bring into the proceedings his authority peremptorily and reaffirm his alpha position in the social order. However, Bryce Ryan (1953) identified an instance in 1945 when a man from the *pātha rata*, Maritime Provinces, where Variga Sabhāwa traditions were not practiced, migrated to Nuwarakalaviya, and came before such Sabhawa.   In Nuwarakalaviya he would be called a *pāthayā*, denoting a different caste identity. He married a woman from a certain *Varige*, but elders of the wife's *Varige* refused her husband's entry into the clan. Moreover, he was a *pita-varigakkārayā* (exo-variga person). The marriage was not recognized in conformity with the Variga customs.

Fuming with anger with the Variga customs the confrontational husband called out the decision and screamed, that "they (his family) were being hoodwinked in a ceremonious carnival of justice." [24]   Hurling such disparaging remarks back and forth was not surprising. In 1853, a prominent resident in Maritime Provinces, Jeronis Pieris, soaked in ingratiation with the British and living his expedient membership of the bourgeoisie society of the 19th century called the old customs of the Kandyans as "nasty," and habits as "brutal."[25]

Even after the wife of the man from the Maritime Provinces paid the Rs. 200 fines, recognizing the man's hostile attitude towards Variga Sabhāwa customs and disparaging them, they added an additional punishment. The Sabhāwa directed the *henayā* to suspend all *tovil tahanam* to the husband who refused to concur with caste norms he was subjected to. Instead, he got his dhobi services for pay. But time healed differences, and a few years later, he was allowed as a variga member (Ryan, 1953. p. 250). The fine of Rs. 200 was hefty figure in 1947.[26] This turned out to be the last known Rata Sabhāwa, a coda for its fine run lasting centuries.

A little- known formality found in earlier times in Kandyan country draws manifestly striking association with *henayā's* role in signing such documents. Nearly all *Sannas*, ola or deeds executed centuries ago, some reproduced in the *Gazetteer* of A. C. Lawrie, have multiple names who witnessed the writing. Examination of hundreds of these *Sannas* produced as evidence in colonial courts of law in 19th century show one common denominator, a pattern, appearing in them – the name of a person of a peculiar lower social status known to the grantor of the document. Review of type of these names among signatories show a particular characteristic of the name: this individual was of different caste, usually of lower in standing than the grantor as existed under the social norms at the time. Inclusion of a name usually identified as a lower or different caste in a document meant to be perpetual and special to the family of the grantor or grantee shows that it was an important traditional component to make the process complete and absolute. In other words, valid and acceptable to all. It is hard to believe a lower caste person or someone in vassalage in the walawwa would sign on a personal and long-term legal transaction of the family of a nobility unless the tradition required and in agreement with it. Thus, having the *henayā* validate the Sabhā decision is a confirmation of a Kandyan tradition practiced in Nuwarakalaviya in binding agreements.

---

[24] As seen from an entry made by John D'Oyly (1917) in his *Diary*, this seems to have been the prevalent attitude in the up-country in general at the time of fall of Kandy. On March 19, 1815, a group of *Mohottālas* from Hath Korale, Uva and Sabaragamuwa Dissavanis and Tun Kōrale districts have complained to D'Oyly through two Adikārs that "they hear, Low Country Modrs (Mudliyars) of Karāva, Durawe, Halagama and other Low Castes have been created, & are accustomed there to travel in Palanquins – in the Kandyan Territory, such Things are never permitted, and they request, that no Persons of these low Castes may be allowed to assume such Honours within the Kandyan Territory, but only the *niyama* (rightful) Mudiyansela of Goyigama – [*sic*]." The Governor concurred and made this proclamation – "Your ancient Customs shall undoubtedly be observed, & the Persons of such inferior castes shall be forbidden to use such Honors & Distinctions within the Kandyan Provinces [*sic*], p. 240 (parentheses by author).
[25] Jayawardena, 2003, p. 251.
[26] Chief Police Inspector L. B. S. Wickramasinghe told me that his salary as a Police Constable in 1947 was Rs. 40 per month.

Even a stranger may be summoned from the street to sign. Review of court records in Kandy conducted by Lawrie (1896) show that in 1806, Ehelepola Dissava of Uva wrote a promissory note on an *ola* page when receiving a loan of 600 parangiwatta pagodas (pagodi) from Paebin Thambi of Borawa Veediya in Kandy. After the *Dissava* died a prisoner in Mauritius island in 1829, a man named Thambi Kandu Muhandiram of Borawaveediya in Kandy brought a lawsuit against the latter in 1833 to recover money owed by the late *Dissava* (p. 206). Names written on it as witnesses were Eladetta Nilame, Rada Badde Vidāne and Talawela Vidāne (last two residing in the walawwa, likely as servants and of lower caste), and Olissa Kumanda, a passer-by randomly drawn from the street at the time the note was written (p. 201).

When the hearing takes place in the walawwa compound, *Ratemahattayā* usually conducts the proceedings from the bench.[27] It is unusual if a Chief would allow someone else of subaltern standing to conduct a hearing within the confines of his walawwa – the symbol of his power. If Maha Vanniya or *Ratemahattayā* was not directing a session, or unable to be present, *Walawwe Mohottāla* and *Arachis* in attendance held Rata Sabhāwa. When *Ratemahattayā* holds a hearing, *Walawwe Mohottāla* keeps records that are written on *Vanni Lēkam Miti* or *lēkam miti* – records written on strips of palm leaves declaring a fact. A *lēkam mitiya* written for a fine was called *dada mudippuwa*. At Rata Sabhāwa in the village, after the decisions were recorded by the *Lēkama*, that record too was called *lēkam mitiya*. The Cadastral register of the shareholders of the tract of paddy fields was also called *Lēkam Mitiya* or *pangu layistuwa*. At the conclusion of the session, the cases decided were announced and reported in writing to the walawwa or in the case of *Gam Sabe* in Kandyan Provinces, to the appropriate department in the palace or the Chief.

PUNISHMENT. After someone was found guilty at a Rata Sabhāwa hearing, he or she can ask for time to pay the fine. If that concession was granted, and if the guilty person is a male, he must then remove the *uramāle* (head scarf). This act is known as *isipili galawanawā* or *isakada arawanawā* (removal of the head scarf). He now carries the *uramāle* in his hand. He covers his head again only after paying the fine.[28] In this sequence, the person ordered to take off the head cover is stamped as one falling into a lowest state until the conditions of the Rata Sabhāwa edict are fulfilled. His position juxtaposed a caste practice existed at the time: a Rodi caste person had no right to wear any form of head cover.[29] Only way out of this harsh social reminder is to pay the fine.

If the fine is not paid, *Baddarāla* goes to the house of the guilty person and takes possession of all moveable property and hand them over to Maha Vanniyā or *Ratemahattayā*. This was called *meti ahu tiyanawa*. What is then left of the house is only the bare walls. Essayists contributing to the *SSS* in 1932 wrote that this custom is so cruel, it must have been practiced only in the times of Sinhala Kings. From the writings in *SSS*, it appears that this punishment was not in practice at Rata Sabhāwa in 1930s when it ended.

---

[27] In the Kandyan highlands it was called *Dissave Naduwa* (Court of the Dissava).

[28] Hettiarachchi, D. E., ed. 2019, 1979, P. 8.

[29] Tennent, 1860, Vol. II p. 188).

In additions to the fine, other methods were in existence more to discipline a person than punish. Taking an oath or *diviya – Keta Padi Alleema –* is one such instance when the convicted person was asked to touch an object such as a *keta* (a pebble). He puts his hand on the pebble and admits and promises not to repeat the alleged wrongdoing. As described earlier, this method is a less inconvenient alternative available to villagers without going through the Sabhāwa process and suffering financial hardship. But in Kapuruhami's *Rata Sabhāwa* thesis, fine was the only punishment for violations that fell under the purview of the Sabhāwa. Thus, Rata Sabhā may have contrived *Keta Padi Alleema* as a simpler way to resolve a dispute.

Variga Sabhāwa or Rata Sabhāwa did not have authority to send a guilty person to prison. Granted, according to D'Oyly (1929), imprisonment in different form took place at the walawwa (p. 58). On certain occasions, need arises to detain a person temporarily in the *Atapattu Maduwa* in the walawwa compound until he pays the fine. The extent of detention was limited to asking the convicted villager to remain in a circle drawn around him in the sand until he pays the fine.

Ridi was the currency used to pay the fine to Maha Vanniyā, *Ratemahattayā* or *Mohottāla*. Since the middle of 19th century, rupee replaced ridi as the currency to pay the fines. The fine was presented on a hand of betel leaves, a few areca nuts, a piece of dried tobacco, a modicum of chunam and *Mohottāla's naga pirambuwa* cane, all placed on a white piece of linen spread over a brass betel salver. This tray was called *tahanam arina vattiya* (ban lifting tray).

Afterwards, the *Mohottāla* pronounces the following *tahanam arina vākkiya* (proscription   lifting incantation) aloud confirming the decision and any actions taken, punishments imposed, and instructions for villagers thenceforth to refrain from mocking and teasing the respondents or litigants involved in the proceedings.

> *"On this day, mulādänivaru headed by Mohottāla heard and deliberated on the evidence pertaining to the accusation of alleged immoral conduct levelled by Punchirāla against Ranmenika. This body has concluded fittingly and acknowledges accordingly the receipt of just fines. The accusations have been proved to be false and maligned. Therefore, it is hereby proclaimed that the bans that were in force on Ranmenika and her blood relatives are removed forthwith. What this means is that this ban remains voided so long as the golden-pinnacled Pattirippuwa is in existence in the city of Senkadagala Nuwara. Henceforth, no male, female or boy shall invoke this accusation during a dispute over firewood, water,[30] while playing games or at any other quotidian moment.[31] This ban shall remain in force by the power of the Sinhale King's golden crown and golden sword; the Great Government Agent of the province; Assistant Government Agent; King Mahasammata; the Vanni Bandara reigning over this province; the Governor in Colombo; the Great Silk Hat of Nuwarawawe Kalukumara Mudyanse and Dissa Mahattaya who initiated this Order. This ban is in effect once, twice, and*

---

[30] Sometimes quarrels can break out during outings to collect firewood or while watering plots of paddies.

[31] Day-to-day affairs (of villagers).

thrice"[32] (Adapted from Kapuruhami 42-68 and *Sinhala Sirith Sangrahaya*).

In *SSS*, following is another ban lifting invocation recited in Kabithigollewa area:
> *"May you live long! May you live long! May you live long! The great quartet of deities* – Drutharāsta, Viruda, Virupāksa *and* Vaisravana, *and* Gama Hat Rajjuruwo *who watches over this kingdom of lakes, and all other great and lesser deities have witnessed us today lifting this vilification. By decree of the Great King of Sinhale and the five walawwas* (walaw pahe)[33] *this slander shall not be pronounced again at a dispute, or for any other reason."*[34]

Mix of phrases like 'power of the Sinhale King's golden crown…' or 'great government agent…' in this invocation are not nuances, but metaphorically expressive assertions highlighting the authority of the Rata Sabhāwa. Here, the supremacy of the Sinhala King or the Colonial government in the Sinhala Pattuwa in Vavuniya District is invoked in allegorical terms. Furthermore, King Mahasammata referred to in the above invocation is an important regnal figure in Nuwarakalaviya folklore.[35] He is the first in line of Kings that belongs to Sākya race. He is the first King who instituted the caste system, which is an important founding ingredient of the Rata Sabhāwa tradition.

Although there was little attention to rules of evidence, procedural remarks and other technicalities and occasional chicanery, traditionally, all agreed that the 'judges' could be relied upon to give a reasonable decision in the end.[36] But few exceptions have been recorded. Some have observed that impartiality while resolving cases at the Variga Sabhāwa is often questionable. There have been instances when different standards were applied during hearings to identical situations at the Variga Sabhāwa. Leach (1968) tells the story of Ranhamy from Nawana, Kurunegala and a relative of the priest at Pul Eliya temple, 130 kilometers to the North and Walli Etani, daughter of *gamarāla*, feudal head of the same village.

---

[32] "රංමැණිකාට පුංචිරාල විසින් අඩගහ කියා තිබුනු කුලදුස්සිය වචනේ ගැන අද දවසේ […] මොහොට්ටාල ප්‍රධාන මුලාදෑනිවරු ඇහුම් බැලුම් කර බලා නිසි දඩ මුඩ අයකර එක බොරු වචනයක් හැටියට ඔප්පුවූ නියාවට මුලින් රංමැණිකාටත්, ඒ ඇත්තීගේ ලේ නෑයින්ටද දී තිබුනු අණ තහනම් උඩ නිසා (තියා) අහක්කර තිබෙන වගයි. එනම් සෙංකඩගල නුවර රංකොත් පත්තිරිප්පුව පවතිනතුරු තහනම නැත. අද දවසේ පටන් ඒ ඇත්තීට මේ වචනය පිරිමියෙක් හරි, ගෑනියෙක් හරි, කොල්ලෙක් හරි දර දබරයකින්වත්, දිය දබරකින්වත්, අඩ දබරකින්වත්, කෙලි පොලකදීවත් අඩගහ කියන්ඩ තහනම්. සිංහලේ මහ රජ්ජුරුවන්නේ රං කඩුවේ හෝ රං ඔටුන්නේ අණ දන්නවා නම් තහනම්. මේ පළාතේ මහ ඒජන්ත උන්නාන්සේගේ, හෝ දෙවෙනි ඒජන්ත උන්නාන්සේගේ අණ දන්නවා නම් තහනම්. නුවර වැවේ කුමාරසිංහ මුදියන්සේගේ තොප්පිහළුවේ අණ දන්නවා නම් තහනම්. මේ අනාඥාව පනවාපු දිසා මහත්මයාගේ අණ දන්නවා නම් තහනම්. දෙවෙනිවත්ව, තුන්වෙනිවත්ව තහනම්, තහනම්, තහනම් [*sic*]"

[33] There is no specific information about the identities of these five walawwas. At the time Rata Sabhāwa ceased to function in 1930s, well-known walawwas in Nuwarakalaviya were Nuwarawawe, Bulankulame, Hurulle of Morakewa, Nikawewa of Ulagalla and Madukanda. But there were other walawwas in the region that are not under the purview of this review.

[34] "ආයුබෝවේවා, ආයුබෝවේවා, ආයුබෝවේවා, ධාතරාෂ්ට, විරුඩ, විරූපාක්ෂ, වෛශ්‍රවණ යන සතර වරම් දෙව්වරුන්ද, මේ වැව් බැඳි රාජ්‍ය වඩා වර්ධනය කරන්නාවූ ගම හත් රජ්ජුරුවන්ද, අල්පේශාක්‍ය, මහේශාක්‍ය, සියලුම දෙව්වරුන්ද, අද මේ කුලය තැනූ බවට සාක්ෂියි. අඩක් දබරයකදීවත්, වෙනයම් කිසිම කරුණක් නිසාවත් මේ කුලය අඩගහ කියන්ට සිංහලේ මහ රජ්ජුරුවන්ගේ අණින්, වලව් පහේ අණින් තහනම් තහනම්," (Hettiarachchi, D. E., ed. 1979, 2019, P. 54).

[35] Thambiah 1989, p. 119.

[36] Goonesekere, 1958 p. 140.

After Ranhamy and Walli Etani married, Pul Eliya villagers labelled the former as a *pita-varigakkārayā* based on the substantial distance to his birth village of Nawana. They brought him before the Sabhāwa for violating variga norms. It was clear that the groom being a relative of the priest, and bride a relative of the influential members in the village would make the decision quite easy. Ranhamy was admitted to the Pul Eliya *Varige* with only a fine! Later in another instance in the same village, the son of the priest's gardener, also from a village close to Ranhamy's in Kurunegala was not so lucky. When he married a woman without any influential relatives in Pul Eliya, Variga Sabhāwa refused his entry into the *Varige* regardless of his eligibility and capability to pay the fine like Ranhamy did. Both the wife and the husband were expelled from the village (p. 72).

FEAST. It had been long few days up to now in the village. So, who does not like to have a good feast and then watch fun games played during and after the curtain call? At the conclusion of the Rata Sabhā session, the accused and his or her relatives will get the opportunity to invite the *mulādānivaru*, guests and villagers to participate in a sumptuous feast – the last item to end the core activities of the Sabhāwa. From what Kapuruhami Madukanda Ratemahattayā (1948) wrote about this feast (p. 42-68), it appears that its protocol followed similar customs as found in group or community feastings held elsewhere during Kandyan Kings' time.[37]

After a *Navandannā Ayagé Sabhāwa* held in a low caste village, the meal to the *Mohottāla* who participated in the hearing was given by the residents of a higher-caste village nearby, usually of Goyigama caste. For both instances of Sabhā, Rata Sabhāwa and *Navandannā Ayagé Sabhāwa*, the five *naidés* supplied cooking equipment and supplies for the preparation and serving of food in the following order:

1. *Badahela Naidé* – Pots and pans for cooking.
2. *Ārachchi Hangili Naidé* – Knives and katties to slice vegetable and meat.
3. *Madinā Naidé* – Juggery.
4. *Marakkala Manamāla Naidé* – Fish and meat.
5. *Pattivalayinge Liyana Naidé* – Milk and yoghurt.
6. *Vādi Undiyarāla* – Bee honey.
7. *Gamarāla – Heel Adukkuwa* (breakfast), coconuts and rice as victuals.

If Maha Vanniyā or *Ratemahattayā* attended the Rata Sabhāwa, his food was brought packed in a *dālpayya*, also called *udahālla*.[38] *Mulādānivaru* sat on the floor in the *Maduwa* for the banquet. Young men are the designated servers. They are dressed in formal attire: a new sarong, a white uramale wrapped around his head. To start the dinner, they go round offering water to the *mulādānivaru* in newly baked earthen pots. Sometimes, instead of earthen pots, brass pots or kettles were used.

---

[37] At a dinner given by the last King of Kandy to Adikārs and *Dissavaru* in celebration of one of his marriages, the guests sat on white linen spread over reed mats on the floor of the designated feasting area in the palace. Food served on banana leaves placed on white sheets of linen spread on reed mats rolled out on the floor in front of the guests. A royal feast like this had about 200–300 curries (Davy 1821, 2006 p. 167). There was no record of games played at the palace after such an event.

[38] A woven basket with square base and hung from a rafter by four woven strips extending up from its edges to hold trays made of reed.

The guest raises the pot and pour water into the mouth without his lips touching the rim or the spout, a custom which goes back centuries.[39] The *muládánivaru* step out of the *Maduwa* and wash their hands from a *kendiya* readying for the dinner.[40] Villages who participated in or witnessed the Sabhāwa proceedings also sit to be served on the reed mats spread out closer to the pandal, or in the *Maduwa* if there was space available.

ENTERTAINMENT IN GENERAL. For some who may be unfamiliar with the genre of rural entertainment, post-Rata Sabhāwa session feast is the beginning of entertainment. To an observer, these activities may seem like an odd form of satire. However, for an isolated village with no other form of entertainment which probably may look unorthodox or exotic, Rata Sabhāwa, with all its lively and absorbing functions – before, during and after the session often becomes their carnival without equal.

A brief description of entertainment practices found in villages in 19th and early 20th century villages needs discussion. Observers have noted as far back as 19th century that some activities during and after the Rata Sabhāwa elicited elements of entertainment. Badulla district judge Aelian King noted in 1869 that when a villager brought a grievance to the *Gam Sabhāwa* it generated quite an excitement among his fellows. It in itself was an entertaining idea. R. Morris, the Government Agent in Kurunegala noted that the enthusiasm generated in cases like this was partly due to the paucity of widespread entertainment events and opportunities like folk theater and amusement productions.[41] These observations have merits, but villages in Nuwarakalaviya were not entirely devoid of divergent genres of uniquely merry moments in the past. Some continue to the present. Peripatetic minstrels like song bills (*kavi kola kārayő*), fortune tellers, snake-charmers or just the lovable monkey dancer (*rila nettuwa*) were utilities that enthused the public with some of the simplest form of travelling circus acts brought to villages and bazaars. Also providing amusing moments and leisure to villagers were nightly reciting of *Pel Kavi* (poems of the watch-hut), *goyam kavi* (poems of the rice planting), *nelum kavi* (poems of the harvesting), *kamath kavi* (poems of the threshing floor), *karatta kavi* (poems of the carters), *bali netum* (propitiation ritual dances), and numerous folk games as simple as *Gal Keliya* and complex as *Nerenchi Keliya*.[42]

To give a comparative idea of the genre of entertainment concept of ordinary people, it is worth noting life's activities that sum up as entertainment in other parts of the country as well. Carters on the road were one such genre. Carts being the main form of transport, they were on the road all over and all the time. In a dispatch to the Colonial Office dated April 27, 1827, Governor Edward Barnes wrote the number of carts in Colombo doubled after the opening of Kandy-

---

[39] See Knox, opp. p. 87 for a mid-17th century illustration of a Kandyan man drinking water from the spout of a kettle.

[40] Using forks at the dinner table was not a custom in Sri Lanka until well into the colonial times. That too was limited to elitist section of the native population, some of them desiring to emulate Western style of living, exuviated a good deal of their indigeneity.

[41] King, Aelian, AR 188, 1869; Morris AR 120, 1869, both qtd. in Pieris, R., 1956, p. 254 n 72.

[42] A diagram of this game is carved out on step number 191 on the first flight of steps on Mihintale hill.

Colombo Road.[43] In 1860, number of carts in Sri Lanka was 11,000. It increased to 15470 in 1891.[44] Carters carried food, fuel, and other provisions between communities crossing boundaries between Maritime Provinces and Kandyan region. It is natural they engendered their own form of entertainment. In the nights, as the carters lugged along the lonely Colombo-Kandy Road or on any other road in their rain-bow-roofed carts laden with bags full of coffee and other commercial items, they recited *karatta kavi* to kill boredom. As the carts passed the houses by the road, the residents trying to fall asleep listened to the refreshing poems sounding like lullabies. Boaters on rivers and canals too sang their own version of songs and poems called *Pāru Kavi* to pass time and entertain residents along the banks of these waterways. Not just people in the village, but carters on the road recited *Kada-Im Kavi* (poems of the boundaries) also for entertainment as they passed a boundary or a well-known boundary marker.[45]

A wedding in the village, the ceremony to celebrate a girl coming of age, *Muttinevum Mangalle* (ceremony of the turning of the rice-pot) held on the tank bund, or a *bali yāga* are common occasions that drew merriment. Annual *Kiribandi Pujāwa* in Welimapothana near Horowpothana, the annual perahera at Hurulu Wawe Dévāle, and the *Gambādi Rājakāriya* in Samādhigama, and lately the burgeoning Poson Perahera in Mihintale are few such public events in the region. They too often have a feast during or at the end of it. We know how exciting would be an annual *bana pinkama* (religious sermon) with its lively folk theater features in the village. Not all villages have Buddhist temples in Nuwarakalaviya. So, every year after the harvest season, villages invite a monk to come and conduct Buddhist sermons for 2-3 nights. Villages in the surrounding areas also came to participate in this event. Its theatrical performances during breaks between sermons brought color and pageantry to the night. In 18th century, a laity who was called *ganinnanse* in the temple performing religious activities recited verses in Pali while another sitting next to him interpreted it in Sinhala in melodic verses as he played *udakkiya*, the handheld two-faced drum to the amusement of the listeners.[46] At the Kandy Perahera, although primarily a religious event, the entertainment it brought to the spectators is remarkable. Entertainment in a village ranged as simple as two girls sitting on a mat in the front yard playing *Gal Keliya*, throwing five pebbles up with one hand and catching them with the other, to a *chuck gudu* game in the *tisbambe*[47] section of the village.

When a Rata Sabhāwa assembly was scheduled in a village, besides the interest it generated with the preparation of the 'courthouse' (*Maduwa*) and other logistical exercises, if the inquest before the public gathering concerns an improper conduct

---

[43] Sivasundaram, 2013, p. 11.

[44] Munasinghe, 1972, p. 407.

[45] See H. C. P. Bell, 1904 pp. 130-131 for few of these ballads in Kegalle District; Sivasundaram, 2013, p. 215.

[46] Wachissara, K. 1961, p. 128.

[47] A park-like clearance of 30-fathom required around a *gamgoda* (village compound) "to admit of a free current of air passing through the village" and, "a broad strip shall be cleared from the tank to the field so as to admit of a free current of air passing through the village," (Ceylon Government Gazette No. 3996, June 20, 1874, p. 1238)."

of someone, or a conflict involving illicit sex or other lascivious act, or any other incident that has the potential to create twists and sensationalism, they are fodder for intrigue and no doubt entertaining for the spectators like tabloid-type news streaming on reality television programs and social media today. The chance to hear narratives of those accused of or those pressing charges and questioning by the panel of *mulādänivaru* are enthusing spectacles for villagers. It was a community event what James Brow called an "occasion of collective ceremony."

The community looked forward to the visit of the *mulādenivaru*, to wit, *Mohottāla*, *Baddarāla*, and *Lékama* dressed in humble attire representing their authority. These officials were expected to stay in the village during the day or two while Sabhāwa activities continued.

To top it off, the arrival of Maha Vanniyā or *Ratemahattayā* seated in a palanquin with the full panoply of his titular regalia showing ostentation of a peacock, and escorted by his entourage of dancers, horn-blowers, drummers, and whip crackers was a sight to behold. The palanquin bearers, usually of the Padu (*paddoo*) caste, carry palanquins of the royalty and the nobles[48] sing songs while carrying the load[49] which entertains the villagers who wait for the opportunity in warmed up expectation. Henry Marshall wrote the finery of the Kandyan Chiefs as "picturesque." But occasionally, his contemporary European writers who no doubt had seen odd forms of aristocracy in their countries as well, seem to have arrived with a Western orientalist perception of these moments.[50]   Englishman Davy (1821, 2006) wrote about the arrival of a *Dissava*:

> Persons of refined taste may justly find fault with this oriental mode of travelling, and exclaim, "what barbarous pomp!" The exclamation is just; but it's the pomp which the natives are accustomed to respect and associate with power, and in consequence it would not be very politic to neglect the observance of it." (p. 358)

Davy (1818) did not seem to have had nicer things to say about Sri Lankan cultural and religious landscape. He wrote "…worship (on Adam's Peak) is strong example too of the lowness of their faith, … and prostrate before a thing deserving only contempt (pp. 25-30)."

I can only say that in the eyes of villagers, the Chief's dress was fantastic, extreme, remarkable, and so unrestrained. The panorama of his descent to the village could only be called exceptionally colorful. In 1932, *Mulādänivaru* of

---

[48] Cordiner, 1807, p. 93.

[49] The bearers of the palanquin sang poems and songs to soften the exhaustion of the occupant and themselves or fit the occasion. In India, when a bride was carried on a festooned palanquin to her new home, the palanquin bearers sang songs to alleviate her sorrow for leaving home. In *Palanquin Bearers*, Sarojini Naidu (1879-1949) wrote her enduring lyrics, "*Lightly o lightly, we bear her along, She always like a flower, in the wind of our song… We bear her along, Like a pearl in a string…, …,*" celebrating the bride's enchanting journey to her husband's home.

[50] For the historical, cultural, and political perceptions of the East by the West, see, Edward W. Said, *Orientalism* (1979), New York: Vintage Books.

Nuwarakalaviya described the dress of a *Maha Vanni Unnehe* as a magnificent sight.[51]

After the greeting protocols that usually consist of offering a water pitcher (*watura sangraha*) and betel quid (*bulath vita*), washing the feet at the entrance to the *Maduwa*, the Chief removes his *hataramulu toppiya*, sword and snake-head cane and hands over to his attendants who daintily deposit them on a mid-sized table with a white sheet of linen spread over it. He then sits on the seat of honor, "the bench." Awed and with anticipation, the optics of this occasion make villagers think the 'royalty' had landed on their turf with a veneer of opulence. Such a gala-like sight is entertaining and a reward not to miss.

The theme of the games during the feast involved fun activities. *Terum māpinna* (mystery dish), *tarakwelā kāma* or *tara kota bat kāma* (eating upon a challenge), and *tun wattamé, hatara wattamé,* or *dāhatara wattamé bat kāma* (third, fourth, or fourteenth round of eating) are some of them. Those who are careless or inconsiderate enough to make an improper comment or move during the Rata Sabhāwa formalities or the feast get fined on-the-spot. This fine is called *varada bat ahura* (eating a fist of rice for the breach). This fine is paid not by ridi as the custom after the hearing just concluded, but by asking the offended to eat more rice with great difficulty to the delight of the participants and spectators! It is instant entertainment for the gathering to see the offender struggling to stuff in mouthful of rice balls, just after completing a full meal a moment earlier!

Thus far women sidelined into the kitchen to prepare the feast get their chance finally to make fun of the men folks waiting while salivating to enjoy the food. The women bring their own form of trickery challenging men to figure out a puzzle they have put together. It is a curry cooked with an assortment of ingredients only they knew. They bring this mystery dish (*terum māpinna*) and deposit it before the seated men and ask them to name its ingredients. Until someone seated names the ingredients correctly, they will not get served, and are doomed to remain hungry. Women have the last laugh literally, watching men stumble and fumble, often making fools of themselves by trying to figure out the contents of the dish by naming outrageous ingredients!

---

[51] Hettiarachchi, D. E., ed. 2019, 1979, p. 194. Also see Appendix D.

12. DISENGAGEMENT OR REALIGNMENT: *MULĀDENIVARU*, ELITES AND THE REST

*A*fter the British colonial administration abolished the old Chiefdom system and introduced Divisional Revenue Officers, it in effect ended the titulary culture and institutions that were part of the ancient system, including the Rata Sabhāwa which faced the inevitability – it disappeared being part of the villagers' lives. Leach observed in 1961 that "… around 1938, power of the *variga* court" at Pul Eliya village near Anuradhapura was "waning" to the point that judgements issued by it were becoming ineffective.[1] Just about the same time as in the old Pul Eliya, in other villages too, e.g., Kukulawa, 40 kilometers to the east Anuradhapura, the 1938 change was taking hold of the life of their residents. Older villagers in Kukulawa and nearby Samādhigama in 1983 told James Brow that attitude towards cross-caste and cross-variga marriage had begun to change, and opposition to such marriages began to decline starting from around 1940s.[2]

Therefore, what happened to the former *mulādenivaru, kāriyakarawannō* and Chiefs in Nuwarakalaviya after the Rata Sabhāwa tradition ended is an interesting story. This can be looked in a similar way studying what happened in the past to certain homogenous communities that often went through what Nira Wickramasinghe called an 'eclipse' of their former self.[3] This happened in different ways for different people. Under certain circumstances they were given or found opportunities to change the expression of their ethnicity, caste or standing among the peoples. Marginal people like slaves in the early 19th century became invisible after getting their freedom. *Mulādenivaru* became non-existent after the colonial laws abolished the main source of their patronage – the Chiefdoms in the provinces, and major traditions they were responsible for or belonged to. The status conscious sector of society was overwhelmed by the infusion of cultural changes and capitalist economic winds that spread across the country with colonial laws and influence of the Western ways. Obeyesekere (1984) discusses 'External Historical Process' of the influence of immigration of different ethnic groups to Sri Lanka, particularly Arabs, and those from the Subcontinent. He also discusses the faith infusion into existing practices of indigenous people in Sri Lanka in the past millennia realigning or even acquiring new forms of beliefs (306-312).

Disengagement happened in multiple ways. And not only in *mulādenivaru* and Rata Sabhāwa related community participation but in other groups as well. *Mulādenivaru* lost an honored designation in the community. They merged in the community as untitled ordinary citizens after the colonial laws made the source of a major rural law – Rata Sabhāwa and Variga Sabhāwa irrelevant.

NOTES

[1] Leach, 1961, p. 73.

[2] Brow, 1996, p. 117.

[3] See Nira Wickaramasinghe, 2020, for realignment of slaves into mainstream society following different paths of manumission.

Villagers who were part of the traditions like these of the past saw their 'laws' handed down through generations slowly evanesce following the changes spawned by the flood of legislations instituted by the colonial administrations. These changes were so instrumental in forcing adjustments to their past ways and rearranging the social characteristics. No sector of the population was spared by such influences. But the conglomeration of *Mulādenivaru*, *Kāriyakarawannō* and Chiefs held onto some of their erstwhile accoutrements and recognition as someone noteworthy and special in the community.

A villager who was formerly identified with a geographical area administered by a Rata Sabhāwa or Variga Sabhāwa retained the identity although it carried no special privileges now. Thus, the collection of villages which my kins lived in called *'Gam Daha Ata Varige* – we of the varige of the eighteen villages' still use it to declare that we come from the same geographical unit with close links but may not necessarily have close familial relationships now.

The lower-level officials, *sulu mulādenivaru*, in the pre-1938 Sri Lanka did not get many opportunities of advancement or reallocation (of careers) in the post-Rata Sabhāwa social landscape. But along with the disengagement and diffusion of their authority, the former *mulādenivaru* were still in demand in the community, not to the same level as during their Rata Sabha tenures. For example, villagers sometimes sought the wisdom of *mulādenivaru* as arbiters in personal issues like petty disputes needing a third-party involvement. They were still addressed by the same suffixes of their former titles such as *Mohottāla* (Seneviratne Mohottāla), *Kōrāla* (Alittane Kōrāla), and *Ratemahattayā* (Hurulle Ratemahattayā). Understandably, references to their former power and luster did not carry any weight of authority but retained a certain aura of authenticity and acceptance among the villagers.

Meanwhile, those of the higher rung in society explored avenues where they could still maintain some semblance of ancestral prestige they once enjoyed. Being former notables in the community was their currency for reengagement prospects. Better opportunities they enjoyed while in power like access to education in religious settings, e.g., *pirivena* education, or in schools maintained by missionaries in the North were tremendously helpful for them while seeking these avenues for re-alignment. Also, the field of qualified candidates in the region to represent the villagers in the burgeoning democratic national politics was small. Thus, former Chiefs and their descendants, arguably the best placed, well provided, and least opposed, stepped in to feel their place in these changing tides.

For many Chiefs, however, success from this effort was hard to come by as was seen from the 1956 general elections results. However, subsequent elections saw these failed candidates dropping out from politics and seeking roles as administrators. Vacancies for regional administrative jobs – DRO positions, the colonial substitute for the 'eclipsed' Chiefs, Land Development positions in the emerging agricultural projects, and positions to fill expanding judicial districts opened. The region was still the backcountry. Competition for these new engagements from the outer districts was negligible even prior to disbanding of the Chiefs as the province was still burdened by the stigma of its insalubrious past like malaria, cholera, and yaws (*parangi*). Besides these hard choices, colonial rulers also believed that though it was not a prerequisite, once having been a *mulādāni* or a Chief or his direct descendant would remain a great asset for consideration for these exclusive jobs.

More and more colonial laws renamed districts and drew their boundary lines anew. For example, the word *Pattuwa* (Province) is rarely used now. It is now Tulana, Korale, or the Palatha (Province). Former Korale districts are divided into a conglomeration of new administrative bodies called Pradeseeya Sabha. Maha Vanniya's former charge is now Provincial Sabhāwa, administered by a team of a new generation of elected members with the Chief Minister as its head, all politically savvy but from ordinary walks of life.

Particularly for the Chiefs, disengaged from their gloried past, assimilation into the 20th century bourgeoisie was thus imminent, slow, obvious, and turned into an altered form of engagement. Nearly a century later, such assimilation carries on its weight yet as chances of a descendant of a Chief becoming a ruler, regional or national, are clearly amassed ahead of an ordinary citizen.

Adjusting to the Post-Ratemahattayā period after 1938 must have been a difficult transition for the Chiefs. They lost the authority and power they wielded in the region. With their acreage of influence getting inconsequential, people's admiration began to trail fast, change of lifestyle and waning caste practices brought pressures they were unaccustomed to as before. Because by then, the cast of this story had begun the predictable medium to exist.

To calibrate into the next fitting standing, many Chiefs found opportunities to merge into the colonial administrative stream by trying employment like Divisional Revenue Officer (DRO), the best comparable positions available. Alternatively, they looked to enter the enticing and lucrative political landscape to mine its riches. As they did for the last 150 years by tinkering with powers of the Sri Lankan nobility, colonial government made sure the disbanding of the nobility happened gradually. They were not going to draw the displeasure of the Chiefs who, to paraphrase Kumari Jayawardena, suddenly found faced with the possibility of being "nobodies." In doing so, their authority over the district became limited and they were subjected to a more organized, formal, and centralized administrative formula directed by the Governor in Colombo and executed by his Agent in the province. Those who chose politics fell under the hierarchy of the party organization, leaders of which were rooted in Colombo, not in the Chief's ancestral comfort zones.

With the reforms of the Donoughmore Constitution in 1927, as the parliamentary form of government was expanded to be more inclusive, soon, the former Chiefs or their descendants lined up to represent people with democratic principles, a drastic contradistinction from their ancestral role of supposedly being sole caretakers of the traditions. And many took the opportunity. But culture still clung to some old ways: during the few early election cycles, Chiefs or their family members stood a good chance to be chosen by the party leadership as candidates for democratic contests. Pared from their privileged past, they found common crowd with no 'blue blood' ancestry, too, begin to flock in to join the fray in political arena in Nuwarakalaviya and elsewhere in the country. P.B. Bulankulame, once the Dissava of Anuradhapura, had a short-lived career in politics during the 1940s and early 1950s. Although the areas they proposed representing as members of the parliament were smaller, the dynamics of the competition they faced was something they had least expected or used to. For example, 20 years after *Ratemahattayā* tradition ended, and only eight years after the British had left, the 1956 General Election hinted the direction Nuwarakalaviya was taking. In the five electorates in the Nuwarakalaviya and Tamankaduwa districts that formed the North Central Province, the contestant list consisted of 13 individuals. Each electorate had at least one candidate who was either a former Chief or one of his direct descendants. After the ballots were counted by the morning after the election day, it spoke of the changes that had taken inroads into the province. Only one candidate with aristocratic family descent, E. L. B. Hurulle, who proved to be an avuncular stateman, came out as the winner representing Horowpothana electorate!

Not all Chiefs took to politics. Some withered into retirement and joined the last Rata Sabhāwa generation to cherish its history. The likes of Kapuruhami Madukanda Ratemahattayā never sought alternatives to titles they enjoyed for generations. He stayed true to his interests – to promote literature and culture of Nuwarakalaviya. Years before political winds took effect, he celebrated this by assisting the two brilliant ethnologists and historians at the time, H. W. Codrington (1879-1942) of the Ceylon Civil Service and Paul E. Pieris (1874-1959) to prepare the landmark manuscript, *Rata Sabhāwa*, for publication to enshrine it as a valued resource for the posterity showing its vitality as a potent institution of rural jurisprudence existed for centuries in the region.

These changes stirred waves of erosion of caste, gender recognition and relationships, group interactions, and past conventions that shaped their existence. Even quotidian affairs like simply the way of life of the lowest rungs of people shed any liaison to the past. These changes paved the way to introduce new customs, religious persuasions, and styles of living now termed as progressive, and rearranged the building blocks of the social organization. The life they engineered in effect helped speed up the reappropriation of the shared social standing of a particular group or an individual.

Bryce Ryan commented in 1953 that caste influence "will have been a significant fact in Ceylon long after the last of its specific characteristics are lost, for its conditioning effect upon alternative forms of social organization cannot be escaped (p. 89)." Thus, with each passing generation, some markers that often helped give clues to a person's past group affiliation faded away from the folk memory due to the influence of caste vicissitudes Ryan anticipated. Nira Wickramasinghe's term 'eclipse' articulates similar situations with certain ethnic groups, e.g., like slaves in early British rule in Sri Lanka.

This ecliptic process and its setting shades were different for different peoples. It seems one of these markers was the configuration of a person's name that may give clues about his or her ancestry. The disappearance of this onus made it easy for people of different alliances, including professions and vocations, to cross the social barriers to bond and blend in turn diluting any strictures of their past and reshaping socio-cultural landscape. Dissolution or realignment of these barriers allowed the pathology of social interactions to ease the state of the otherness of the communities. Slowly but certainly, familial relationships that were unthinkable generations earlier between these groups began to take root. With the termination of the service tenure traditions or feudal obligations in general becoming insignificant, regardless how prominent, or modest the ancestral standings had been, even now, changes occurring even in the outermost corners of the society from top to bottom show they are not immune from this new metrics of integration.

In the nineteenth century or just prior, the Dutch and Portuguese households, elite Vellala Tamils in the Jaffna peninsula and Sinhala and Moor elites in the littoral and Kandyan country owned slaves, or descendants of freed slaves who were still in some degree of bondage. Many slaves were descendants of erstwhile forms of slavery existed in Sri Lanka or brought as slaves from Kerala, Malabar Coast, Coromandel coast in India, Batavia, from some parts of the African continent, or accompanied Dutch officials posted to Sri Lanka by the Dutch East India Company.

In general, slaves did not belong to or share the resources and perks of a conventional village. They were commodities owned by rich families who kept them in bondage usually allowing them to live in the family compound until death or deeded away to a family member as inheritance or sold away. In 1824, Galagoda claimed his female slave was valued at 100 ridi.[4] Inheriting not just adult slaves, but their children, too, through family line or as any other property succession, was common.

Integration of the slaves into the free mainstream society in Sri Lanka during 17th - 19th centuries is a fascinating story. However, few decades into the British administration, by law, slaves themselves or their children became free after the death of the owner. According to a 72-page pamphlet titled *Slavery and Slave Trade in British India, Ceylon, Malacca, and Penang,* published in 1841 in London by the British and Foreign Anti-Slavery Society, efforts to abolish slavery in Maritime Provinces in Sri Lanka had been shaping up since 1806.[5] In 1814, out of 17,538 slaves in the country, 15,341 were in Jaffna peninsula.[6] The Society wrote that there were 22,000 slaves in Jaffna and Trincomalee in 1818. In 1837 records show there were 27397 slaves in Sri Lanka – 24545 of them in Northern Province, including Nuwarakalaviya. Kandy Board of Commissioners report dated August 25, 1829, records 2113 slaves in Kandyan Provinces.[7]

Although the exact number was not known, there were three types of slaves in Nuwarakalaviya. It was comprised of 1. *Bath Vāāllu* (slaves), 2. *Karae Poth Vāāllu* and 3. *Kankota Vāāllu.*[8] In this province too, these slaves have disappeared by merging into the mainstream society shedding off all their ancestral markers. But Obeyesekere (1967) does not believe slavery had altogether disappeared. He found mid-20th century household workers, euphemistically identified with the vernacular

---

[4] Lawrie, 1896, Vol. 1, p. 248.

[5] For a lengthy discussion of slavery in Sri Lanka, see Pridham, 1849, pp. 223-233; Lawrie, 1896, 1898, Vol I & II; and Wickramasinghe, 2020.

[6] Wickramasinghe, 2020, p. 41, citing SLNA *Returns of the Population of the Island of Ceylon 1827,57-59. 67-68* SLNA.

[7] D'Oyly, 1929, p. 80.

[8] Galmaduve Wannihamy Vel Vidāne of Manankattiya, cited in Hettiarachchi, ed. 2019, 1979, p. 236

vedakārayō (servants), were without de facto rights like *vahallu* (*vāāllu*), a modern type of slaves (p. 16).[9]

Act No. 20 of 1844 abolished all forms of slavery in Sri Lanka. But in the North, the disengagement of former slaves from its stigma did not happen in a steadfast manner. It followed a twisted course. While developments like Chilaw Experiment[10] in 1820 or Abolition Law 1844 guaranteed documented and absolute freedom after receiving manumission, many Jaffna slaves found themselves continuing in their masters' homes working as domestic servants or in the fields. The colonial government at the time did not foresee how the existing or future interactions between the former slaves and their masters and the larger community would shape up after the way of life of bonded people ended. Deeply embedded cultural and social currents took a perverse trajectory and sequestered them in the anathema of their slave past. One thing was certain though: colonial law guaranteed these 'former slaves' would not become commercial objects for sale or purchase. But with the new economic challenges ditched upon them, e.g., like not owning a square inch of the earth to work on, forced them to retain some level of servitude under the former masters and their descendants who owned the lands.[11] Poignantly, somewhat similar situation was described by Booker T. Washington, a slave once lived in a plantation in the state of Virginia and later became an educator. He wrote, when his fellow plantation slaves returned to their cabins after listening to the Emancipation Declaration on January 1, 1853, by 'a stranger' who he presumed to be a United States officer:

> … there was a change in their feelings. The great responsibility of being free of having charge of themselves, of having to think and plan for themselves and their children, seemed to take possession of them. It was very much like suddenly turning a youth of ten or twelve years out into the world to provide for himself. In a few hours, the great questions with which the Anglo–Saxon race had been grappling for centuries had been thrown upon these people to be solved. These were the questions of a home, a living, the rearing of children, education, citizenship and the establishment and support for the church. (p. 21).

Similarly, unencumbered living was a distant goal for the slave men and women in Jaffna to reach. Former masters of these slaves also held high positions in temple management advocating arcane faith conventions which prohibited the practice of religion freely for lower caste people, including the former slaves whose manumission did not address their caste order and associated stigma in the community. As the caste and religious subtleties were not addressed in the abolition law, fundamental challenges to livelihood of the former slaves in this region remained unchanged. One can argue, therefore, that the altered expressions of

---

[9] There are major differences between the two categories of these persons. Most pertinent is that *vedakārayō,* or any person for that matter. He or she cannot be sold, owned, or deeded away under the current laws in Sri Lanka. Conflating of words *vedakārayō* and 'slaves' in any form can lead to confusion in vassalage-related narratives.

[10] Wickramasinghe, 2020, p. 126.

[11] Wickramasinghe, 2020, p. 204.

slavery persisted, as in the case of *Vedakārayō* suggested by Gananath Obeyesekere largely leaving the disengagement meaningless.

Wickramasinghe found parallel situations how a group of marginalized people like slaves merged into the larger society over time shedding markers that were embodied in their past. This made it possible for them to distance themselves from any stigma of slavery and integrate into the mainstream society by initiating into a recognized religious sector practice, e.g., baptism. An example of one such earliest religious sect is the Dutch Reform Church in Wolfendaal, Colombo. Practicing certain exclusive and longstanding customs of another non-slave ethnic group, e.g., circumcision of children by Moors is another.[12]

Freed descendants of enslaved people in the 16th – 19th centuries in Sri Lanka baptized the children fathered by their owners. As a consequent, the child naturally acquired at least a part of the father's name - Dutch, Portuguese, British, Moorish, Tamil, or Sinhalese. Thus, we see Dutch names like Ferdinando, de Sadrado, Hendriksz, Jansz, Fransz, Philippsz, listed in slave registers.[13] This assimilation by circumstances opened the door for freed slaves and their descendants to acquire the "trappings of (non-slave) communities," and "erase their slave inheritance and becoming another"[14] even a few generations later. After becoming 'another,' with each passing day, they cast away any ties to their slave past. A few generations later indices that identified them as slaves or slave descendants have disappeared completely so much so, some would have cringed to hear or read their past story. L.A. Wickramaratne claims descendants of slaves who were with the Dutch families "were designated as Burghers." But Nira Wickramasinghe notes with a caveat that such assertions may not necessarily "cover the variety of trajectories followed by freed men and women."[15]

With the immediate aftermath of the end of Dutch rule in Sri Lanka, "all political and commercial servants of the Dutch East India Company (were) allowed to remain as private individuals in Colombo."[16] But the slaves in these households or in the quarter in Colombo still called Slave Island, were still far from being treated differently. Some Burgher families (who were of Dutch descent) who owned slaves "hired out them as bricklayers, palanquin-bearers, domestic servants, etc., and lived on the wages earned by them."[17]

The slaves who did not acquire a religious identity or unable to secure freedom by any other means retained their birth names like Babby, Camba, Callua, Cethy, Dinghy, Sompania, and Seekka.[18] Wickramasinghe called erasing any markers of their slave ancestry by acquired assimilation as "eclipse of the slave."[19] Example of

---

[12] Wickramasinghe, 2020, p. 160.

[13] Wickramasinghe, 2020, p. 199.

[14] Wickramasinghe, 2020, p. 195.

[15] L.A. Wickramaratne, 1973, p. 167. Qtd. in Wickramasinghe, 2020, p. 202.

[16] Toussaint, J. R. 1935, The Burghers in Early British Times, Lecture given at the Dutch Burgher Union Hall on August 30th, 1935, *Journal of the Dutch Burgher Union of Ceylon,* Vol. 25, October 1935, No. 2, p. 43.

[17] Toussaint, J. R. 1935, p. 44.

[18] Wickramasinghe, 2020, p. 58.

[19] Wickramasinghe, 2020, p. 189.

other forms of trends in disengagement of people from their past stigma in the general population enhanced the pace of building the caste or creed free society in Sri Lanka we see today. Ironically, today's lightning speed of global communication has made this a captivating reality. Most parents now buy a name online and it is becoming a trendy practice! It rarely adheres to established naming traditions and any allusion to the parents' ancestry.

A caste free society forced on by changing laws and customs also threatened the established homogeneity of some groups by opening paths towards an egalitarian structure in once disparate clan structures. Late in the 20th century, an obituary in an English Daily showed how true this had become.[20] As is the tradition, the obituary listed deceased's living relatives and those who had passed away decades ago. While remembering the life and acknowledging the achievements of the deceased, the announcement brought to light an important fact, a social shift, that was painting the Sri Lanka since lately with a new layer of brush strokes obfuscating the homogeneity of his kins' ancestry. The list started with names of deceased's kins who were prominent five generations ago titled in the Kandyan Court and later the British reign. The taxonomy of these names unmistakably revealed their gilded past of elite family establishment. Then starting around the mid-19th century, gradually each passing classificatory kinship level showed names which appear signs of slipping of the clan homogeneity towards a heterogenic construct. Some kin's names usually hinted as associated with different caste, religious, ethnic, or professional identities in line with their own disparate ancestral reputation. The brew of names of the kins in the later generations began to look a lot like today's Sri Lanka: a medley of Dutch, Portuguese, Kandyan, British, Low Country, Up Country, Malay, Tamil, Karava, Durava, Vellala names, etc.

---

[20] Newspaper reference withheld to protect privacy.

13. CONCLUSION

$\mathcal{F}$rom what we have discussed so far, it is fair to say Rata Sabhāwa or Variga Sabhāwa traditions or their variations have evolved over a long period, starting even before the Middle Ages. Rata Sabhāwa or Variga Sabhāwa was a social institution nourished and sanctioned by oral traditions and practices, acutely nurtured by feudatory ways with vicissitudes specific to regions. Thus, it is correct to say that it was a significant part of the heritage of a people in this part of Sri Lanka. After the end of Medieval Ages when colonial powers subdued parts of the country, they still showed no discernible interest, acknowledgement, or accreditation of these Sabhā because they were willing to remain uninvolved with traditional ways of the colony as a political stratagem. In the contours of Sri Lankan history, it was the standard bearer to help guard and maintain cultural strictures and systems propped up with the laws that were either customs and traditions or edicts of the rulers including those who had control over semi-independent regions like Nuwarakalaviya during those times. Accumulated wisdom, the core of governmentality of these institutions, became weathervane of people's self-definition and direction to which justice emphasizing ability to counter often internecine issues that threatened the solidarity of their communities pointed. While entrenched in the land for four centuries, as a practical matter, they wanted no friction between the indigeneity of the subjects as wheels of Roman Dutch law turned. These laws too were often marred with shades that were imbued with medieval-like elements. This attitude continued in diverse ways until the early decades of the 20th century.

Major Forbes (1841) called the Rata Sabhā "free institutions." He noted that by 1828, they were only operating in the "remote province of Nuwarakalaviya (p. 71)." Inherently being independent and having acquired a provinciality of its own, the institutions may have acted irrational in the opinion of some. Thus, that the Rata Sabhāwa and Variga Sabhāwa traditions did not have flaws is an incomplete assertion. But they served their role in becoming one of the quintessential instruments to play the social medley of their time. They were hardly Potemkin institutions – institutions that looked real but not in fact real. Nothing was hidden in actions taken in these quaint social conventions, for they were innocuous in what they meant to do – being direct and straight forward to uphold the dignified customs and traditions of its people. Although, as a byproduct, it helped the elite class to hold on to their inherited privileges.

In the same token, no one fancied and claimed it as the best judiciary they had for their moments of diverse conflicts. But in ways large and small, given the best and worse circumstances they were accustomed to, this institution delivered a definitive and magnificent service for the villagers. Let there be no doubt, with its indelibly framed practices that some may call old-fashioned or medieval-styled conflict resolution ways, it did a remarkable service to the community as good as we now expect from all our modern-day gilded volumes of codified ways reinforced by rules of evidence and thousands of case law experience. Case law of Rata Sabhāwa was the people's deep-rooted customs, traditions, and the community experience. The 70-year-old man who came to the Provincial Day to ask the young DRO in 1973 in Horowpothana was dreaming for the justice the Rata Sabhāwa delivered with modesty and humility which he witnessed when he was young (See page 214). He was not ready or willing to let go of his Rata Sabhāwa inheritance and experience.

Even before the total erasure of Rata Sabhāwa in the 20th century, the indigenous nobility found its grip of old ways loosening slowly. This small segment of society had little help or power to arrest the influence of changes in tribal and caste ways taking place across the land. Their proprietary role involving how common people led their lives came lose asunder. While their hold on feudal ways had begun the dissolving process a century ago, the institution of Rata Sabhāwa, their mainstay to keep the social codes, became less and less important as more modern and stable statutory philosophies that professed a casteless and non-clannish humanity filled its void. People began to get comfortable and trusting with such ways more and more. Furthermore, people came face to face with the reality that the Rata Sabhāwa had run its course. To the casual observer, the end of Chieftain tradition may seem like a speck in the blue horizon of the history of Nuwarakalaviya. But closer look points to its momentousness and remarkable impact on the life and culture of the people in the province. As outlined earlier, often their avidity of the old ways cannot be missed when we get the opportunity to talk to villagers in rural communities where a host of anthropologists like Bryce Ryan, E. R. Leach, James Brow, M. U. A. Tennakoon, T. M. Madduma Bandara, Ukkubanda Karunananda and others embedded in the region also had the privilege to meet and write about them.

The depth of influence and usefulness of Rata Sabhāwa or Variga Sabhāwa of Nuwarakalaviya was so striking, it endured extended periods interspersed by marginal support of native Kings who often showed little or no interest in the tradition. This region found strength to continue it, nevertheless. After three centuries of indifferent and lukewarm interest of colonial rulers in the region lasting until the early decades of 20th century, their changing governing formula became a consuming threat to an age-old cultural institution. The result was that they wrote the swan song of the Rata Sabhāwa and Variga Sabhāwa and forced them into oblivion. There are signs that yearning for the old ways are getting a reexamination: M. U. A. Tennakoon had proposed (See page xviii) a type of rural Sabha called *"Ellanga Sabha,"* a concept based and using the resources that exist in and around the Tank Cascade Systems[1] in the Nuwarakalaviya and Tamankaduwa regions. It is not necessarily a judicial body, but a concept that encompasses all things Ellangawa-related involving multiple villages in a shared watercourse. This no doubt will give a broader role to the villagers in their affairs than occupants of a State House whose only visit to the village unctuously schemed, no less, is during an election cycle.

A new class of civil servants called DRO – Divisional Revenue Officers – took over the functions and prestige enjoyed by the Chiefs, but they lacked the authority or mandate under the colonial government or the social codes of the community to help continue the age-old traditions, including Rata Sabhāwa. DRO's functions did

---

[1] Madduma Bandara, 1985, pp. 99-113.

not require the continuation of most native traditions. This was a departure from the colonial attitude on native traditions agreed upon in Article 4 of the Kandyan Treaty 120 years earlier. The result was that the villagers began to feel what was once a concern becoming a reality which led them to take up arms in 1818. The colonial administration's goodwill that existed towards the ways they practiced waned as decades passed after the fall of Kandy.

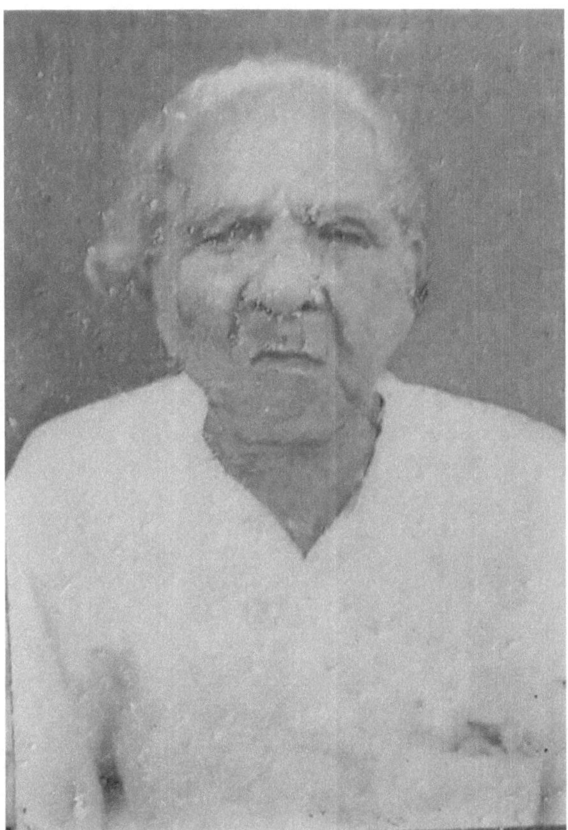

Fig. 48. Alittane Malhami Punchi Bandara Alittane Kōrāla, (1897-1976). Tirappane. Photo: Anula Kumarihamy Herath

With the disbanding of the feudal Chiefs, the concept of *Varige* and its seldom totemic functions began to suffer. With it, coupled with the existential influence of emerging economic, cultural, and political trends in the late 19th and early part of the 20th centuries, old institutions, including caste system an issue under the purview of the Rata Sabhāwa, fell out of favor. But its intrinsic value to the Nuwarakalaviya people was unmistakable as there are records of this fading tradition pulsating with little life still as late as 1945. Bryce Ryan (1953) found that the Variga Court was held a decade after it was disbanded while *Ratemahatvaru*, already retired, had blended into modern way of life including politics or government service (p. 250). Pieris (1956) noted that another Variga Sabhāwa was held in 1954 when the Chiefs were only a memory reminiscing about their past. At the end of this Sabhāwa, an 'outsider' was allowed into a *Varige* after paying a fine of Rs. 37.50 – equal to 150 *ridi* (p. 256 n76). This is not difficult to explain. Regardless of the Rata Sabhāwa not being a legal body anymore, the *mulādenivaru* who officiated it were still alive and well, and the good old days of Sabhāwa functions had not lost in the community memory, resorting to simpler ways acceptable to villagers to resolve issues was still inviting as a good investment than paying lawyers and going through the trouble of visiting a town miles away where the magistrate's court convened making the process no longer a community affair.

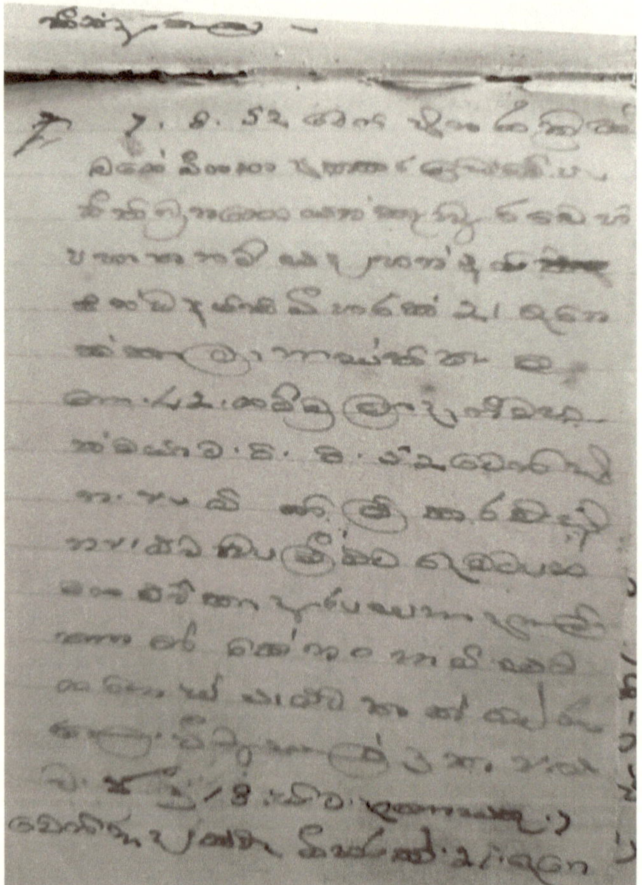

Fig. 49. Diary notes of Alittane Malhamy Punchi Bandara Kōrāla, August 7, 1952. Photo: Anula Kumarihamy.

It is possible the village elders who were once *mulādänivaru/kāriyakarawannō* themselves with past Rata Sabhā experience could have stepped forward to resolve conflicts involving old caste codes. As these instances were reported to anthropologists, I believe their interpreters, usually with urbanized background could have easily ascribed these gatherings incorrectly to a Rata Sabhāwa which, they believed had been somehow sanctioned still to be functional. Despite this seemingly startling oddity in the eyes of the scholars, the villagers, still fresh with memories of a good old system, had no misgivings about using the inexpensive, user-friendly, and time-honored practice to settle a dispute. In any case, these instances illustrate a nostalgic and fitting curtain call of the remarkable run of a truly traditional institution in Nuwarakalaviya.

But *Kōrāla*s who had participated in Rata Sabhāwa traditions until 1938 and living in retirement in later years continued to assist and record settlements (*sittu*) of disputes between villagers. Diary notes from Alittane Malhamy Punchi Bandara Kōrāla (1897-1976) (Fig. 48, 49) tells of a dispute of crop damage by a herd of 21 buffaloes belonging to a K. Nanhamy. Nanhamy must have been dealt with, but unfortunately Kōrāla's grandson told me that English translation of the text).

IDEOLOGIES INFUSION. Ideologies came to fill the vacuum created in the village after the demise of the old caste and feudatory systems, including the archaic institution of Rata Sabhāwa which thrived unchanged for centuries. The urban intellectuals and aspiring rulers found easy targets to manipulate in rural communities where, though, appeal for archaic culture was still strong. In places where once Kings and *Vannihuru* graced, politicians, some living in far away regions, walked in. But unlike the Kings and Chiefs, these individuals and their competing ranks invented catchphrases and pledged dogmas with beguiling phrases like *Dharmista Samajaya* (Righteous Society), socialist forms of community governing or chauvinistic social attributes or so-called potential 'Pacts' to govern by tinkering parliamentary principles, all of which in general acted like a pervasive haze across dissimilar caste and cultural landscape. For villagers whose inventory of memories filled with simplicity of Rata Sabhāwa, and now unaccustomed to the depths of unfamiliar rhetorical republicanism and party politics, the alternative presented in these governing approaches were unavoidably alien.

Villages dispersedly located in Nuwarakalaviya had been 'republics' of their own,[2] managing own affairs and co-existing with the neighboring villages. As Rata Sabhāwa faded and years passed, and as shown by sociologists in 80s and 90s, these small communities, not just in Nuwarakalaviya, but elsewhere as well drew urban intellectuals with political motivations and persuasions. They came armed with formulations that were less articulated but often confusing than what villagers and their ancestors were accustomed to.[3] One example is the hegemonic and nationalist ideologies introduced by these masterminds who were craving for power. Some were Western educated and beset with venal attributes. They all were aiming and appealing to a universally passionate human nature – the betterment of life. They induced it with dogmas with pulsing phrases like the 1956 Bandaranayake (S.W.R.D) '*Sanga, Veda, Guru, Govi, Kamkaru*' (monks, indigenous doctors, teachers, and workers) election manifesto or Chelvanayagam Pact acting as indomitable forces permeating across the village. The result of this novelty was the planting of seeds of political and ethnically based divisions, twice as destructive as caste-based co-existence. These divisions furthermore carried socially acrimonious undertones fueled also by micro-politics in small communities. This was evident unfettered so much so, a village of 25 families, all with kinship affiliations and housing compounds

---

[2] Pieris, R, 1956, p. 233; Brow, 1996, p. 39.

[3] For further reading on infusion of party politics into village, see James Brow, 1996, pp. 73-87.

sitting side by side, could easily separate into fractious groups delineated by partisan ideologies. Caste and ethnicity of pre-parliamentary Sri Lankan village did not have such divisive air, though. Politics was not something they were accustomed to. They existed harmoniously but diverse in caste and cultural practices.

As the political winds changed in post-colonial Sri Lanka, villagers found State resources to take advantage of, and ideas for how to compete for them to be very enticing. Soon, the burgeoning political ways and ideologies found a vehicle into the village through its residents' evolution of thinking which thus far had been well versed and content with the defunct Rata Sabhāwa system. Consequently, the seeds of partitive culture inherent in party politics came to life in the village and it effectively "made mockery of the image of the harmonious village community."[4]

But after its demise and through a generation later, its pennant of reputation – the general willingness of most of the participating villagers to accept its decisions without contesting them remained dear to all. Through decades, the spirit of Rata Sabhāwa or Variga Sabhāwa remained a dormant image in the community memory. An example of this was evident as noted in previous pages with the 70-year-old man in Horowpothana, four decades after Rata Sabhāwa ceased to function. During their contacts with villagers who wished for the old ways, officials saw embers of this spirit ready to light up in a moment's chance.[5]

In the first decades of 20th century when Kapuruhami Madukanda Ratemahattayā (1948) jotted down his extraordinary notes about Rata Sabhāwa, he prophesied about the would-be fate of this historic Nuwarakalaviya institution. He found traditions involving caste participation with this institution was falling short since late 1900s as Chieftains had no choice but line up ready to acquiesce British administrators more and more. Finding that the end of Rata Sabhāwa was imminently foreseeable, Kapuruhami Ratemahattayā wrote:

> "[…] the Chiefs who care but very little for the purity and fair administration of this Rata Sabhāwa system […]. The lack of sympathy and support is the main cause. Thus exposed, the time-honored Rata Sabhāwa system is bound to decay and disappear in the course of time." (pp. 42-68)

At long last, the Rata Sabhāwa came face to face with its inescapable destiny. The British colonial administration which would see its own final days perched on the horizon dissolved the Rata Sabhāwa in an indirect way by terminating the Sri Lanka's aristocratic order. But in the final summation, I have no other way to explain the vigor, the purpose and audacity of this institution it shared with the people of yesteryears maintaining the force that bound them together and stronger.

In its glory days, it was impossible to think of trading the Rata Sabhāwa with something else, even for a minute. In a world of myriad of cultures interconnected with touch of a screen on one's palms, it surely may be spurned now. Let us not

---

[4] Brow, 1996, p. 87.
[5] Gunasekara, 2004, p. 131.

forget that it was astonishingly a workable system at that time, and a social force, the Rata Sabhāwa of Nuwarakalaviya!

When we look at the portrait of the Rata Sabhāwa, we see a tradition of a time that held the social order of the people sailing through good times and bad times. It was the alternative for a land without written conventions of law. For someone unfamiliar with villages in pre-modern Nuwarakalaviya might think of its ancient Rata Sabhā tradition and customs as a pointillist painting – dots and strokes with no discernible meaning. But a keen observation from afar will show it as art blended to form a remarkable scene of moments in time we left behind.

It held together a people by verbal guidelines of feudal ways, the main purpose of which was to ensure heritable rights and privileges of all levels of the community maintain the status quo. It was not a perfect paragon of conflict resolution. But after a Rata Sabhāwa session, villagers went home happy and contented. I hope I made it easy for us now to see the forest of history of Nuwarakalaviya region through the trees of the social and traditional institutions, biggest of it in my mind – again, the Rata Sabhāwa of Nuwarakalaviya.

14. OFFENCES AND VIOLATIONS UNDER RATA SABHAWA

By K.A. Kapuruhami, Madukanda Ratemahattaya
(Later Dissava of Vavuniya Sinhala Pattuwa)

Partial Extract from Rata Sabhāwa. *Journal of Royal Asiatic Society (Ceylon)*, Vol. 38, No. 106, (1948). pp. 42-68.

OFFENCES THAT FALL WITHIN THE JURISDICTION OF A RATA SABHĀWA

****

... 1-13.

---

14. It takes cognizance of such offences as are calculated from a social point of view to be disgraceful acts.

The following is a short summary of them:

1. A woman eloping with a low caste man or a low-country Sinhalese whose status is not known.
2. A man or woman living with another of a low caste as husband and wife.
3. A woman having illicit connection with a low caste man openly.
4. A woman suspected of having illicit connection with a low caste man.
5. A woman conceiving having no legal or known husband.
6. Inter-marrying with persons of another *Varige*.
7. Contracting a marriage within the prohibited degrees or relationship.
8. Making a proposal by giving rise to a marriage within the prohibited degrees of relationship.
9. Having illegal connection with one who comes within the prohibited degrees of relationship.
10. Eating in the house of a low caste man food prepared by a low caste man or woman and in their cooking vessels.
11. Drinking water from a vessel used by a low caste man.
12. Doing menial service to or in the house of a low caste man.
13. Getting beaten by a low caste man.
14. Accusing a person of an offence which has been adjudicated upon and settled in a Rata Sabhāwa or by the Chief.
15. Associating with persons who have been banned temporarily or permanently in funeral and marriage ceremonies.

16 Doing services or acts which fall to the lot of low caste persons.

17 Practicing *huniyam* (හූනියම්) in its several branches [*sic*]

18 Accusing a person in the course of an altercation of offences calculated to be disgraceful which are clearly false and malicious and uttered at the impulse of the moment

19 Disregarding to do, at the biding of a Rata Sabhāwa such services (රාජකාරී) one is bound to do.

20 Failure to provide meals or provisions (අඩුක්කු පැහිදුම්) to the Rata Sabhāwa when it is one's turn (මුරපේරුව) to supply them and due notice has been given beforehand.

21 Irregularities occurring in the course of supplying meals or provisions.

22 Irregularities in preparing meals (අඩුක්කු).

23 Improper movements and acts done in the Rata Sabhāwa or using improper words and terms while talking.

24 Any act considered to be slighting the Rata Sabhāwa officers (in their official capacity) in receiving, accommodating, or feeding them.

25 Minor offences *i.e.* (අත්වැරදි) - offences by acts, offences by words (කට වැරදි) offences of eating, all committed through sheer ignorance and not willfully, and similar other offences.

---

(15) [- - -] Offences (19 to 25) apply in the case of Chiefs moving in the country with their retinue. These together with (18) can be inquired into by Chief alone without the aid of a Rata Sabhāwa and inflict fines which if not paid immediately restriction (a) mentioned below can be enforced but not (b).

Restrictions (banning): තහනම් දීම

(16). Anyone who commits or is suspected to have committed offences like those mentioned above is banned or kept apart temporarily till a Rata Sabhāwa inquires into the offence complained of. The restrictions put on the offender are of two kinds:

(a) **Banning participating in**: funerals(ඉලව්) and marriage (මඟුල්), ඉලව් මඟුල් තහනම් කිරීම. The other members of the offender's *Varige* are prohibited from admitting the offender to their funerals (ඉලව්) and marriage (මඟුල්) ceremonies or attending to such of his ceremonies themselves.

(2) By this restriction the members of the offender's *Varige* are not prohibited from going to his house, talking to him or rendering him any necessary assistance, or vice versa; but they are not to eat of him or give him to eat in their plates, etc. (තැටිපිඟාන). This is very strictly observed in funerals and marriage ceremonies. No one should eat at his funerals feasts (ඉලව් බත) or marriage feasts (මඟුල් බත) nor admit him to such ceremonies of theirs.

(b) The *dhoby* is prohibited from washing his clothes and doing the usual service at his funerals and marriages. This is called තොවිල් තහනම් කරණවා.

(2) (*sic*). At the present day, තොවිල් තහනම් කිරීම is taken to be the prohibiting of the *dhobi* only from doing the usual services. No notice is taken of the other four castes: mostly because an ordinary villager has very little need of the services of these, and therefore their presence is also not considered to be necessary at the Rata Sabhāwa. But of course, it is understood that a banned person cannot command the services of any of these low castes, e.g., a *kadaya* will never take a *kada* (කඩ) for a banned person.

(3) The apparent reason for excluding these from the Rata Sabhāwa appears to be that the free service system having long been discontinued, the low caste people, except the dhobi whose services are indispensable, have neglected to render the services they were bound to do for the *Rate áttō* who not being very much in need of such services, as payment on hand provides them now-a-days with all that they want, did not insist on exacting such services thinking it less troublesome and expensive.

(17). Restrictions (a) and (b) are enforced only when the offence committed is of a grave nature such as offences (1) to (7). When the offence is not a serious one, restrictions (a) and (b) will not and cannot be enforced; but only (a). In such offences (18) to (25), restriction (a) is enforced only in case the offender refuses or neglects to pay the fine [*sic*].

APPENDIX – A

Kapuruhami Madukanda Maha Dissava[1]
Poet & the Pioneer Ethnographer of Nuwarakalaviya

*J*n 2016, when I was searching for literature for a chapter on Rata Sabhāwa for a proposed book project, one name popped up over and over as the primary source of reference on the subject looked for by nearly everyone who had interest in it in the 20th century. It was a little-known name, Subasingha Kapurubandara Kapuruhami Ratemahattayā of Madukanda, a village on Horowpothana road, about seven kilometers east of Vavuniya in Northern Province.

Fig. 50. Madukanda Maha Dissava (seated) and his son (*Ratemahattayā*). Photo: Madukanda Family Archives.

It was the seat of northern-most Kandyan aristocratic district in Sri Lanka during colonial times. The colonial government endowed him as the Dissava of Sinhala Pattuwa of Northern Province later in his life.

NOTES

[1] Adapted from Tillakaratne, Lokubanda, *Daily Mirror*, Sri Lanka, February 15, 2017.

As this aristocrat's writings had contributed mightily to the knowledge of Rata Sabhāwa, once an important social and judicial institution in Sri Lanka, I felt it was imperative on me to search for more information to get a broader understanding of him and his work. Therefore, I called Madukanda Post Office one day hoping to find out whether relatives of this man still live there. The postmistress Kumarihamy's answer to me had never been more exciting: Yes, the 5th generation direct descendants of this aristocratic son of the village are still living in his ancestral home!

Little had been written or known about him outside his district. Unlike some of his peers, he was not much into politics, a common way to get yourself known. There is no evidence that he owned excessive feudal land holdings. Alternatively, was he not fawning enough to the colonial powers or even with gravitas fit for a *Dissava* did he choose to remain low key? But the crux of what I expected to delve into was not an attempt to compliment the feudalism he represented. What drew my attention was his efforts to unfurl this archaic culture in contemporary Nuwarakalaviya, and to see it through his widely read and referenced scholarly work, the *Rata Sabhāwa*.

Fig. 51. Madukanda Maha Walawwa Looking out from the inside.
Photo: Niranjala Tillakaratne

Sometime between 1910 and 1930s Madukanda Dissava wrote his authoritative disquisition on Rata Sabhāwa, the arcane rural judicial system that had been in practice in Nuwarakalaviya and some parts of Matale and Kurunegala districts up to 1930s and 40s. Until then, no comprehensive study had been done detailing how it operated. It existed based purely on oral traditions and longstanding customs under the guidance and supervision of *Ratemahattayā* of a district or *Dissava* in a province. It existed independent of the King's quaint systems of law or colonial judicial structure in force at the time.

In scholarly circles all over the world, this article became the *opus* on Rata Sabhāwa. Also, the eclectic ensemble of 32 unassuming village elders who contributed to the SSS deserve equal credit for describing various regional practices and traditions, including Rata Sabhāwa, unknown to many outside of

Nuwarakalaviya. But many admit that Madukanda Dissava's remarkable scholarly work on this tradition went above and beyond in breadth and context.

The thesis on Rata Sabhāwa is only a part of *Dissava*'s collection of compositions. A palm leaf book of encomium to parents written by him in 1891 and the elegiac poems he wrote for his wife Giranga following her death during childbirth confirm him not just a scholar, but a poet capturing the depth of human despair. These poems are called *Madukande Gedara Kavi*, widely read in villages in Nuwarakalaviya. I remember well my mother often reciting these heartbreaking poems to me. I was fortunate to get these poems (unpublished) from P.B. "Chutta" Senevirathna of Maradankalla who wrote them to me by rote. They give us a glimpse of his silent but erudite presence in the scarcely known literary and social marrow of this area. His dear-to-heart writings must be construed as products not so much as just hobbies or pastimes, but luminous contributions to ethnographic landscape in Sri Lanka. However, he lived without receiving accolades he rightfully deserved for his corpus of literary and community work.

Fig. 52. Madukanda Kuda Walawwa. Photo: Niranjala Tillakaratne

Although his education had been in English, the *Dissava*'s prose have been in Sinhala. While he was creating poetry volumes and remarkable essays, according to contemporary written accounts (Ievers 1899), some of his peers could hardly read or write their name in Sinhala (p. 70), aptly illustrating his extraordinary and broad learnedness.

His granddaughter Nanda Kumari Mahadivulwewa Wijeratne told me that Madukanda Dissava was born at Madukanda early in the last quarter of the 19th century. He attended St. John's College, Jaffna. Schools like this in Jaffna were the traditional choice for boys of well to do families in Raja Rata in 19th and early 20th centuries. After he returned home, he inherited the title of *Ratemahattayā* of Madukanda, as was the custom then. He took up residence at Maha Walawwa (Fig. 17, 51). Later, when colonial government appointed him as *Maha Dissava*, his son

Ukkubanda Madukanda inherited the title of *Ratemahattayā* and took up residence at Kuda Walawwa next door (Fig. 52). Dissava died in 1943.

He presided over an area rich with antiquities and legends. Stone walls, stone steps, guardian stones and other lithic structures scattered in the Madukanda temple grounds lend credence to its link to a distant past. Madukanda village received the Sacred Tooth Relic while it was on its way from India to Anuradhapura.[2] The village temple received the Relic and deposited it for a while in a chamber (*Maduwa*) flanked with double-walls designed to generate climate-control effects. A ditch between these walls carried water to cool and circulate air in and out of the room with intermittent openings on the inner wall.

Inscriptions on the rocky outcrop named Thonigala (Dhonigala?) located not far from this village (not to be confused with Thonigala inscriptions near Anamaduwa in Northwestern Province), takes us to the textual past of this area. Ven. Kirigollawe Wimalasara Thero (Madukande Hamuduruwo) in the temple and a specialist in rock inscriptions said that it is a memo about, among other things, bartering and banking believed to be the first of its kind in the country. During the height of the armed conflict with Tamil Tigers terrorist group in the last decades of the 20th century and continued to early decades of the 21st, residents in the area took extraordinary steps to protect the inscriptions from destruction by terrorist activities. For obvious reasons, I am obliged not to discuss these steps.

Usually, Sri Lankan monarchs or their colonial equals in the littoral ennobled indigenous individuals to overlordships at their pleasure and demarcated their respective aristocracies in *Thombos*, Deeds of Grant, *Sannas* or other forms of proclamations. Descendants of these noblemen inherited the title as well as the district as a sure birthright.

But as of 1810, there was no Chief in Madukanda village and surrounding area. Notwithstanding the Madukanda legends described above, its location shrouded in a sylvan landscape occupying the farthest fringes of Kandyan kingdom and colonial territories seemed to have generated no interest in contemporary rulers to declare it as an aristocratic constituency. But villagers had other ideas to get their own seat of aristocracy. In an earlier page, I discussed how they got their Mudliyar, a title in British-controlled districts on par with *Ratemahattayā* in Nuwarakalaviya.

The Court House where Rata Sabhā sessions convened as described earlier, still stands abreast the main compound of the Kuda Walawwa (Fig. 52). Both residences show architecture intrinsic to manor houses of the time. Unfluted square columns with simple entablatures guard the ornate entryways. Steps to the porch have masonry simulating *korawak* stones like those found flanking doorways in ancient buildings. They show attempts to emulate ancient stonework entrances to large building compounds. The long hallways crisscrossing the interior of the house and crenellations atop the walls dividing inner rooms are a feature no doubt designed for efficient air circulation – a must for a residence in a hot climate. A collage of photos of the *Dissava* adorns the long sitting room. Some photos are

---

[2] Lewis, J.P. (1894). Archaeology of Wanni, *The Journal of the Ceylon Branch of the Royal Asiatic Society of Great Britain & Ireland*, Vol. 13, No. 45 (1894), pp. 151-178.

frazzled with age. But the glitter of his four-corner hat, fluffy upper jacket, cylindrical eyeglasses, and the trouser wrapped with a frilled silvery fabric that can fence a mid-sized paddy field are unmistakably fitting display of elegance of this Chief, an extraordinary writer.

Besides the formality of her grandfather's ducal-cum-scholarly mien, Nanda Kumari Mahadivulweva Wijeratne remembers her mother saying that Maha Dissava was an avid landscaper. Horticulture must have been in the veins of the area back then too, as there are records of an experimental botanical garden started by the British in 1891 in nearby Vavuniya town. Maha Dissava built three wells on the property and added a sophisticated irrigation system as a solution to scarce water resources in the area. Living proof of his gardening activities is still visible. A visitor need not look beyond the verdant grove of aged fruit trees to see faint paint of fact that Maha Dissava was indeed a dedicated and assiduous gardener. Two 30-feet tall Madu trees (*Cycas Zeylanicus*), stand strategically on both sides of the gate-towers like two diligent sentinels still welcoming visitors to the renowned glory of the house. Madu tree must have been a feature in the area, so much so, the *Maduwa* to deposit the Tooth Relic once long time ago; abundance of Madu trees on the rocky outcrop Thonigala near the spillway of the village tank; and the name of the aristocratic district Madukanda, all have one common descriptor – alliterated sound of the word "Madu."

Fig. 53. A partial collection of regalia of Madukanda Maha Dissava. Family Archive. Photo: Niranjala Tillakaratne.

Finally, a former principal of the Madukanda School, Mr. R. B. Dissanayaka gave me a hint of a man bent on education advancement of his district. There is an entry in the school logbook made by Dissava for the birthday of King George VI. It highlights the day's celebrations and the importance of education. *Dissava* asks the students to study hard and keep the schoolyard and classroom well swept and clean. Such was the meticulous and exemplary life of one of the great poets, legal scholars, and a community leader in the country of Nuwarakalaviya.

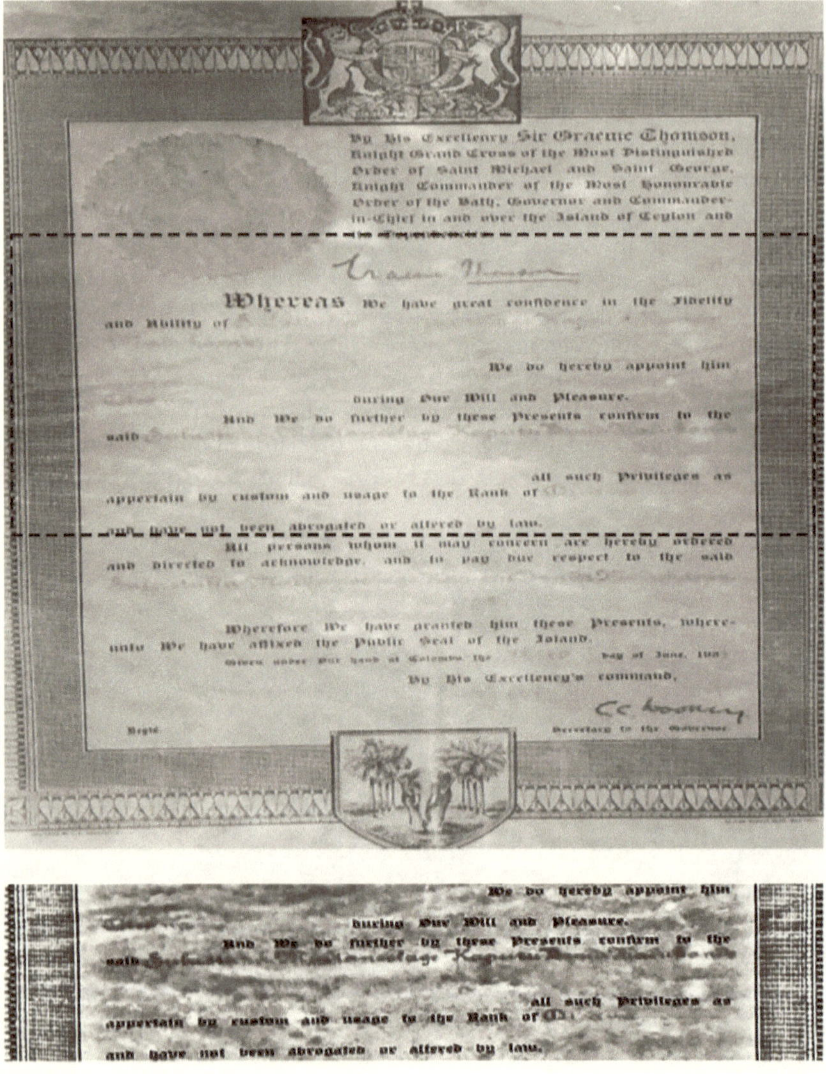

Fig. 54. Grant Deed of Title of *Dissava* to Subasinghe Mudiyanselage Kapurubandara Kapuruhami Madukanda Dissava issued By Governor Graeme Thomson. Handwritten text is barely visible. The rectangle marked with dash lines is magnified below showing the details. Photo: Nanda Kumari Mahadivulwewa Wijeratne, from the family archives. Enhanced image and transcription by Niranjala Tillakaratne.

Deed of Title of Dissava granted to Subasinghe Mudiyanselage Kapurubandara Madukanda Dissava

By His Excellency Sir Graeme Thomson, Knight Grand Cross of the Most Distinguished Order of Saint Michael, and Saint George. Knight Commander of the Honorable Order of the Bath. Governor and Commander-in-Chief in and over the Island of Ceylon and its Dependencies.

Graeme Thomson

WHEREAS We have great confidence in the Fidelity and Ability of

Subasinghe Mudiyanselage Kapuru Bandara Madukanda.

We do hereby appoint him *Dissava* during Our Will and Pleasure. And We do further by these presents confirm to the said

Subasinghe Mudiyanselage Kapuru Bandara Madukanda

all such Privileges as appertain by custom and usage to the Rank of *Dissava* and have not been abrogated or altered by law.

All persons whom it may concern are hereby ordered and directed to acknowledge and to pay due respect to the said

Subasinghe Mudiyanselage Kapuru Bandara Madukanda.

Wherefore We have granted him these Presents Whereunto We have affixed the Public Seal of the Island.

Written under Our hand in Colombo 14. Third day of June 1933.

By His Excellency's Command.
Signed: Illegible
Secretary to the Governor

APPENDIX – B

Once Upon a Time – Ulagalla Walawwa
Adapted from Sanath Panabokke

This is a short account of the Nikawewa family in Nuwarakalaviya and the advent of the Panabokke clan to Rajarata.

Ulagalla, the seat of the Nikawewa family, is a small village 2 kilometers east of the nondescript town of Tirappane on A9 highway. From historic times, lands where its walawwa occupied were owned by this family which produced many Chieftains in Nuwarakalaviya. Usually, under normal circumstances, father to son continuum of Chieftain succession remained through the years. The area of their rule is said to extend from Ulagalla to Padaviya tank, with Ulagalla as the seat of government where the residence of the Chief was. Thus, the walawwa was the place where the local laws were laid down as customs and traditions.

Through the years, although taking care of the matters of the area in just and fair manner continued, the Nikawewa family began to reduce in size. By around the 1870s, the family had only one child of marriageable age. That too was a girl. Thus, the end of the Nikawewa dynasty was lurking on the horizon. She was known by the name Nikawewa Anula Kumarihamy. She was home-schooled by leading scholars as there were no schools in the area then.[1] She quickly became a well-read student. The marriage of Anula Kumarihamy took precedence in the matters of the Nikawewa Chieftain and his wife. Emissaries were sent out but finding an eligible partner proved difficult.

Once upon a time, travelling in this area was by bullock carts and palanquins. Then one day there came to pass through this area of the Nikawewa charge an aristocratic family from Kandy on their way to Anuradhapura on a pilgrimage. As would be expected, their retinue was large. Unfortunately, or fortunately, whilst passing Tirappane, a sleepy bazaar on a clay road colonial government called Migrant Highway which evolved as the present day A9 route, one family member fell ill. This predicament interrupted the travelers' journey onward, and they had to find a comfortable and compatible place to stop till the patient recovered. On inquiring around they were told of the Ulagalla Walawwa, a kilometer off the bazaar.

The walawwa was approached and the Nikawewa Chief at once agreed to have the family stay till the patient got well. The visitors from Kandy were of the Panabokke clan, a well-known Kandyan Chieftain family. This is the first recorded visit of the Panabokke clan to the Rajarata. What followed next seems to indicate the interruption of the trip was pre-destined!

As luck would have it there was a young man in the Panabokke family who found the enchanting and pretty Anula Kumarihamy attractive. The elders of both

---

NOTES

[1] Nearest school at Tirappane was started in 1886.

families conferred, and a marriage was arranged. Consequently, the young Panabokke, Kuda Banda Panabokke by name, became the Chieftain of the Nikawewa dynasty ably assisted by Anula Kumarihamy. At the time of their marriage, they were residing in the old walawwa. That too was a sprawling structure with court houses and other residential structures for the house staff. But in time, this building proved inadequate for the demands of Panabokke's duties. So, the present building was planned and constructed in around 1885. All construction material and workmanship were supplied by the people of the villagers owned by the family. The legend has it that the lime for the building was brought from Matale in the Kandy district. This entailed much travelling as the distance was far and the mode of transportation was the cart. The old walawwa regrettably is no more.

Panabokke held Court in his new walawwa (Fig. 10). His travels to outlying areas were done on horseback, bullock cart and sometimes on elephants. Unfortunately, he died at the young age of 48 leaving Anula Kumarihamy and 6 children. Of the 6 children, only one boy and 2 girls survived. The two girls married into the Bulankulame and Poholiyadda families. The boy married into the Rambukwella family from Kandy after completing his post graduate studies at Cambridge University. Anula Kumarihamy lived at the walawwa with the surviving son's family till a ripe old age. She passed to the great beyond in 1957.

APPENDIX – C

Mulādänivaru contributing to 1932 *Sinhala Sirith Sangrahaya*

1. R.K. Tillakaratne Mohotti[1]   Kahatagasdigiliya
2. T.B. Ekanayake   Kekirawa
3. D.B. Rajakaruna, Indigenous Doctor   Kekatiyagollewa
4. S.B. Ratwatte Kōrāla   Kalaweva
5. Baddarāla Appuhamy   Gonuhendanawa
6. M.P. Bandara, Former Kōrāla   Habadivulwewa
7. Kapurāla Baddarāla   Udadutuwewa
8. Ukkurāla Baddarāla   Welimuwapothana
9. Sadhatissa Upasaka   Ihala Hammillewa
10. R. Mudiyanse   Manewa
11. Vannihamy Vel Vidāne   Galmaduwe
12. R.S.B. Herathhamy Vedarāla   Mahakumbukgollewa
13. N.B. Senarathna Mohottāla   Welimuwapothana
14. Punchiappu Lékama   Diganhammillewa
15. U.B. Kanakaratna former Kōrāla   Mahapothana Konwewa
16. Disanayake Wijesundara Banda   Walaswewa
17. P.M. Banda   Kadiragama
18. B.M.U. Sriwardena   Kebitigollewa
19. Wijesinghe Kirinaidurāla Mohottāla   Galmaduwagama
20. P.B. Awusadhahamy   Meewamalwewa
21. Punchiappularage Pinhamy   Nelugollekada
22. H.M.K. Mohottāla Kōrale Lékama   Horowpothana
23. Ilangasinghe Kalubanda Vel Vidāne   Sivalakulama
24. D.M.L. Banda   Madatugama
25. Ukkurāla Baddarāla   Panwella
26. Wijeratne Mohottāla   Galkadawala
27. Senevirathna Banda Vel Vidāne[2]   Maradankadawala
28. Velathe Lékama Kapuruhami Gamarāla   Pandarellawa
29. Senevirathna Appuhamy   Nochchikulama
30. P. Ukkubanda   Timbiriwewa
31. B.S. Appuhamy Vel Vidāne   Mahawewa
32. A.M. Kandappu   Kahatagasdigiliya

NOTES

[1] Winner of Rs. 50 first prize for the best essay submission.

[2] Writer's great-grandfather. He was later the Kálä Kōrāla of forest resources of Kanadarā Kōrale. Name of this village was changed as Maradankalla in 1956 (see page 35).

APPENDIX – D

Dress of Maha Vanniyā as described in *Sinhala Sirith Sangrahaya*.[1]

රන් නූලෙන් විසිතුරු කොට මසන ලඳල ක්‍රමයෙන් උස් වූල මුදුනෙහි මල් ගසන ආකාර දක්වන මැණික් ඔබ්බවා රන්කමින් නිමකළ කොතකින් ද, අලංකාරවත් වූ තොප්පියක් ද, හිස පලඳින ලදි. රන් කවනියෙන් සැදූ ජැකැට්ටුව, අත්කොට හැට්ටය ද, යටට අඳින කංචුකයක් හෙවත් බැනියමක් ද, තුප්පොට්ටිය යටින් ඇඳීමට ජංසා දෙසට රැලිකොට මසන ලද කලිසමක් ද, රන් කවනි තුප්පොට්ටියක් ද, සුදු තොප්පොට්ටි තුනක් ද, සුදු රෙදියෙන් මසන ලද පටි දෙකක් හා රන් නූලෙන් අලංකාර කොට විල්ලුද වස්තුවලින් මැණික් ගල් අතරට ඔබ්බවා සාදන ලද පටියක් ද, කර පලඳින රන් මාලපටක් ඒ තුමාගේ මුළු ඇඳුමෙහි කොටස් විය. එසේ ම විල්ලුද බහා රන් නූලෙන් මසන ලද පා වැසුම් ද විය.

ඒ තුමාගේ සාමාන්‍ය ඇඳුම නම් සුදු තොප්පොට්ටිය යට බැනියම සහිත සුදු හැට්ටය පසුමුල් තොප්පිය පා වැස්ම හා සැරමිටිය විය. උන්තැනේගේ චාන් ඇඳුම සුදු රෙද්දක් හා බැනියමක් ද කරවට ලන පට වස්ත්‍රයක් ද විය [*sic*].

NOTES

[1] Hettiarachchi, D. E., ed. 2019, p. 194.

APPENDIX – E

Hurulu Pattuwa and Hurulle of Morakewa

*A*ccording to the family folklore and history provided to me by Themiya Loku Bandara Hurulle, grandson of the last *Ratemahattayā* of Hurulu Pattuwa, this family descends from a line of Chiefs that ruled the Hurulu Palatha (Knox in 1681 called it *Hourly*). According to the folklore in the area, the Hurulu Pattuwa name is associated with the Mahasen lore. The area these Chiefs controlled is nearly half of the expansive stretch of the forested country of Nuwarakalaviya. In general, boundary lines of the Hurulu Pattuwa connect Hurulu Wewa in the South, Kantale wewa in the East, Padaviya Wewa in the North and Mahakanadarāwa Wewa in the West. Yan Oya, 140 kilometers long and the primary water source for the eastern half of the North Central Province, flows through it. As the name suggests, this district was anchored by Hurulu Wewa built by King Mahasen (274-301). He is credited as the builder of 16 major irrigation tanks which won him the moniker *Hath Rajjuruwo* (the Seven King).[1]

Hurulle family not only had the caretaker role of Hurulu Wewa, but the responsibility as the default head of the Rata Sabhāwa tradition in the Hurulu Pattuwa. In accordance with the same traditions related to major irrigation tanks in Sri Lanka, The Padaviya Wewa in the northern border of Hurulu Pattuwa has had a namesake Chief who was an ancestor of the Hurulle of Morakewa family. His name is Padaviya Mudiyanse Vanni Unnehe. Bertolocci (1817) quoted Bournand, an officer of the Dutch government in Sri Lanka as saying around 1789 that there were two "Wanniships of *Soerlie* (Hurulle) and *Nogerie* (Nuwaragam)."[2] Thus, I suggest Nuwarawawe Vanniya and Hurulle Vanniya had the full control of the Nuwarakalaviya through at least few centuries before its pre-modern history.

By examining the style of stone-blocks that are part of the sluice of the Morakewa tank and just below it the strategically planted large mee trees at the gate to the walawwa in the Hurulle of Morakewa family estate, it appears the family may have had some presence or habitation in the area running back to the beginning of medieval times. This family had a residence near Hurlu Dewale or on a location below the Hurulu Wewa tank bund in Hurulle, the community where the Wewa is located about 40 kilometers south of Morakewa. The family moved to the current location on Anuradhapura-Trincomalee Road sometime in the 19th century (Fig. 14-16). It is possible that this move must have been begun because of the family having ancestral lands in Morakewa, easy road access to Anuradhapura where the Sri Maha Bodhi Tree was located and Maha Vanniyā lived.

The Hurulle of Morakewa family archives have written information from 10 generations back, i.e., before the year 1600. Granted, if I may go forensic, the flora in the property is impressive, abundant and with large canopies, I believe that some

NOTES

[1] Parker, p. 158.

[2] Cited in Bertolacci, 1817, p. 64.

of them, i.e., the mee trees must be old at least for a couple of centuries. They also suggest that owners must have had fabulous taste of inviting landscape design ideas.[3]

The walawwa, a Victorian architectural classic in Nuwarakalaviya is believed to have been built in the 19th century. Some of its furniture, and building materials were brought over from India. In the debris field of the burn out walawwa I saw a roof tile from the house embossed as '*1865*' probably the year of manufacture. As there was no known *rata-ulu* factory in Sri Lanka at that time, this suggests that some building materials were imported from the Indian subcontinent for construction of the house.

Fig. 55. Henerath Bandara Hurulle c 1901, Vanni Mudiyanse (*Ratemahattayā*) of Hurulu Pattuwa

The classic arched entryway, and an all-embracing wide corridor supported by 18-inch-a-side columns with square capitals, and 20-feet tall ceiling in the living room are examples of a lifestyle of ages gone by. These walls and columns must have witnessed gamboling children playing hide and seek whispering to each other, and adults sitting on armchairs in relaxed conversations watching bullock carts laboring past on the unpaved road in front of the house. Although the house and the culture of politics it belonged to were different from today's more egalitarian social basics, we should not forget that it was once the much-loved home of a family and link to their storied ancestry.

---

[3] *Mee*, like *palu, buruta, teak* and *ehatu,* is a hard wood tree native to dry zone of Sri Lanka and parts of South India. Villagers are reluctant to cut it for timber because of valued products extracted from it for medicinal purposes: mee-oil from its seed, and mee-honey from flowers. Indigenous medicinal applications use these widely.

Sadly, though, The Walawwa with its furniture, historic artifacts and documents were destroyed in 1988 when the inglorious and violent political culture pervasive since early second half of the 20th century descended upon it. Thugs blinded with hatred following the indoctrination of repulsive political agendas set the house on fire. In doing so, they desecrated an architectural treasure of Nuwarakalaviya and wiped out a piece of its history. Themiya L. B. Hurulle shared with me a photo of the house as it looked before the destruction (Fig. 14). Except the colonial governments' loathsome destruction of homes[4] in early 19th century,[5] I cannot find evidence of another instance of political savagery directed at an ancient home like Morakewa in recent Sri Lanka.

The Morakewa area represents the bucolic beauty and quiet dignity characteristic of Raja Rata which the Nuwarakalaviya was a part of. The late patriarch of the family, E. L. B. Hurulle, fondly known in the area as 'Hurulle Unnehe,' served as a Member of the Parliament for Horowpothana since 1956. He was a cabinet minister for a long time, a well-loved person by its people and deeply attached to his native province. There is no better way to demonstrate this than the 1956 general election when he entered politics from Horowpothana constituency. It was an inflective election in the post-colonial Sri Lanka. At the monumental election that year which introduced dynastic political culture ushering Bandaranayakes, out of the 95 electoral districts in the parliament, UNP suffered a stunningly crushing defeat. E. L. B. Hurulle was one of the eight contestants standing with the victory sign!

As discussed earlier, Hurulle *Ratemahattayā* was one of the three Ratamahattayas participating with a bevy of others in selection process of Atamasthānadhipathi of Anuradhapura, the priestly head of the eight preeminent places of Buddhist worship in Nuwarakalaviya.[6]

During a speech given in 1983 on the opening of the Kukulawa Samādhigama, a village built in Horowpothana electorate under the Udāgama concept, E. L. B. Hurulle, MP, told the crowd about his family's association with the community of Kukulawa. He said that the family had been in the province for a long time. For centuries, Hurulle of Morakewa family had provided Kukulawa folks with comfort, and refuge.[7] It was an apt and succinct description of the Morakewa affiliation with larger Hurulu Palatha.

---

[4] Soldiers of the Colonial government burned the walawwa of Nugaliyadda Muhandiram in 1818 after he was accused of participating in the Kandyan War (Judicial Commissioner 16th and 25th November 1820, cited in Lawrie, 1898, Vol. II, p. 649).

[5] Recently homes of politicians were set on fire during public protests.

[6] Centuries before, this committee consisted of the Maha Vanniyā, and on behalf of the people of Nuwarakalaviya, three *Ratemahatvaru* and 17 *Kōrālas* (Ievers, 1899. P. 42). Chief Priests of Malwatte and Asgiriya Chapters seem to have entered the selection process only during the colonial times. Prior to the government's entry into this process, in Kings' times, it is hard to believe a Chief Monk (usually of old age) in Kandy would take a dangerous road trip to participate in the selection process in Anuradhapura, a city known as insalubrious, and disconnected from Kandy.

[7] Brow, 1996, p. 104.

GENEALOGY NOTES

The following is a concise genealogy chart of Hurulle of Morakewa family up to 10th generation provided to me by Themiya L. B. Hurulle.

1   – Henerath Bandara.[8]

2   – Padaviya Mudiyanse Vanni Unnehe.

3   – Hurulle Loku Mudiyanse (Hurulu Hat Pattuwe Vanni Unnehe 1833 AD).

4   – Hurulle Kuda Mudiyanse.

5   – Hurulle Loku Bandara (c 1820/24).

6   – Hurulle Tikiri Bandara Kōrāla.

7   – Ilangasinghe Kalukumara Raja Singhe Henarath Bandara Hurulle *Ratemahattayā* (1901 AD). In 1908, he was appointed as one of the three Ratemahatvaru representing Nuwarakalaviya people and Chairman of the Atamasthāna Committee under the Buddhist Temple Temporalities Act (Fig. 55).

8   – Tikiri Bandara Hurulle *Ratemahattayā* (The last Chief in Hurulu Pattuwa as of 1935). Colonial government ends the Old Chiefdom Tradition in 1938) (Fig. 56).

9   – Edwin Loku Bandara Hurulle, M.P. (held A series of government cabinet portfolios.

10   – I.   Sarasvati Maya (Hurulle) Madawala.

           – II.   Sakuntala Deepthi (Hurulle) Dunuwille.

           – III.   Themiya Loku Bandara Hurulle, M.P. Held post of the Minister of Science & Technology.

           – IV.   Vajira Kumara Hurulle.

           – V.   Kanishka Arjun Shanaka Hurulle.

---

[8] Seven Vanni Bandaras landed in Jaffna or Mutu Varaya in Northwest coast during King Maha Sen (274-301 AD). They were sons of a King Bodhi Mallawa in Mallawa Rata in India escaping the harassments of the King who replaced their father. For two of them, Kumara Bandara and Gunasobhana Henerath Bandara, he bestowed Manankattiya in Hurulu Palatha. Hurulle of Morakewa and Nikawewa Ulagalla families descend from the latter (Ievers, 1899, p. 92; *SSS*, p. 35-37).

Fig. 56. Tikiri Bandara Hurulle *Ratemahattayā* and Alice Bulankulame Hurulle Kumarihamy with son c 1916.   Photo: Themiya L. B. Hurulle.

APPENDIX – F

Nuwaraweva Bulankulame Family

Since the pre-colonial times, head of the Nuwarawawe family held the title of Maha Vanniyā, Chief of all *Vannivaru* (Vanni Mudiyanse, Vanni Bandara) and *Ratemahatvaru* in Nuwarakalaviya and adjacent Vanni areas. The preamble to an unpublished family document called 'family constitution' (c 2014) shared by Bulankulame and Nuwarawawe clan members shows that they were concerned that if a unified front by them who are linked with a common heritage and generations of kinships was not formed, some traditional rights, prestige, and privileges dear to them involving the Atamasthāna could be jeopardized by the agency of 'non-national' sources.[1] What is 'non-national' is not defined in this 'constitution.' Following a parley and a feast, the two families declared 'we are one' from thenceforth and assented collectively. This development has not yet fully permeated into community perception in the region. It is not known whether this document has been deposited as a public record in some form.

I believe this concern of the families was based on the current political and State behavior where its unpredictable and moving variables can encroach and dilute the standing of Nuwarawawe Bulankulame's association with the Sacred Bodhi Tree, chief of the committee that selects the *Atamasthānādhipathi*,[2] and other social perks. Presently, the statutory authority of the State legislation concerning any religious institution, e.g., the Buddhist Temporalities Act, already in the books in force since the first half of 19th century and its later manifestations have taken larger role in the affairs of the Bodhi Tree. Government's involvement increased by wielding considerable influence manifestly on par with the traditional roles of the two other factions, the Chief Incumbent of Atamasthāna and the Nuwarawawe Bulankulame. However, ordinary devotees who visit the Atamasthāna have no concerns about such changes since it is a priory that the Sacred Bodhi Tree and Atamasthāna belong to the heritage of the people and not one person or a family.

This family claims its primogeniture to guardians who accompanied the Bodhi Tree to the island (c 267 BC). It is one of the most prominent and oldest Buddhist icons in Sri Lanka. Oral, folkloric, and cultural traditions in the region bear witness to the historic relationship of Nuwarawawe Bulankulame family with the Sri Maha Bodhi Tree and Udamaluwa (upper sanctum of the Bodhi complex). It is recorded in *Dipawamsa* that eight princes accompanied the Sri Maha Bodhi Tree as Bodhi Guards of warrior clans during King Devanmpiyatissa's reign.[3] Two of these princes, Bodhigutta (Guardian of the Sacred Bodhi Tree), also named as Bohotta in

---

NOTES

[1] Ravana (Ravi) Wijeyeratne shared a copy of this document with me.

[2] In early days, this committee consisted of the Maha Vanniyā and the people of Nuwarakalaviya who were represented by three *Ratemahatvaru*, and 17 *Kōrālas* (Ievers, 1899. P. 42).

[3] Oldenberg, 1879, 2001, p. 195.

Kada-im Poth, and Sumitta, and host of other Brahmana Rālas (nobles called *Mudalihuru*)[4] and commoners of 18 castes too were part of this entourage. King Devanmpiyatissa appointed Bodhigutta and Sumitta to supervise wards in the purlieu of Anuradhapura city – Nuwarawawe (perhaps two of the four suburbs created by his grandfather, King Pandukabhaya) stated in *Mahawansa*).[5] Bodhigutta was called *lakmahalena* and Sumitta was called *jayamahalena* (Chief Secretary for War).[6] The two princes were also entrusted with administering the people of 18 castes.[7] Nuwarawawe Bulankulame family claims that its role as custodianship of the Sacred Bodhi Tree is inherited from the time of Bodhigutta.

Ryan (1953) notes that, "Nominally they (*Vanniya*s) are feudal aristocracy tracing their descent from the royal overlords of the region during the period in which the area was a no man's land between Sinhalese and Tamil invaders (p. 243)." At some point in history, role of Nuwarawawe Bulankulame families expanded to include the selection process of Anunāyake of Atamasthāna, the head of the Eight Holy Places in Anuradhapura. Accordingly, Nuwarawawe Bulankulame family holds unique position like no other, in that it is the only family in Sri Lanka that has the distinction of being the traditional caretaker tenure of a prominent religious establishment retained unbroken for centuries.

According to Lawrie (1896) Ayittaliyadda, Nuwarakalaviya Dissava in 1824, and Nuwarawawe Bulankulame family are known to each other with family connections. *Dissava*'s grandfather Ayittaliyadda Muhandiram of Henepola went to Siam in 1750 and again in 1753 at the urging of Weliwita Saranankara Sangharaja and King Kirthi Sri Rajasinghe (1747-1782) to bring *upasampada* (Buddhist higher ordination) to Sri Lanka. Ayittaliyadda Dissava's great-grandfather was Owille Dissanayake Nilame of Kohonsiya Pattuwa, Matale (p. 343). A century ago, naming conventions of higher caste families usually followed the tradition that along the family line a person was named after the village of origin of the common primogeniture. This practice remained the same along the family line regardless of how many sub-divisions later generations added. Following this premise, Ayittaliyadda Dissava and Owille Kumarihamy, widow of *Maha Vanniya*, c 1872, may be linked to a common ancestor, perhaps the aforesaid Owille Dissanayake Nilame, grandfather of Ayittaliyadda. According to an unverified account of Ievers (1899), Nuwarawawe Mudiyanse Maha Vanniyā built the 15-foot wall around the Bodhi tree complex from ancient granite blocks removed from surrounding ruins (p. 50). If so, in my view, this is one of the major public works projects a Chief in Nuwarakalaviya completed. It may not be a coincidence that Ilupangamuwe terunnanse, student of the Sangharaja came to Anuradhapura to renovate the granite wall of the Bodhi complex where *Maha Vanniya* was a caretaker and married to an Owille Kumarihamy. And Ayittaliyadda from Owille family line was sent by the Sangharaja to Siam!

Traditionally, from the earliest days, chores of the Sacred Bodhi Tree complex had been attended by members of a caste called Velli-Durai. They too claim descent

---

[4] Abeyawardana, 1978, p.224.

[5] *Mahawansa*, 1912, 2003, X. 88.74.

[6] *Perakumbasiritha.* "kulaparapuren ena lesa demin jayamahalena tanaturu" (granting Jaya Mahalena titles to run through generations) cited in Ariyapala, 1956, 1997. P. 116.

[7] Hettiarachchi, D. E., ed. 1979, p. 2.

from one of the 18 castes.[8] This suggests that prior to abolishment of the feudal system in 1930s, as lay-caretaker of the Bodhi Tree, Nuwarawawe Bulankulame family seems to have had a managerial role on this group of people as well. The relationship between Velli-Durai and this family had not been free of controversies as Ievers (1899) had reported. Citing Assistant Government Agent's diary entries and correspondence with the Government Agent in Jaffna, Ievers noted disputes between the monks in the Bodhi Tree complex called Udamaluwa, temple tenants called 'Padaviya People' and Nuwarawawe Chief on issues relating to the disposal of offerings (p. 42).

The presence of Maha Vanniyā's family in whatever role in the context of Atamasthāna must have been important due to ground realities in early centuries when the city was in ruins, the religious and cultural establishments enveloped in dense forest teeming with wildlife, diseases rampant, regional hostilities abundant and, as Knox (1861, 1995) noted in the middle of the 17th century, majority of the native population speaking a version of pidgin language not understood by the Sinhala people in Kandyan highlands (p.175). This is not surprising, rather quite possible. The isolation of the province was so acute, naturally over time the mix of other languages from the Indian subcontinent were continually finding receivers in villages. The Atamasthāna holy places in dire state were islands in the impossibly expansive jungles, inaccessible and connected only by footpaths at best. Through such bleak circumstances, the role this family undertook to keep the heritage and history of the region intact is commendable.

Often government intrusion to religious affairs proved to be difficult to Nuwaraweva Bulankulame family. As happened in the colonial times in early 19th century, and continues to the present, government's penchant for interference in cultural and traditional ways of Sri Lankan life is well known. If a government suddenly decides to wield its statutory authority shielding behind the Buddhist Temporalities Act or little-known provisions of the 20th century Cultural and Buddha Sasana ministries, it is not lost in the minds of this family that it could face the threat of being sidelined from the relationship with the Bodhi Tree and other related roles. It is not that such fears are not worrisome. Sivasundaram (2013) noted that as far back as in 1840s, British Colonial government tried to "appoint day managers of land belonging to Temples… (p. 321)." This is contrary to what Colonial Administration in England was espousing. Even decades later, members of the House of Commons questioned: "Is not the (Buddhist Temporalities) Ordinance a distinct departure from the principle of non-interference on the part of the Local Government with Buddhist affairs?"[9]

A century later, an amendment to this rule by the Sri Lankan government in Ordinance Number 3 of 1992, Part V, Section 40, explicitly stated that: "No person shall be a member of the Atamasthāna Committee [...] unless he is of the male sex." Nuwarawawe Bulankulame heads the civilian committee that professes policies contrary to the commonsense principle of equal access. Although few know of this

---

[8] Ryan, 1953, p. 122.

[9] Sir J.K. Kennaway, MP, questioning Baron H. de Worms, *Hansard*, Ceylon, 22 August 1889, vol. 340 cc. 97-98.

reality, many in the know despise this misogynic policy which can drive the committee, as happened in courts in 1859, to conflicting and confusing proprietary situations concerning its patriarchal order and the Trusteeship and succession issues of the family. With such potential for confusion and threat to centuries old participation in the trusteeship process, it is not difficult to think Maha Vanniyā's descendants' unease has merits.

Few examples of how the Government intrusion like above had impacted some entities are the Sri Lankan Cricket Board, Olympic Committee, and the selection of the Diyawadana Nilame of the Temple of the Tooth Relic. These bodies that enjoyed no government participation suddenly got in the grip of it. The government reach on these bodies is so influential, common belief is that it weakened the brand of these entities: competitiveness of cricket in international arena, athletic performance in Olympics and the decision-making authority of Diyawadana Nilame and his selection process as the caretaker of the Temple of the Tooth Relic shaded with political whims. Just as in Atamasthāna Trusteeship process, the Diyawadana Nilame selection process too has maintained a misogynic status quo that recognizes no woman shall be eligible to hold this office nor participate in the selection process in any official capacity![10]

The 'constitution' circulated among Nuwaraweva Bulankulame family members declared that their ancestors "had adopted the name Nuwarawawe Suriyakumara Wannisinghe by the time of King Rajadhi Raja Singhe (1793 AD) and one among the family was appointed to the post of Maha Vanniyā upon a Copper *Sannas* [*sic*] (vide Sri Lanka National Archives volume 41/58)."

I hazard to suggest as done earlier, that given the independence enjoyed by the *Vanniya* in the province, his position is nothing less than a 'princely.' The making or granting of a royal document to him could, therefore, be considered a ceremonial and a goodwill gesture of diplomacy by the King to a visiting dignitary. In other words, it is an acknowledgement of the already established tradition of *Vanniya* being the de facto ruler of this special part of the country and his guardianship of the Atamasthāna. Granted, a trip from Anuradhapura to Kandy sitting on a bumpy palanquin[11] and often walking for days along footpaths, treacherous mountain passes and swollen rivers to pay courtesies itself was a remarkable feat for the King to be pleased and show his appreciation with a royal acknowledgement.

Upon further examination, folk or written lore is silent on the King's role in the welfare of the Sri Maha Bodhi Tree, let alone the Nuwarakalaviya which was isolated and distanced for centuries by the Kingdoms in the South. As stated earlier, in all of 18th century, only three Kandyan Kings had visited Anuradhapura, each making just one appearance! But Maha Vanniyā's association with the Bodhi Tree seems to have remained a constant since the 13th century when *Vanniya* title as feudatory Chieftains first appears in historical accounts.

---

[10] In 1960, Sri Lanka elected the 1st woman Prime Minister in the world.

[11] Often Chief Monks travelled in palanquins. When Valivita Saranankara Sangharaja was invited for a preaching at Kanukatigedara in Hath Korale, he went there in a palanquin (Kotagama Wachissara, 1961, p. 278).

Dutch era documents refer to a High Sheriff or Governor of Nuwarakalaviya. For instance, 130 years before King Rajadhi Raja Singhe's copper *Sannasa*, Robert Knox (1681, 1995) on his last attempt[12] to escape from Kandy, passed *Bonder Cooswat* (Bandara Koswatta) and *Nicavar* (Nikaweratiya) in Hath Kōrale before stopping at the house of the *High Sheriff* at Colliwilla (Kaluwila?), nine kilometers south of Anuradhapura (p. 156). Knox noted the Governor's house as fairly large. The High Sheriff received the visitors in the visitor's lounge of the house. Ievers (1899) believes it is one of the houses (walawwa) of Nuwarawawe Vanni Unnehe. Knox and his companion Stephen stayed there for a few days. Knox also called him 'Prince *Coilat Wannea*' (Kaluwila Vanniya?) who was independent from King of Kandy and Dutch colonists in the Maritime provinces. He wrote further that *Coilat Wannea* paid an acknowledgement (*dekma*) only to the Hollanders (p. 175). Since Knox travelled past *Parroah* (Paravahagama?) and *Eopoulpot* (Eppawala Pattuwa), it is fairly certain the sheriff referred by him was at Kaluwila where Nuwarawawe family was believed to own a *nindagama* as well.[13] According to Knox, Dutch had tried to subdue Coilat Wannea without success. He said the Kandy King and this *Prince* "maintained a friendship and correspondence together."

Knox (1681, 1995) wrote:

> "They (Nuwarakalaviya citizens) pay greater tax than *Chingulays* (Sinhalay) due to their King. But he is nothing so cruel. He ('Prince *Coilat Wannea*') victuelleth his soldiers during the time they are upon the guard either about palace or abroad at wars… They are now fed at his charge, whereas 'tis contrary in King's country, for Chingulays soldiers bear their own expenses [*sic*]." (p. 175)

Unlike the *Dissavaru* and Chiefs in Kandy, Nuwarakalaviya Chiefs seem to have not paid a *Wāhala Kada*, the pingo of victuals to the palace in Kandy.[14]

After restocking food supplies, Knox started to *Anarodgburro* (Anuradhapura). Upon arriving at Nuwarawawe he met the 'Governor' of the area.[15] It seems possible the Governors Coilat Wannea and Nuwarawawe no doubt related to each other thus were equal Chiefs (holding hereditary titles) sharing nindagam, showing their role in the larger context of Nuwarakalaviya. Therefore, the Nuwarawawe Vanniya, or the High Sheriff of Nuwarakalaviya as Knox called him in September 1679, also had been the leading person worthy of the title of Prince in the region. And as stated in pages earlier, a Chief in Kandy directly under the King would only fancy to hold power the Maha Vanniyā enjoyed historically. Thus, by default, Coilat Wannea and his family in Nuwarawawe also had a major (and independent) role in the administration of the province and direct association with the religious establishment in Anuradhapura. As the city remained enveloped in jungle, it is possible the incumbent priests of Atamasthāna turned to the two prominent

---

[12] Knox made eight or ten test-runs to Nuwarakalaviya, once up to Hurulle (*Hourly*) to get acclimated what to expect along the route he would take to escape. Finally, he was successful and walked for freedom through Nuwarakalaviya all the way to the Dutch garrison at Arippu on the Northwest coast.

[13] Ievers, 1899. P. 40.

[14] Vimalananda, 1963, p. 408

[15] Knox, 1681, 1995 p. 159.

families, Nuwarawawe and Bulankulame in the city for protection and support to continue traditions, customs, and even to a degree, maintenance of these establishments. Since sacerdotal participation in the project no doubt was an imperative, as stated earlier Ilupángamuwe terunnanse must have played a larger role in planning and construction, while Mudiyanse, the chief lay person in Anuradhapura assisted in many ways to complete it.

Association with the Atamasthāna evolved with the two families helping the core mission – supporting the Sacred Bodhi Tree complex till the Buddhist Temporalities Act and other sources came threatening to inconvenient the proprietary role enjoyed by them. This shows the Nuwarawawe Bulankulame clan can rest assured that their ancestors administered the Nuwarakalaviya country quite independently of the decrees or the practices of the Dutch, King of Kandy, task Kandyan Chief holding office under the King would not dare even to dream.

Finally, according to folklore of Nuwarakalaviya, and asserted by Nuwarawawe Bulankulame family, it did have the authority granted from the Kings, millennia before Kandy had a King. Thus, any subsequent document in any form and source does not negate or change the well-established traditional relationship Maha Vanniyā had with the Atamasthāna and Nuwarakalaviya.

APPENDIX – G

Page from the diary of Alittane Kōrala (Fig. 49).

7.8.52 වෙනි දින රාත්‍රියේ මගේ මී ගහ අක්කර ඉඩමේ පැසී තිබුන ගොයන් කුඹුර මෙහි පහත සඳහන් අයින්ඩ අයිති මී හරක් 21 දෙනෙක් කාලා නාස්ති කලාය.
නො. 42 ගම්මුලාදෑනි මහත්මයාට පැමිණිලි කර එතන පාළුව බැලීමට ---- සහ ආලිත්තානෙන් කේ. නංහාමි සමග ගොස් පාළුව තක්සේරු කලා ය. වී බුසල් 3 ක පාළුව. ජුලි 13 දා සිට අගෝස්තු 2 දක්වා මී හරක් 21 දෙනෙ---- [*sic*].

7.8.52 The 21 water buffaloes belonging to the below mentioned had destroyed the ripened rice in my field Mee Tree acre. After complaining to No. 42 (Tulana) Gam Muladeni Mahatmaya went with .... and Alittane K. Nanhamy and estimated the damage. The damage is three bushels of rice. From July 13th to August 2nd the 21 water buffaloes ....

Note: Second page of this memo is torn off from the diary.

APPENDIX – H

Ehelepola Kumarihamy's Drowning: Bogambara Weva or Boraweva? A Re-examination.[1]

How much disastrous and despicable weight the caste norms had placed on a woman in Kandyan times is well demonstrated in the saga of Ehelepola Kumarihamy. In 1811, she was drowned by the orders of King Sri Wickrama Rajasinghe as a punishment for her husband Ehelepola Adikārama (Fig. 57) who bolted to Colombo and asked the British for protection and helped them with sensitive logistical information about the Kingdom to overthrow the King. This incident throws light on the abhorrent cruelty of the last King of Kandy and how people were influenced rather forced to make fateful decisions due to pressure from caste traditions, even moments before the sure death.

After consulting a host of reliable and most enlightened sources, and most likely eye witness accounts, John Davy (1821), a British Army doctor stationed in Kandy from August 1816 to February 1820, described the episode of beheading few years earlier of Kumarihamy's children in the palace square and parading her and drowning in the Bogambara Weva "in the immediate neighbourhood of Kandy [*sic*] (p. 323.)" Some folklore accounts suggest, the King gave her the option of being married away to a Rodiya (untouchable caste person) and she refused it. Burdened with the vitriolic substance of the caste norms of the day, Kumarihamy chose to perish with her four children to protect her husband's honor. Meanwhile even after hearing the deadly threat to his family, Ehelepola Adikārama decided to stay in Colombo under the safety of the colonial government. Had he returned to Kandy, he probably could have saved his wife and children. This episode also shows depravity of the type of punishments that existed at the time and depth of the caste influence on people.

Lately, questioning the reliability of historical sources, Obeyesekere (2017) has expressed doubts about the location where the actual drowning took place. He believes the King would have resisted polluting Bogambara Weva leaving convicts to rot in its depths (p. 208).

Accordingly, in preference to Bogambara Weva, bodies could have been thrown to another body of water, Boraweva , a small pond (now extinct) northeast of the city.[2] As the name suggests, this pond must have been prone to be muddy (*bora*), so indeed the public avoided using its water except for paddy fields below it. There are reasons to think that this is an implausible supposition. I wonder a King

---

NOTES

[1] Tillakaratne, Lokubanda, Adapted from Ehelepola Kumarihamy Drowning: Bogambara Weva or Boraweva? A Re-examination. *Ceylon Today*, November 25, 2022.

[2] Borawewa, a small pond, was believed to have been at the end of former Borawey Veediya (also known as Nagaha Veediya, present-day D.S. Senanayake Veediya).

who demonstrated ample evidence proving that lives of his subjects could be expendable and portrayed "the last state of individual depravity and wickedness, the obliteration of every trace of conscience"[3] would be sophisticated and considerate enough to have concerns about the water quality of his city.

On the other hand, King would be least likely to use Boraweva for the drowning episode because it was very close to two locations dear and sacred to him: Royal burial grounds within hearing distance of it, and about 400 meters away a highly venerated sacerdotal institution which is also a binary caretaker of the Temple of Tooth Relic – the Asgiriya Vihara. With all his cruelties, the King dumping dead bodies near such places cardinal to him would be incompatible to ground realities existed at the time.

Bogambara Weva was the main water source of the city folks at the time. It covered the present-day Kandy City Center, George E. De. Silva Park and extended up to the neighborhood of the clock tower. But the palace on its part, no doubt used exclusively the virgin water supply from the aptly named Raja Pihilla (Royal Spring), the perennial stream entering the Kandy Lake at a place about a kilometer northeast of the palace. It is also possible, that water from this stream could have been diverted southwest at a place about a kilometer upstream northeast of the city and brought down south to the palace in a canal (*wélla*) cut along the hillside what would be above the shoreline of the present-day Kandy Lake. There is evidence inferring the existence of a canal circling the palace in past as Duncan (1990) had suggested citing the Spilberger map of 1602, Robert Knox (1681, 1995, p. 44) and *Pujavaliya* (p. 67).

The aforesaid Raja Pihilla Royal Stream after filling the Kandy Lake, spilled out to the Bogambara Weva immediately below replenishing its water in the latter continuously indeed. Excess water from Bogambara Weva continued to flow out through the lower spillway somewhere near present day clock tower by the police station and headed to Mahaweli river four kilometers south. There must have been a regulated spillway in place in Bogambara Weva. Robert Knox wrote in 1681 that tanks at that time were drained easily. Constant discharge of water over the lower spillway minimized chances of any undue pollution lingering and accumulating in the upper section of the Bogambara Weva immediately below the Kandy Lake, leaving that area clean for public use. So, the King probably ordered or his Katupulle people involved in the execution took it upon themselves to select a spot closer to the lower spillway to throw the bodies. This is not unusual. As recently as 1950s, villagers in Nuwarakalaviya collected drinking water from *diyamankada* in their tank, their stationary body of water. *Diyamankada* was located at least 50 meters up the bund from *nānamankada* and *harakmankada*, locations that were prone to get fouled generally. Elsewhere in the country, other streams, too, carried all manner of detritus, and people downriver still took this water for personal use.

---

[3] Official Bulletin No. 1, British Headquarters, Kandy 2, March 1815, reproduced in Davy, 1821, 2006, p.497.

Fig. 57. Ehelepola Nilame, c 1810, stucco. Name engraved in Sinhala. Herbert R. Cole Estate. Gift to Los Angeles County Museum of Art (2018).[4]

---

[4] While Ehelepola's refusal to come to Kandy and face King's ire resulted in his wife being forced to surrender to pernicious caste norms with fateful outcome for herself and children, it is surprising that some writings like *Ehelepola Hatana* c 1816 and sculpturing like this have attempted to portray him with glowing praise.

APPENDIX – I

List of Figures and Illustrations

BIBLIOGRAPHY

1. Author: Unknown (1851). The English in Ceylon. Cornell University Digital Library Collections on Making of America. In *United States Magazine and Democratic Review. 28* Vol. XXVIII, No. CLV. 1851 May: 409-412.

2. Abeysinghe, T.B.H. (1985/86). Embassies as Instruments of Diplomacy: A Case Study from Sri Lanka in the First Half of the Seventeenth Century. *Journal of the Royal Asiatic Society Sri Lanka Branch,* 1985/86, New Series, 30, 1-40.

3. ---------, (1964). Myth of the Malvana Convention. *Ceylon Journal of Historical and Social Studies,* 7(1), Jan-June, 67-72.

4. Abeyawardene, H.A.P. (1978). කඩඉම් පොත් විමර්ශණය *Kada-Im Poth Vimarsanaya* (A Critical Study of Kada-Im Poth). Colombo: Department of Cultural Affairs.

5. *An Account of the Religious and Literary Life of Adam Clarke,* By a Member of His Family. 1833, London: T.S. Clarke, Printer and Publisher.

6. Applbaum, Arthur Isak. (2019). *Legitimacy: Right to Rule in a Wanton World.* Cambridge: Harvard University Press.

7. Arangala, Ratnasiri. (2014). *Initiating into the Print Culture and the Challenges in the Book Publishing in 19th & 20th Century Sri Lanka.* Keynote speech at the 2014 Godage Literary Award Ceremony. https://www.academia.edu/38563377/Initiating_into_the_Print_Culture_and_the_Challenges_in_the_Book_Publishing_in_21st_Century_Sri_Lanka.pdf. Last accessed on June 6, 2020.

8. Ariyapala, M.B. (1956, 1997). *Society in Mediaeval Ceylon.* Colombo: Department of Cultural Affairs.

9. Arunachalam, P. (1906). *Sketches of Ceylon History* 2nd Ed., Colombo: Colombo Apothecaries Co. Ltd.

10. ----------, (1910). Kandyan Provinces. *Journal of the Ceylon Branch of the Royal Asiatic Society,* 22(63), 103-123.

11. *Asiatic Journal and Monthly Register for British India and its Dependencies, 8, (1819). London: Black, Kingsbury, Parbury, & Allen.*

12. ----------, 2, (1819).

13. Attygalle, J. (1913). Medical Literature of the Sinhalese by W.A. De Silva. *Journal of the Royal Asiatic Society (Ceylon),* 23(66), 34-50.

14. Bahr, Philip H. (1915). Notes on Yaws in Ceylon, with Special Reference to its Distribution on that Island and its Tertiary Manifestations. *Annals of Tropical Medicine & Parasitology,* 8(4), *675-682,* DOI:10.1080/00034983.1915.11687671.

15. Baker, Samuel (1855, 1983). *Eight Years in Ceylon.* Dehiwala: Tisara Publishers.

16. Baillies, H, MP. *Hansard*, Ceylon. https://api.parliament.uk/historic-hansard/commons/1851/may/27/Ceylon. Columns 20-26. Last accessed on Dec. 27, 2021.

17. Bandaranayake, Shirani Anushmala (1986). *The Devolution of Government in Sri Lanka: Legal Aspects of the Relationship Between Central and Local Government; An Historical and Comparative Study.* (Unpublished Doctoral Dissertation). University of London. Publication Number 11010518, ProQuest Dissertation and Thesis Data Base.

18. Beligatamulla, Gnanaharsha, et al. (2015). A Critical Reading of Seating in Non-Secular Buddhist Contexts in Colonial Sri Lanka. *Making Built Environments Responsive.ed.* Rajapaksha, Upendra. Proceedings of 8th Int'l. Conf. of Faculty of Arch. U. University of Moratuwa, pp. 491-505.

19. Bell, H.C.P. (1904). *Report of the Kegalle District of the Province of Sabaragamuwa.* Colombo: George J.A. Skeen, Government Printer.

20. Bennett, Michael. 2020, *War Against Smallpox: Edward Jenner and the Global Spread of Vaccination.* Cambridge: Cambridge University Press.

21. Berkwitz, Stephen C. (2017). Sinhala Sandésa Poetry in a Cosmopolitan Context. *Sri Lanka at the Crossroads of History*, Eds. Zoltan Bledermann and Alan Strathern. London:University College London Press.

22. Bertolacci, A. (1817). *A View of the Agricultural, Commercial and Financial Interests of Ceylon.* London: Black, Parbury and Allen.

23. British and Foreign Anti-Slavery Society. (1841). *Slavery and the Slave Trade in British India, Ceylon, Malacca, and Penang.* London: Thomas Ward & Co. Paternoster Row,

24. Brito, C. (1879, 2007). *Yalpana-Vaipava-Malai or The History of the Kingdom of Jaffna.* New Delhi: Asian Educational Service (AES).

25. Brodie, A.O. (1894). Topographical and Statistical Account of the District of Nuwarakalaviya. *Journal of the Royal Asiatic Society (Ceylon) 1856-1858*, 3(9), 136-161.

26. Brow, James. (2011). Reconstituting Village Communities: Sir William Gregory's Efforts to Renovate Village Agricultural Systems in Ceylon's North Central Province. In H.L. Seneviratne Ed., *The Anthropologist and the Native: Essays for Gananath Obeyesekere*, pp. 125-135. London: Anthem Press.

27. ----------, (1996). *Demons and Development: The Struggle for Community in a Sri Lankan Village,* Tucson: University of Arizona Press.

28. ----------, (1978). *Vedda Villages of Anuradhapura: A Historical Anthropology of a Community in Sri Lanka.* University of Washington Press, Seattle.

29. Caplan, Lincoln. (2022), Justice Elena Kagan in Dissent, qtd. in *Harvard Magazine*, November-December 2022.

30. *Census of the Island of Ceylon 1871: General Report* (1873). Government Printer, Colombo.

31. Chitty, Simon Casie. (1834, 1989). *Ceylon Gazetteer,* New Delhi: Navrang.

32. Christenson, Allen J. (2003). *Popol Vu: The Sacred Book of the Maya.* Norman: University of Oklahoma Press.

33. Codrington, H.W. (1938), *Ancient Land Tenure and Revenue in Ceylon,* Colombo: Ceylon Government Press.

34. Cohen, Bernard S. (1996). *Colonization and Its Forms of Knowledge: The British in India.* Princeton: Princeton University Press.

35. *Collection of Legislative of Act of the Government of Ceylon, 1, 1796-1833*, (1854). Colombo: William Skeen Government Printer.

36. Coperehewa, Sandagomi. Colonialism and Problems of Language Policy: Formulation of a Colonial Language Policy in Sri Lanka. *Sri Lanka Journal of Advanced Social Studies* 1(1), Jan – June 2011, 27-52.

37. Cordiner, James. (1807). *A Description of Ceylon: An Account of Country, Inhabitants, Natural Productions,* Vol. 1, Aberdeen. London: Longman, Hurst, Rees, and Oeme Paternoster Row; and A. Brown,

38. Cumming, Gordon C.F. (1892). *Two Happy Years in Ceylon* Vol. II, Edinburgh: William Blackwood & Sons.

39. Cunningham, Major Alexander. (1854*), Bhilsa Topes or Buddhist Monuments in Central India.* London: Smith and Elder.

40. Daniels, Lakshmi Kiran. (1992). *Privilege and Policy: The Indigenous Elite and the Colonial Education System in Ceylon, 1912-1948.* (Unpublished Doctoral Dissertation). Oxford University. Retrieved from *https://ora.ox.ac.uk/objects/uuid:652d093a-bcd6-49ca-aa17-787cd251e4c3*

41. Davids, Rhys T.W. (1903, 1911). *Buddhist India.* New York: G.P. Putnam's Sons.

42. Davy, John. (1821, 2006). *An Account of the Interior of Ceylon,* New Delhi: Asian Education Service.

43. --------, (1818). A Description of Adam's Peak. *The Journal of Science and the Arts,* 5(9), 25-30.

44. De Butts, Lieut. (1841). *Rambles in Ceylon.* London: Wm. H. Allen and Co.

45. De Silva, Charles. (1914). The Date of Buddha's Death, Appendix I. *Journal of the Royal Asiatic Society (Ceylon),* 23(62), 141-273.

46. De Silva, K.M.D. (1981). *A History of Sri Lanka.* Delhi: Oxford University Press.

47. De Silva, R.K. and Buemer, W.G.M. (1988). *Illustrations and Views of Dutch Ceylon 1602 -1796,* London: Serendib Publishers.

48. De Soyza, John Siriman. (1960). Rock Inscriptions of Anuradhapura Period. *Sahitya: Tri-Monthly Magazine.* Literature Day 1960 Special Volume.

49. De Zilwa, L. (1967). *Scenes of a Lifetime: The Autobiography of Dr. Lucian de Zilwa.* Colombo: H. W. Cave.

50. De Zoysa, Luis. (1873). Transcript of an Old Copperplate Sannasa. *Journal of the Royal Society of Arts* (JRSA), 1873, Part 1, 75-79.

51. Dickens, Charles (1853). The Noble Savage, *Household Words,* June 11, 1853, 337-339.

52. Dirks, Nicholas B. (2006, 2008) *The Scandal of Empire: India and the Creation of the Imperial Britain.* Cambridge, Massachusetts: Harvard University Press.

53. D'Oyly, Sir John. (1929). *A Sketch of the Constitution of the Kandyan Kingdom: And Other Relevant Papers.* Colombo: Government Printer.

54. ----------, (1917). *The Diary of Mr. John D'Oyly, 1810-1815: With Introduction and Notes by H. W. Codrington,* Colombo: Colombo Apothecaries Co., Ltd.

55. ----------, (1833, 1835). A Sketch of the Constitution of the Kandyan Kingdom. Communicated by A. Johnston, *Transactions of the Royal Asiatic Society of Great Britain & Ireland*, 3, 191-252.

56. Dumas, Alexander. (1844, 2003). *The Count of Monte Cristo*, New York: Bantam Books.

57. Duncan, James S. (1990). *The City as Text: The Politics of Landscape Interpretation in the Kandyan Kingdom*. Cambridge: Cambridge University Press.

58. Ekanayake, A. De Silva. (1876). On the form of Government under the Native Sovereigns of Ceylon. *Journal of the Royal Asiatic Society of Great Britain and Ireland*, 8, 297-304.

59. Fairfield, Edward. (1880). *The Colonial Office List for 1880: Comprising Historical and Statistical Information*. London: Harrison & Sons.

60. Fallon, Richard, H. Jr. (2018). *Law and Legitimacy in the Supreme Court*. Cambridge: Harvard University Press.

61. Farmer, B. H. (1952). Colonization of the Dry Zone of Ceylon. *Journal of the Royal Society of Arts* (JRSA). 100 (4876), 27th June 1952, 547-564. https://www.jstor.org/stable/41365405 Last accessed on Jan. 15, 2021.

62. Farrer, Reginald. (1908). *In Old Ceylon*. London: Edward Arnold.

63. Fennell, James & Bunbury, Turtle. (2006). *Living in Sri Lanka*, New York: Thames & Hudson

64. Ferguson, A.M. (1868). *Ceylon Directory: Calendar and Compendium of Useful Information for 1866 and 1868*, Colombo: Observer Press

65. Ferguson, John. (1893). *Ceylon in 1893*, Colombo: A.M & J. Ferguson, Observer Press.

66. Forbes, Major. (1841). *Eleven Years in Ceylon* Vol. I. London: Richard Bentley.

67. Foucault, Michel. (1977, 1995). *Discipline & Punish: The Birth of Prison*. New York: Random House, Inc.

68. Gamage, H.H. (1988). *Andare Saha Gajaman Nona*. Maradana, Colombo: Indika Press.

69. Gamlath, Sucharita & E.A. Wickramasinghe. (1996). Eds. *Ayittaliyadda Muhandiramge Sangharaja Sadhu Chariyawa*, Colombo: S. Godage Brothers.

70. Godakumbura, C.E. (1960). Anuradhapura Yugaye Purawasthu. *Sahitya: Three Monthly Magazine*. Literature Day 1960 Special Volume. Colombo: Department of Cultural Affairs.

71. Gooneratne, Brendon and Yasmine. (1999). *This Inscrutable Englishman: Sir John D'Oyly (1774-1824)*. London: Cassell.

72. Gooneratne, Yasmine. (1970). The Mudliyar Class of Ceylon: Its Origins, Advance, and Consolidation. *Vidyodaya Journal of Science, Arts, and Letters*, 3(2), 116-123.

73. Goonesekere, R.K.W. (1958). The Eclipse of the Village Court. *Ceylon Journal of Historical and Social Studies*, 1(2), 138-154.

74. Gowariker, A. 2004. *Swades* (film), Mumbai: Ashutosh Gowariker Productions & Netflix.

75. Gunasekara, A.P.A. (2004). *Horowpothane Palaveni DRO*. Colombo: S. Godage Brothers.

76. Gunasekara, B. (1900, 1954).ed. *Rajavaliya or Historical Narrative of Sinhalese Kings from Vijaya to Vimala Dharma Suriya II,* Colombo: Government Press.

77. Harari, Yuval Noah. 2015, *Sapiens: A Brief History of Humankind.*

78. Harvard, W.M. (1823, 2016) *A Narrative of Establishment and Progress of the Mission to Ceylon and India.* London: Harvard, W.M. and T. Blanshard.

79. Herber, Reginald. (1828). *Narrative of Journey Through the Upper provinces of India from Calcutta to Bombay 1824-1825 (With Notes Upon Ceylon).* Philadelphia: Carey, Lea and Carey.

80. Hettiarachchi, D.E. ed. (2019). *Sinhala Sirith Sangrahaya,* Nalin Publishers: Bibila.

81. ----------, (1979). *Sinhala Sirith Sangrahaya:* From C.L. Wickramasinghe Manuscripts, Colombo: Wesley Printers.

82. ----------, (1978-79). C.L. Wickramasinghe Collection of Manuscripts Relating to the Traditionary Customs of Nuwarakalaviya (Presidential Address). *Journal of the Royal Asiatic Society (Sri Lanka),* 24, (new series) (1978-79), 1-14.

83. Howland, W.W. (1877). Caste as Affecting Christians in Ceylon. *The Missionary Herald,* 73(3) August.

84. Ievers, R.W. (1899). *Manual of the North Central Province.* Colombo: Government Press.

85. International Labor Organization. https://www.ilo.org/dyn/natlex/natlex4.detail?p_isn=67628&p_lang=en.

86. Jayawardena, Kumari. (2003). *Nobodies to Somebodies: Rise of Colonial Bourgeoisie of Sri Lanka.* Colombo: Social Scientists' Association and Sanjiva Books.

87. Jayewardene, H.D. ed. (1907, 1951). *The New Law Reports of Cases Decided by the Supreme Court of Ceylon* (9), Colombo: Government Printer.

88. Jayewardene, Kathleen. (2008). Nilwala Ganga Kivindiyo. In Watagedara, Sugath, et. al. eds. *Matara Wansaya,* Vol. 2. Battaramulla: Ministry of Cultural & National Heritage, (pp. 75-83).

89. Jennings, Sir Ivor. (July 1952). Notes on Kandyan Laws Collected by Sir Archibald C. Lawrie, LL.D. *University of Ceylon Review,* 10(3), 185-220.

90. Johnston, Alexander. (1835). A Sketch of the Constitution of the Kandyan Kingdom. *Transactions of the Royal Asiatic Society of Great Britain and Ireland,* 3, 191-252.

91. Jonville, Mons. (1948). Narrative of a Journey… *The Journal of the Ceylon Branch of the Royal Asiatic Society of Great Britain & Ireland* Vol. 38, No. 105 (1948), pp. 1-21

92. Kapuruhami, K.A. (1948). Rata Sabhāwa, *Journal of the Royal Asiatic Society (Ceylon),* 38(106), 42 68.

93. Karunananda, U.B. (1993). The Administration of the Atamasthāna at Anuradhapura. *Rohana Research Journal,* 4(8), 137-156.

94. ----------, (1990). *Nuwarakalaviya 1815-1900,* Kelaniya: Shiela Printing Works.

95. ----------, (2009). *Tamankaduwa 1815-1900.* Colombo: Ministry of Culture and Heritage.

96. Karunaratne, Kusuma. (2008). Matara Era Literature and Literati. In Watagedara, Sugath, et. al. Eds. *Matara Wansaya*, Vol. 2. Battaramulla: Ministry of Cultural & National Heritage, pp. 15-28.

97. Karunaratne, M.W.E. (Undated Pamphlet in Sinhala) *Historic Maduwanwela Walawwa 1700 AD to 1905 AD*. Enderamulla, Wattala: Sponsored by Department of Archaeology.

98. Kettell, Thomas Prentice. (1851). English in Ceylon. In *United States Magazine, and Democratic Review*, 1851, 28, 409-412. https://ia600900.us.archive.org/23/items/unitedstatesmag00sciegoog/unitedstatesmag00sciegoog.pdf.

99. Knox, Robert. (1681, 1995). *A Historical Account of the Island Ceylon in the East Indies*, New Delhi: Navrang.

100. Kulasekera, K.M.P. (1984, 2018). *British Administration in the Kandyan Provinces of Sri Lanka, 1815-1833, With Special Reference to Social Change.* (Unpublished Doctoral Dissertation). University of London. Publication Number 11010526, ProQuest Dissertation and Thesis Data Base. https://eprints.soas.ac.uk/33753/1/11010526.pdf. Last accessed on Aug. 16, 2021

101. Lawrie, A.C. (1898). *A Gazetteer of the Central Province of Ceylon Excluding Walapane* Vol. II. Colombo: Government Printer.

102. ----------, (1896). *A Gazetteer of the Central Province of Ceylon Excluding Walapane* Vol. I. Colombo: Government Printer.

103. Lawson, Tom. (2014). *The Last Man: A British Genocide in Tasmania.* London: Bloomsbury Publishing.

104. Leach, E.R. (1961, 1968). *Pul Eliya: A Village in Ceylon. A Study of Land Tenure and Kinship.* Cambridge: Cambridge University Press.

105. *Legal Enactments of Ceylon 1707-1879* (1907). Colombo: Government Printer.

106. *Legislative Enactments of Ceylon – 1870-75.* (1875). Colombo: Government Printer.

107. LeMesurier, C. J. R. and Panabokke T. B. Trans. (1880). *Niti Nighanduwa or The Vocabulary of Law*, Colombo: Government Printer.

108. Leupe, P.A. (1891). Short Summary of the History of the establishment of the Honorable Company in the Island of Ceilon. *Journal of the Royal Asiatic Society (Ceylon)*, 1889, 11(38), 2-147.

109. Lewis, J.P. (1913). List of Inscriptions on Tombstones and Monuments in Ceylon, Colombo: Government Printer.

110. ----------, (1895a, 1993). *A Manual of the Vanni Districts of the Northern Province, Ceylon.* New Delhi: Navrang.

111. ----------, (1895b). Folklore from North Ceylon, *Folklore*, 6(2) (June 1895), 176-185.

112. ----------, (1894). Archaelogy of Wanni, *The Journal of the Ceylon Branch of the Royal Asiatic Society of Great Britain & Ireland*, Vol. 13, No. 45 (1894), pp. 151-178.

113. ----------, (1891). Buddhist Ruins Near Vavuniya. *Journal of the Ceylon Branch of the Royal Asiatic Society*, 12(42), 111-112.

114. Liyanage, Jagath Padmasiri. (2008). Adhikarana Kriyadamaye Vikashanaya. In Watagedara, Sugath, et. al. (Eds.), *Matara Wansaya*. Vol. 1. Battaramulla: Ministry of Culture Affairs and National Heritage, 328-333.

115. Madduma Bandara, C.M. (1985). Catchment Ecosystems and Village Tank Cascades in the Dry Zone of Sri Lanka. In J. Lundquist et. al. U. Lohm and M. Falkenmark (eds.), *Strategies for River Basin Development*. Reidel Publishing Co., Dordretch, pp. 99-113.

116. *Mahawansa or The Great Chronicle of Ceylon*, n.d., (1912, 2003). Trans. Wilhelm Geiger, New Delhi: Asian Educational Service.

117. Marshall, Henry. (1846, 1954). *CEYLON: A General Description of the Island and Its Inhabitants*. Kandy: Kandy Printers Ltd.

118. Mbeki, Linda & van Rossum, Matthias. (2017). Private slave trade in the Dutch Indian Ocean world: a study into the networks and backgrounds of the slavers and the enslaved in South Asia and South Africa, *Slavery & Abolition*, 38(1), 95-116. https://doi.org/10.1080/0144039x.2016.1159004.

119. Mills, Lennox A. (1933, 2012). *Ceylon Under British Rule 1795-1932: With and Account of the East India Company Embassies to Kandy 1762-1795*. Oxford: Rutledge.

120. Moder, Frank. (1899). Kandyan Law. In Isaac Thambyah (Ed.). *The Ceylon Law Review* I (1), 24-28.

121. Moumakwa, P.C. (2010). *Kgolta System: A Mechanism for Traditional Conflict Resolution in Modern Botswana. A Case Study of the Kanye Kgolta*. (Unpublished Master's Thesis). University of TromsØ. TromsØ, Norway. https://munin.uit.no/bitstream/handle/10037/3211/thesis.pdf?sequence =1 2022.

122. Muller, Edward. (1883). *Ancient Inscriptions in Ceylon: Collected and Published for the Government*, London: Trubner & Co., Ludgate Hill.

123. Munasinghe, Indrani T.G. (1972). *The Development and History of Transportation in Ceylon: A Study of Roads and Railways 1800-1905*. (Unpublished Doctoral Dissertation). University of London. Publication Number 11010407, ProQuest Dissertation and Thesis Data Base.

124. Nadaraja, T. (1972). *The Legal System of Ceylon in Its Historical Setting*.

125. Navaratnam, C.S. (1960). *Vanni and the Vanniyas with Map of the Vanni Districts*. Jaffna: Ealanadu Ltd.

126. Nevil, Hugh. (1869-1886). Sinhala Verse (Kavi). In P.E.P. Deraniyagala (Ed.), *Ethnolgoy*. 3, (1955). Poem 783, p. 206.

127. Nicholas, C.W. and Paranavitana, S. (1961). *Concise History of Ceylon*, Colombo: Ceylon University Press.

128. Obeyesekere, Donald. (1911, 1999). *Outlines of Ceylon History*, New Delhi: Asian Educational Service.

129. Obeyesekere, Gananath. (2017). *The Doomed King: A Requiem for Sri Wickrama Rajasinghe*, Colombo: Sailfish.

130. ----------, (1992, 1997). *The Apotheosis of Captain Cook: European Mythmaking in the Pacific*. Princeton: Princeton University Press.

131. ---------, (1984), *Cult of Goddess Pattini*, Chicago: University of Chicago Press.

132. ----------, (1967). *Land Tenure in Village Ceylon*. Cambridge: Cambridge University Press.

133. Oldenberg, Hermann. (1879). *Deepawamsa: An Ancient Buddhist Historical Record*, London: William and Norgate.

134. Panabokke, C.R. et al. (2002). *Evolution, Present Status, and Issues Concerning Small Tank Systems in Sri Lanka*. Colombo: IWMI.

135. Parker, H. (1910, 1982). *Village Folktales of Ceylon* Vol. I, Dehiwala: Tisara Prakasakayo Ltd.

136. Percival, Robert. (1803). *An Account of the Island of Ceylon*, London: C., and R. Balwin.

137. Pereira, James Cecil Walter. (1899). Sources of our Laws. *The Ceylon Law Review*, 1(1), 5-8.

138. Perera, Arthur A. (1917). *Sinhalese Folklore Notes Ceylon*, Bombay: British India Press Mazgaon.

139. Perera, Edward W. (1910). The Age of Sri Parakrama Bahu VI 1412-7 A.D. *Journal of the Royal Asiatic Society* (Ceylon), 22(63), 6-45.

140. Perera, Joseph Martinus. (1861). *Armour's Grammar of the Kandyan Law, Methodically Arranged and Digested with a Copious Index, Glossary, and Appendix,* Colombo: "Examiner" Press.

141. Pieris, P.E. (1918, 2018). *Ceylon and the Hollanders 1658-1796*, Tellippalai: American Ceylon Mission Press.

142. ----------, (1950). *Sinhale and the Patriots 1815-1818*, Colombo: Colombo Apotecarios.

143. ----------, (1920). *Ceylon and the Portuguese 1508-1658*, Tellippalai: American Ceylon Mission Press.

144. Pieris, Ralph. (1956). *Sinhalese Social Organization: The Kandyan Period,* Colombo: The Ceylon University Press Board.

145. Pieters, Sophia. (1908). Tr. *Instructions from Governor-General of India to Governor of Ceylon 1656-1665*. Colombo: H.S. Cottle, Government Printer.

146. Pridham, Charles. (1849). *A Historical, Political and Statistical Account of Ceylon and its Dependencies* Vol. I, London: T. and W. Boone.

147. Priyanka, Benille. (2010). *Recently Deciphered Records from the Mirror Wall at Sigiriya*, Colombo: Godage International Publishers.

148. Raghavan, M.D. (1961). *The Karava of Ceylon: Society & Culture*, Colombo: K. V. G. de Silva & Sons.

149. Rajakaruna, Ariya. (1958, 1962). Martin Wickramasinghe Hā Parani Kāvya Sampradaya. *Sankruthi – Tri Monthly*, 6(4), 56-75.

150. Ranaweera, L. et al. (2014). Mitochondrial DNA history of Sri Lankan ethnic people: their relations within the island and with the Indian subcontinental populations. *Journal of Human Genetics* (59), 28–36 https://doi.org/10.1038/jhg.2013.112. Last accessed on Feb. 8, 2023.

151. Ricci, Ronit. (2019). *Banishment and Belonging: Exile and Diaspora in Serendib, Lanka, and Ceylon*. Cambridge: Cambridge University Press.

152. Robertson, William. (1791). *Historical Disquisition Concerning India*. London: A. Strahan and T. Cadell.

153. Robinson, Marguerite S. (1968). Some Observations on the Kandyan Sinhalese Kinship System. *Man.* Sep. 3(3), 402-423.

154. Ryan, Bryce. (1953). *Caste in Modern Ceylon: The Sinhalese System in Transition,* New Brunswick: Rutgers University Press.

155. Said, Edward W. (1979). *Orientalism.* New York: Vintage Books,

156. Schrikker, Alicia. (2007). *Dutch and British Colonial Intervention in Sri Lanka 1780-1815: Expansion and Reform.* Leiden: Brill.

157. Schrikker, Alicia and Kate J. Ekama, (2017). "Through the Lens of Slavery: Dutch Sri Lanka in the Eighteenth Century" in *Sri Lanka at the Crossroads of History,* Eds. Biedermann, Zoltan and Strathern, Alan, London: University College London Press.

158. Seligmann, C.G. and Seligmann, Brenda Z. (1911, 1993). *The Veddas,* New Delhi: Navrang.

159. Senaveratne, John M. (1914). The Date of Buddha's Death and Ceylon Chronology: Appendix I. *Journal of the Royal Asiatic Society (Ceylon).* 23(67), 141-273.

160. Seneviratna, Anuradha. (1994). *Ancient Anuradhapura: The Monastic City.* Colombo: Department of Archaeological Survey.

161. Seneviratne, H.L. (1978). *Rituals of the Kandyan State,* Cambridge: Cambridge University Press.

162. Sivasundaram, Sujit. (2013). *Islanded.* Chicago: University of Chicago Press.

163. --------, (2007). Tales of the Land: British Geography and Kandyan Resistance in Sri Lanka, c 1803-1850. *Modern Asian Studies* 41(5), 925-965.

164. Stewart, John MP, *Hansard,* Island of Ceylon, May 27, 1830, Columns 1155-1162. https://api.parliament.uk/historic-hansard/commons/1830/may/27/island-of-ceylon.

165. Tambiah, H. W. 1962, Buddhist Ecclesiastical Law. *Journal of Royal Asiatic Society.* 8 (1), 71-107.

166. Tennakoon, M.U.A. (1974). *Traditional Dry Zone Irrigation: Eco-systematic Concepts Revisited and Reconceptualized.* Colombo: South Asia Partnership Sri Lanka.

167. Tennent, Sir James Emerson. (1860). *Ceylon: An Account of the Island, Physical, Historical and Topographical* Vol. II, 3rd Ed. London: Longman, Green, Longman, and Roberts.

168. Thambiah, Stanley J. (1989). King Mahasammata: The First King in the Buddhist Story of Creation, and His Persisting Relevance. *Journal of the Anthropological Society of Oxford ,*20(2), 101-122.

169. Thomas, Elizabeth Marshall. (2006). *The Old Way.* New York: Sara Crichton Books.

170. Tillakaratne, Lokubanda (2022, November 25). Ehelepola Kumarihamy Drowning: Bogambara Weva or Boraweva? A Re-examination. *Ceylon Today.*

171. --------, (2020, July 13). A Bit of Unorthodox History of the Police. *Ceylon Today.*

172. --------, (2017, February 15). Madukanda Maha Dissava. *Daily Mirror,* A12.

173. --------, (2015). *Echoes of the Millstone: An Ethnographic Account of Life in a Village in Sri Lanka.* North Charleston: CreateSpace.

174. --------, (2010, October 03). Hurulle Walawwa: A Piece of History Through the Ashes of Destruction. *The Sunday Times*.

175. Tissera, Shirley Pulle (2013). *The Colombo Chetties of Sri Lanka.* _https://thuppahis.com/2013/07/14/the-colombo-chetties-of-sri-lanka-three-essays/

176. Toussaint, J.R. 1935, The Burghers in Early British Times. Lecture given at the Dutch Burgher Union Hall on August 30th, 1935, *Journal of the Dutch Burgher Union of Ceylon*, 25(2), *October 1935*, 41-55.

177. Toussaint, J.R. (1934). Literature and the Ceylon Civil Service. *Journal of the Dutch Burgher Union of Ceylon.* 23(3), 113-143.

178. Trimen, Henry. (1894). Book-notes, News & Etc. *The Journal of Botany, British and Foreign.* 32(380), Aug. 1894, 255-256.

179. Turner, L.J.B. (1919). Some Aspects of the Economics of the Maritime Provinces of Ceylon 1798-1805. *The Ceylon Antiquity and Literary Register.* 4(4). April 1919, 183-196.

180. -------, (1918). The Town of Kandy About the Year 1815 A.D. *The Ceylon Antiquity and Literary Register.* 4(2), July 1918, 76-82.

181. Turnour, George. (1836). Trans. *An Epitome of The History of Ceylon, Compiled from Native Annals: And the First Twenty Chapters of the Mahawanso.* Ceylon: Cotta Church Mission.

182. Upananda, Ven. Matale Sri. *Devayo and Mahavansa* (Undated Booklet). Rajagiriya: Semage Industries Press.

183. Valentia, George Viscount. (1809). *Voyages and Travels to India, Ceylon, The Red Sea, Abyssinia, and Egypt.* London: William Miller.

184. Vimalananda, T. (1970). *The Great Rebellion of 1818.* Colombo: M.D. Gunasena & Co.

185. --------, (1963). *Udarata Maha Keralla,* Colombo: M.D. Gunasena & Co.

186. Wachissara, Ven. Kotagama. (1961). *Valivita Saranankara and the Revival of Buddhism in Ceylon.* (Unpublished Doctoral Dissertation). University of London. Publication Number 11010440, ProQuest Dissertation and Thesis Data Base.

187. Washington, Booker T. (1944). *Up From Slavery: An Autobiography.* New York: Doubleday, Doran & Co.

188. Watson, Paul. (2017). *Ice Ghosts.* New York: W.W. Norton & Company.

189. Weber, Max. (1978). *Economy and Society: An Outline of Interpretive Sociology.,* Eds. Guenther Roth and Claus Wittich. Berkeley and Los Angeles: University of California Press.

190. White, Herbert. (1893). *Manual of the Province of Uva.* Colombo: Government Printer.

191. Wickramaratne, L.A. (1973). Education and Social Change 1832 to c 1900. In *University of Ceylon History of Ceylon,* Vol. 3, *From Beginning of the Nineteenth Century to 1948.* Ed. K. M. De Silva, 165-186.

192. Wickremasinghe, Don Martino de Zilva. (1900). Catalogue *of Sinhalese Manuscripts in the British Museum,* London: Gilbert and Rivington, Ltd.

193. Wickramasinghe, Nira. (2020). *Slave in a Palanquin.* New York: Colombia University Press.

194. Wijesekara, Nandadewa. (1990). *The Sinhalese.* Colombo: M.D. Gunasena & Co. Ltd.

195. Wijetunge, M.N.R. (2012). *Domestic Architecture of the Sinhalese Elite in the Age of Nationalism.* (Unpublished Doctoral Dissertation). Nottingham Trent University. http://irep.ntu.ac.uk/id/eprint/305/1/216257_ntuthesis_wijetunge_domestic_architecture_20150211.pdf.

196. Wilkerson, Isabel. (2023). Division & Destiny: How to Build a Truly Equal American Democracy. *Time,* Vol. 201(5-6), Feb. 13-20, 2023, 34-40.

197. Wimalakeerthi, Ven. Medauyangoda, (1955). *Sinhala Ānduwa.* Colombo: Anula Printers.

198. Winick, Charles. (1970). *Dictionary of Anthropology.* Totowa, New Jersey: Littlefield, Adam & Co.

199. Woolf, Leonard. (1961). *Growing: An Autography of the Years 1904 to 1911.* San Diego: Harcourt Brace Jovanovich, Publishers.

200. Yalman, Nur, (1967). *Under the Bo Tree.* Berkeley: UC Press.

201. Yang, Anand A. (1987). Conversation of Rumors: The Language of Popular Mentalites in Late Nineteenth-Century Colonial India. *Journal of Social History,* 20(3), 485-505